T0188073

INSIDE THE ENEMY'S COMPUTER

CLEMENT GUITTON

Inside the Enemy's Computer

Identifying Cyber Attackers

HURST & COMPANY, LONDON

First published in the United Kingdom in 2017 by
C. Hurst & Co. (Publishers) Ltd.,
41 Great Russell Street, London, WC1B 3PL
© Clement Guitton, 2017
All rights reserved.
Printed in India

Distributed in the United States, Canada and Latin America by
Oxford University Press, 198 Madison Avenue, New York, NY 10016,
United States of America.

The right of Clement Guitton to be identified as the author
of this publication is asserted by him in accordance with the
Copyright, Designs and Patents Act, 1988.

A Cataloguing-in-Publication data record for this book
is available from the British Library.

ISBN: 9781849045544

This book is printed using paper from registered sustainable
and managed sources.

www.hurstpublishers.com

In memory of my mother (1956–2016)

CONTENTS

CONTENTS

ACKNOWLEDGEMENTS

I owe an important debt of gratitude to many people who have supported me in various ways throughout the various stages of this long undertaking. First and foremost, Thomas Rid, professor of security studies at King's College London, has been very patient in reading, commenting and guiding me through this lengthy process to improve my arguments and my writing. It is certain that his guidance was of the utmost help in this experience. I am also very much indebted to the valuable comments made by a few other scholars, including Peter McBurney, Ian Brown, Marco Roscini, David Betz, Michael Goodman and Richard Overill. Conversations on the topic of cyber security with then fellow doctoral students Tim Stevens, Martin Chapman and Mirva Salminen have also proved very helpful. A large thank you also goes to Elaine Korzak who helped me shape part of the argument in the chapter on standards of proof and with whom I had the chance to publish a related article in the *RUSI Journal*.

I am very grateful to the people who allowed me to interview them, many of whom cannot be named here, but who have however tremendously informed the content of the book through valuable discussions. I am indebted to them. In particular, thank you Richard Bejtlich for offering to help me better understand the inner working of Mandiant.

My thanks also go to two anonymous reviewers and to the Hurst team for their efforts to improve the manuscript as much as possible.

I would also like to thank Kushwant Mussai for his sound advice, and Fiona Gamble who was of immense help when it came to supporting me through difficult times, and who generously went through the painful proofreading of several of my very rough drafts.

ACKNOWLEDGEMENTS

Finally, I owe much to my partner, Juliane Hauptmann, whose emotional support cannot be expressed in words.

I dedicate this book to my family.

INTRODUCTION

The pervasiveness of computers has brought with it a wealth of threats. Many of these have targeted everyday users of computers, as well as users of now widely cherished smartphones. For instance, in April 2013, the Finnish security company F-Secure discovered a piece of malware, Pincer, targeting users of mobile phones running Google's operating system. The malware, once on the device, would intercept text messages and forward them to a central server—nothing unusual for malware targeting a smartphone.[1] The malware could also perform many other functions depending on commands received from the server. In an age where many people perform a multitude of tasks on their phone, Pincer could turn quite nasty. It had the potential to garner people's most private moments, passwords and bank credentials, and even potentially to access confidential data when phone users connected to their employer's network.

In the fight against Pincer, Brian Krebs, a former journalist for *The Washington Post*, started tearing the code apart and analysing it. In it, he found a username: the author of the malware had left a trace. Very quickly, Krebs was able to identify the man, Yuri Shmakov, at a far remote place in the middle of Russia.[2] Krebs sent an email to Shmakov, frankly asking him if he had authored the malware. Shmakov answered equally frankly: he had written a module for the malware, based on specifications given by a client. In other words, he had made a major contribution to building the malware but had been unaware of the larger goal his contribution would serve. An unknown person who used an anonymised email service had contacted him and had requested his freelance services, to

1

which he had agreed. This unknown person had then tweaked Shmakov's code to transform it into the Pincer malware.

Can we consider that Shmakov is the 'author' of Pincer, used to launch nefarious cyber attacks? This question, the question of finding the authors of cyber attacks, is commonly referred to as 'attribution'. As this first small case illustrates, the answer to the question of authorship is not easy, and needs a nuanced approach.

The Pincer case contains traits similar to the investigation of many other cyber attacks: an individual, and not the police, found a piece of information that was key for attribution; the attack involved near-professional, organised criminals, with specialised experts working on the different aspects of the steps required to successfully launch the attack; the investigators, the victims and the writers were scattered across the world; and the name of the criminal who released the malware, in the end, still remained unknown.[3]

By finding the authors of cyber attacks, it is possible to initiate the first phase of a judicial process. The state can prosecute the authors, possibly convict them and hence prevent them from continuing to pursue further cyber attacks. As the criminal who distributed Pincer is probably still at large, he can continue to release malware, causing much disruption to personal lives.

Focusing on finding the instigators of cyber attacks has another important aspect that this case does not illustrate: not all of them are professional private actors or even amateur criminals. There are many more kinds of actors launching cyber attacks, all wishing to take advantage of the medium, in particular companies and state actors. As Christopher Painter, Coordinator for Cyber Issues for the US State Department, mentioned, 'Knowing whether a state or non-state actors are involved' in an attack is already 'a huge problem in cyber security'.[4]

In dealing with the category of state actors, as much as in making the distinction between Shmakov and the other author behind the Pincer malware, much nuance is required. It is useful to discern between states' intelligence services directly launching an attack, a state hiring the services of hackers, or even patriotic hackers acting without command from any state organ but nonetheless shielded from prosecution thanks to the protection of a corrupt government official. Making such distinctions is important insofar as it may warrant a different response to the attack on the part of the victim. A state actor undergoing a cyber attack might decide to prosecute an individual who launched it, but might decide to retaliate in kind if the attack came from another state. Knowing the identity of the attacker can therefore allow different responses to cyber attacks: an attack of a purely criminal nature may only necessitate the involvement of law enforcement agencies; but a state-sponsored attack—an attack in which a state agency has had an active role, from actively encouraging it to shaping, coordinating, ordering, conducting or executing part of it —may necessitate other retaliatory measures coming from the government and not from the police, be they diplomatic, economic or military.[5]

Knowing who the attackers are also has a value for private companies. The questions asked following an attack on a company have changed very little in twenty years of the development of information security as a field, with 'Who is the attacker?' remaining one of the first questions of interest—the term 'attacker' referring to anyone breaching the confidentiality, integrity or availability of an information system (the term is further discussed below).[6] What has changed, however, is companies' willingness to invest resources in answering this question, although a deeper understanding of attribution mechanisms has not always followed this willingness. By focusing on the identity of attackers, companies can design defence mechanisms adapted to the attackers, their motivations and their resources. Increasingly, attackers carry out attack campaigns where they target a company not once but several times.[7] By knowing what the attackers are after, their motivation in other words, companies can focus on defending themselves more effectively; especially when the attackers come back several times, companies need to go beyond only increasing network security at the technical level. Companies can think more widely by considering a whole range of strategic options, from bringing a court case against a competitor to working closely with their government if the attack is state-sponsored.

Further highlighting the importance of attribution are the statements of many current and former policy-makers. Shawn Henry, the Federal Bureau of Investigation's (FBI) former executive assistant director in charge of cyber crime, acknowledged the importance of attribution in a conference in 2012: 'The most significant challenge that we face in this space [cyberspace] is attribution'.[8] Many have agreed with Henry. A 2011 report from the North Atlantic Treaty Organization (NATO) Parliamentary Assembly read: 'The problem of attribution is widely recognised as the biggest obstacle for effective cyber defence'.[9] More recently, Jane Holl Lute, a deputy at the Department of Homeland Security from 2009 to 2013, confirmed the importance of the topic at a security conference by asking the question, 'Who's doing it [launching cyber attacks]?' and answering: 'Everybody begins every cyber article you'll read with ever more breathless representations of the dreaded foes out there: profit driven criminals, electronic saboteurs, and spying governments'.[10] The types of actor are in fact even more numerous than that, with a wide range of motivations. In 2010, the United States former Deputy Secretary of Defense William J. Lynn told an audience in Australia that 'because of the difficulty in attribution, the reality is that we cannot defend our networks by ourselves'.[11] A year later, however, he recognised that reducing the difficulty of defending against cyber attacks only to the problems with attribution is dangerous and insufficient. He revised his statement as follows: 'Our ability to identify and respond to a serious cyber attack is only part of our strategy'.[12] Other analysts such as Joel Brenner, a former senior official within the US intelligence services, also repeated that defence is difficult without attribution. Brenner wrote: '[O]ur inability to figure out who's responsible for illegal behavior on our electronic networks is a fundamental reason why we can't safeguard our personal data, corporate intellectual property, or national defense secrets.'[13]

Attribution is hence central to defence strategies against cyber attacks. More specifically, not knowing the identity of an attacker with a high degree of certainty from the outset raises several problems for states wishing to retaliate. For example, against whom should they retaliate? And can they be sure that they will be retaliating against the right enemy? In addition, if states cannot correctly identify attackers, are future attackers likely to think that they too can launch cyber attacks with impunity? In other words, how can the victim deter other states from launching similar cyber attacks? Over the past few years, scholars have produced an important and growing body of literature on cyber attack deterrence.[14] Each time, the question of attribution is at the core of the debate. The threat of retaliation, which has to be credible to act as a deterrent, 'depends on attribution', according to Michael V. Hayden, director of the Central Intelligence Agency (CIA) under the Bush administration between 2006 and 2009.[15] The 2011 US strategy for cyberspace also included deterrence via attribution mechanisms. The strategy read:

> In the case of criminals and other non-state actors who would threaten our national and economic security, domestic deterrence requires all states [to] have processes that permit them to investigate, apprehend, and prosecute those who intrude or disrupt networks at home or abroad.[16]

As mentioned in the strategy, the investigation and prosecution of crimes are part of the attribution process. The strategy vividly echoed the words of Robert Knake of the Council on Foreign Relations, who had declared during a hearing in front of the US House of Representatives a year earlier that: 'For deterrence to work, it is critically important that we know who has carried out the attack and thus attribution is a central component of deterrence strategy'.[17] Many other academics in technical circles have also repeatedly emphasised the importance of attribution for deterrence.[18]

Yet, and unfortunately given that it is so crucial for many security policies, attribution is 'unbelievably difficult', in the words of Alan West, the UK minister for security and counter-terrorism under Gordon Brown.[19] Instead of focusing on attribution *per se* and how to approach it, much research has accepted the premise that attribution is difficult and has tried to work out the implications of this difficult situation: a need to rethink deterrence, a need to find means to protect networks that do not rely on attribution and a need to assign blame despite a lack of attribution. In contrast, very little research has actually addressed attribution itself, or looked closely at what makes attribution so difficult.[20]

Consistently, three common misconceptions have permeated the debate on attribution: that it is a technical problem; that it is unsolvable; and that it is unique. This book will strive to show that these are indeed misconceptions, and that they are also misleading.

Several recent policy documents from the United States, a country often regarded as the leading authority on cyber security, have wrongly emphasised the technical side of attribution.[21] Attribution is mentioned only once in the US 'Blueprint for a Secure Cyber Future' published in

5

2011, when it refers to the innovation of technology for attribution.[22] Other policy documents, such as the 2009 'Cyberspace Policy Review' and the 2011 Department of Defense 'Cyberspace Policy Report', have similarly supported technical solutions for attribution.[23] A draft of the Cybersecurity Information Sharing Act, a 2015 voted bill that is supposed to enhance the protection of critical infrastructure in the United States, also mentioned attribution only to support technological research to solve the problem.[24] Lastly, the former US official Shawn Henry stated: '[Attribution] involves using *technology* to identify the attacker through hints, such as signatures, command-and-control infrastructure, tactics and funding sources' [emphasis added].[25] And the former FBI deputy assistant director Steven Chabinsky, while defending a policy based on attribution, stated that: 'We [need to build] the software, hardware, protocols necessary for assurance, attribution, and penalty-based deterrence'.[26] His defence of attribution as a solution stems from the observation that to tackle the risks of cyber attacks, it is only possible to mitigate the consequences of attacks, to 'lower the threat', or to 'lower vulnerability'.[27] Unfortunately, there has been a lot of work that only focuses on fixing vulnerabilities, almost as if 'it would be ever possible to create software and hardware that would be impenetrable'.[28] A focus on lowering the threat involves attributing attacks to their instigators and imposing penalties on the attackers. Although Chabinsky's rationale for focusing on attribution is sound, his approach to attribution, grounded as it is in suggesting technical solutions, is problematic. Internet architecture integrates a certain conception of values such as civil liberties, while policies on use of technology play at least an equally important role in achieving attribution.[29] Worse, the assessment that technical constraints are primary lacks crucial nuance, as the rest of this book will strive to demonstrate.

As well as seeing attribution as a technological problem, many have expressed the view that it is a problem that cannot be solved. In 2008, technical cyber security expert Jeffrey Hunker asked the question: 'Given that we need attribution, but that in general attribution is impossible, what should we do?'[30] In 2010, Bruce Schneier, a leading expert on cyber security, wrote that: 'Universal identification is impossible. Even attribution—knowing who is responsible for particular Internet packets—is *impossible* [emphasis added].'[31]

His point was echoed by Peter Sommer and Ian Brown, two cyber security experts, who wrote in a report published by the Organisation for Economic Co-operation and Development (OECD) that: 'In terms of cyber attacks the one overwhelming characteristic is that most of the time it will be *impossible* for victims to ascertain the identity of the attacker [emphasis added].'[32]

Similarly, Jack Goldsmith, a professor of law at Harvard, acknowledged in *The Washington Post* that 'attribution for [a] cyber attack takes time and is sometimes *impossible* to determine with certainty' [emphasis added].[33] In 2012, a panel of three professors discussing 'Attribution—How to Live Without It?' also concluded that 'most experts share the view that attribution is impossible'.[34] Reflecting this consensus, Julian Richards, a political scientist, wrote in his 2012 book on national security that the 'precise attribution of attacks is virtually impossible'.[35] The list of other sources mentioning this impossibility, from blog posts to other media sources, is in fact quite long.[36] Following the rationale that attribution is important, but impossible, even led Mike McConnell, former director of the National Security Agency (NSA), to consider that the United States 'is fighting a cyberwar today', and that they 'are losing it'.[37] He explained that the lack of attribution was central to why the United States is losing the 'cyberwar'—whatever he meant by using this term.

The third common misconception is that the attribution of cyber attacks is somewhat unique. US officials, again, have asserted the difference between the attribution problem in 'cyberspace' and the attribution of other types of attack. Steve Schleien, principal director for cyberspace in the US Office of the Undersecretary of Defense for Policy, highlighted the uniqueness of the attribution problem in cyberspace: 'The challenge of attribution is one that we are working on, but it is much different than what we're familiar with in other domains'.[38] Likewise, the US senator Sheldon Whitehouse, speaking at a military academy in 2012, declared: 'Clarity does not exist in cyberspace, in part because of attribution problems, and in part because principles in geographic space do not translate readily to cyberspace. Without this clarity, we cannot adequately deter cyber threats'.[39] The uniqueness of cyber attack attribution is mostly based on the assumed uniqueness of the properties of 'cyberspace', which is considered different from other 'spaces'. For example,

Lieutenant General Charles Croom, referring to a policy statement issued by the White House in a conference organised by the Atlantic Council, mentioned the uniqueness of cyberspace:

> Is it a global commons? Is it the fifth dimension, as the military would say? Air, land, sea, space and cyber? Is it the frontier? Is it the Wild West? The White House came out with a policy statement in the last few days that clarified that totally. It said it's not a cyber domain, it's not a war-fighting domain, it's not a military domain, it's not an operational domain, but it is cyberspace.[40]

This leads us to consider the following: what makes the attribution of cyber attacks so unique? Are there specific elements that constrain the attribution of cyber attacks and not the attribution of any other types of attack, be they criminal attacks or other forms of politically violent incident? Furthermore, coupled with the claims of insolvability of the attribution problem, the claims of uniqueness raise the question of whether there are genuinely any constraints unique to cyber attacks that cannot be overcome.[41] The first central question addressed in the book is therefore: what constrains attribution? In other words, besides technical elements that make attribution of cyber attacks difficult, is it possible to identify other elements? Most notably, political and legal constraints must arise in relation to cyber attacks, but what are they specifically?

The second question relates to the way attribution and its constraints are approached: it should be viewed not as a problem, but as a process. Approaching attribution as a process has two methodological advantages. Firstly, it allows the consideration of a range of nuances for attribution, and not only to simply see attribution as 'solved' or 'unsolved', a misleading but common characterisation.[42] One of the issues of classifying attribution as 'solved' or 'unsolved' is that analysts and journalists may soon stop questioning the evidence that points in the direction of the authors behind an attack. They may simply consider that the authors of the attack have now indisputably been exposed— that the 'attribution problem' has been solved—when it is still necessary to consider all the important details and nuances of the case. However, in contrast, attribution is a process that constantly evolves and changes with time. In other words, it is not a one-off problem with one single solution. Depending on the time and context, the certainty required to consider the process completed may necessitate a high level of proof; at other times, it may not. Further, the process evolves as more and more information is gathered, linked together by various entities, and weighed, judged and publicly claimed, until, sometimes, a consensus emerges reflecting an audience's conviction that a certain presented narrative is genuine.

The attribution of the now infamous Stuxnet, which targeted the Iranian nuclear power plant at Natanz, is a perfect example. As soon as its existence came to light in June 2010, experts suspected US and Israeli involvement in the operation.[43] Two years later, these suspicions were first confirmed when a journalist at *The New York Times*, David Sanger, claimed to have had access to confidential sources confirming the operation in detail.[44] Obama's administration, in what could be seen as confirmation of the claim's veracity, started legal proceedings to find the leakers who had talked to David Sanger and there were suspicions that former General James Cartwright was the main source of the leak (Cartwright admitted in October 2016 talking with Sanger and lying to the FBI about it, although he claimed that he was not the 'source of the story' and only did so in order 'to protect American interests and lives').[45] Again a year later, Edward Snowden, a former CIA employee and NSA contractor at Booz Allen Hamilton, a company contracted out by intelligence services, confirmed the revelations to the German magazine *Der Spiegel*.[46] Neither the United States nor Israel has acknowledged being the authors of Stuxnet. But attribution has become clearer and clearer as the process has moved along. Far from knowing with great certainty from the outset who the authors were, therefore, achieving attribution has necessitated several steps. With time, the attribution evolved, and in this case, the evidence came to strengthen the hypothesis. Stuxnet is not an isolated case when it comes to defining attribution as a process, but a rather representative one. As the rest of the cases studied here will demonstrate, achieving attribution requires going through a distinct process, which is at times closely linked with criminal processes, and at other times more closely related to political processes.

The second advantage of considering attribution as a process is the framework this provides for distinguishing the needs of the many different parties involved in attribution, ranging from cyber security companies, intelligence services, law enforcement agencies and private individuals (such as Brian Krebs in the Shmakov case). Each entity functions differently and under different constraints. For cyber security companies, the most important constraint may well be technical. But for law enforcement agencies and courts, these constraints are at the legal and political levels; for example, they relate to the exchange of information in order to trace an IP address internationally, and to the extradition of offenders. For decision-makers, the constraints of merely acquiring information are not nearly as important as taking the political decision to publicly attribute an attack.

Therefore, if we consider a framework for attribution, where attribution is defined as a process, processes can be broken down into different steps. The first step of the attribution process is clear: discovery of the breach of an information system. But the remaining steps vary significantly from case to case. In fact, the intermediary steps, and the certainty reached at the end of the process, depend mostly on whether the incident is solely criminal, or if it represents a potential threat to national security. From a legal standpoint, this degree of certainty can be, for instance, the irrefutable deduction of a party's guilt based on verifiable evidence. From a political standpoint, the mere possession of intelligence pointing to a state may be sufficient to create a stand-off with another state.

This decision to regard a state as an enemy and formally attribute the attack to it is a political decision, and is likely to be taken only by senior elected officials (Chapter 2, on judgement, will further examine the definition of 'political'). As Francis Maude, then minister for the Cabinet Office, pointed out in a hearing at the House of Commons in June 2012, 'if something looked like it could be a sovereign attack', the judgement about deciding sponsorship 'would clearly be for the Prime Minister' to make.[47] Such a step has precedence. In a case detailed below, where the film producing company Sony Pictures Entertainment came under cyber attack at the end of 2014, the president of the United States publicly attributed the attacks to the North Korean government.[48] Obama's actions and Maude's comment highlight the strong political nature of attribution in certain cases where it does not make much sense to talk of attribution as a political act that would be 'solved' or 'unsolved'; instead, it is more meaningful to explain the different steps of the process and consider what constrains each of these. This process looks very different again in the Shmakov case, where hardly any political features could be identified. These differences in the steps of the process lead to the second central question of this book: what does the attribution process entail?

This book's first original approach concerns the modelling of attribution as a process. It identifies five aspects that differ according to whether attribution takes place in a criminal or national security context. These aspects are: the authority responsible for attribution (judiciary vs. executive); the type of evidence the authority uses (digital forensics vs. intelligence intercepts, and whistle-blowers); the standard of evidence ('beyond reasonable doubt' and 'preponderance of the evidence' vs. dependent upon convictions); the timing for attribution (irrelevant vs. urgent); and the issues at stake (individual vs. political). These five aspects conflict with the three commonly expressed beliefs about attribution: that it is a technical problem, is unsolvable and has unique properties. They highlight the fact that the technicality of cyber attacks and the anonymity supported by the Internet's network structure are not the most significant constraints on attribution. For national security incidents, for example, contextual and political elements are the most important constraints informing the decision of whether or not to pursue the attribution.

The central argument of this book, and a short answer to the two research questions it investigates, is therefore that the attribution of cyber attacks is a two-pronged political process. The processes are never entirely 'solved', but evolve through different stages depending on the nature of the incident. In many such incidents, the process closely follows a legal path; in others, the incident and its attribution remain within the realm of the executive. However, in both processes the attribution of cyber attacks is not unique, and shares a wealth of common properties with the attribution of either criminal or national security incidents.

The political nature of attribution is also reflected in the two processes (the next chapter will examine this in greater detail): in criminal cases, laws reflect prevailing norms and power in society, while in national security cases, attribution is the reflection of a state's will to maintain, increase or assert its power. Furthermore, when cyber attacks occur at national security level, investigators benefit from accessing specific resources. For example, intelligence agencies intervene and use their widespread networks to gather useful information. Another key difference is that once a case occurs at national security level, the government decides on what constitutes an appropriate and efficient standard of evidence for attribution. It then must convince an audience of the appropriateness of its claims. This contrasts with attribution in criminal cases, where courts rely on stringent and set standards, and primarily on forensic evidence—although attribution outside a court setting is also possible.

To support this central argument, the book draws its conclusions from the analysis of short case studies—a detailed examination of aspects of cyber attack cases in order to test hypotheses 'that may be generalizable to other' attacks.[49] Each case study examines the particularities of the attribution process, and is chosen because it can highlight a new aspect of what limited or enabled attribution. Each study thoroughly analyses the process that led to attribution of the cyber attack to an individual, a corporation or a state actor. This process encompasses the discovery of the incident, the collection of evidence and intelligence, cooperation with other entities to exchange evidence, the interpretation of the evidence, and questioning the reliability of the evidence. Together, the case studies provide a 'real-life insight' into how the attribution process has evolved historically and is taking place currently, and highlight causal relations between different variables. Such a causal relation could, for example, be whether cooperation on cyber attacks between countries depends on political factors unrelated to the incidents being considered. Case studies can support or help refute this association.

A case study methodology is in sharp contrast to a quantitative approach to attribution, where it is possible to compare numbers of attributed cases. Yet such a method fails to grasp the nuances of the many cases that stand somewhere between being 'solved' or 'unsolved'. Furthermore, for each case, it is necessary to examine the specifics to know who considered the case solved, and on what grounds and evidence. It is not possible, by looking at general statistics, to obtain the type of detail necessary to observe the important constraints shaping the process. As such, any statistics invite strong methodological concern. Moreover, one of the few ways to obtain statistics would be via departments of justice. Yet when courts find an individual innocent, that does not imply that the attack can't still be attributed to the individual. Considering statistics would therefore be highly misrepresentative.

INTRODUCTION

The case studies are used here to build the theory surrounding attribution following the grounded theory method, which uses case studies as instances of the constructed theory.[50] This is both a strength and a weakness of the grounded theory method. On the one hand, the constructed theory aims to be as general as possible by identifying common patterns between the selected cases, and is thus empirically valid. On the other hand, induction is limited, and the constructed theory cannot by design be universal and applicable to all cases. This also implies that the sampling method does not influence the representativeness of the cases, which have been chosen for their ability to highlight a particular phenomenon and illustrate a particular theoretical aspect. With grounded theory, the constructed theory is refined and revisited as a function of the possible contradictory conclusions stemming from the set of considered case studies.[51] The flexibility of the method allows the consideration of emerging and unanticipated issues, the formation of original hypotheses, and the investigation of evidence supporting the hypotheses within the set of case studies.

The materials and data for the case studies come from newspapers, police reports, court documents and interviews, when needed. By putting the information together and cross-checking facts between the different sources, the narratives of the case studies attempt to be as close to the facts as possible. But in certain cases, it is not possible to re-trace how the police followed a hacker's trail. For such cases, interviews with the main parties involved (the hacker, companies supporting the investigation, or defence forensic experts) provide the main elements for the narratives recreating the attribution process.

Interviews with investigators involved in attribution procedures, ranging from law enforcement agents to forensic researchers for private companies, also helped verify hypotheses—but only to a limited degree, for two reasons. Firstly, many interviewees were wary of walking the thin line between discussing what was already in the public domain and revealing new information that could upset either a party they were working with, the public (as some of the topics touched upon are privacy-sensitive) or their hierarchy. Further, the interviews were conducted in the midst of bulk revelations on surveillance programmes conducted by the NSA, adding to the interviewees' caution and to their fear that their words could be misunderstood. Secondly, most investigators' and experts' views on attribution largely depend upon the confined environment in which the investigators and experts work. A researcher working for a commercial cyber security company may well be oblivious to the functioning of politics in a government. Experts, in other words, cannot be expert on the whole attribution process, and their views will necessarily be biased or limited.

Case studies also generate an important bias when used to generalise.[52] For a start, it is problematic that few examples exist of state-sponsored cyber attacks—far fewer than examples of criminal cyber attacks—even if they are growing. But alternatives to considering case studies are even less appropriate in the context of an academic study. For instance, the popular book *Cyber War* by Richard Clarke (former national coordinator for security, infrastructure protection and counterterrorism under President Bill Clinton) and Robert Knake of the Council on Foreign Relations relies heavily on future hypothetical scenarios.[53] Throughout his long experience in government and as a national security advisor, Clarke has certainly gained useful insights that bolster his analysis. He may have had access to secret and confidential briefings, which may in turn have shaped the book's tone of urgency and, at times, of apocalypse. Also, Clarke was one of the very few people who consistently tried to warn the National Security Council, prior to 9/11, of the Al Qaeda threat.[54] His authority gives weight to his analysis to some extent. But two points explain why such a methodology is ill-fitted to this particular research.

Firstly, hypothetical scenarios cannot be considered as reliable evidence for elaborating sound hypotheses. Created hypothetical scenarios, in Clarke and Knake's book and numerous other works, usually seek to emphasise the importance that the threat of cyber attacks represents.[55] To do so, they only consider extreme cases and tend to be detached from common reality. Far from facing cyber attacks targeting industrial control systems with devastating consequences, most threats concern espionage rather than sabotage, are considerably more low-profile, and do not beget complete social chaos. Considering extremes loses the nuance, which is precisely what this book is about: analysing the subtleties of attribution in different cases. Some of the hypothetical scenarios used in Clarke and Knake's book are only taken seriously because of the authors' credentials. This leads us to the second reason for not following Clarke and Knake's methodology: the author of this book does not have the same credibility or experience in decision-making as Clarke does. Creating scenarios would hence be void of any sense, and the conclusions drawn from them would be baseless.

Having dismissed quantitative methodologies, and the use of hypothetical scenarios, it is important to note that there is a further advantage to considering case studies, especially for criminal cases: there exist many examples throughout the world of police investigating and successfully identifying criminals behind cyber attacks. Looking at differences between these criminal cases, and those more recent cases that seem to involve states, has helped to inform the arguments of this book, and reduces the bias towards generalisation. The evidence drawn from each case counterbalances other conclusions from other cases in order to present the different sides of the argument, and attempts, again, to reduce the bias stemming from the use of a particular collection of case studies. Cases that do not support the hypotheses help to inform the extent of the hypotheses' validity, and help to limit the theories' scope of application.

Hence, the methodology includes a comparative element between the different case studies. The comparison of the different variables attempts to discern the constraints and limits of the attribution process, the tactics used by the hackers to mask their trails, the techniques (including political manoeuvres) used by the investigators to unravel the hackers' identities, and the criteria used for determining the sponsorship of attacks.

Before outlining the next chapters, it is important to focus on a couple of definitions, which set the limits and scope of the present work. This book focuses solely on cyber attacks. The term 'cyber attack' is far from self-explanatory, largely because of inconsistency in the use of the prefix 'cyber' not only in academic literature, but also in common parlance.

The term 'attack' can have different meanings. In a legal context, a group of scholars who are experts on international law and cyber security have agreed to define a cyber attack as an operation 'that is reasonably expected to cause injury or death to persons or damage or destruction to objects'.[56] Such a definition of cyber attacks excludes any use of a cyber attack for espionage purposes. As this group of scholars was specifically analysing the threshold that cyber operations must cross to be regarded as 'use of force', the exclusion is justifiable by linking the term 'attack' with the violence an act begets in terms of consequences.[57] (A fair criticism of such a definition, grounded in consequentialism, is that espionage can beget great harm or be used to spark further forms of indirect violence, and should hence be included within the definition of the term 'attack'.)

The experts further suggested that, with such a definition, a denial-of-service 'attack' should not be considered as such.[58] Other legal scholars have disputed this interpretation and have contended that it is not acceptable only to count as attacks those acts begetting physical damage, and that a lower threshold should be used.[59] As this study is concerned with all types of threats posed to computer systems, a more holistic definition, based on a primarily technical understanding of the term, is appropriate. Therefore, in this work, an 'attack' here refers to the intentional breach, for assumed malicious purposes, of an information system's components of information security.[60] These components are confidentiality, integrity, availability, authenticity and non-repudiation.[61] Espionage operations breach the confidentiality element of this model. Furthermore, the two last components, authenticity and non-repudiation, can help with the technical attribution of attacks. Techniques for authenticity aim at ensuring that the identity of a person or device is as it is claimed to be. Non-repudiation mechanisms aim at ascertaining that a person or device is the author of a specific message or packet, and ensures that the author cannot later deny creating the message or packet.

The term 'cyber' in 'cyber attacks' similarly requires definition. The word 'cyber' tends to be used as a contraction of 'cyberspace'— although it has gone through different meanings over time, including one phase where it was used as a verb to refer to 'having cybersex', or virtual sex.[62] When used to mean 'cyberspace', the types of network encompassed within the word 'cyberspace' are entirely heterogeneous. There is no single, globally accepted definition of cyberspace. Cyberspace can include a wide range of devices that operate through different networks with many protocols, and includes, for instance, the Internet, local area networks, mobile networks and industrial control systems. To study attribution on all these different networks can at first seem an ambitious task because it implies studying the technical particularities of each type of network. But there are wider considerations (legal, economic and political) that constrain attribution, regardless of the type of networks and their operating protocols. Several authors have focused on the technical aspects, as aforementioned. Similarly, others have emphasised the legal aspects of attribution.[63] 'Attribution is a legal exercise', wrote the London-based scholar Marco Roscini in his 2014 book.[64] Attribution combines all technical, legal and political aspects, but this book, motivated by the dearth of research on this angle, focuses specifically on the political aspects. In fact, as will be argued later, technical elements are not even a key tenet for the attribution of attacks to a sponsor. Considering all types of networks within the term 'cyberspace', regardless of their operating protocols, is thus meaningful for this study.

The larger field of study concerned with the protection of information systems against cyber attacks is that of cyber security. Cyber security encompasses computer and network security, which aims, as the name indicates, to protect computing devices or a network. But while computer and network security focuses on the technical system, the term 'cyber security' encompasses not only the technical protection of all communication networks in their widest meaning, but also a wide range of other economic, legal and political measures that can ensure the maintenance of the five information assurance components introduced above. The International Telecommunication Union provides this definition: 'Cybersecurity is the collection of tools, policies, security concepts, security safeguards, guidelines, risk management approaches, actions, training, best practices, assurance and technologies that can be used to protect the cyber environment and organization and user's assets.'[65]

The term 'cyber security' is in fact so general that it comprises not only the protection of cyberspace against cyber attacks but also against cyber crime in the broadest sense; that is, not only crime that targets information systems, but also crime that is facilitated by them.[66] The problem of identifying cyber criminals shares many similarities with that of identifying the instigators of cyber attacks. The identification of criminals involves a mix of technical, legal and political elements, and the process often starts with the discovery of an IP address whose user is unknown.

Yet the political aspect of attributing cyber crime involves balancing many civil liberties that the attribution of cyber attacks does not affect. For instance, cyber crime includes online harassment and racial discrimination. Policies to identify authors of acts of harassment need to balance an individual's right of expression, of privacy, and of association with the harm these rights can beget. Policies to identify instigators of cyber attacks, which mostly fall within the category of espionage and sabotage operations, rarely pertain to issues of freedom of speech. Furthermore, it is unlikely that a corporation or a state would sponsor harassment, whereas such entities do sponsor cyber attacks, and are at the core of this book's study of attribution.

Despite cyber attacks only being a subset of cyber crime, many of the findings on the identified constraints, limits and solutions for attribution of cyber attacks are likely to be replicable to some extent for cyber crime in general. As the problem of cooperation and exchanging information is central to both cyber crime and cyber attacks, the solutions must likewise be relatively important for the identification of any cyber criminals, and more specifically for the identification of attackers.

The process of attributing cyber attacks also shares many common points with the larger debate on identifying people online. For instance, this includes companies trying to analyse users' behaviours in order to target advertisements to potential clients by gathering a large amount of data. The process of identification can be slightly different from that used for cyber attacks, although it raises similar issues at the crossing of privacy, policy and national security. For example, the terms of use of websites visited online are influenced by national privacy standards and laws on data protection.[67] Furthermore, security agencies have used the impetus from the terrorist attacks in the first decade of this century to access the data these companies gather, partially to identify people, and partially to identify new forms of threat.[68] Overall, this has led to warnings such as the one given by the UK Information Commissioner that his country was slowly 'sleepwalking into a surveillance society'.[69] Such shared interests arguably lead to considering a certain complicity between state and company interests; such complicity is also part of an analysis of attribution, where state actors can turn a blind eye to, or directly provide stimulus for, the instigation of attacks.[70]

INTRODUCTION

One of the key differences with attribution of cyber attacks within this debate, however, is the question of choice. '[U]sers should feel they have the effective possibility to choose whether they want to be tracked and profiled or not', declared Neelie Kroes, the vice president of the European Commission responsible for the Digital Agenda.[71] In other words, users can change their privacy preferences in order to evade companies' tracking systems. On the other hand, one cannot simply 'opt-out' of a hacker's decision in targeting his or her victim. In reality, it may be that users' preferences have, at the moment, little impact in light of the technology and ingenuity deployed by companies.[72] Users are influenced by technology and policies they have little understanding about or control over. Also, in comparison with cyber attacks, hackers generally have good technical knowledge of computer systems. And when hackers are state-sponsored, they are further secure in the knowledge that the state has direct control over policies regulating their practices.

Therefore, the set of cases considered within the scope of this book is considerably reduced in order not to address too many issues at once. The book focuses solely on cyber attacks and their attribution. The cases considered range across a wide time frame and include various forms of attack vectors, investigation techniques and countries. However, despite considering cyberspace in its wider meaning, most of the cases still focus on hackers attacking via the Internet. The Internet has become such a preponderant means of communication that such a focus is only natural. This focus should not be problematic because the most relevant aspect of attribution considered is not technological but political.

Last but not least, the term 'attribution' also needs defining. There already exist several definitions of attribution, including the 'attribution problem'. David Wheeler, a computer scientist, defined attribution as 'determining the identity or location of an attacker or an attacker's intermediary'.[73] Similarly, the scholars Isaac Ben Israel and Lior Tabansky defined the attribution problem as the issue of 'know[ing] the attacker's source and identity and on behalf of whom he operated'.[74] Both definitions raise a similar question. The terms 'identification', or 'investigation of instigators of attacks', or even 'investigation of sponsors of attacks', all commonly used in different contexts that are not related to cyber attacks, could potentially convey the same meaning. So, what does the term 'attribution' bring as a nuance to these other terms? Does it bring any nuance? To answer these questions, it is necessary to look at how the term emerged in the debate on cyber attacks.

Interestingly, in the 1990s, for most scholars and policy-makers, attribution referred to either a psychological or a legal concept. In psychology, attribution theory tried to explain how and what motivated individuals to act.[75] The theory was applied early on to computer crime, by, for instance, the security expert Sanford Sherizen, who, when analysing criminological concepts to control cyber crime, wrote in 1990 that 'a social rule, called attribution' can help prevent computer crimes, as we could explain how organisations decide to 'respond to computer crime incidents'.[76] The current use of the term retains some of this meaning as attribution entails finding out what motivated the instigators in launching the attacks. Other references to attribution can be found within the legal literature with two different meanings. One of these is linked to clearly stating and identifying the author of a document. For instance, a 1995 legal article about aspects of international law on the Internet did not refer to attribution in the sense of knowing who the attacker is, but dealt with copyrights.[77] The second legal meaning concerns the assignment of responsibility.

This second legal meaning is not completely detached from its psychological equivalent: by trying to explain causes for an incident, it is possible to understand who should bear the blame for it. Already, in 1985, William Bechtel, a philosopher who was then at Georgia State University and was concerned with ethical questions, asked whether 'attributing responsibility to computer systems' was possible. Bechtel did not look at cyber attacks in his paper, but was actually looking at faulty computer programmes.[78] The use of the term to refer to an intentionally, rather than unintentionally, caused incident is not a major leap. However, for Bechtel, the answer of who is to blame would ironically be far easier to answer in the case of a perpetrator intentionally launching an attack. Several other scholars, notably in the mid-1990s, then used attribution with the meaning of ascribing responsibility, rather than identification.[79] This was also a common use of the term to refer to responsibility in the contexts of 'transnational threats' and of nuclear weapons.[80] Yet before the end of the 1990s, it was still very common for resources touching upon the topic of the identification of criminals not to use the term 'attribution' when not set within the legal literature.[81]

The very end of the 1990s marked two gradual changes, which were not inherently related but largely explain a shift in the meaning of attribution and in the underlying assumptions that come with it. These assumptions notably concern the framing of attribution as technical and unique, and in this regard necessitating the allocation of distinct and important resources. From 1999, attribution started referring to identification rather than assignment of responsibility, in the context of both cyber attacks and nuclear threats.[82] And from this year on, a tool potentially hindering attribution, cryptography, became more widely available. (Although in practice the change of regime came only a year later, the change of mentality also started that year, with public officials stating that they would relax the laws.) The debate around cryptography touched upon anonymity, privacy, criminality and national security—the same topics that attribution directly relates to. The policy shift regarding cryptography therefore signalled an important change in how the United States was to approach attribution as an area where the government and its intelligence services acknowledged their key role in gathering forensics via the monitoring of telecommunications infrastructures.[83]

December 1999 marked the end of the long battle of US software companies and privacy activists against the government and the NSA to change the export status of cryptography, regulated until then as weapon munitions. From 1992, in opposition to the NSA and the government, there was a movement known as 'cypherpunk'. The movement's core contention was that it regarded cryptography as key to allowing people to 'interact with each other in a totally anonymous manner'.[84] The design of specific schemes dating from the previous decade, based on cryptography, allowed users to hide their identity, besides masking the content of online conversations to any unwanted intruder.[85] But the US government viewed cryptography very differently, namely as a military tool that should not be put in the hands of foreigners, and that should be monitored closely. As such, the export of any cryptographic material outside the United States was heavily restricted, and the publication of cryptographic software within the country was also subject to censure. The NSA wanted to ensure that it would still be able to decipher any code in the world if it needed to.

21

Many who associated themselves with the cypherpunk movement regarded cryptography as serving a lot more than a military function. Many of the writings of the movement's founders have a revolutionary tone attached to them, presenting encryption as the 'tool' enabling this revolution. At a conference in 1991, John Gilmore, a well-known member of the cypherpunk movement, said, 'I want to guarantee—with physics and mathematics, not with laws—things like real privacy of personal communications ... real privacy of personal records ... real freedom of trade ... real financial privacy ... [and] real control of identification'.[86] Similarly, another famous member, Tim May, also talked of 'the end of the nation-state' with the cryptography revolution—which did nothing to reassure the NSA about the changes ahead.[87] 'These developments will alter completely the nature of government regulation, the ability to tax and control economic interactions, the ability to keep information secret, and will even alter the nature of trust and reputation,' May further wrote in the *Crypto Anarchist Manifesto* in 1992.[88] The over-emphasis on technical points to thwart traceability is therefore not new to the debate on attribution; nor are the many arguments put forward by the government to prevent a change of regime with regard to the liberalisation of cryptographic standards.

On the whole, the US government relentlessly put forward two closely connected arguments in the 1990s when refusing to change regulations controlling the export of cryptography. Interestingly for attribution, these two arguments have largely resurfaced twenty years later in the debate concerning the collection of metadata to help identify Internet users. The first argument the US government put forward to explain its reluctance was that if more people used cryptography, the amount of useful data that intelligence services could capture would decrease, and would therefore result in creating a greater threat to national security. In other words, a change in the current regime would hinder law enforcement agencies from conducting their duty effectively.[89] Illustrative of this argument is the charge brought in 1993 against Phil Zimmermann, the creator of a widely distributed encryption programme called Pretty Good Privacy. During a hearing, the court blamed him because the police could not read a paedophile's diary encrypted with his software.[90] Zimmermann answered that 'all technology has trade-offs', including what he had developed.[91] The second argument, summarised as 'if you knew what I knew', was that the public does not have full knowledge of the actual level of the security threat, but that if people were aware of it, they would never suggest cutting back the resources of security services.[92]

In the end, though, the US government gave in to the cypherpunk movement's main request to relax export laws on cryptography. The change in the export regime, allowing companies to use and ship cryptography products abroad, took time to take effect. An initial move by the NSA, announced in 1993, was to suggest that telecommunication companies could use encryption, but that they should, on a voluntarily basis, include a chip, the Clipper Chip, in the process, to help the NSA decipher the encrypted communication. The chip would split the encryption key into two parts, and put one part in escrow accessible by the NSA only. The telecommunication companies had a threefold interest in the chip: it kept communication secure for its customers against third parties other than law enforcement agencies, helped law enforcement agencies, and, most important of all, kept the government as a customer of their services.[93]

But the cypherpunks did not see the situation in quite the same way; instead, they regarded it as 'Big Brother' trying to spy on everyone's conversations.[94] Opposition grew quickly against the chip, and had reached 80 per cent by 1994.[95] For a start, the name was not good for presentation, and led to puns such as 'Clipper, clips the wing of individual liberty'.[96] On top of this, the discovery of flaws in the chip did not help the government sell the argument that the chip would help make communications more secure in general.[97] In November 1993, Representative Maria Cantwell tried to put a bill forward to change the export status of encryption as munitions. Although it was unlikely to pass, Vice President Al Gore suggested she drop the bill if the Clinton administration changed their position on the Clipper Chip.[98] She agreed, and the Clipper Chip was no longer politically viable.

At the same time that Cantwell was drafting her bill, Congress commissioned a report to study the question. The report came out three years later, was very thorough in its analysis, and extended beyond 700 pages.[99] The committee concluded that 'the complete elimination of export controls on products with encryption capabilities does not seem reasonable in the short term', but criticised the current government's approach, hence advocating a relaxed regime of export control and greater use of cryptographic solutions by domestic companies.[100] Several projects helped spread the use of encryption within the United States and abroad, most notably Pretty Good Privacy and Netscape, which certainly helped popularise encryption. Yet the end of robust regulation of encryption is due to a much smaller project, Snuffle, whose creator, Daniel Bernstein, a graduate from Berkeley, wanted to publish. After enquiring about the process, and being denied the right to publish, Bernstein filed a suit with the help of John Gilmore, a founder of the Electronic Frontier Foundation. In April 1996, in the first ruling of its kind by a District Court, Judge Marilyn Patel ruled that code is a form of speech, and thus the export control rules were partially unconstitutional.[101] The government naturally challenged this opinion, stating that the Court had no authority to rule on the matter, and the case went on to the Supreme Court. In May 1999, the Court gave its verdict, ruling in favour of Bernstein.[102] From there, the path was clear.

The Clinton administration considered two arguments. Firstly, with the rise of online commerce, people needed protection on the Internet. Secondly, if encryption were to become prevalent, 'people may die', as security services would not be able to unravel a plot targeting a digital infrastructure. But equally, if the digital infrastructure could not protect itself because of a lack of cryptography, 'people may die'.[103] In December 1999, Al Gore finally unveiled a new set of regulations that relaxed export control.

The change of policy did not mean the end of the nation-state or any revolution that the cypherpunk movement had hoped for or predicted. But, interestingly, this change in policy came at the same time as the change in the usage of the word 'attribution': from a legal meaning indicating blame, to a definition relating to identification. The two changes may not be connected, but they translate similar aspects of cyber attack investigations.

Firstly, policy-makers were increasingly aware of the need to make resources available for investigation and cooperation, and the use of a different term marked a change in their policy: instead of simply dismissing cases of cyber attacks, they started seriously investigating them in the 1990s and providing the resources to do so, even if encryption stood in their way. Secondly, policy-makers perceived the attribution of cyber attacks as being somewhat different and unique from investigations of other attacks, such as criminal assaults and bombing incidents—as already noted in the first part of this introduction—probably due to the technicalities of cyber attacks. 'We often think of cyber investigations as unique in nature, and most of them do require a certain technical expertise,' said Robert Mueller, director of the FBI, at an international conference in August 2013.[104] (In all fairness, Mueller is also well aware that this difference between the identification of criminals and of instigators of cyber attacks has it limits: 'But our effectiveness in cyber investigations rests on the same techniques we have used in cases throughout the FBI's history—physical surveillance, forensics, cooperating witnesses, sources, and court-ordered wire intercepts'.)[105] This uniqueness warranted new definitions, according to scholars, who defined attribution by accenting its technical traits.

For instance, David D. Clark and Susan Landau defined the attribution problem by separating the technological side of attribution from its human component.[106] W. Earl Boebert, an information security expert, also made the distinction between technical and non-technical attribution, phrasing the two corresponding problems as: 'Can you determine which machine or machines are generating or controlling the intrusion? Can you determine the party that should be held responsible for the intrusion?'[107] Yet the technical traits of attribution, in many cases pertaining to finding sponsors, are hardly relevant, and justify defining attribution separately from technical tenets.

The last aspect that this change in meaning illustrates is that attribution is not merely the identification of attackers, but the process of unravelling the entire chain of individuals, organisations and states involved in the attacks. This definition of attribution is the one used in the book. Different state organisations' policies directly influence attribution—for instance, policies regarding cryptography, and other policies of data retention or extradition—thus constituting a chain of entities that play a direct role in how attribution occurs. Consequently, the roles of policy and of these organisations need to be properly examined in a study of the matter. Our broader definition of attribution allows this. It is also worth noting that in the debate on nuclear strategy, use of the word 'attribution' reflected this emphasis on the chain of people involved, as a report published by the Harvard Kennedy School pointed out: 'Attribution ideally would identify not only the original source of the fissile material but also its chain of custody, so that system "holes" could be identified'.[108]

Attribution is therefore a process to unravel the identity of the chain of actors involved in a cyber attack. The process starts with a security breach being discovered, and finishes with its authors and sponsors being found, or not. Who discovers the breach, who investigates it, and what happens between the discovery and the outcome of the attribution process can be meandering. The following chapters will aim at clarifying this meandering process.

Chapter 1 starts by separating attribution into two distinct processes. One concerns the attribution of criminal cyber attacks, and closely follows a judicial process that is successful in many cases, with a high level of certainty. The other concerns cases of importance for national security, involving the assessment of potential threats to the state. Both processes differ on five levels, characterised as: the authority responsible for attribution, the type of evidence the investigator uses, the standard of evidence, the timing for attribution, and the issues at stake. The chapter's main argument is that investigations of cyber attacks at the level of national security threat benefit from significantly superior resources to those behind the investigation of mere criminal cases, especially as investigators can resort to intelligence garnered with methods bordering legality, and for which they may not be accountable. Yet this broader investigative power does not make it easier to find instigators: in national security incidents, making initial assumptions about who the enemy is by using judgement can be easy, but conclusively proving the identity of the enemy is more difficult than in criminal cases, despite the use of significant resources.

Chapter 2 examines the reliance of attribution on judgement, especially in the context of national security. Judgement is commonly accepted as being part of the judicial process, but less so when it comes to attributing attacks to states. The reliance on judgement has allowed accused states to ward off such claims easily, by calling the accusations 'unprofessional'. Yet, this is arguably not the case; judgement is inherent to the attribution process. Many steps of this process entail judgement calls, not from the point of view of legal, ethical or moral understanding, but in order to interpret states' behaviours and officials' statements. The chapter argues that political judgement for attribution is fallible but inescapable. The role of judgement needs to be acknowledged so as not to fall into a false expectation that attribution will be 'unprofessional' because it relies on judgement, and in order to consider the problems of authority and trust that it raises.

Chapter 3 looks at the standard of evidence specifically required for attribution. There is great variety in legal standards, from proving beyond reasonable doubt, to merely having some intelligence on an instigator. It can be tempting to consider that one 'appropriate' standard for attribution is needed, especially in the national security context where officials need to make quick decisions often based on little reliable information. Yet standards of evidence do not really matter for attribution: states can easily choose the standard that most fits their purposes. Unfortunately, once a government makes attribution claims based on a chosen standard, there is often very little critical debate about that standard and about the evidence pointing in the direction of particular attackers, except in highly technical expert circles. The focus is rather on the actions called for as a result of the attribution. This demonstrates the malleability of standards for attribution, which can facilitate the manipulation of evidence, or of its presentation, by the state.

Chapter 4 considers one important actor in the attribution process: private companies, which face a few particular issues. As they publish reports on attribution, the accused party often uses the same arguments to try to undermine the authority of their claims: that the companies are not independent, but act on behalf of a government. They use the way private companies inherently operate to give grounds to their argument, albeit distorting the reality. And this matters, given the central role that certain private companies' reports can play in reshaping the diplomatic agenda. Private companies hope, with their reports, to counter the argument of an attacking state that no one has proof of such alleged activity. These criticisms reflect, therefore, the attacking state's unwillingness to accept reports as the valid evidence it demands. However, as with judgement inherent to attribution, the chapter shows that the close collaboration of private companies with intelligence services is an inescapable characteristic of the process.

Chapter 5 examines the time factor from two different perspectives: time understood as a measurable unit, and time understood in terms of context. Attribution, recognised as a time-consuming process, warrants effort to try to reduce the time it requires. But the efforts need to be correctly oriented. With calls for attribution to be 'in real time', many who advocate technical solutions completely dismiss the context in which attribution takes place, which can be far more important than merely reducing attribution time. Furthermore, these technical solutions run against one of the lessons of reduction in attribution time: in the past, gains in time have been largely due to improvements in bureaucratic processes rather than improved technical solutions.

Chapter 6 argues that states do not seek plausible deniability, or evade attribution for all types of cyber attack. In fact, when they do, the incentives may be greater because of domestic pressure rather than international pressure, especially for sabotage operations. In order to coerce a state actor via the use of cyber attacks as an instrument for political change, an attacker has to partially reveal their identity. This is in contrast with a state carrying out espionage operations that wish to remain covert, and from which domestic political fallouts can be costly. By analysing the meaning of plausible deniability, the chapter also contributes to demystifying the situation that attribution and deniability are both anchored in how the Internet is structured: deniability involves bureaucratic trickeries rather than technological prowess.

Lastly, the conclusion starts by summarising the contributions of this book, before considering what the future of attribution may look like. It briefly analyses the consequences for privacy of large metadata collection, and the effects on Internet governance of attribution mechanisms being revealed. More specifically, it contends that the potential breaking up of the Internet into multiple 'Internets' will reshape the practice of cyber security to some extent, but that the political limitations of attribution will remain very similar. This last chapter also briefly outlines the basis for future work by showing that attribution is not only limited to cyber attacks but also emerges in many other situations, involving the need to strike a 'right' balance between anonymity, privacy and security, which is one of the key challenges of the twenty-first century. Hence, the approach to attribution will reflect how society wishes to address the anonymity-privacy-security triangle, and how it has the potential to shape the balance between these three questions for years to come.

1

MODELLING ATTRIBUTION

In August 2012, the Shamoon malware infected the computers of Saudi Arabia's national oil company, Saudi Aramco, and prevented 30,000 computers from starting by overwriting a segment of their hard drive.[1] The attack was not very sophisticated; the attackers got lucky as they stumbled upon a document entitled 'Administrator passwords'.[2] Sophistication aside, the damage was still important. The *Financial Times* reported:

> While its industrial oil production systems were unaffected, Aramco was nearly fatally compromised because so much of its corporate infrastructure was destroyed. Company officials had to use typewriters and faxes to try and keep billions of dollars of oil trades from falling through. Domestically, the company gave oil away for several days following the attack because it could not process transactions.[3]

The attack even prompted the then US secretary of defense, Leon Panetta, to discuss the attack in a well-noted speech in front of business executives, and to answer further questions in a briefing at the Pentagon.[4] While Panetta's speech stopped short of accusing Iran of the attacks, a journalist, quoting an unnamed US government official, claimed that Iranian hackers carried out the attack with support from the Iranian government.[5] Officially, the attack remains unattributed to this day. In comparison, a great deal of other malware has in the past infected a significantly larger number of computers without prompting high political officials to react regarding the identity of the instigators. For instance, in 2004, the Sasser worm infected millions of computers, including those of rail systems in New South Wales, the Italian Interior Ministry, the European Commission, and British coastguard stations, without prompting such a response.[6] The police later found its author, Sven Jaschan, thanks to an information reward programme set up by Microsoft.[7] The attribution of these two different cyber attacks presents stringent dissimilarities, which raise several notable questions.

How and why does the attribution of an incident become the responsibility of the executive rather than the judiciary? How do the processes of attributing a criminal incident and attributing a national security incident differ?

This chapter offers a two-pronged model for attribution, based on the nature of the process either as criminal or as a threat to national security. Criminal cases rarely rise to the level of 'national threat', and are mostly dealt with by law enforcement agencies and subsequently by judiciary organisations. Several cases, based on certain criteria, fall within the remit of the executive rather than the judiciary, because government officials regard them as threats to national security.[8] This transfer has several consequences. First and foremost, the question of knowing the full name of the attacker becomes less relevant than knowing who the enemy is and who the sponsors are; for instance, a state actor or a terrorist organisation. Second, a national security incident usually implies broader investigative powers, especially those of intelligence services, which can use secret methods bordering legality. In cases threatening national security, it can be easy to make initial assumptions about who the enemy is, using judgement; but conclusively proving the identity of the enemy is more difficult than in criminal cases. Making assumptions without robustly proving them can be sufficient: how to act upon these assumptions is a matter of judgement left to the executive branch, which is not subject to a strict level of judicial proof. The process within which the attribution of a case falls is therefore influenced by many determinants: the authority responsible for attribution, the type of evidence the authority uses, the standard of evidence, the timing for attribution, and the issues at stake.

This chapter presents the two attribution processes in two steps. First, it shows the criteria that lead to incidents being considered national security threats, rather than mere criminal attacks. Second, it examines the different characteristics of each distinct process. The chapter concludes that criminal cases face constraints that can be more easily overcome than those confronting cases of national security.

Attribution by the executive: a set of conditions for the model

Four main models have previously emerged to characterise attribution; one has its roots in computer science, one in political science, and two others have origins in both fields.

In the first model, cyber security expert Tom Parker suggested assigning values to three variables to characterise the attacker: the attacker's intrinsic characteristics (such as resources and motivation), the target and the general environment of the attack.[9] Analysts compute the values using Bayesian probabilities, and are hence forced to assess the certainty of the assumptions and known information. Parker published his model in 2003, but it is still influential.[10] Such a model suffers from two main pitfalls: many variables do not lend themselves to being ascribed numerical values; and Parker's attempt to draw the line between criminal and terrorist cyber attacks based on the unknown motivation of the attacker leaves too much room for guesswork. The verification of the attacker's motivation always follows at least partial attribution, and cannot precede it. In fact, according to manuals given to police officers, the role of the police in proving that a person committed an offence does not include motives.[11] Investigations focus on only two elements, ability and opportunity, noting that '[o]ften, the motive for a crime is never known'.[12]

Furthermore, the model of characterising attackers by using properties of the attacks does not take into consideration new modes of developing attack techniques. Experienced hackers now sell a variety of malware and attack techniques (such as the infamous ZeuS malware) online.[13] An entity sustaining attacks could think that the same attacker is behind all of them because the modus operandi is the same. In reality, it may be that two different attackers are targeting the same entity, using the same product purchased online. A better model for attribution therefore needs to differentiate, at least for criminal attacks, between who carries out the attack, and who developed the tools for supporting it; in other words, between the operator and the customer.[14] At another level, the model also needs to distinguish when states are involved, and their different types of involvement (for instance, attacks can occur without any affiliation to a state, or a state may turn a blind eye to an attack, fund it or even direct it).[15] Parker's model of profiling fails to grasp these nuances, as do the few other cited studies that base their approach on it: they focus on techniques, rather than on a political approach to the issue of attribution.

The lawyer Susan W. Brenner proposed a second model for attribution, conceived as a political decision based on the trichotomy of war–terrorism–crime, whose relevance, she acknowledges, erodes in cyberspace.[16] Brenner suggested starting by attempting to classify the incident within this trichotomy, using three variables: the origin, the target and the motive for the attack. Yet determining if an incident is an act of crime or of terrorism rests solely on knowing whether the motives behind it are political. Again, the motives cannot be known before at least partial attribution. In such a model, the motive for the attack is simultaneously the solution to the problem and the variable on which the problem depends, as surmising motives is already moving towards achieving attribution. This is a major flaw in modelling attribution. Brenner's solution to the eroding relevance of the trichotomy focuses on the dilemma it poses at an institutional level, between military and civilian entities responding to the threat, rather than on the core problem it poses for attribution as a whole. When a case arises, before knowing the instigator's motive or whether they were a state actor, civilian law enforcement agencies and the military, traditionally involved only with state actors, can engage in a turf war over who is to investigate the case. By focusing on the institutional problem this creates, Brenner advocates a greater incorporation of civilians in a network-type voluntary militia. But her solution does not address the flaw in her model, leaving room for another, more coherent model to describe attribution.

Thirdly, computer scientists have pointed out that the attribution problem in fact encompasses three sub-problems: identifying the machine, identifying its owner, and identifying the sponsor.[17] The computer scientists David Clark, Susan Landau and Earl Boebert examined technical procedures in order to attribute to a machine, and left aside the details of identifying individuals and sponsors, the latter being a political problem. Thus, they only examined one of the three areas covered by their classification, the technical one. While much research has been carried out to improve the tracing of attacks, many researchers have also acknowledged that technical considerations alone cannot be sufficient to solve the attribution problem.[18] It is therefore important to continue expanding the model for cyber attack attribution without focusing on its technological aspect. The focus away from technology is further justified because political considerations dwarf technical ones when the incident meets certain criteria, thereby constraining access to evidence.

Finally, Thomas Rid and Ben Buchanan, scholars at King's College London, devised what is probably the most comprehensive, albeit imperfect, model for attribution yet.[19] They called it the 'Q Model'. The model divides attribution into three layers—technical (tactical), operational, and strategic—with an additional layer concerning communication. They remark that the further considerations are from the technical layer, the more judgement and interpretation are required. Their points of departure in building the model coincide with the ones laid out in this book; they simply take another road to structure their analysis of attribution. A possible criticism of the model, however, is a certain over-emphasis on cyber attacks representing a national threat, at the expense of criminal cyber attacks. The authors note, for instance, that '[t]he ultimate goal of attribution is identifying an organisation or government, not individuals'.[20] Though this rings true for many cases of national security, the goal of criminal investigations is precisely to pinpoint the individuals responsible. But even cases of national security merit a caveat. Since 2014, the US Department of Justice has indicted specific named individuals believed to be behind state-sponsored operations: five members of the Chinese army in 2014 and, in March 2016, three members of the Syrian Electronic Army (one already extradited from Germany to the US) and seven Iranians believed to hack on behalf of their government.[21] The rationale behind targeting these individuals was to instil fear in the hackers that if they were to travel, they could be deported to the US, where they would then be prosecuted. Individuals would then be either more reluctant to launch cyber attacks for their government, or much more careful. The book will come back to this theme when discussing the use of proxy actors in cyber attacks.

To remedy the shortcomings of each of the four aforementioned existing models, attribution can be approached as two distinct processes: the first follows well-established criminal procedures; the second is confined to the executive branch, and concerns threats deemed to be national security issues, requiring a governing entity to take decisions such as classifying an incident as an act of war or terrorism.[22] Considering attribution as a process and not as a problem allows the identification of steps where different questions arise, with different saliency, within the process. For instance, domestic criminal courts would only rarely deal with questions of the state's degree of involvement, and even more rarely would they focus on strategic questions about the instrumental use of cyber attacks as a covert means to achieve foreign policy objectives.[23]

In both types of attack, criminal and national security threats, the attribution process is political. This is core to the model and a key argument in this book. Practically as theoretically, however, this is far from evident. The next paragraphs will attempt to show what, from a theoretical perspective, is meant by political—a contested concept, given the various understandings attached to it.[24] It is useful for the discussion to keep the distinction between criminal cases, dealt with by a judiciary that implements the outcome of the legislative process (the law, in other words), and cases threatening national security, dealt by the executive.

To start with, why is attribution of a purely criminal case political? An activity is criminal because it breaches criminal law; laws are the outcome of a political process. This process of voting law is political for two different possible reasons. One is that laws shape the state, where the state is a modern version of the Greek term *polis*, the etymological root of politics.[25] A second logic understands the term 'political' as meaning divisive between groups of friends and enemies. Political issues, in other words, are at core 'polemical'.[26] Many ideas about cyber attacks and their attribution are in fact polemical, or at least far from being unanimously accepted.

One such idea concerns encryption. Encryption can preserve people's anonymity and consequently their privacy. But with encryption, it is also possible to hide traces of what one is doing, or where the traffic really flows (for instance, when someone extracts traffic from a compromised computer). Fights with US governments in the 1990s to relax encryption laws exemplify this political aspect of encryption.

Another polemical idea pertaining to attribution is the right of anonymity. A famous case can illustrate this contention. In 1992, Johan Helsingius, a Finn, had set up a server functioning like a proxy, anon. penet.fi, and allowed people to interact anonymously on forums. People were anonymous to one another, but because the system allowed users to answer each other, the system had to maintain a way of identifying them.[27] Complications began when, on 2 February 1995, a member of the Church of Scientology contacted Helsingius to find out the email address linked with a pseudonym used on a particular forum. The person had posted information only available within the Church's computer, and they therefore told the police to investigate a case of burglary. As Helsingius refused to cooperate, the US police sent an official request to the Finnish police via Interpol on the same day. On 6 February, the Finnish police used a warrant to seize all Helsingius's servers, and could therefore have identified all the users of his service. After negotiating with the police, Helsingius obtained a compromise, and was able to give the police only the email of the poster in question.[28] The user of the handle '-AB-' turned out to be the man responsible for the maintenance of the Church computer system, Tom Rummelhart.[29] The case illustrates squarely the political nature of attribution even for simple criminal cases. The cypherpunk movement has even integrated the political issue at the core of the fight in the anon.penet.fi case in their motto: 'privacy for the weak, transparency for the powerful'.[30] The motto can even, if interpreted in an extreme way, indicate that no cyber attacks should be criminalised when they are targeted against 'the powerful', meaning governments and large corporations.

The attribution process of cases relating to national security is also political. The executive, a set of state institutions, performs the attribution of national security cases. The mandate of the institutions operating for the state can be sufficient to understand their work as political, in the etymological sense of the word. But it is also tautological, if one understands the state as a political entity by definition. Going beyond these observations, the set of state institutions actually involved in the executive process of attribution is in fact rather small, and comprises security services (law enforcement agencies, intelligence services), the office of the prime minister or head of state, possibly the ministry of defence, and the ministry of foreign affairs. Non-state actors, as examined in Chapter 4, also increasingly have significant powers to set the political agenda of these state institutions by investigating and naming the international actors behind attacks.

For national security cases, the political aspect can have two different contexts: international or domestic. Attributing an act to another state adversary will invariably come down to the question of the state's willingness to engage with that adversary to prove sponsorship—regardless of whichever level that may be, ranging from turning a blind eye to directing the activity—and to act upon the proof. This willingness depends on an evaluation of the benefits the state can gain from attribution, especially whether it will be able to maintain, increase or assert its power, namely its capability of achieving certain goals—the very definition given by the famous international relations theorist Hans Morgenthau.[31] Regarding the attribution of national security threats to domestic actors, the process eventually branches back to criminal procedures, where the political dimension has already been considered.

Attribution is therefore a political affair. This does not automatically imply that its constraints have to be political too. Parts of the issues surrounding attribution are in fact technical and legal. But interestingly, a certain number of the constraints surrounding attribution are factors often found in many other political matters as well. The analysis of five of them in the coming chapters aims at counterbalancing the overwhelming dominance of the technical aspects of attribution.

Firstly, many political matters rely on judgement, not in the moral sense of the term, but in the sense of requiring an assessment of the situation and formulating an opinion. Such political matters do not have a right or wrong approach, but depend on persuading an otherwise disagreeing entity (adverse political parties within the victim state, foreign allies) that the intuitive understanding and knowledge-based evaluation of the situation are correct. Secondly, legal standards, due to the nature of the law being closed to politics, also play a role in many political disputes. Thirdly, companies do not have any binding authority as the state does; but in the case of attribution, they have a certain power to set the political agenda. Fourthly, time is 'a basic dimension of political activity', as governments have to manage their agenda and their time effectively.[32] And finally, the constraint of plausible deniability for attribution relies on deception, an aspect of politics drawn out by Niccolò Machiavelli in *The Prince*, and with which politics is strongly associated in common parlance, as its definition in the dictionaries illustrates.[33]

One of the distinctions between the two attribution processes resides in the institutions involved, which in turn have an effect on the resources invested into cases. For example, within the executive, the invested resources go well beyond those used in criminal cases. The incentives behind attribution are also divergent: finding a criminal or facing a political adversary. As noted by the former director of the NSA (2005–14) and former director of the US Cyber Command, General Keith B. Alexander, 'not every event that affects our networks rises to the level of a national security threat'.[34] Those that do not reach this level follow the attribution process of criminal incidents, given that the importance of the investigation largely outweighs the cost of the attacks; otherwise, law enforcement agencies may not deem the cost of attribution in the state's interests.

Classifying incidents as national security threats certainly has a symbolic value, and as stated by Arnold Wolfers in his seminal 1952 article on the topic, 'if used without specifications it leaves room for more confusion than sound political counsel or scientific usage can afford'.[35] This confusion is often instrumental in giving agencies more capabilities and in curbing civil liberties.[36] Tellingly, the cypherpunk movement has a term to regroup the pretexts most commonly used under the heading of 'national security threat' in order to increase surveillance and restrict individual privacy: 'the Four Horsemen of the Infopocalypse', which include money laundering, drugs, terrorism and child pornography.[37]

What constitutes a case of national security? Assessing the threat and damage that can result from cyber attacks cannot be a sufficient factor, as this assessment can be far from straightforward to carry out. There are those on one side who write using near-apocalyptic scenarios that are not based on empirical evidence, and whose main consequences are to elicit an unwarranted level of fear.[38] On the other side are those who warn that certain speeches and acts elevate an incident to a security issue, even though the incident does not warrant such a label.[39] Part of the problem with classifying cyber attacks as national security threats is that they span a wide range of possible types of attack, from small annoyances with denial-of-service attacks to the potentially much scarier disruption of industrial control systems in Stuxnet-type attacks.

Another part of the problem is that while there is much conjecture about what could happen as a result of cyber attacks, there are a lot less actual data to help understand these risks. In this context, the unclear term of 'national security' can refer to the security of information systems, people, the economy or sometimes, as implied in Clarke and Knake's book, the security of the very foundations of our society, thereby resulting in chaos.[40] A computer security expert gives another explanation in the *Harvard National Security Journal* as to why cyber attacks belong in the category of national security threats: 'Because the United States's ability to project power depends on information technology, cyber insecurity is the paramount national security risk'.[41] Focused on power and the state, such an explanation sets the debate within a neorealist agenda. In fact, this debate about defining security, including national security, is not limited to cyber attacks. There is a much wider debate, with extensive literature, that seeks on one side to restrain the referent object to the military and the state, and on the other, to widen it to include political, economic, societal and environmental issues concerning people and systems.[42]

This book does not aim to look at why many governments have brought cyber attacks under the umbrella of national security threats; other very good studies have already done this.[43] Rather, it looks at how—based on which criteria and practices—governments and their 'national security community' distinguish the different levels of cyber attacks so as to consider only a certain portion of them as threatening national security, and to treat the other cases merely as criminal. National security is used here to reflect the current varied and common concerns and security priorities 'put forward by the political leaders' of several states about cyber attacks.[44] An analysis of the criteria used by political leaders to make the distinction between criminal and national security cases will allow a certain understanding of what they mean by 'national security'—a mixture of the preservation of the status quo concerning public institutions and infrastructures, and of people's standards of living.

The distinction between the cases must start with the observation that the attribution of cyber attacks is not systematically difficult. In many Western countries, the successful sentencing of many individual criminals who have launched cyber attacks attests that non-severe attacks can be easily attributable. In several cases, the attack remained within the boundaries of the country, and the criminals did not use any specific techniques to try to obfuscate their trails.[45] Once the victim noticed such an attack and reported it to the police, the police simply needed to look for the IP address of the instigator. Once they had the IP address, they checked which Internet service provider issued the address. By contacting the provider, they obtained a match between the IP address and the name. In these incidents, the providers were in the same country as the investigators, and the attackers were not astute enough to hide their IP address.[46]

This contrasts with the many factors that influence an incident becoming the preserve of the executive rather than of the criminal justice system. These factors are: the scale and severity of damage, the nature of the victim's organisation, the apparent origin of the instigator, the means of the attack and any claim of the attack by a political group. Most importantly, these factors are assessable from the outset of the investigation and do not rely on formulating early assumptions, as Brenner's model required for determining the motive of the attack. The factors are also strongly contingent upon perception, and can be approached in different ways. For instance, an incident could be presented as highly damaging, with strong rhetoric about its consequences, when the damage was, in fact, rather limited. These five factors are therefore not definitive or systematically indicative that the executive will deal with a case; a certain will to reap the political benefits of the case still needs to exist as well. Each of these factors will be further explained in turn.

Firstly, the severity of an attack is initially a strong indicator for justifying a case as threatening national security.[47] However, it must be noted that the assessment of an attack's severity is not always evident. In espionage cases, the severity depends upon the information accessed by the hackers, which can be difficult to gauge. Then, identifying the type of entity targeted (a security contractor, for instance) will establish if the damage could potentially be important. Also noteworthy is that the threshold for the severity of damage does not always need to be very high for the case to become political, and hence the framing of the damage also plays an important role.[48] A short case, widely mediatised, can illustrate this: the attacks on Sony Pictures Entertainment at the end of 2014. The real physical damage remained very much contained to the company itself, but the case spilled over so much that it became a national security matter, with the US president intervening.

The attack probably started in September 2014, but became visible only on 24 November of that year. That day, when employees arrived at work and turned on their computers, the computers displayed images of Sony's CEO, Michael Lynton, with his head severed.[49] A group called Guardians of Peace claimed the attack and demanded a ransom for data not to be released. This was not the first time in the past few days that the company had received such a threat. Three days earlier, a group called God's Apstls had sent a similar e-mail to the company, but no one had paid attention to it. On 27 November, the hackers released stolen data: five new upcoming films, the salary details of 6,000 employees, the bonuses of seventeen executives, and e-mails, many of which were embarrassing. And the attacks continued. By 1 December, Lynton, who had first thought of the intrusion as a mere 'nuisance', realised that 75 per cent of Sony's servers had been wiped out. Two weeks later, another e-mail from Guardians of Peace arrived: it contained terrorist threats if Sony went ahead with the release of a film called *The Interview*.

This was the first time that the hackers had mentioned this film, a first hint at their real motive. The movie was a bad comedy in which two journalists were to go to North Korea to murder the country's leader, Kim Jong-un. Throughout the film, Jong-un is ridiculed; he dies at the end. This upset the North Korean government, which had already expressed its discontentment in June 2014 via a press release from its foreign ministry and a letter to the UN secretary-general, Ban Ki-moon. More specifically, a spokesman said that North Korea would undertake "'a decisive and merciless countermeasure" if the United States government permitted Sony to make its planned Christmas release of the comedy "The Interview"'.[50] After some hesitation, the film was still released on Christmas Day.

The case escalated to the point where President Barack Obama, FBI director James Comey and James Clapper, the director of national intelligence, all called the North Korean government responsible for the attack.[51] This was highly unusual. Clapper even added that a Korean general, Kim Youn Chol, was specifically responsible.[52] How the US was so confident in attributing the attack remains partially unknown—which led to much criticism, although it is understandable that the US did not want to give away its sources.[53] It would appear that the NSA had had access to computers within North Korea, and also that a few of the users' real IPs were revealed due to sloppy operational security from the attackers.[54] Lastly, the attackers also reused modules from another attack, believed by many also to have been engineered by North Korea, DarkSeoul (see Chapter 2).

This case of 'cyber vandalism', as Obama called it, exemplifies how a case starting as purely criminal and without obvious ties to the national security of a country can escalate, but also how such a case can force a government to react even if no critical infrastructure has been targeted.[55] The main driver behind this escalation seems to have been that the US administration did not want a foreign country to bully one of its enterprises. It feared that letting this happen would set a precedent and that in future much more vulnerable companies could be targeted. In the end, the US government took a still relatively minor step, deciding on new sanctions against ten North Korean government officials and against three state-run organisations.[56]

A second factor indicating that a case will be regarded as a threat to national security, and almost self-evidently, is the political character of the target. The political character can be twofold: a political institution, but also an organisation whose targeting could constitute a threat to national security. Critical national infrastructure falls within the latter. Furthermore, states such as the United Kingdom and the United States now regard a situation where companies lose intellectual property on a large scale as a threat to national security. The loss of intellectual property influences companies' productivity, and in turn harms the national economies of countries hosting them.[57]

A third factor, the apparent origin of an attack, although easily falsifiable, can justify the intervention of high-level officials to resolve deadlocks in order to obtain information. In cases where the apparent origin is an existing enemy of the state, or a state with which the victim does not have either official channels for contact or partnerships, law enforcement agents are unlikely to receive cooperation. The victim states can then try to force the hand of the information holder by involving government officials. Involving the executive is justified to try to limit the possible escalation of conflict if the political situation between the two states is already unstable. The involvement of political actors is necessary to decide whether pursuing the investigation is possible, and whether it is worth taking the risk of receiving a refusal of help and cooperation. For instance, there are currently tensions between the Republic of China, also known as Taiwan, and the People's Republic of China over recognition of each other's governments. Many criminal cyber attacks motivated by financial gain take place between China and Taiwan, and many of these attacks have absolutely no connection with government. Yet prosecution never follows.[58] As a member of a Taiwanese law enforcement agency explains: 'There is no mutual help between Taiwan and China. We try to tell them and ask for their help, but basically there is no response'.[59] For any exchange of information to happen, authorities must trust each other to some extent. In this climate of tensions, trust is at a minimum, or even non-existent. Cooperation on cyber incidents between the two countries cannot happen without a relaxation of tensions over other unrelated, political issues. In this context, it is unavoidable that each cyber attack seemingly originating from the other side of the strait may be perceived as a provocation, potentially further straining relations between the countries.

The fourth factor explaining a case being regarded as a national security threat is the means of attack; if the attack is perceived as being 'sophisticated', this is likely to trigger wild and biased speculations of state involvement. The rationale behind this is that crafting a 'sophisticated' piece of malware requires extensive resources that only a state can invest in. One of the key incidents that set the trend was Stuxnet, in which case analysts very quickly agreed that the sophistication of the malware indicated state sponsorship.[60] In this case, the analysts were right. But sadly, as Chapter 3 will show, this indicator is decidedly inconclusive in a rigorous assessment of state sponsorship. In light of the prevailing use of this criterion, however, any new 'sophisticated' malware is still likely to trigger suspicion that a state was behind it, forcing intelligence services to investigate the case.

Finally, any cyber attack claimed to have been carried out for political reasons and substantiated by enough evidence has to be assessed within its political context. The claim may be unfounded or even unrealistic. But such a claim necessitates a certain assessment involving political judgement, and not solely the analysis of technical and forensic evidence. Within a purely criminal context, however, the police and cyber security firms lack this political judgement and the authority to wield it. The involvement of organisations with expertise and authority in the field—in other words, political entities—is therefore necessary. The level of confidence in a claim's credibility plays a role in considering whether the attack lies within the realms of criminal justice or national security. A different level of certainty is required for criminal and national security attributions, with attribution on a political level not implying attribution on a legal one. Therefore, making claims can be an important strategic decision for many groups launching cyber attacks, besides trying to achieve fame and recognition. Making a false claim under a false name can have dire consequences for the wronged organisation or state. But it will be up to a state official to make the political decision of attribution and to answer the following question: is the cost of misattributing the attack to the claimed group, and taking retaliatory measures against it, greater than the cost of not attributing the attack and not responding to it?

In the case of Shamoon, commented on by Secretary of Defense Leon Panetta, several groups had claimed the attack, but only one was really credible.[61] 'The Cutting Sword of Justice' claimed to have targeted Saudi Aramco for political reasons because the company is the main source of revenue for Saudi Arabia, which is involved in 'crimes and atrocities taking place in various countries around the world'.[62] To support its claim, 'The Cutting Sword of Justice' released all of the IP addresses of Saudi Aramco's compromised servers, with the date and time of their breach. Saudi Aramco confirmed that the released data were accurate.[63] Interestingly, many different sources also named Iran as being behind the attack. On 11 October 2012, an unnamed former US government official talked to a journalist from The Associated Press and pointed to Iranian hackers as being responsible for Shamoon. He added that the hackers benefited from the support of a state.[64] Panetta, in his well-noted speech about cyber security, fell short of accusing Iran of the misdeeds.[65] Nonetheless, many newspapers repeated the mantra that the attack was actually of Iranian origin.[66]

Based on these five criteria, investigators have to decide at an early stage if the motives of an attack are purely criminal, or if they extend to threatening national security. At this early stage of the process, investigators have very little information about the attack. They may know the modus operandi of the attack (targeted or non-targeted), the result of the attack (espionage or sabotage), and the nature of the victim. This information forms the basis of the criteria for assessing if the attack is criminal or has further national security implications.

Also, the two processes described for attribution do not have to be mutually exclusive. As it is not possible to determine from the start of an investigation whether the threat level has been correctly assessed, this can lead to several military and civilian agencies investigating the same case at once. General Keith Alexander suggested in 2013 that legislation be passed for 'all reports of intrusions' to 'go to the FBI, the Department of Homeland Security and the NSA simultaneously so that the appropriate agency could take any required action'.[67] At worst, this creates a duplication of work, as well as a turf war about the investigation of the case.[68] At best, the combined methodologies and resources used by the different entities can lead to a better analysis, and to an assessment of the instigator that is as close to the truth as possible.[69] A directive from 2008 marked top secret also explained that the CIA, the NSA and the FBI may come together in a 'National Cyber Investigative Joint Task Force' to collaborate on cases and share information, in an attempt to avoid overlap as far as possible.[70]

Furthermore, discerning if the attribution of a case follows a judiciary or an executive path can be confusing for a country like China. In China, as noted by the Taiwanese scholar Lennon Yao-chung Chang, cyber attacks are a sensitive issue, as they are—seemingly indiscriminately—considered 'a national security issue'.[71] This was highlighted by President Xi Jinping's 2014 statement that 'no Internet safety means no national security'.[72] Approaching all cyber attacks as national threats could imply that all attacks fall more or less under the executive's jurisdiction, but this is not genuinely the case. In most instances, the police still look to identify individuals if and when they investigate, rather than sponsors of attacks. They still operate within a criminal framework, meaning that they are unlikely to obtain assistance from intelligence services providing them with captured traffic. Moreover, government officials are also unlikely to work on attributing the cases. Hence, despite the classification of an incident as a 'national threat', the attribution process remains similar to a criminal process.

The policy in China highlights two particular points. First, the line between criminal and national security is not strict; many cases lie somewhere in between. Second, China's policy indicates that a case must have certain features for it to be considered within the executive's remit. These features mostly depend on the estimated political fallout that could result from the case, and the benefits of investigating it. For instance, an incentive to investigate could be the genuine fear that an enemy of the state sponsored the attack. Any democratic government —this does not include China—needs to effectively perform its function of protecting its citizens. If it fails to do so, the electorate can then decide to hold the government accountable by not re-electing it. Investigating an attack is therefore a first step for a government to show that it takes its responsibility seriously, and responds to attacks that could potentially damage national security.

As a result of the executive's involvement in attribution, the process becomes significantly different from the attribution process of purely criminal incidents. In and of themselves, the five factors presented here do not allow the drawing of any conclusions. But they do allow for the discernment of two questions. What is so different about the attribution process of criminal acts and the attribution process of threats to national security? And, more importantly, is it more difficult to attribute a criminal case, or a case linked to national security? As a case follows the path of judicial or executive attribution, an important distinction emerges: more resources are deployed to investigate cyber attacks regarded as national security threats, because they are framed in terms of finding an 'enemy of the state'. Consequently, it is easier to make a first guess about who this enemy is, but it is harder to conclusively prove it. Conclusively proving the identity of a criminal attacker, on the other hand, is much easier, once investigators have a genuine lead to follow.

Two attribution processes: characteristics and deployed resources

Starting from the common element that both processes share is the easiest approach, before explaining where they diverge. Both processes begin with the difficult step of uncovering an attack. Many cyber attacks, especially those involving espionage, are very stealthy, and can stay undetected for years. They involve infecting a system with a Trojan, for instance, siphoning information out, and removing all traces of the breach. Once the hackers have deleted the malicious software, it is very difficult for anyone to even know that a breach occurred. Also, not every breach of an information system is an attack. A cyber attack is a breach assumed to be of a malicious and intentional nature. When a system administrator discovers an information system has been breached, he cannot know at first if it was merely an accident, or if he faces a cyber attack. Information systems fail from time to time, either because individuals make mistakes, or simply because information systems are not perfect finished products and can simply malfunction. Establishing that a breach is an attack falls mainly to the field of technical observations. A system administrator or an engineer analyses the characteristics of the breach, then determines first whether the system's dysfunction was likely to be caused by a human, and then, by looking at the behaviour of the individual, whether it looks intentional or not.

At this point, the two processes diverge, especially as they have different goals: identifying individuals in a criminal case, and identifying sponsors in a national security context. To identify an individual, investigators must attempt to gain information, especially the attacker's IP address. This information does not usually prove 'beyond reasonable doubt' an individual's involvement in an attack, but evidence seized on his computer can more often than not be the link between the individual and the attack, although it may be more circumstantial than a 'smoking gun'.[73] Types of evidence include, for instance, stolen documents found on the computer, or traffic logs or computer history matching the patterns observed during the attack.

Finding evidence by seizing incriminating material on a person's computer can, however, be tricky when an attacker is located in a non-cooperating country; but this is still possible even when there are no agreements between two countries to cooperate on criminal matters (the capture of Julio Cesar Ardita, discussed in Chapter 5, illustrates this). The seizure of evidence should help conclusively prove authorship of the attack in front of a court—'conclusively' meaning that there is little doubt that other hypotheses could point to a different perpetrator. The court validates the inferences made from the collected evidence, proving that the person was indeed the criminal using the computer from which the cyber attack was launched. Attribution of criminal attacks therefore follows an established judicial process: 'identifying the criminal conduct', 'gathering forensic material', turning it into evidence and 'presenting it before a court of law'.[74]

But within the national security context, access to evidence is much more difficult. The evidence should shed light on sponsors rather than on mere individuals. Even if the possibility of seizing the attacking computer existed, the seizure would be unlikely to reveal the real sponsors of the attack. Investigators need to seek other information to find the sponsors: contracts, if they exist; intercepted messages between the attacker and the sponsor; or, somewhat impractically, it could be necessary to patiently wait for a whistle-blower to come forward. The four-step process for the attribution of criminal cases (discovery of the attack, finding information, finding evidence and conviction) then becomes the following four-step process: discovery of the attack, finding information, formulation of an assessment and publicly acting on the assessment.

Another distinction concerns the process through which information will be released. In a national security context, information will have to go through a chain of decision-makers within an organisation who will decide whether it is appropriate to release it. One of the fears decision-makers assess is whether such a release could reveal means of intelligence collection otherwise kept secret.[75] This process for releasing information, part of the attribution process, is, however, in its infancy. The United States is notably still grappling with the many paradoxes it poses, with the traditionally opaque structure operated by intelligence services on the one hand, and, on the other, the need for information dissemination in order better to counter cyber attacks. For instance, following a series of repeated denial-of-service attacks on US banks, the US intelligence services thought it appropriate at one point to brief executives of the banks concerned 'on what they knew about the attacks and "who was behind the keyboards"'.[76] However, giving access to this type of information required the executives attending the meeting to have security clearance. Consequently, the FBI created an 'extraordinary' one-day security clearance, revealing a certain mismatch between how formal procedures function and what attribution can require.

In both processes, investigators generally have two main options for obtaining information at the very beginning of the enquiry: to discover forensics left behind from the attack, and to liaise with informants.[77] But the resources at their disposal vary greatly depending on whether it is a criminal or a national security case. One of the direct consequences of a case being regarded as a threat to national security is that the means to investigate are completely different. Most law enforcement agencies, such as the FBI, are accountable entities, and operate under public scrutiny. They need to ensure constantly that they are collecting evidence in a legal fashion in order to be able to present this in front of a court. But within the national security context, the higher stakes mean a readiness to use more invasive methods to collect intelligence. The main goal is to discover who the enemies and their sponsors are, not to hold a fair public trial. Against this backdrop of potentially high political stakes, investigators and government officials show a readiness to resort to extraordinary and less accountable investigative means, mainly provided by intelligence services, especially when it comes to using technical forensics.

One legal and accountable option for obtaining information is the use of informants, which is common practice in regular intelligence collection and the traditional work of the police. The mechanism for using informants is simple: a reward is offered, as an incentive for cooperation, to the person who supplies information. The reward that the police offer is often in the form of penalty reductions, rather than monetary.[78] Informants have to rationally weigh the benefits of their cooperation against the benefits of withholding information. For rewards to work, the police, as much as private actors like Microsoft, have to make these benefits exceed those of non-cooperation. For criminal gangs making money by using malware, a monetary reward could encourage one of the money mules—people charged by the criminal gang, on a low wage, to withdraw in cash the revenue from illegal activities—to defect from the group and snitch on his gang.

The FBI has used former hackers many times to help them in cases of cyber attacks. The hacker David Lee Smith, who created the Melissa worm, was arrested in 1999 but went on to help the FBI and collected 1,745 samples of malware for them.[79] The prosecutor who handled David Smith's case said, 'There are very few people who can walk the walk and talk the talk of a sophisticated malicious code writer. The average FBI agent with good training is not one of those people.'[80]

One of the people that Smith helped arrest was the 22-year-old British citizen Simon Vallor, author of three items of malware called Redesi, Gokar and Admirer that the FBI had started investigating in December 2001.[81] David Smith started talking on IRC, a seemingly anonymous chat channel, to an individual under the pseudonym Gobo who was proudly claiming to be the author of these viruses. Smith recorded this conversation. Meanwhile, the police were trying to find Gobo's IP address. It took them three weeks to trace him back to his BT Internet connection.[82] The FBI contacted the cyber crime unit of the Metropolitan Police, and on 14 February 2002, Scotland Yard arrested Gobo, also known as Simon Vallor, in Wales. On 20 December 2002, Vallor admitted creating the viruses and pleaded guilty. The Court sentenced Vallor to two years in prison, a sentence that many experts regarded as stiff. But Vallor was also found in possession of indecent pictures of children, which added to his sentence. The viruses had infected roughly 29,000 computers in forty-one countries.

A more recent example is the 2011 arrest of Sabu, whose real name is Hector Xavier Monsegur. Sabu was one of the six members of a hacking group called LulzSec (the police arrested five of its six members), and an active member of Anonymous.[83] In March 2011, Sabu mistakenly typed the address of his personal website into a chat room. Another hacker recorded the data and leaked it to Jennifer Emick, a writer specialising in religious movements who wanted to take revenge against Sabu after finding out that Anonymous was 'full of hackers and people who don't do nice things for fun'.[84] She quickly found out Sabu's personal name and address, but the police did not arrest Sabu quite yet.[85] Instead, they waited for concrete evidence, and arrested Sabu in June 2011 after he had mistakenly left his IP address in a chat channel with other hackers.[86] The police detained him for less than 24 hours: they had to get him to cooperate quickly, otherwise other members of the hacking group would find it suspicious that Sabu had disappeared offline for so long. Playing on Sabu's fears of going to prison and not seeing his children, the police were successful in obtaining Sabu's help.

In the end, Sabu gave the FBI information on members of the hacking group LulzSec that led to the arrest of eleven other hackers involved, inter alia, in denial-of-service attacks against Visa and MasterCard in the US and the UK. But Sabu did not just help catch other hackers. Because of his recognised role within Anonymous, hackers would often come to him about vulnerabilities they had found on websites, and attacks they planned to execute using these vulnerabilities. Each time a hacker informed him of an imminent attack, Sabu would relay the information to the FBI, which would then relay it to the organisation under threat. Just a month after his arrest by the FBI, Sabu had already helped prevent attacks on 300 organisations by revealing 150 vulnerabilities.[87] For his cooperation, Sabu received a six-month reduction in his sentence.[88] (More controversially, Sabu also conducted attacks mainly against foreign targets to gather intelligence while under surveillance—a point further addressed in Chapter 6 about states' use of proxy groups).[89]

The second aspect to obtaining information is a focus on technical forensics; the resources deployed by different investigators (such as the FBI, CIA or even private companies) varies significantly in this area. By using technical forensics, investigators can link an attack to previous ones, which can yield information. When a hacker or hacking group consistently reuses a set of tools or exploits, these tools become strongly associated with them.[90] Law enforcement agencies, and also private companies, keep track of many attacks, and use tools to try to correlate the different information that they can garner from each attack.[91] Tracing back an attack by drawing correlations with previous attacks requires large databases and, ultimately, the ability to obtain a match between an IP address and a name.[92] Intelligence services have an advantage with both of these steps: they do not need to follow formal channels to obtain information, because they do not need to ensure that it will be acceptable in a court setting.

In order to collect forensics, police investigating a criminal attack can use social media to find information that already exists on the Internet.[93] As such, a member of the British law enforcement agencies characterised the rise of social media as a real 'boon' for collecting data.[94] Sloppy criminals leave an important digital footprint on the Internet, including on social media sites, which investigators can easily reuse. This does not, however, compare with the large capabilities of intelligence services—although it is not entirely clear how much information intelligence services share with the police, as will be discussed later in this chapter. Furthermore, it is worth noting that intelligence services have also adapted, and now use, social media in combination with their other collection tools as part of what has been coined 'SOCMINT', or 'social media intelligence'.[95]

Jake Davis, a former British hacker known as Topiary, summarised very well the hacker community's fears about US capabilities for attribution when he commented that he is 'almost certain' that the police 'know the identities of nearly every hacker that surfaces around the social networking world'[96] Several statements from high officials in the United States have echoed these fears, and have also revealed how US intelligence services envision the development of attribution methods. In January 2008, the director of national intelligence, Michael McConnell, suggested in a New Yorker interview that 'in order for cyberspace to be policed, Internet activity will have to be closely monitored'.[97] By 'closely monitored', McConnell meant 'giving the government the authority to examine the content of any email, file transfer or Web search'.[98] The comments were surreal to hear at the time—although the fact that they came from McConnell, an early supporter of the Clipper Chip mentioned in the previous chapter, was not surprising.[99]

Recent leaks by former NSA contractor Edward Snowden indicate that McConnell's comments were taken seriously. Over the past few years, the United States has significantly expanded its surveillance capabilities to monitor Internet traffic. Three years after McConnell's interview, The Associated Press reported that 'U.S. military and law enforcement officials say the government has made significant strides in figuring out who is responsible for complex cyber attacks'.[100] These strides are highlighted by the testimony of a cyber security company CEO, Kevin Mandia, who described the monitoring capacity and efforts of the United States to detect cyber attacks, the first step in the attribution process. Mandia testified in front of the Committee on Intelligence at the US House of Representatives that '90 per cent of the breaches Mandiant responds to are first detected by the government, not the victim companies'.[101] In October 2012, in a speech to business executives, Secretary of Defense Leon Panetta also publicly commented on the US government's 'significant strides'. He reported that 'the Department [of Defense] has made significant advances in solving a problem that makes deterring cyber adversaries more complex: the difficulty of identifying the origins of an attack'.[102]

There is a large gap between what these 'significant strides' look like when comparing official documents and leaks by the former NSA contractor Edward Snowden. In 2011, a report by the US Department of Defense mentioned three ways in which the United States was improving attribution: investing in research to physically trace attacks and develop behaviour-based algorithms, hiring forensic experts, and increasing cooperation with other countries to exchange information.[103] Also hidden in the report was a mention of the fact that the United States was working on acquiring intelligence to 'understand other nations' cyber capabilities'.[104] Furthermore, Michael S. Rogers, the new head of the NSA from 2014, also hinted while still a nominee for the job that he intended to focus more on infiltrating groups in order to identify attacks before they take place. 'We must ensure we leverage the newest technology to identify our attackers before and during an attack—not just after,' he said.[105] This implies the monitoring of discussions on hacking forums, for instance, or even the use of networks of informants to gather intelligence—a method already used by the police, as aforementioned, and not only in the United States.[106] Such an approach would be the natural continuation of a policy already started under Rogers's predecessor, when a secret review had concluded that the US President had the authority to order a 'pre-emptive' strike if there was enough evidence of a planned cyber attack that could beget significant damage.[107]

Recent leaks by Snowden, however, show a different picture. They notably illustrate that the attribution methods developed by the United States rely a lot more on the significant capture and analysis of data. For instance, there is a programme, MonsterMind, for detecting an attack as early as possible by analysing all the possible traffic that travels into the United States—in other words, a programme that requires considerable investments in infrastructure and problematic partnerships with telecommunication providers.[108] The Snowden leaks, in general, also show that while government programmes are very appropriate for finding the identity of individuals, it is unclear to what extent they can be useful for discovering sponsors of attacks, a question of burning interest for policy-makers once a case is raised to the level of national security. By focusing on the capture of metadata, for instance, it is rather difficult to find connections revealing links to sponsorship. Metadata may give clues, but focusing on content analysis would be much more valuable.

The NSA has engaged in the collection of significant amounts of data from telecommunication and service providers, at home and abroad, putting a large emphasis on metadata.[109] Describing the collection and analysis programmes, *The New York Times* commented that the NSA 'clearly views its collections of metadata as one of its most powerful resources'.[110] Furthermore, the 2013 budget request of the NSA to Congress shows that it seeks to invest in manpower and technology to harvest and process 20 billion 'record events' a day, and then to make them available to intelligence analysts within one hour.[111] Concerning metadata collection abroad, *Le Monde* alleged that, either as a result of cooperation with foreign intelligence services or by infiltrating the communication providers, the NSA had gathered more than 70 million recordings in one month in France, and accessed 60 million Spanish calls in the same period.[112]

Furthermore, when the NSA cannot obtain the metadata it is after, or when it does not manage to launch a successful cyber attack, it has a further recourse: it can send a CIA team to break into the apartment of a suspect—usually a senior target suspected of terrorism—to directly inject malware into the suspect's computer.[113] The NSA has also already planted thousands of Trojans in computers and routers, and plans to expand this to the millions, which could allow it to intercept a considerable volume of traffic.[114]

It is also worth noting that the NSA has invested heavily in order to be able to decrypt traffic it could not otherwise read. The method of decrypting messages is a mix of traditional brute force and more controversial collaborations with private companies.[115] The NSA reportedly spends $250 million a year to influence the design of companies' encryption mechanisms.[116] The budget includes, for instance, spending to plant a controversial vulnerability in an encryption algorithm that has been recognised by a highly trusted agency, the National Institute of Standards and Technology (NIST).[117]

The extent of the NSA collection programmes is such that they allegedly cover 75 per cent of all communication traffic passing through the US infrastructure, which constitutes an important backbone for worldwide traffic.[118] *The Wall Street Journal* even contended that this figure represented the capture of not just metadata, but also communication content.[119] This could be the case with programmes like Prism, under which the NSA accesses data retained by large Internet companies such as Facebook and Google, more or less systematically. It would appear, contrary to initial report, that the NSA has no direct access to the companies' servers, but rather that Prism was merely a standardised platform for handling an information exchange request after the issue of a warrant by a judge.[120] Notably, with a large portion of Internet traffic passing through many of the US nodes, the NSA can also capture much traffic between two foreign countries. Further, the NSA uses the vast amount of data collected to retrace the data flows of networks around the world in a programme called Packaged Good.[121]

Unsurprisingly, bearing in mind the long tradition of signals intelligence in other countries, the United States is not alone in engaging in this type of extensive data collection from Internet traffic. France has also admitted to 'examining, every day, the flow of Internet traffic between France and other countries, outside of any legal framework'.[122] In an attempt to bring such programmes within appropriate legal frameworks, in December 2013 the French government drafted a law giving more power to different law enforcement agencies to access communication content, for reasons broader than terrorism, as originally intended, and without judicial authorisation.[123] For instance, officials working for the organisation tackling cyber security, the French Network and Information Security Agency (ANSSI), would be able to request the identification of IP addresses.

Similarly, in the UK, as part of a project called Tempora, the British signals intelligence agency Government Communications Headquarters (GCHQ) infiltrates the fibre-optic cables that directly transport Internet traffic between the UK and both the American continent and mainland Europe.[124] Every day, GCHQ is able to accumulate so much data that the *Guardian* compared it in 2013 to the equivalent of 'all the information in all the books in the British Library', sent '192 times every 24 hours'.[125] Embarrassingly, in a rare press release in 2009, GCHQ had declared: 'GCHQ is not developing technology to enable the monitoring of all Internet use and phone calls in Britain, or to target everyone in the UK. Similarly, GCHQ has no ambitions, expectations or plans for a database or databases to store centrally all communications data in Britain.'[126]

Today, this press release appears as a misrepresentation of GCHQ's activities. Even if they do not monitor *all* Internet usage and do not store *all* communications, they do appear to be storing some, and to be tapping Internet cables to look for specific keywords and selectors. Many people were not completely fooled about what was actually going on, even before the Snowden revelations. Noting that a very large portion of Internet traffic is transited via the United States and the United Kingdom, Ian Brown, a researcher at the Oxford Internet Institute wrote that: 'It is likely [the NSA and GCHQ] take full advantage of their ability to access international traffic flowing through domestic ISPs'.[127]

On top of collecting important data, the NSA has also invested in programmes to efficiently store and process the data. XKeyscore, for instance, is a large distributed database gathering many different types of technical data and metadata that the NSA has collected via various programmes. Analysts can frequently search through and examine the different collected data without having to request a warrant from a judge.[128] One of the slides leaked by Snowden shows that the programme allows analysts to search 'nearly everything a typical user does on the internet'.[129]

The interesting question for attribution is to know whether intelligence services actually use these vast resources and the collected data for attributing cyber attacks—Edward Snowden himself, for instance, has claimed that XKeyscore could easily be used for that purpose, although other experts have expressed doubts.[130] The answer is not in the public domain and is not straightforward because of conflicting accounts. Various officials and senators have vehemently defended the NSA surveillance programmes on the grounds that they have served to foil terrorist plots. But on 8 July 2013, *The NewYork Times* reported that the surveillance programmes were not only limited to cases of terrorism, but also used to pursue people suspected of cyber attacks.[131] An NSA spokeswoman also confirmed that the NSA's 'activities are centred on counterterrorism, counter-proliferation and cyber security', with a focus on foreign intelligence.[132] For instance, an NSA programme called 'Follow the Money Trail', which monitored banks and financial transactions, was targeting terrorists, the sale of illegal arms and, interestingly, cyber crime.[133] Following the money trail is a common tactic used by law enforcement agencies, and demonstrates once again that if the capabilities of the NSA are used at all, they are geared more towards finding the instigators of criminal cyber attacks than identifying the sponsors of national security incidents, which is much more difficult. Examples of successful attribution of cyber attacks by following the money abound. For instance, in 2012 and 2013, the UK police arrested 255 people linked to financial cyber attacks that had caused an estimated £1.01 billion of damage.[134] A caveat must, however, be made: payment system regulation, especially since the rise of anonymous payment systems such as Bitcoins, has not always kept up with the criminals' pace of innovation, making the technique of following the money trail 'decreasingly effective in the cyber crime era'.[135]

Evidence that NSA programmes are used for cyber attacks includes a 2012 classified strategic document about the NSA's goals for the following year. One of these was '[to defeat] the cyber security practices of adversaries in order to acquire the data the agency needs from "anyone, anytime, anywhere"'.[136] In a 2014 speech about changes to signals intelligence practices, President Obama reiterated this goal, and the role of intelligence in achieving them:

> We cannot prevent terrorist attacks or cyber threats without some capability to penetrate digital communications—whether it's to unravel a terrorist plot; to intercept malware that targets a stock exchange; to make sure air traffic control systems are not compromised; or to ensure that hackers do not empty your bank accounts.[137]

More specifically, despite claims that the NSA's capabilities are used for cyber attacks, it is difficult to know if the NSA passes information to law enforcement agencies for the identification and arrest of criminals. Since 9/11, when the FBI had information about hijackers and did not pass it to the CIA, and similarly, the NSA refused to give full information to the CIA about an earlier Al Qaeda meeting, many reforms have taken place to ensure that there is greater information exchange between members of security services. 9/11 was truly a watershed moment in many regards for the intelligence community. In the same aforementioned presidential speech, Obama reminded the audience that the metadata collection programme emerged because the NSA was not able to 'see that [a] call', between Khalid al-Mihdhar and Al Qaeda in Yemen, 'was coming from an individual already in the United States'.[138] The NSA therefore changed its practice to account for such situations. More specifically, a leak from Snowden showed that before 2002, an intelligence agency could pass information to a law enforcement agency if this action was approved by a court, but the intelligence agency had to delete all irrelevant private details falling outside the scope of the warrant. After 2002, the Foreign Intelligence Surveillance Act changed this and allowed the sharing of unfiltered information, potentially opening the door for a lot more sharing between the FBI, the CIA and the NSA, inter alia.[139]

With regard to the collection programme revealed by Snowden, *The NewYork Times* acknowledged that the NSA had rejected many requests for access to the collected data from other law enforcement agencies. The requests did not meet the criteria set by the law or in the form of policy directives for exchanging information. These basically require that the requesting party show 'links to terrorism or foreign intelligence'.[140] Many cyber attacks dealt with by the FBI may only be classified under the 'terrorism' label with difficulty, because they are mostly non-violent, and do not even fall under the heading of foreign intelligence; for instance, sabotage operations routed through a proxy in the United States would not, *a priori*, meet the NSA requirements for access.[141] This view of limited data sharing is contradicted, however, by a leak showing an NSA-created search engine similar to Google, ICREACH, which law enforcement agencies such as the FBI can easily access and search.[142] ICREACH connects to various databases pertaining to 'foreign intelligence' and displays them to analysts. The role of the NSA in this case is described as that of a 'data broker', in that it has a very central relation with its clients, and not only a vertical one. (In a vertical and more classical scheme, the NSA would respond to questions of interest stemming from its clients.) Hence, it is difficult to assess the extent of the use of NSA data by other law enforcement agencies.

In the United Kingdom, the extent to which intelligence services' resources are used to track the authors of cyber attacks is also unclear. The main focus is on terrorism, but during the first public hearing of its kind, the director of GCHQ Iain Lobban mentioned to Parliament that GCHQ's programmes allowed the agency 'to reveal the identity of those involved online in the sexual exploitation of children'.[143] He also mentioned that, in relation to the threat of cyber attacks, the role of GCHQ was 'to anticipate, discover, analyse, *investigate* and respond' [emphasis added] and that GCHQ has 'to do so globally because the threat is coming at us [the United Kingdom] globally'.[144] Again, the leap from finding the identity of online paedophiles to finding the identity of cyber attackers is not great, especially considering the role of GCHQ as an *investigator* of attacks. If the extent of the metadata collection programmes is as it seems, and the NSA along with GCHQ can genuinely track anything a user does online, this implies that the gathered and analysed data can easily help to solve many criminal cases, including the discovery of cyber attack instigators. This means that correlating information to find people's real identity online is much easier than for law enforcement agencies operating without this collecting capability.[145]

This display of impressive attribution capabilities largely operates away from public scrutiny. For criminal cases, whether in the United Kingdom or the United States, legally collecting evidence is important so that it is acceptable in court.[146] But for cases involving national security threats, legality and accountability are secondary. In the words of Julian Assange, 'it is too cheap and too easy to get around political accountability and to actually perform interception'.[147] Two points show this lack of scrutiny. First of all, many NSA programmes operate within the remit of secret laws, whereby intelligence officers make requests to the Foreign Intelligence Surveillance Court, which 'sits in secret session, holds no adversary hearings, and, with one exception, publicly issues no opinions or reports'.[148] Secondly, the political backlash that followed the revelations prompted US President Obama to outline changes to the overall surveillance programme. These changes did not, however, mention holding any entity accountable, despite the apparent illegality of several of the individual programmes.[149] Leaks by Snowden in fact showed that several of the NSA programmes may be illegal. (Similarly, the legality of programmes run by GCHQ is unclear, and an advisory opinion distributed to members of parliament in January 2014 suggested that the programmes relied 'on the gaps in the current statutory framework to commit serious crime with impunity'.) The investigatory powers tribunal confirmed in October 2016 that GCHQ did collect metadata illegally for ten years.[150]

The relevance of secret laws is questionable. Secret laws emerged with the National Security Act of 1947 and go against a principle of law: *ignorantia juris non excusat*, ignorance of the law excuses no one. With the laws being non-public, it is not possible to know if someone breaches them. Worse, it is also not possible to know if the law furthers the cause of national security or hinders it.[151] Secrecy makes accountability much more difficult. The procedures that are supposed to ensure oversight of these programmes are also far from well balanced. For an agency to operate under the Foreign Intelligence Surveillance Act, it merely needs to go to court to convince a single judge to grant it authority; in this court, no other party counter-argues the position of the government.[152] Consequently, oversight is minimal, and almost certainly ensures that the NSA is able to carry out an operation, as long as it has the capability to do so.

The four US surveillance programmes concerned with the collection of data and metadata of phone calls and Internet traffic originally started well outside any laws. Then, between 2001 and 2007, the Bush administration spent a great deal of effort introducing amendments to a 1978 act regulating intelligence collection from US citizens at home, the Foreign Intelligence Surveillance Act.[153] Under the new Act, the NSA could intercept metadata if it had a 'reasonable, articulable suspicion'.[154] This clause was important. As *New Yorker* journalist Ryan Lizza eloquently described it, this clause constituted: 'The thin wall between a legal programme with some oversight and one with the potential for domestic spying and tremendous privacy violations'.[155] Moreover, according to Judge Richard Leon of the Federal District Court for the District of Columbia (and according to an independent federal watchdog), the phone data collection programme constituted an infringement of the fourth amendment against unreasonable search and seizure by the government.[156] This legal decision stood against what other judges on the Foreign Intelligence Surveillance Court had stipulated by basing their reasoning on a 1979 case ruled by the Supreme Court, a court which has authority over district courts. In the 1979 *Smith v. Maryland* law case, the Supreme Court had decided that the use of a 'pen register, which records the numbers dialled from a telephone, did not constitute a search and hence did not necessitate a warrant under the U.S. Constitution'.[157] On the other hand, Judge Leon felt that the scope of the programme and the 'evolving role of phones and technology' warranted a revision of the ruling.[158] Metadata, especially when used in conjunction with other data mining programmes, can be very revealing about a person's private life.[159]

A few weeks later, another judge, William H. Pauley III, ruled again on the matter, but this time, in the exact opposite direction.[160] Pauley ruled that the NSA programmes revealed by Snowden were constitutional. These differences of opinion highlight the problem of finding a clear answer to the question of the legality of the programmes. The answer is not straightforward. In addition, admissions that violations of the principle of probable cause had occurred have emerged. In July 2012, the director of national intelligence James Clapper admitted that some collection had been 'unreasonable'.[161]

The well-developed resources of the intelligence community constitute non-negligible sources of information for attribution. However, one of the consequences of these techniques' revelation has been to undermine trust in the United States and its companies. Attribution, especially for the exchange of information in criminal cases, relies on trust. But the revelations have prompted other countries to challenge the United States, without drawing a clear difference between its intelligence services and its law enforcement agencies. This creates the risk that cooperation between law enforcement agencies will become more difficult. The attribution of even a relatively inconsequential cyber attack could then rise to the level of national security, requiring the involvement of a member of the executive to discuss the issue with a foreign counterpart in order to negotiate the exchange of necessary information.

The difference between the capabilities used for criminal cases and for cases threatening national security is best illustrated by examples of successful arrests. The following criminal case, successfully attributed, highlights the important discrepancy between the professional tools described earlier, used by intelligence services, and the time-consuming and painstaking searching undertaken manually by the police and private companies.

On 14 August 2005, the Zotob malware started spreading. The worm built a botnet by infecting computers. When the FBI started investigating the worm, two elements linked it to a previous worm. First, the author of Zotob had left a signature saying 'by Diabl0'.[162] In February 2003, the worm Mytob also included the same signature. While this fact was not very informative on its own, the FBI also knew Diabl0's first name, Farid. Diabl0 had used Microsoft Visual Studio software to program his worm, which left the directory path in the code when he compiled the worm. It read: 'C:\Documents and Settings\Farid'.[163] The second element linking Zotob to Mytob was that they both communicated via the same Internet Relay Chat server. The FBI observed these links without relying on a huge database such as those of the Prism or Tempora programmes: the establishment of correlations between the current and the past incident was almost amateurish, relying on investigators' prowess rather than on computerised capabilities.

Mytob, the worm linked to Zotob, contacted many servers, which were registered under false identities, although they contained the name of the writer of the worm, as in 'diabl0.turkcoders.net' and 'ilovediabl0.net'. But one hacker registered one of the domains with the email address masteratilla@yahoo.com. Yahoo is registered in the US, and the FBI could easily ask Yahoo to hand over information about the account via a warrant. It also discovered another hacker involved with the worm, 'C0der'. According to Steve Santerolli, an investigator at the time with Microsoft, he had been tracking 'C0der' for a while and knew about the name.[164] But it is unclear how he knew about it, or how the police learnt about C0der prior to accessing the emails. One possibility is that C0der registered several of the servers contacted by Zotob to download the payload, and that C0der left his pseudonym during the registration. In the emails, the police found exchanges between Diabl0 and C0der about Zotob, and stolen information from more than a thousand credit cards.[165] The tracing of the IP addresses from C0der's emails led the police to Turkey.

On 18 August 2005, via the US Embassy in Ankara, the FBI contacted the cyber crime unit of the Turkish national police. The FBI could not make any arrest in Turkey, and there was no legal basis for them to request the identification of the individual behind C0der's IP address. However, the FBI could offer its help, which it did. The Turkish police accepted, and on the same day, they identified C0der as Atilla Ekici. Microsoft had also further identified many of the servers that Zotob contacted to download the payload, and many of the addresses of these servers contained Ekici's name. These servers, such as atillaekici.net and ekiciailesi.com, registered by C0der in May 2003, saw a surge in traffic after the Zotob infection started.[166] Following their identification as part of Zotob, Microsoft asked the Luxembourg-based Internet host, EuroDNS, to shut them down. The FBI repeated the same process with the Moroccan authorities. On 21 August, a team of FBI agents and Microsoft employees flew to Morocco and Turkey to present their evidence.

When a local Turkish newspaper published an article about the possible location of Zotob's author in Turkey, Diabl0 and C0der decided to erase the hard drive containing proof of their authorship of the worms. But this was not enough. On 25 August, the Turkish police arrested Atilla Ekici, 21, the son of a farmer. At the same time, in Rabbat, the police arrested Diabl0, also known as Farid Essebar, 18, a Moroccan national born in Russia. He was working with another accomplice whom the police had also identified. The police arrested this accomplice at the same time, Achraf Bahloul, 20, an old friend of Essebar. Microsoft and the FBI were able to retrieve most of the source code that Essebar attempted to delete, supporting the trail of evidence already incriminating him. On the other hand, Ekici had thrown out his hard drive, and it was more difficult to bring evidence against him.[167]

Microsoft and the FBI helped to bring this evidence to support their prosecution. Ekici commissioned Essebar to write the worms, allegedly with stolen credit card information.[168] In a conversation with a security researcher, David Taylor, who had logged onto the IRC Channel that Mytob contacted, Diabl0 explained that the worm lowered the settings for Internet Explorer to let advertisements appear. Even when a user deleted the worm, the adware remained, and brought the criminals money.[169] On 15 September 2005, a Moroccan court sentenced Essebar to two years in jail for virus writing, illegal access to computers and conspiracy to commit credit card fraud, and sentenced Bahloul to one year in prison for conspiracy to commit fraud.[170] Ekici, on the other hand, was never condemned, due to the lack of acceptable evidence in court. The information the FBI and Microsoft had collected during the investigation did not meet the strict criteria to qualify as such.

The investigation of the Zotob worm brings a certain nuance to the use of informal channels for attributing attacks: they are used not only by non-transparent intelligence services to find out enemies of the state, but also by law enforcement agencies. Of particular relevance is that informal cooperation still, to a great extent and despite the lack of a full court ruling, allowed attribution to take place. The lack of sentencing by the court does not diminish its relevance, even if in criminal cases, the highest and most relevant authority that can attribute is within the judicial system, namely a court.

The new proposed model for attribution challenges three previously accepted arguments. Firstly, it challenges the argument that attribution is a problem and posits that it is better described as a process. Secondly, it challenges the argument that attribution is mainly a technical issue, although the large number of NSA programmes shows that policy-makers still approach attribution as such. Lastly, it challenges the argument that identifying a criminal and identifying the sponsor of an attack follow similar characteristics. By using the common umbrella term 'attribution problem', many officials and researchers have advocated the same solutions for what appear in fact to be two distinct attribution processes.

This distinction has led to a consideration of the following argument: in cases of national security, the resources deployed can be significantly more impressive than in criminal cases. Especially in the United States and the United Kingdom, intelligence services can use important Internet monitoring capabilities to trace an attack. Although these technical capabilities could be very helpful when it comes to finding individuals, it is unclear to what extent law enforcement agencies can have access to them. Yet as cooperation between states is unlikely for cases threatening national security, and bearing in mind the stealth of the attacks as well, a first conclusion is that the definitive attribution of criminal attacks, despite the higher standard of evidence needed and despite the recourse to less extensive resources, is actually easier. The many difficult political constraints present in cases of national security are examined in the next few chapters. The issues discussed include dealing with the uncertainty of attribution's political fallout, using private companies in attribution cases, juggling with different standards of proof and gauging if the standards really matter, using time as an advantage, and, finally, deciding if plausibly denying attacks is worthwhile.

2

RELIANCE ON JUDGEMENT

In many instances, it is easy to challenge the evidence supporting attribution, especially in cases involving a potential sponsor, and hereby to undermine the legitimacy of the victim wishing to take action against the alleged perpetrator. For example, following a series of attacks on journalists working for *The New York Times*, whose instigators were believed to have ties with the Chinese government, a Chinese Foreign Ministry spokesman declared: 'To presume the source of a hacking attack based on speculation is irresponsible and unprofessional'.[1] Following the discovery of the hacks, The Associated Press reported that the US administration was preparing a report 'to better understand and analyze the persistency of cyber attacks against America which come from China'.[2] The report came out a couple of days later but stayed confidential, although a leak mentioned that China was carrying out significant espionage operations via cyber attacks.[3] This was not the first report to point directly to China as an instigator of cyber attacks for espionage, and the situation developed further towards taking action following more formal attribution of the attacks.[4] A week later, on 18 February 2013, a private security firm named Mandiant issued a report showing technical evidence of coordinated cyber attacks against many US corporations traced back to a large business area in China which included, among others, a building occupied by the Chinese military.[5] A Chinese Foreign Ministry spokesman responded to the accusations by claiming once more that 'making baseless accusations based on premature analysis is irresponsible and unprofessional'.[6] The spokesman added that 'the report, in only relying on linking IP addresses to reach a conclusion [that] the hacking attacks originated from China, lacks technical proof'.[7]

The lack of 'professionalism' pointed out by the Chinese is a cunning response that helps undermine trust in the reports by framing them as methodologically flawed and hence baseless. But the methodological flaws may not be as important as the Chinese portray them to be. The methodological flaws stem from the very nature of attribution, especially in cases threatening national security, because they require judgement to assess the situation—a mixture of common sense and in-depth knowledge of a topic. Unfortunately, judgements are inherently fallible. The larger looming questions, therefore, do not relate to knowing whether using judgement is unprofessional—because the use of it is inevitable—but rather: what constitutes an authoritative judgement for attribution? Is that the same thing as a sound and universally true judgement? Furthermore, what are the political implications of acknowledging that attribution relies on judgement?

Taking account of political judgement can bring an important contribution to the debate on attribution by displacing the usual focus on technical constraints to a focus on political ones. Adapting a sentence from the widely cited researcher on intelligence analysis, Richard Heuer, it transpires that *political judgement for attribution is neither good nor bad; it is fallible but inescapable.*[8] Attribution is a process that constantly evolves and is never perfect, due to its inherent reliance on judgement. This reliance on judgement in order to attribute cases threatening national security explains a useful trend: attribution is always possible, but with differing degrees depending on the authority and trust conferred on the entity expressing the judgment. In fact, though, the veracity of the judgement expressed is only secondary to its authoritative value: the role of attribution is primarily to convince an audience that its consequences were called for. Technical forensic evidence for attribution is therefore important; but so is the extent to which the public will be convinced of the guilt of the alleged instigator. In light of such an argument, the case of Chinese espionage shows that *The New York Times* and Mandiant both displayed political judgement rather than the unprofessionalism referred to by Chinese officials.

This chapter demonstrates the argument in two steps. Firstly, it shows why judgement calls are inescapable but fallible for attribution. Secondly, it examines the political consequences for trust and authority that the reliance on judgement raises.

Attribution as an inescapable judgement call

As established in the introduction of this book, attribution as a technical problem is a very common misconception, within both academia and policy circles.[9] The professor of philosophy Christopher Eberle even explicitly commented: 'Attribution is a "technical" problem, to be resolved by those with the relevant computer and forensic skills'.[10] Myriam Dunn Cavelty, another scholar and a cyber security expert, also wrote that 'the attribution problem arises from technological protocols that guarantee a great deal of anonymity for its users'.[11] Similarly, on the policy side, Christopher Painter, State Department Coordinator for Cyber Issues, stated in a briefing: 'One of the problems in cyberspace is attribution. It's difficult because of the way the internet is constructed'.[12] Mike McConnell, former director of the National Security Agency under George W. Bush, also followed that line of thinking when suggesting in a 2010 *Washington Post* interview that 'we need to reengineer the Internet to make attribution more manageable'.[13] Such statements are misleading. They foster the perception that technology can make attribution perfect and systematic. But finding an authentic IP address can only, with difficulty, provide the sponsor of an attack. For instance, a state actor could mandate a person located in a foreign state to attack an enemy, and no technological solutions would be able to show the connection between the attacker and the mandating state. The argument that judgement, while not conclusive, is necessary for attribution hence goes against the approach to attribution as a technical problem, and recognises from the outset that attribution is necessarily imperfect.

Judgement is needed at several stages of the attribution process, mainly to either formulate an assessment of an attacker's identity, or decide to make attribution public.

Firstly, following a cyber attack that a government considers a threat to its national security, there is usually a list of suspects even before any investigation begins. 'Every state has its enemies or untrustworthy friends,' wrote cyber security expert Martin Libicki from the Rand Corporation, 'and if anything untoward happens, the usual suspects will be trotted out for examination'.[14] The examination of suspects relies on evidence, but also on an analysis of the current geopolitical context, an informative criterion for attribution but far from conclusive.[15] Past incidents of wrong attribution solely on this basis (such as Solar Sunrise in 1998—see Chapter 4) suggest the need for caution and to look beyond the obvious.[16]

Secondly, most attacks are routed via foreign countries, a situation which gives rise to four possible scenarios concerning the exchange of information that leads to attribution: the foreign country is willing to share genuine information with the targeted country; the foreign country knowingly provides false information to the targeted country; the foreign country does not possess the required technical information; or, the foreign country refuses to cooperate. The targeted country will have to interpret the non-possession of information and the refusal to share it in these ways and within its political context. The foreign country, for example, may be utilising the incident for its own purposes, raising the question of how to respond to such a move. There is a rising fear about non-cooperating states acting as 'sanctuaries'. 'The benefit is that they can use cyber criminals as a proxy force, irregulars who can engage in espionage or attack opponents at the government's behest, while providing a degree of plausible deniability,' wrote James Lewis, a cyber security expert and director at the Center for Strategic and International Studies.[17]

Facing such an obstacle to moving the attribution process forward, the targeted state nonetheless has to take decisions within an environment permeated by informational obscurity. It has to decide whether it is possible that the foreign state genuinely does not possess the requested information, and how to engage with the state. This decision must be the result of a careful distinction between what the foreign state with potential information wants the victim to believe, and what the victim state wants to (but may not) show about its own belief. The foreign state's refusal to cooperate could have three main explanations: there are political tensions between the foreign government and the victim state, albeit unrelated to the cyber attack; the foreign government ordered or conducted the attack; or it indirectly benefited from the cyber attack but did not sponsor it. Differentiating between all these possibilities calls for a need to identify their probability by assessing and accommodating many factors, which are far from being solely technical. Furthermore, the targeted state faces new questions once it has strong suspicions of the existence of a foreign state's sponsorship. Should it publicly attribute the incident to the foreign state? How will the foreign state react to the attribution of the incident? Is this reaction desirable? The attribution of incidents threatening national security requires judgement in understanding the differences between these scenarios, and, in fact, is the only possible recourse.

The type of judgement involved is not moralistic or legal. Instead, it refers to a thought process conducive to a decision, relying on a mixture of knowledge and experience, and taking place in an environment where it is difficult to assess the correctness of the information at hand.[18] This type of judgement is political in two different regards.

Firstly, attribution is political, and not only because almost every attribution claim divides the security community. When representatives of the state—elected or senior political figures—publicly attribute cases, it carries a different weight than when done by private companies—a point discussed further in Chapter 4. The political nature of attribution means that the type of judgement it involves is, by extension, also political.[19] Secondly, attribution is political because of the features inherent to the type of judgement it requires. Political judgement can imply a judgement not about a specific domain, the political in this case, but a form of judgement that presents specific characteristics. Political judgements primarily present two such characteristics: they are needed when there is an acute lack of information, and when further action needs to be taken following an assessment of attribution.[20] These circumstances apply to attribution of cyber attacks. Information obscurity is present at each step: it is, for instance, difficult to know if IP addresses are genuine or if attackers have redirected their traffic via several compromised computers. It is equally difficult to prove the involvement of a state, and next to impossible to do so only on the basis of technical elements. At each step of the attribution process, evaluation of the quality of the information requires judgement.

This latter aspect of political judgement is also evident in purely criminal contexts, although it is widely accepted from the outset of an investigation that judgement will also play a more general role.[21] The entity responsible for asserting attribution cannot avoid making a judgement on the certainty of the information obtained, and cannot avoid making a judgement to decide whether to act upon the assessment of this information. In the setting of a court trial, the assessment of the information can be easier than in a case involving a decision about state sponsorship, because the prosecution may be able to present evidence that would not be possible to collect in the latter case. In the end, however, the outcome of testing the reliability of the evidence will be the expression of a judgement stating whether the evidence is sufficient to corroborate a thesis, namely that the defendant is guilty. Similarly, a court's decisions over whether to incriminate a defendant and what sentence to impose occur as a result of weighing different parameters (such as intentionality and damage caused), and of judging the relevance of these parameters in sentencing. Hence, even in a legal context, a judgement presents several of the characteristics of political judgement as understood in its two different definitions.

What defines political judgement is also what makes it fallible. Because attribution relies on political judgement, this also explains why it is similarly fallible and relatively easy to undermine. For instance, many experts expressed their support in the conclusions drawn in the aforementioned Mandiant report, including Michael Hayden, the former director of the CIA and the NSA.[22] The conclusion stated that the Chinese military was behind attacks on 141 US companies. In order to appear credible and so rational, the experts highlighted the reasons for supporting this conclusion. But in the end, because they lacked the conclusive evidence linking the attacks with the military (such as an interview with Chinese officials with knowledge of the case confirming the involvement of the government, or an army or government mission statement listing the operation), their reasoning also entailed an element of judgement.[23] It is worth noting that this type of evidence is very difficult, even close to impossible, to obtain for any operation instigated by the Chinese army. Very often, therefore, the phrasing of hypotheses about the identity of cyber attack instigators incidentally involves some mention of 'beliefs'.[24]

An analyst has some belief about the certainty of the information he deals with, of the inferences he formulates, and of the effects attribution may have on an entity's behaviour. One should note that in a legal context, a court also express beliefs to some extent. Judges and jury members express the belief that 'the event happened, making for themselves the inductive leap from the evidence about the event to a statement about what happened'.[25] Furthermore, expert witnesses, for the defence and the prosecution, will influence the decisions of the jury in these criminal matters, even though technical complexity can often be rather difficult for any layperson to grasp. Although experts have a greater ability to understand technical matters, thereby giving them greater authority, they too express opinions and interpretations of the technical elements of a case.[26] These opinions are also a form of judgement.

In fact, two factors determine political judgement: intuition, and a deep insight into the topic at hand.[27] For instance, Mandiant has extensive knowledge about different aspects of cyber security. The quality of its judgement is enhanced by this knowledge; if Mandiant was not well versed in cyber security, its judgement would be less credible and of lesser quality. Yet such knowledge may not always be beneficial for attribution, and can influence intuition in the wrong direction. Expert knowledge can also further expectations, which makes a judgement based on it subject to expectation biases.

In fact, more information does not lead to a more correct judgement, because of individual biases and the way in which organisational decision-making functions.[28] Biases are inevitable because human beings' observations form the basis of judgements.[29] Several psychological studies have shown the saliency of expectation biases at the level of both individuals and organisations. Figure 1 is such an example, taken from an article by Richard Heurer, a former analyst at the CIA. He asks the question: 'What can you see?'[30]

Figure 1: Expectation in observations and analysis

In each triangle, the words 'a' and 'the' are written twice. Most people will have overlooked this fact, as 'we tend to perceive what we expect to perceive'.[31] Once an analyst forms a hypothesis for attribution, he will have expectations of what to perceive, and will yearn to find evidence supporting this hypothesis. The debacle of the Iraqi 'weapons of mass destruction', in which policy-makers cherry-picked the information that supported their hypothesis and their interest, remains a prominent example.[32] An analyst may reject evidence that does not match his hypothesis as he tries to confirm it, rather than finding evidence that affirms it. In fact, the cognitive psychologist Peter Wason found that in a majority of cases, people try to confirm their hypotheses rather than trying to disconfirm them, which results in their analyses being wrong.[33] Trying to disconfirm one's expectation is more difficult than trying to confirm it, because it goes against one's intuition, and dismissing the hypothesis will require a lot more work.[34] This is in accord with the phenomenon that the social psychologist Leon Festinger called cognitive dissonance: individuals try to reduce or reject dissonant elements to create a consistent 'belief system'.[35]

The theory of bounded rationality also supports the idea that more information does not lead to better judgements. It argues that analysts and decision-makers make heuristics and simplifications to be able to reach decisions; in addition, the rationality of their decisions is bounded by the 'incomplete information about alternatives' that they possess.[36] When analysts receive more information, they may not be able to process it all and will therefore exclude information from their analyses. Hence, according to the theory, analysts do not seek to maximise the quality of the analysis, but 'settle for a satisfactory decision' about who the instigator is. This is what Simon called 'satisficing'.[37]

A 2013 cyber attack against South Korea is a case in point, and illustrates the following three arguments: expectations can work towards adapting whatever evidence one has to confirm a hypothesis; judgement is detached from making logical inferences; and more information may not necessarily lead to better judgement. On 20 March 2013 in South Korea, three banks and three broadcasters experienced a common cyber attack. The DarkSeoul malware (also dubbed Jokra by Symantec) wiped out the hard drives of 32,000 computers.[38] The attackers programmed the malware with a specific date and time for activation so that it would synchronously make all the infected computers unusable, thereby triggering a sense of overwhelming crisis.

Forensic examiners trying to determine where the malware came from had to attempt to trace how the malware was able to infect all the computers—particularly as such a large number were concerned. The main hypothesis is that a spear-phishing attack took place the day prior to the malware's activation date.[39] From the email, investigators were able first to trace the attack to computers in China. Despite this, many analysts still accused North Korea of being behind the attack.[40] The only Internet connection that North Korea receives is in fact via China, so the Chinese origin was not surprising. Furthermore, the main argument driving the accusations was drawn from the geopolitical context: attacks came in the midst of an escalation of tensions between North and South Korea. This had culminated in North Korea revoking the 1953 Korean War armistice ten days prior to the cyber attack, interpreted as a sign of provocation by South Korea.[41]

But, embarrassingly, the investigators later confessed a mistake: the traced IP addresses that delivered the malware did not originate from China, but from the internal network of one of the banks. This new information did not change many analysts' view that North Korea was behind the attack. For instance, in a conference taking place after the announcement, a retired British army colonel, John Doody—despite the uncertainty surrounding the instigator of the attacks and despite the very limited scale of the damage—bluntly claimed: 'This is cyber war'.[42] The authors of the attack may simply have been teenagers targeting non-political entities.[43] But the expectation bias of seeing North Korea as the attacker was so prevalent that any information would either be interpreted as supporting the hypothesis, or dismissed altogether.

A couple of weeks later, South Korean state officials repeated the accusation against North Korea in the midst of ever increasing tensions between the two countries. The Associated Press article that broke the story even quoted a South Korean professor, Lim Chae-ho, saying: 'Future evidence will strengthen the case rather than reverse it'.[44] But Lim Chae-ho's statement is methodologically flawed according to the aforementioned theory of bounded rationality: future evidence, in a context of high expectations, will only reinforce the case for attributing the attacks to North Korea if one tries to refute the hypothesis rather than confirm it. In this process of falsifying the hypothesis, if it becomes too difficult to refute the considered hypothesis, then this is a further indication of its probable correctness. Simply introducing more evidence without challenging it is therefore not confirmation of the hypothesis.

In this particular example, further 'evidence' did come out. The South Korean Yonhap News Agency revealed that investigators had found an IP address that they were able to trace to North Korea, and which they thought was exposed 'due to technical problems in a communication network'.[45] This IP address was used in thirteen other cyber attacks that investigators also believed had been orchestrated by North Korea. Also, the investigators revealed that of the seventy-six modules constituting the malware, thirty had already been used in previous attacks, which were 'believed' to originate from North Korea.[46] But this reasoning was also logically flawed, because none of the previous hacking attempts were formally attributed to North Korea with a high degree of certainty. The new released evidence contributed to constructing an image of the North Korean state as the instigator of the attacks, yet at each layer of the construct the evidence was shoddy. Investigators suspected the North Korean government to be the instigator of these previous attacks based largely on the context; the investigators were once again quick to dismiss other hypotheses.

One example of the fallacy in their reasoning was the fact that the investigators detected only one North Korean IP address amongst the forty-nine routes that the attackers took to direct their traffic. This IP address could have been reused by the same group that had previously targeted South Korea's organisations. It could also have simply been a proxy and not the final destination of the traffic. In the end, the new information still did not prove beyond doubt the involvement of the North Korean state, especially as the proof remained at a technical level, which can neither inform nor prove sponsorship. The use of judgement in this case overwhelmingly informed the attribution to North Korea, which is unavoidable. Yet this does not mean that it is acceptable for logical fallacies to permeate the judgement.

It follows that within the context of attribution, even if an analyst is in possession of more knowledge or information, it is not a given that the analysis leading to attribution will be 'better'. More knowledge can increase the constructed expectation bias because the experts work on different and unrelated cases from which they draw parallels, while more information impels analysts to construe the information within their own set of particular expectations and beliefs. More information about DarkScoul merely served to reinforce the analysts' theory of North Korean sponsorship, instead of prompting them to try to test other hypotheses.

To ensure a minimisation of biases and flaws inevitably linked with judgement, as with the DarkSeoul incident, analysts can follow strict methodologies, especially ones that have been developed for and by the intelligence community. Several 'tools' exist based on the following premise: if one is able to trace the analytical thought process, and how analysts dismiss hypotheses to arrive at a conclusion about the identity of an instigator, it will be easier to reach less biased conclusions, which, in turn, may make it easier to convince other parties that the judgement is correct. These 'tools' include quantifying the level of a statement's probability in regard to the language used—with, for instance, the wording 'almost certain' for a threshold of 93 per cent certainty—in order to improve precision.[47] Other such 'tools' are: applying situational logic, applying theory, drawing comparisons with other historical situations, and the Analysis of Competing Hypotheses (see below).[48] Situational logic is the process whereby an analyst tries to 'work backwards to explain the origins or causes of the current situation'.[49] Situational logic and theoretical frameworks, and their comparison as tools for analysis, do not prevent the type of observation biases exemplified by Figure 1. But they allow us to be at least cognisant of the methodology applied, and they aim to reduce any bias.

On the other hand, the Analysis of Competing Hypotheses, often abbreviated as ACH, highlights the cognitive process underlying attribution; it is more tedious to apply, although it can also bear more fruitful results. Several researchers have already advocated its use in the context of the attribution of cyber attacks.[50] The Analysis of Competing Hypotheses seeks to incentivise analysts to consider alternative hypotheses and to find elements to disprove them. The goal of the exercise is to recognise that there are alternative hypotheses, and to avoid 'satisficing', namely taking the first hypothesis that appears to be 'good enough' for granted. As Heuer notes: 'If deception is planned well and properly implemented, one should not expect to find evidence of it readily at hand'.[51] Analysts should therefore strive to find evidence that is inconsistent with a hypothesis, to try to disconfirm it. If they cannot find such evidence, they should ask, 'can I realistically expect to see evidence of it?'[52]

Applying the Analysis of Competing Hypotheses can be time-consuming and requires specific training. In the end, even Heuer confirms that the bias cannot be completely removed: 'The result, after all, still depends on fallible intuitive judgment applied to incomplete and ambiguous information', with which logic cannot help.[53] This conclusion echoes that of the political theorist Peter Steinberger on political judgement. He notes that the relevant skills and tools can only be developed up to a certain point:

> Political judgement—like any other kind of judgement—can be nurtured and honed, largely through a curriculum of experience, expert guidance, and habituation. But just as some people have perfect pitch, while others are tone-deaf, so do some individuals have a certain knack for the practice of politics that others can never acquire.[54]

Hence, the role of scientific tools remains limited to being able to formulate correct attribution. Yet instead of focusing on the correctness of attribution, the inescapability of the use of judgement raises several other political concerns about the entity formulating them, especially in terms of trust and authority.

Political implications: authority and trust

Anyone can form and express a judgement, but only the judgements of a few matter for attribution. Accepting that attribution is based on judgement therefore raises an important issue in terms of who formulates the judgement, whether this entity has any authority to do so, and whether this entity should be trusted or not. It is worth noting that when attribution is presented as a technical problem, these questions of trust and authority do not arise. In fact, their dismissal is also very common when discussing how information and communication technologies have supported various societal changes, in a global context.[55] For the attribution of cyber attacks, an entity's judgement matters on two grounds: if the entity can convince an audience of the correctness of its judgement; and if it can act on it.

Judgements are not universal truths but rely prominently on convincing 'others'. And to be convincing, authority is required. It involves arguing that, in the given circumstances, the choice of actor(s) to whom the action has been attributed is the appropriate one, and trumped all other alternatives. Ultimately, the decision can only be rationally affirmed, but not proven.[56] Highlighting the different rationales behind the identification of a party as the attacker attempts to prove attribution. But in this context of high uncertainty, with little and possibly false information, the rationale is likely to favour one amongst other options pointing in the direction of certain parties, and to dismiss other interpretations of the evidence. The trust that an audience places in institutions formulating the judgement is hence of primary importance.

Governmental agencies, and to some extent private companies (including media companies), are the two main entities whose judgement really matters when it comes to attributing attacks threatening national security: the former because state actors are the only authoritative actors on the international scene who can take decisions and act upon them; the latter because companies have the power to reshape the political agenda on an international level. For example, the wave of diplomatic reaction triggered by Mandiant's report on Chinese state-sponsored espionage did not have to take place. Both parties could merely have dismissed the report as one amongst so many published every day by different organisations. But the United States chose to lend its support to the Mandiant report, adding credibility and authority to it while also being able to deflect criticisms because it did not author it. As a consequence, Mandiant's judgement played an indirect but important role in initiating discussions between the United States and China, a role that cannot be ignored.

Trusting a private company about issues pertaining to attribution is not without its set of issues, and nor is trusting a state's judgement. Companies' main interests reside in making financial gains. When companies publish reports pointing in the direction of a state, all of a sudden they come under the spotlight and can reap non-negligible marketing benefits. This increased visibility can incentivise them not to share information with competitors about the threat they are monitoring, an otherwise usual practice. When companies restrict the circulation of threat information, it arguably puts many more victims at risk from the investigated, but not yet publicised, cyber attack. More importantly, the increased visibility companies obtain can also prompt them to inflate the importance of evidence towards denouncing a state and consequently to impair their faculty of judgement.

Trusting state actors for judgements can also be problematic, in light of their heavy reliance on intelligence services and the associated opacity. Intelligence services play a key role in cyber security, especially signals intelligence agencies such as the NSA in the United States or GCHQ in the United Kingdom. These have grown from their traditional technical expertise in communication systems. This expertise in gathering and analysing technical information makes them ideal candidates for blending the mixture of political and technical elements necessary in order to assess the identity of cyber attack instigators. Yet their judgement is far from universally convincing, for two main reasons.

Firstly, they often invoke the argument that their judgements are based on non-publicly verifiable confidential information. Attribution based on non-public intelligence raises several trust-related questions: does the intelligence community really have more information than is publicly made available? Is the information they have conclusive? And are they oblivious to their own bias (to 'satisficing' or 'perseveration', in other words)? No one from outside the intelligence community can seriously investigate or know the answer to these questions. Therefore, relying on non-public evidence for attribution actually shifts attribution from a process focused on collecting and analysing data to a process of convincing a population on a basis of trust. The reliance of attribution on trust adds another nuance to attribution being political: the trust in the entity formulating judgement creates divisive and potentially polemical lines of interaction between supporters and non-believers of the attribution claims.[57]

A second issue with state attribution is that intelligence services are not immune to organisational weaknesses, especially the phenomenon known as 'groupthink'.[58] This term was popularised after the failure of the intelligence community in assessing the risk of weapons of mass destruction in Iraq in 2003—a failure that for many is an indication that intelligence services are not credible for attribution, although, counter-intuitively, the opposite might be true: the 2003 debacle has arguably led them to be considerably more careful about stating their judgement. Whenever the US intelligence community expresses their views—as was the case when they denounced the Russian intelligence services as behind a cyber attack of the Democratic National Committee during the 2016 US presidential campaign—it can be expected that they would not do so lightly especially following the case of Iraqi weapons of mass destruction.[59] In his commentary about Iraq's possession of weapons of mass destruction, Paul R. Pillar, a senior intelligence officer at the CIA and at the Director of National Intelligence, rebuked the claim that intelligence analysts modified their assessment because of political pressure. Instead, 'the actual politicization of intelligence occurs subtly', he claimed. He writes: 'Intelligence analysts—for whom attention, especially favourable attention, from policy-makers is a measure of success—felt a strong wind consistently blowing in one direction. The desire to bend with such a wind is natural and strong, even if unconscious.'[60]

Furthermore, Pillar argued that the administration willingly cherry-picked information to make their case for the war, and largely ignored other judgements from the intelligence community.[61] That there was no pressure and that intelligence analysts did not modify their assessment as the result of this is corroborated by Michael Hayden's version in his memoir, director of the NSA between 1999 and 2005 and of the CIA between 2006 and 2009:

> The urban legend has it that we [the intelligence community] were pressured by the White House, and especially by Vice President Cheney, to write a case for war. I never experienced such pressure, and when I got to CIA and talked to those more directly involved, they reported that they felt no such pressure either. We just got it wrong.[62]

Notably, even the French and German intelligence services believed there were weapons of mass destruction in Iraq, although they did not support the war. While it is difficult to go against a prevailing 'groupthink', French president Jacques Chirac was allegedly highly suspicious of the intelligence reports, understanding how the intelligence community functions.[63] This single case of failure has made the public far more wary and suspicious of claims by intelligence services, a wariness which does not bode well for attribution. This wariness in specific relation to attribution of cyber attacks was highlighted by the 2014 attack on Sony, about which several prominent members of the intelligence community expressed judgements that nevertheless drew criticisms. Robert Steele, a scholar working on intelligence, summarises this scepticism when he writes: 'Where intelligence is used at all it is generally to confirm pre-existing policy positions rather than what governing elites need to know'.[64]

On the other hand, following revelations from the former NSA contractor Edward Snowden, the public now know that the United States and the United Kingdom have deployed impressive capabilities to monitor networks—although, as outlined in the previous chapter, it is not entirely clear whether the intelligence services use them to track instigators of cyber attacks. The revelations have been a boon to the credibility of the intelligence services. Even if they do not possess further secret intelligence, the public can easily be mistaken in believing that they do, because the services' monitoring capabilities are now perceived as quasi-ubiquitous. Hence, the Snowden revelations may have partly counterbalanced the history of shortcomings resulting from the 2003 'groupthink' effect, and may even have enabled the United States to recover some of the lost authority so dearly needed for attribution.

For a government wishing to attribute an attack, overcoming the trust issues in order to be convincing to its electorate and to other states is important. An electorate can hold its government accountable if it deems that the government did not take the right course of action. On the other hand, it is admittedly difficult for the public to be able to exert such a judgement, because information opacity mostly prevails in cases of cyber attacks. In fact, it is as difficult for members of the public to evaluate the little information they are presented with as to evaluate the level of trust that they should accord to the judgement formulated by intelligence services or their government. Furthermore, a government needs to convince other states that its attribution claims rest on solid ground in order to harvest support from the international community and not be regarded as taking arbitrary decisions. Convincing the international community cements a government's 'attribution power', strengthening the perception that it can correctly identify instigators of attacks, a potentially strong argument in favour of its deterrence strategy.

To avoid this reliance on trust, on the fallibility of judgements, and on the resulting shift of attribution towards a distinctly political process, legal scholars have been trying to set authoritative standards for attribution. Legal standards for attribution, be they within domestic or international law, strive to be high, and try to minimise the recourse to judgement. Yet these standards cannot avoid judgements either, depending on where they place the threshold to consider a state responsible. Also, a focus on standards short-circuits the political process required for a decision to be reached on whether to formally attribute an attack or not. Illustrative of these standards is what the Tallinn Manual, a publication written by international law and cyber security experts, notes about attacks being traced back to state-owned infrastructures: 'The mere fact that a cyber operation has been launched or otherwise originates from a governmental cyber infrastructure is not sufficient evidence for attributing the operation to that State, but is an indication that the State in question is associated with the operation.'[65]

Mandiant made such an association when it traced the attacks on 141 US companies to a Chinese military area comprising 5 million people and, among others, the Chinese signals intelligence agency. It made the connection between the area, the agency, and the sponsor of the attacks, namely the Chinese state. Chinese officials criticised the company's methods, but this did not prevent several other security experts, such as Michael Hayden, from considering that the judgement, albeit logically flawed in its presentation of evidence, was correct. Naturally, there is the possibility that independent non-state actors took over the state-owned infrastructure. The mere possibility that hackers compromised a state-owned infrastructure can prevent the law—domestic or international—from being conclusive about attribution, if too high a standard for evidence, such as 'beyond reasonable doubt', is applied. However, at this point, political judgement becomes relevant: a relevant authority can assess the probability of non-state actors compromising government computers as low, and may subsequently consider the evidence as conclusive for attribution. Mandiant's judgement, endorsed by the United States, did just that.

Hence, attribution is never completely impossible as several analysts mentioned in the introduction have declared. However, the possibility of attribution is contingent upon the levels of trust and authority accorded to the entities formulating the core judgement. Part of this judgement is to decide on which evidentiary standards to base attribution, and whether attribution should include any types of sanction associated with these standards. The importance of acknowledging the possibility of attribution is threefold. Firstly, by giving substance to the political (and fallible) character of attribution, the emphasis shifts from approaching it as a 'universal truth' to seeing it merely as a game to convince an audience. Secondly, this implies that any government badly hit by a cyber attack is not deprived of all recourse: it can retaliate in kind, economically or diplomatically, against an alleged adversary as long as it successfully garners the trust and authority required to convince its audience. This leads us to the third point: gathering evidence is important to formulate a correct judgement; but resources and time must be spent on successfully influencing public opinion and other state actors of the validity of the judgement. This last task can be especially difficult, and does not rely solely on the attack at hand. Previous cases strongly influence a public's perception of an entity's capability to formulate a correct judgement, and therefore its trust in the entity. Any attribution mistake can therefore be very damaging in the long run. Such an analysis of attribution strongly displaces the main constraint on attribution from what many see as being technical to the political.

Attribution is not perfect; and neither is political judgement, on which it relies. Yet we cannot fail to notice that for every large-scale past incident, analysts have expressed judgements about the origin of the attacks, consequently achieving at least some degree of attribution. Though imperfect, political judgements have allowed analysts to form strong suspicions of who was behind an attack. At times, the judgements may not have been good, but at least they moved the attribution process forward to some extent.

In contrast to the common understanding that 'hid[ing] your identity in order to attack a person or an institution is unnervingly easy', this chapter has shown that it is not completely impossible to assess the identity of attack sponsors.[66] This possibility is predicated upon the fact that attribution of national security incidents does not rely on a set of well-defined rules for collection of evidence and its interpretation. In a national security context, therefore, the capacity of states to formulate convincing political judgements on the identity of attackers should not be underestimated. The words of William J. Lynn III, deputy secretary of defense under President Obama from 2009 until 2011, strongly reflect this: 'If you're a major nation-state, you're probably not going to bet the farm on the fact that we [the US] wouldn't be able to trace it back.'[67] Yet this nuance also matters: the veracity of the trace is secondary to the ability of the United States, or any other state for that matter, to successfully convince people of it.

Judgements can be wrong, as noted. There is an interesting trend, however, of states reacting to shield themselves from errors, thanks to private companies such as Mandiant that report on attacks and attribute them. States can push the responsibility for errors, incomplete data or logical flaws onto these private companies, while still yielding the benefits of unofficial attribution if they support a report's conclusion. As cyber attacks become an increasingly common tool for foreign policy, it is questionable whether state institutions will become more willing to publicly share their judgements on the identities of their attackers, or if they will leave the bulk of this work to private companies. The indictment of several hackers by the US Department of Justice seems to indicate that the US, at least, is willing to directly confront attacking states. In fact, the Justice Department has been specially training prosecutors to follow up on cyber attacks and bring cases.[68] But not all states have the leverage power of the US; some may favour quieter responses or none at all.

3

STANDARDS OF PROOF

When accused of sponsoring attacks, states usually vehemently deny involvement, and they are able to do this all the more easily because the judgemental element in attribution facilitates undermining such accusations. No public courts are involved in the assessment of guilt, and accusing states may need to take swift decisions, sometimes on unsound grounds, about whether to attribute attacks. This rapid decision process contrasts with the care taken by the judicial process, but is not unique to the attribution of cyber attacks—the attribution of other national security incidents often functions in a similar way. Furthermore, more often than not, it is not entirely clear when it is possible to consider an attack 'attributed', to an individual or a state actor. Courts play a role in the process, but it would be very narrow to reduce attribution purely to court decisions. Discrepancies between judicial procedures and attribution exist. For instance, in a criminal and domestic context, cases have emerged where courts did not condemn individuals, though they had confessed to the attacks. This apparent contradiction between the legal grounds for accountability and attribution raises several questions. When can we consider that an attack is attributed, if attribution is not dependent on court proceedings? Do we need 'appropriate' standards for the attribution of cyber attacks? What would such standards look like?

This chapter starts by noting that there is a mismatch between how attribution functions, and how the law operates. Attribution is not contingent on legal proceedings, and can occur despite a lack of condemnation by a court. This lack of reliance on strict standards of evidence leads us to consider the following argument: that attribution is easily malleable. On top of the reliance of attribution on judgement, two factors notably underpin this malleability: an apparent lack of scrutiny for the evidence presented in cases of cyber attacks, and the use of non-conclusive criteria that are nevertheless presented as decisive. This malleability can be of great help to officials who seek to convince an audience of their attribution claims.

The argument will be considered in two steps. Firstly, the chapter will show that the standards used in court settings are inappropriate for attribution. Secondly, it will show the negligible role played by the quality of the evidence gathered for attributing an attack.

Domestic and international legal standards for attribution: a mismatch

If one looks at the standards used in domestic criminal courts and in international law, it is clear that there is a wide discrepancy. Different standards exist to translate different needs—and legal needs do not always align with those of attribution. This has led several analysts to call for the establishment of an appropriate standard for attribution.[1] For example, Jason Healey suggested that states should hold other states accountable for the use of their territory to launch cyber attacks.[2] This is a narrow and specific interpretation of attribution; it is also problematic when examined under the prism of international norms.[3] Establishing one unique standard for attribution, as suggested, also raises many different challenges within domestic law. This is especially the case because legal and attribution processes operate differently, serving different purposes. In general terms, legal standards seek to maximise the conviction of guilty entities while minimising the conviction of innocents. In order to do so, the standards used in courts can be rather difficult to meet, especially for cyber attacks. Attribution, however, has a much broader scope. It can frame instigators as 'adversaries' or 'enemies of the state', which is useful rhetoric for whoever tries to justify retaliatory actions, and does not require the meeting of stringent standards for doing so.

One example of the rigorous standards used within the context of the law is 'beyond reasonable doubt', the most commonly used standard in domestic criminal cases.[4] It can be very difficult in cyber attack cases for the prosecution to meet this standard and show continuity of evidence, especially when attempting to prove that the indicted individual was the one sitting at the computer during the attack. In this regard, circumstantial evidence usually plays an important role when the accused does not confess to the crime.[5] The defendant is always able to argue that his computer was used for the attack, but that he was not the one operating it, or that a Trojan had hijacked the computer. This strategy of defence has worked in the past, and is commonly and successfully used in child pornography trials in Hong Kong.[6] Looking into the details of a British hacking trial illustrates the stringency of the legal standards for individual criminals, and shows what constitutes 'beyond reasonable doubt' in the context of cyber attacks.

In 1994, Richard Pryce, then aged 16 and using the pseudonym 'DataStream Cowboy', hacked into the servers of the US Air Force's network. After finding an encrypted file containing usernames and passwords, Pryce successfully decrypted it and was able to compromise hundreds of accounts of people who had varied access to military information. Pryce accessed, copied and deleted emails, as well as a battlefield simulation programme.[7] A week after discovering the attacks, investigators at the military base found out that Pryce had also infiltrated the Army Corps of Engineers' network. By monitoring the attack, they were able to retrieve Pryce's pseudonym. DataStream Cowboy initially went through Colombia, before logging into a provider in New York called mindvox.phantom.com in order to mask his origin. But that did not prevent the police from finding him.

Working from the handle, investigators then tried to gather information from the Internet. An informant quickly came forward and told the investigator that he had had an online discussion a few months earlier with an individual using the handle DataStream Cowboy. According to the informant, DataStream Cowboy was a 16-year-old boy living in the UK 'who liked to attack "MIL" sites because they were so insecure'.[8] DataStream Cowboy had also given the informant the address of his own Bulletin Board System, a sort of early version of online forums, which he hosted at his own location. The address used to access the Board was his telephone number, a crucial element for the investigators. The United States asked the British police for help to identify the person behind the phone number, and they were able to arrest him less than two months after his initial break-in.

The police charged Pryce with twelve offences. Yet this did not mean that his condemnation was entirely assured. Defence expert Peter Sommer disputed the quality of many elements brought against Pryce.[9] Firstly, the defence was not given the material on Pryce's hard drive, because Pryce had allegedly downloaded three security-sensitive files. Instead, the prosecution provided printouts, which could not count as evidence because they could not possibly be testable by the defence. Secondly, the pen register on Pryce's phone captured only the number he dialled, showed 'unusual combinations of numbers', and revealed calls that lasted for hours. Taken together with the fact that the police found software to carry out phone-phreaking, the prosecution interpreted the 'unusual combinations of numbers' as proof that Pryce was carrying out such activity. Sommer, however, suggested that the content of the pen register showed that it could not be trusted, may have been malfunctioning, and that the alleged link between the pen register and the offence left room for doubt.

Thirdly, Pryce allegedly phoned a telephone exchange in Colombia to mask his traces. But no evidence was retrieved from the telephone exchange. The next point where a trace of Pryce appeared was via a US ISP called 'Cyberspace', at which DataStream Cowboy had an account. The investigators were unable to make the connection between Cyberspace and the alleged telephone exchange in Colombia. Fourthly, the US Air Force officer who monitored DataStream Cowboy's account with Cyberspace produced evidence of the activity on the account, but also apologised for a recent hard-drive crash at the provider. This crash raised the question of the quality of evidence the US Air Force was able to retrieve. Moreover, the US Air Force did not present the original logs, and could not prove that no one had tampered with them. Fifthly, the US Air Force did not release the source code of the programme with which they captured the packets to ensure that it worked correctly. Therefore, Sommer concluded that the evidence brought forward from the attacked computers could not be trusted and went against forensic rules. One of the general rules given by a reference textbook on presenting data in cases of cyber crimes notably specifies: 'A party may therefore need to be able to show that any system from which evidence is derived was functioning appropriately at the time the evidence was generated, for example through audit records.'[10]

In this case, the computers had been compromised, and the prosecution should have attempted to set up a clean environment to collect presentable evidence for the court. A close examination of the evidence shed doubts on the culpability of the individual, and, in the end, on the attribution of the malicious breach to the individual. On 21 March 1997, the court still condemned Richard Pryce, but fined him the small amount of $1,200 for the twelve charges brought against him.[11]

The five points that Peter Sommer used to challenge the technical evidence of Pryce's involvement demonstrate the difficulty of declaring 'beyond reasonable doubt' that an individual is responsible for a cyber attack. Yet Sommer's successful defence may be more exceptional than the norm. Keith Roscoe, working for the Digital and Electronic Forensic Service at the UK Metropolitan Police Service, confirmed that there are now safeguards in the United Kingdom to ensure that the police have not tampered with collected data. These safeguards also allow the defence to go back to the originals. But in practice, the defence rarely asks to see the originals, and the collected material presented in court often goes undisputed.[12]

The divergence between legal conviction and attribution are further highlighted in cases where a court does not convict a defendant for various reasons, but the defendant admits to the accusation. Several factors can prevent condemnation. The lack of a legal framework was an issue in the mid-1990s in many countries, and still is in developing countries.[13] Other obstacles can include the expense of bringing experts into the country where the defendant is being tried and/or from where the defendant has committed the offence.[14] Yet by using one's own non-authoritative judgement, it may be possible despite no conviction to consider the case as attributed, especially when the defendant has willingly admitted to the cyber attacks.

Naturally, for criminal cases, different courts in different countries have different processes and different standards for ruling on a case. Not all countries have, for instance, stringent standards when it comes to the scrutiny of digital forensics. Also, not all countries have the same ability to hold corporations responsible for breaches of criminal and civil law, and the differences can at times be subtle and complex.

Commonly, a company can be held criminally accountable when senior executives or employees act in their official capacities and commit violations of the law. But the standard can also be lower in some cases. If a company simply failed to put in place mechanisms to detect criminal activities by its employees, and benefited from such activities, courts can identify the company as responsible.[15] There is, therefore, a wide range of regimes for considering a company liable for wrongdoing, ranging from strict liability to duty-based liability, to mixed regimes of liability.[16] This variety makes it impossible to draw one single standard for attribution, but also highlights once again the mismatch between legal standards and attribution. If a company is found not guilty in one court and in one jurisdiction, this does not imply that the company did not sponsor an attack in any form. Attribution with all its nuances needs to be preserved. It is worth noting that in the European Union, companies can explicitly be held liable for offences such as 'illegal access to an information system, illegal system interference, illegal data interference, and illegal interception'.[17] Again, if a court does not recognise a company as culpable, this does not mean that the attribution process ends there. Often, it is necessary to look at the details to know why and if a case can be considered as attributed, or where the process stands.

This mismatch between legal judgement and attribution extends further, to national security incidents and to international law. Within this set of incidents, the problems are three-fold. Firstly, as noted above, there are a multitude of standards in international law as well.[18] Secondly, and much more problematically, the status of cyber attacks within the body of international law is far from clear and lacks precedent.[19] Thirdly, within the national security context, intelligence, rather than testable and high-quality evidence, plays a more predominant role. This stems from the lack of clear consensus on both the applicability of international law for cyber attacks, and the pressing need for attribution of national security incidents.

With intelligence, the level of standard diverges from the high standards in courts, but this represents a need for quick decision-making, even if it means disregarding standards. When analysts try to attribute a case that threatens national security, the attribution process is clearly different from that of criminal cases. In the latter, law enforcement agencies first obtain the name of a culprit, and then try to look for evidence. In a national security context, intelligence analysts are under pressure to feed information to decision-makers about the attacker's identity. However, such analysts rarely need to look for evidence: intelligence, albeit potentially deceiving, can be sufficient.

Also, policy-makers may not look at intelligence with as much scrutiny as Peter Sommer did in the case of Richard Pryce, and intuition may play a much more preponderant role in deciding to retaliate than it could in the context of a courtroom. Examples outside the realm of cyber attacks abound of a government deciding to retaliate against an enemy on the basis of gathered intelligence rather than as the outcome of a planned and lengthy legal process. These examples include the United States bombing Libya in retaliation only two weeks after a bomb exploded in West Germany—killing three people—in April 1986, or the rapid measures taken against Al Qaeda following 9/11.[20] Intelligence also fits the model of attribution much better than discussions about 'evidence' and standards of proof, because in the national security context, it is difficult to evaluate the correctness of the information one possesses. As seen in the previous chapter, the attribution process requires interpretations that qualify in many regards as judgement calls. For instance, if a country refuses to share information, the victim government may decide to see it as a form of sponsorship of the attack, and act accordingly. Establishing 'the facts' can be difficult, and can warrant a relaxation of otherwise stringent standards if sufficient political will exists to retaliate. Retaliation cannot be contingent on a long, albeit careful, legal evaluation of the facts according to certain standards.

In summary, courts' decisions play only a minor role in attribution for two main reasons. Firstly, a court verdict is binary: a court finds an entity either guilty or not guilty of a specific charge. But as this book strives to show, attribution is a lot more complex and nuanced. Even if a court can actually be more flexible with the charges it chooses to bring against an entity, the verdict is still always going to be a choice between those two options. But with regard to state-sponsored activity, for instance, it is important to distinguish if the attacks were simply tolerated by a government that turned a blind eye to them, or if the government directed them.[21] This nuance is especially important to bear in mind when discussing actions to take based on attribution—

which is, after all, why attribution occurs. A government may hold in one case that a state that 'turns a blind eye' to its citizens launching cyber attacks warrants attribution because this suits the victim's best interests, while in another case it may not.

Secondly, as seen in the case of legal attribution to individuals and to states, the lack of consensus on a legal standard does not actually impede attribution from taking place. Individuals not convicted by a court could still have instigated attacks; governments could still respond to attacks using force despite the lack of court rulings. Decisions may very well be based on intelligence that would not prove the attack sponsor's guilt according to a specific legal standard. What is important is that the retaliatory state convinces the international community that its actions were called for. The marginal role courts play in attribution is therefore even smaller for national security incidents than for criminal cases. In this context, political attribution is much more important than legal attribution in deciding whether action against an alleged attacker must be taken, but also consequently much more malleable in the hands of the political elite. This conclusion has two implications: despite many authors' calls for determining an 'appropriate' standard for attribution, this is not feasible; and the lack of standards of evidence implies that government officials have a great deal of flexibility to manipulate the truth in order to achieve a political goal—a consequence that the next section will examine.[22]

State sponsorship: malleable standards and misleading criteria

The argument that the standards are malleable in the case of attribution to state actors follows from two separate points, one conceptual and one empirical, about the lack of scrutiny behind attribution cases.

Conceptually, and despite what may look like objective standards, international law is not completely objective. It inevitably entails 'some measure of politics', as the influential international lawyer and former Finnish diplomat Martti Koskenniemi wrote.[23] Koskenniemi argued that international law is political, and hence 'manipulable'.[24] To be objective, international law needs to meet two criteria: it must be 'concrete' and 'normative'. International law must be focused on actual and verifiable behaviours. It also needs to ensure that it is applicable to all states, even if a state opposes the law. But these two requirements conflict with one another. For a law to be concrete, it needs to be focused, and hence 'close' to states' practices. On the other hand, in order to be normative, a law needs to be 'distant' from states' practices, in other words more general. However, it is not possible to demonstrate that a law does both. In the first case, by demonstrating a law is close to states' practices, the demonstration is vulnerable to the argument that states with the power to craft laws will use them to defend and re-assert their position at the expense of weaker states. Hence, international law is, in this case, an apology to realpolitik. In the second case, by demonstrating that a law is distant to states' practices, the demonstration is vulnerable to claims of utopia and lack of applicability. Koskenniemi hence concludes that international law cannot be objective, and is political. If international law is political, the standards that international law is based on are also political.

The political aspect of standards is exemplified by how a government can use them to legitimise a response against an entity it regards as guilty. The choice of one standard among the many in existence is not anodyne, and is carefully chosen to match and justify intended actions. This means that successful attribution relies heavily on the political elite's ability to garner enough support for their attribution claims. This ability may, however, not be entirely contingent on the evidence behind the claims, but on other larger, trust-related factors that help them turn circumstantial aspects of the attack into presented evidence.

The intelligence community has suffered several backlashes that have undermined the public's trust in their claims, most notably following the Iraqi weapons of mass destruction debacle. Yet surprisingly, it is still fairly unproblematic for US officials, or usually high-quality newspapers, to make claims of attribution for cyber attacks without backing these up with much evidence.

Specific examples illustrate this almost systematic lack of concern for nuance and lack of scrutiny behind evidence. Officials can choose any standards of evidence that fit their claims because their choice is very likely to go under the radar in any case. For instance, US senior officials have repeatedly mentioned Mandiant's report on the attacks on US companies and its conclusions (notably that the attacks were of Chinese origin), but did not mention the evidence used to reach these conclusions. This is telling of the strength and validity of the claims.[25] Similarly, in 2014, the former US representative Michael J. Rogers, also chairman of the Permanent Committee on Intelligence between 2011 and 2015, briefly mentioned certain cyber attacks during the annual Munich Security Conference, among which was Operation Ababil. This operation involved denial-of-service attacks against US banks in retaliation for an inflammatory video called the 'Innocence of Muslims'.[26] Rogers attributed all the attacks he listed to governments, without any nuanced consideration of their real involvement, and without any proof regarding the attacks:

> You have a nation state who has well over 200 times, according to public reports, targeted US financial institutions for disruptive activities: the nation of Iran. You saw North Korea take a, albeit not very good, but aggressive DDoS attack on a financial institution in the South. We watched Russia, that one is earlier, 2013 [sic], do a preparatory cyber attack before it launched its attacks on South Ossetia.[27]

In reality, none of the cases he mentioned are clear-cut, and especially not Operation Ababil. The previous year, Rogers had already made this claim accusing Iran, declaring to the media that banks 'have had trouble keeping up with the recent DDoS attacks that have had the sophistication and the level of resources that a nation-state entity like Iran can devote to them'.[28] Another congressman, Senator Lieberman, likewise put aside any standards of proof behind attribution to express his own judgement about Operation Ababil. A group called Mrt. Izz ad-Din al-Qassam Cyber Fighters took credit for the attacks, but Senator Lieberman, in an interview with C-Span on 21 September 2012, declared:

> I don't believe these were just hackers who were skilled enough to cause a disruption of the websites. I think this was done by Iran and the Quds Force, which has its own developing cyber attack capacity. And I believe it was in response to the increasingly strong economic sanctions that the United States and our European allies have put on Iranian financial institutions.[29]

The Cyber Fighters denied being supported by anyone.[30] The senator said that his sources were individuals within the intelligence community—an obviously problematic statement as it forced the public to trust not only his judgement, but his sources as well. As mentioned, trusting secret sources is not easy following the Iraq case.

On the same day the senator made this statement, Reuters journalists also claimed that Iran was the source of denial-of-service attacks on three large American banks.[31] The journalists did not name a source, but hinted that an individual with national security knowledge had talked to them about the case—possibly the same individual who had talked to Lieberman. Following the statements, Iran denied being the instigator of the attacks.[32] Rogers's aforementioned quote is just one example among many. Another is that of Richard Ledgett, deputy director at the NSA, who stated in March 2014 during a conference: 'You're probably aware that there has been a spate of those [denial-of-service attacks] directed against the US financial sector since 2012. Again, that's a nation state who's executing those attacks and they're doing that as a semi-anonymous way of reprisal.'[33]

It appears that Roger and Ledgett were right. In March 2016, the US Department of Justice indicted seven Iranian members of the army for these hacks and the indictment showed more evidence.[34] The point, however, is that until then, their claims were unsubstantiated, yet repeated by the media. This highlights once more the role of the central element explored in Chapter 2: trust.

Also illustrative of the at-times lack of concern for the evidence is a case from *The New York Times* about the authors of the Shamoon virus, the malware that disrupted Saudi Aramco, and whose authors remain uncertain. A group called 'The Cutting Sword of Justice' asserted that they had targeted Saudi Aramco for political reasons, and they released accurate information to prove their claims.[35] Another hypothesis is that Iran was behind the attack, as it wished to retaliate against the tightening of the sanctions regime.[36] The US government may have further evidence that proves this sponsorship, although the evidence currently available in the public domain is too sparse to support such claims. Despite this uncertainty, *The New York Times*, eschewing journalistic nuance, simply attributed the attacks to the Iranians. In March 2013 it featured an article stating that 'Iranian hackers gained some respect in the technology community when they brought down 30,000 computers belonging to Saudi Aramco'.[37]

It was not the first time that *The New York Times*, a highly respected newspaper, has taken shortcuts. In a much more consequential case, it published what later turned out to be incorrect information about

Iraq's possession of weapons of mass destruction in the run-up to the 2003 war.[38] It would be terribly short-sighted to assign all the blame to *The New York Times*; but more generally, a revelation by an intelligence officer explaining 'why he thought the war was inevitable' highlights the importance of the media in influencing the intelligence cycle. 'My source of information was the *Washington Post*,' said the intelligence officer.[39] The loss of nuanced consideration in the case of Shamoon, which could also be fairly consequential, similarly echoes a lack of scrutiny regarding the evidence that stands behind the case.

The same situation recurred following the discovery of Flame, a highly complex Trojan that targeted Iran, but also Israel, in 2012. *The Times* published a lazy headline that read: 'Iran attacked by "Israeli computer virus"'.[40] There was at the time almost no evidence to substantiate this claim. When it had published its own news reports, security software company Kaspersky Lab had linked the 'sophistication' of the Trojan to a nation-state.[41] This constituted the main evidence for *The Times'* story—and it is rather meagre. In this case, again, *The Times* was actually proved right. Nevertheless, the decision to blame a country as the attack's instigator without presenting compelling evidence shows that the newspaper was relying on readers' trust in the truth of the story. The confirmation that the newspaper was right came shortly after. A Kasperksy report that appeared a week after the *Times* story, on 11 June 2012, announced that Flame was linked to the previously discovered malware Stuxnet and Duqu.[42] By then, the journalist David Sanger had published the results of his investigations (on 1 June 2012), linking Stuxnet and Duqu to the United States and Israel. This meant that the same countries were also behind Flame. Another week later, reporters at *The Washington Post* quoted unnamed 'Western intelligence officials with knowledge of the effort' as evidence that the United States and Israel were behind it.[43]

In addition to this disregard of evaluating the evidence, it is very often difficult to find the evidence that enabled law enforcement agencies or other analysts to conclude that a certain entity was behind an attack. This type of detail is only rarely placed at the forefront of media reports.[44] There is almost a blind trust in the judgement expressed by members of the cyber security community—possibly for fear of failing to grasp the technical relevance of certain pieces put forward as 'evidence'. By presenting attribution claims as certain, reports remove the nuance and uncertainty around them, and readers are less likely to question them. The questionability of such claims, therefore, is instead strongly linked with the trust that one has in an organisation. For news organisations such as *The New York Times*, there is a strong expectation from their readership of high reliability. Sources presenting cases of cyber attacks may have to adapt to maintain this trust, and preserve the nuance behind attribution claims by examining the supporting evidence. Since 2014, the trend has actually been for news media, *The New York Times* included, to improve their reporting about the evidence behind attribution claims.

This lack of scrutiny is even more surprising in light of the careful analysis of the evidence seeking to identify the author of an August 2013 chemical attack in Syria. The British and French intelligence services, in an unusual move, each released reports claiming to have evidence supporting the thesis that the Syrian government had used chemical weapons against insurgents.[45] *The Guardian* noted that there was a 'striking lack of any scientific evidence in the document'.[46] Many more reports expressed doubt about the evidence.[47] Similar scrutiny followed after a report by United Nations experts was published.[48] Josh Lyons, a satellite imagery analyst for Human Rights Watch, noted that the technical data 'isn't conclusive, but it is highly suggestive'.[49] In light of this lack of conclusive proof (or based on a cold political calculation), the secretary-general of the United Nations, Ban Ki-moon, refused to directly attribute the attacks.[50] The Russian president, Vladimir Putin, also disputed the allegations and demanded their withdrawal from the findings of the report, stating that anti-government rebels, not the Syrian state, had deployed the gas.[51]

The difference in the handling of cyber attack attribution and the attribution of this chemical attack is startling, and not easy to explain. It could be argued that the difference in scrutiny came from the difference in the stakes, but this would be misguided. Attribution of the Syrian chemical attack was meant to support military intervention in the country by Western forces, a significant and direct stake in other words. But similarly, attributing intellectual property theft via cyber attacks, which costs industry $20 billion to $100 billion per year, an oft-repeated and potentially dubious claim, is non-negligible.[52] Attributing cyber attacks can also lead to a straining of relations between states, as was the case with China and the United States following the Mandiant report, or Iran and the United States following Shamoon. The stakes are therefore also high in these cases, albeit less directly and with fewer clear consequences. Curbing China's systematic use of espionage or Iran's alleged intent to build nuclear weapons is far from straightforward. In fact, the reaction to cyber attacks is often complex because such attacks transcend other political issues: the problem of espionage and of the economic rise of China, the problem of Iran's acquisition of nuclear weapons, or the ongoing conflict between South and North Korea. The complexity of the possible consequences triggered by a response necessitates thorough discussion. But such discussion can also be dangerously misinformed if one is more concerned with simplicity than with the evidence behind attribution.

As mentioned above, one of the possibilities for this aversion to scrutiny could be that the editors of newspapers are scared to enter a highly technical, and hence unintelligible, discussion on attribution. In itself, this would be a weak justification, especially as attribution to sponsors is rarely technical. Regardless of the motivation behind this lack of scrutiny, one consequence of avoiding discussion of the evidence is to displace the focus onto the actions attribution begets. The importance of the political aspect of designating standards therefore has two major implications for cyber attacks. It facilitates the presentation and manipulation of non-conclusive circumstantial evidence as conclusive. In addition, and also importantly, it steers the focus onto the actions a state subsequently takes. Debates follow about the consequences of these actions, and mostly assume that the attribution claims are irrefutably and perfectly correct.

Furthermore, the lack of concern for evidence and the malleability of standards are best exemplified by analysts' use of criteria to attribute attacks, instead of focusing on gathering and analysing evidence. The use of criteria facilitates the manipulation of a case to fit a preconception of the enemy in order to further realise a political agenda. Intelligence analysts' use of a framework based on criteria—such as 'sophistication'—can help this manipulation. The framework represents the use of a low standard of evidence in sharp contrast with the standards used in domestic or international courts. These criteria may at best qualify as circumstantial evidence, and fail to meet any higher evidential standards. Worst of all, in light of the argument that high legal standards are inappropriate for attribution, these criteria can be misleading. They can easily result in the misinterpretation of information heavily influenced by expectations, an effect famously known in intelligence circles as 'perseveration' and already presented in the previous chapter.[53]

Sophistication is only one criterion amongst several used by cyber security analysts to circumvent evidence and focus instead on circumstantial, non-conclusive evidence. In fact, many experts commonly use six criteria to attribute attacks to states: the geopolitical context, the political character of the victim, the beneficiaries of the attack, the apparent origin of the attacker, the sophistication of an attack and the scale of the attack. In 2010, the United Nations' Group of Governmental Experts on cyber security demonstrated the common use of several of these criteria: 'The origin of a disruption, the identity of the perpetrator or the motivation for it can be difficult to ascertain. Often, the perpetrators of such activities can only be inferred from the target, the effect or other circumstantial evidence, and they can act from virtually anywhere.'[54]

Using circumstantial evidence is common even in a court setting, but it also needs to be corroborated with evidence.[55] What is highly problematic is that for several analysts these criteria are conclusive and their use seems to replace the need for evidence. Yet analyses of the criteria, coupled with counter-examples, provide clear grounds to refute the simple rationales behind their uses.

The first criterion is the geopolitical context: many attacks are attributed on the basis of the situation in which they take place. According to Jason Healey, a director at the Atlantic Council, 'while some attacks are technically difficult to attribute, it is usually a straightforward matter to determine the nation responsible, since the conflict takes place during an on-going geo-political crisis'.[56] However, the Solar Sunrise espionage case in the late 1990s should serve as a dire warning against such a simplistic rationale.

In February 1998, tensions between the United States and Iraq were rising over concerns about the Saddam Hussein regime's alleged attempts to produce weapons of mass destruction. Against this backdrop, the United States and Israel were preparing for physical confrontations with Iraq. On 2 February 1998, Israel deployed US missiles.[57]

And on 3 February, a hacker broke into computers at the military academy at Andrews Air Force Base. In a video later produced by The National Counterintelligence Center, the FBI and the National Infrastructure Protection Center, law enforcement officers explained that the intrusions seemed coordinated, striking at the heart of the military systems.[58] The break-in could have threatened the flow of transportation, personnel and medical supplies. The United States was already preparing the deployment of 2,000 troops in Iraq.[59] As a result of the geopolitical context, policy-makers at the time believed that the Iraqi state was launching the attack. Steven Chabinsky, former deputy assistant director of the FBI in the Cyber Division, recalled:

> We see military computers, dot-mil computers that are being intruded upon, and it's coming from abroad. And it's during some conflict that was occurring at the same time with Iraq, if I recall correctly. And we're seeing the traffic coming in from another Middle Eastern country. On the receiving side, it really very much looks like the dot-mil environment is under attack at this point from this other nation state.[60]

Different law enforcement agencies came together to investigate the breach, in an operation dubbed 'Solar Sunrise'. The name came from the operating system targeted, Sun Solaris. The investigators found that the hackers had used a vulnerability discovered in December of the previous year, which system administrators should have patched but had not. Through this vulnerability, the hackers implemented backdoors in the computers that allowed them to siphon files out. The instigator of the breach rooted the attacks via several gateways, including several servers located in Iraq and its neighbour, the United Arab Emirates. But as Scott C. Charney of the US Department of Justice then rightly stated: 'Where an attack seems to be coming from, and where an attack is actually coming from may be two very different things'.[61] Physical access to the gateways could have allowed law enforcement agencies to further trace the origin of traffic passing through them. But it wasn't possible to access the gateways located outside the United States that the attackers were using, such as the ISP Emirnet in the United Arab Emirates. Fortunately for the investigators, the hackers also routed their traffic via university servers, which usually have less stringent security procedures, and via Sonicnet, a service provider located in the United States. By accessing the log files, the investigators noticed that the hackers had made repeated access to a webpage that offered students the chance to post college services, Maroon.com. The hackers used the website without its owner's knowledge as a platform for the attacks. The investigators asked Maroon.com's owner for authorisation to tap the line, and waited for the hackers to connect again, at which point the investigators were able to trace them. The connection originated from Israel, with the hackers showing a clear determination to access military-related information.

In parallel to tracing the hackers via Maroon.com, the investigators found a second way to identify them. Because of the volume of data, the hackers could not transfer it all out of the computers at the Andrews Air Force Base. Instead, they copied the data onto Sonicnet, a communication service provider based in California. The investigators placed a mechanism on Sonicnet's lines, similar to that placed on Maroon.com, to trace the connections when the hackers came back to consult the files. Sonicnet also received requests from two US universities, MIT and Harvard, about attacks on their websites. Sonicnet easily traced the attacks to two teenagers, Mac and Stimpy. The investigators started reconstructing their sessions, and caught traffic of Mac's conversation with another hacker, The Analyzer, who was teaching him more advanced hacking techniques. The connection with The Analyzer, like the Maroon.com connection, came from Israel. On the same day that the investigators found out about the connection, 13 February 1998, the United States deployed 2,000 more troops to Iraq. But was The Analyzer the same hacker using Maroon.com as a platform to launch the attacks against the Andrews Air Force Base?

On 23 February, the UN secretary-general, Kofi Annan, struck a new deal with Iraq to allow United Nations scrutiny of the allegations that Iraq possessed weapons of mass destruction. As a result, tensions with the United States decreased.[62] Two days later, the investigators still did not have strong evidence about the two teenagers' involvement in the hacking case, and needed a search warrant to gain access to their computers. But the media had heard about the investigation, and were about to make it public. The investigators had very little time left, and the teenagers could simply delete all traces of their involvement in the attacks if they heard that law enforcement agencies were investigating them. The police managed to obtain the warrant before the media released the information. Mac and Stimpy each admitted at their homes to breaking into the Department of Defense's computers. Mac also shared what he knew about The Analyzer: he was 18, and from Israel. A week following the seizure of the teenagers' computers, The Analyzer gave an online chat interview on a website for hackers, AntiOnline. During the interview, he took credit for several hacks within the Department of Defense, but denied having anything in particular against the United States. US law enforcement agencies contacted Israeli authorities, and they found that The Analyzer's true identity was Ehud Tenenbaum.[63] Tenenbaum admitted his crime, as well as hacking into 500 other networks. An Israeli court sentenced him to a year's probation, a two-year suspended prison sentence, and a fine of about $18,000.[64] In 2008, Tenenbaum was involved in a Canadian case of computer fraud estimated at US$1.5 million and a US court sentenced him in July 2012 to repay $500,000 and to serve three years' probation.[65] Meanwhile, Mac and Stimpy received fines, three years' probation, and 100 hours of community service; they also had to forfeit their computers and were barred from using the Internet without adult supervision.

This case is a strong counter-argument to Healey's proposal that the long-term geopolitical context usually permits easy attribution to a sponsoring state; rather, Solar Sunrise illustrates that attacks do not always come from where they seem to. Healey further argued that the geopolitical context might be more informative for attacks aimed at sabotage than for those aimed at espionage, as only state actors reap the benefits from sabotage operations, while non-state actors prefer to steal information. Again, the distinction is not very helpful, and empirical evidence also contradicts Healey's analysis.[66]

The geopolitical context, then, is one of the misleading criteria used by intelligence analysts to evaluate the evidence. The second concerns the political nature of the victim, and is linked directly with the third criterion of *cui bono*—in other words, 'whom the cyber attack benefits'.[67] The argument usually goes as follows: because attacks on governmental and political entities do not bring any direct commercial or financial benefits to attackers, the attackers must be politically motivated: state actors, or at least state-affiliated.[68] But even if economic benefits are not apparent, many other imaginable possibilities remain.[69] The hackers could be professional criminals; that is, non-state actors, reselling their information to whoever is interested. The hacking could also be the recreational work of teenagers, as in the Solar Sunrise case. Even companies could have an interest in finding information kept in governmental networks. Instead of making suppositions about motives based merely on the political character of the target, any entity making claims of attribution should rather aim at gathering and examining evidence to support a claim—given that the victim's political nature only constitutes a circumstantial factor, not evidence.

The fourth criterion commonly used by analysts is the apparent origin of an attacker, which is seemingly independent of the geopolitical context. An official document by the US Department of Defense, albeit from 1999, read that 'state sponsorship might be persuasively established by such factors as signals or human intelligence, *the location of the offending computer within a state-controlled facility*, or public statements by officials' [emphasis added].[70] Yet, once an investigator finds the IP address of an attacker, it can be difficult to know if this is genuinely the final destination of the information, or merely a proxy. That said, in a few cases, the possibility that IP addresses have been faked becomes less likely in the face of other factors. In its famous APT1 report, Mandiant used many IP addresses as evidence to support its stance that China was behind the attack.[71] The report said that the vast majority (83 per cent) of command-and-control servers were in China, that 98 per cent of the IPs used to connect to these servers were in China, and that all the IPs used to route the attacks were Chinese. These were not the only indications. Mandiant was able to monitor one of the hackers registering a new e-mail address, for which he had to provide a phone number to confirm who he was. He gave a Chinese number, received an activation text-message straight away, and immediately input the code. Furthermore, many users logged in into the servers had their keyboard set to 'Chinese simplified'.

An attacker could fake all these indications; he could assume the identity, behaviour and interests of China. That would be a false-flag operation. But to do so repetitively and so consistently over the course of seven years, and without making other mistakes that would give a clue as to their real identity, would be rather exceptional—not to say unprecedented. Another false-flag operation occurred recently, but in comparison, it was outed as such a mere three months after the first attack took place; in the case of APT1, there were no such indications even seven years later. This false-flag operation concerns an attack on the French TV channel TV5 Monde in April 2015, which was able to interrupt broadcasting. An online group claiming to be affiliated with Islamic State first took responsibility for the attack; but it later emerged that the Russian intelligence services seemed to be behind it.[72] Thus, although an IP address is not in itself strong evidence, its value needs to be considered within a set of other indicators and within its context.

Cognisant of the limitations of using IP addresses as indicators for attribution, other cyber security experts have advocated considering lack of cooperation as suggestive of sponsorship. In the case of Mandiant, this implies that unless China can prove the traffic was merely routed via the country, Mandiant's conclusions should stand. Such a policy option is deeply rooted in the post-9/11 security debate. Following the attacks on the Twin Towers, George W. Bush quickly formulated a new doctrine to combat terrorism, part of which was taking into account 'any nation that continues to harbor or support terrorism [to] be regarded by the United States as a hostile regime'.[73] Unsurprisingly, Richard Clarke, former chief counterterrorism adviser under Bush, advocated the application of this doctrine to cyber attacks. He wrote that the United States should 'judge a lack of serious cooperation in investigations of attacks as the equivalent of participation in the attack'.[74] This policy has since then been advocated by many other experts.[75]

However, such a policy for attributing cyber attacks to states that do not engage in information exchange has significant limitations. Firstly, this approach is highly controversial under international law regarding state responsibility because 'lack of cooperation' falls fundamentally short of the standards of 'instruction', 'direction' or 'control' normally used. Secondly, and more importantly, states may not be able to exchange information simply because they do not have this technical information: either there was no trace generated by the malicious activity, or the country does not have robust communication data retention laws to ensure that Internet service providers have the sought-after information. But advocating an increase in data retention also raises privacy concerns, or can be disproportionate to what policy-makers are trying to achieve. For instance, requiring Internet service providers to store not only the minimum data needed for daily business (such as subscriber data) but all communication data is not desirable in countries with a doubtful record on human rights. It follows that the apparent origin of an attack in cases where a state does not cooperate should not be considered a valid criterion for attribution. The making of attribution claims solely on this basis has important consequences; it further normalises the use of this inappropriate criterion, while pushing into the background the issues raised by its use. Only when other indications substantiate the found IP addresses should they become part of an attribution claim.

The fifth criterion often used as proof of state sponsorship is sophistication. The approach of linking an attack's 'sophistication' to a group is a 'capability-centred approach' and relies on the assumption that it is possible to infer an instigator's identity from the fact that capabilities differ between one group and another.[76] The case of Stuxnet (2010) was probably one of the very first in which sophistication started to be linked with state sponsorship. When analysing Stuxnet, Kaspersky Lab declared: 'Stuxnet's sophistication, purpose and the intelligence behind it suggest the involvement of a state'.[77] Many different technical and political experts have since started to use the term, but without a common understanding of its meaning. Asserting that only states can engineer 'sophisticated' attacks is based on the false assumption that attacks need to cross a certain threshold to be 'sophisticated'. In the end, it appears that the label of sophistication is contingent upon a person's own definition of the term.[78] An attack can also be called 'sophisticated' in order to further political objectives, by influencing people's perceptions of the attacker. Moreover, states are not the only actors that create attacks classified as 'sophisticated'. Zeus, for instance, is a piece of malware used by criminals to harvest credit card information, and which fulfills many technical criteria for sophistication. Constantly updated, it incorporates novelties and is modular, and the long period during which it has been in use testifies in favour of its stealth and effectiveness. It would therefore be too restrictive to regard sophistication as an appropriate and decisive criterion for attribution.[79]

Instead of looking only at the sophistication of an attack, one alternative that seems *a priori* less prone to manipulation is to collect information about the capabilities of specific groups and the types of attack they engineer. Accumulating data and cross-correlating them when a new attack happens can serve as a first indication about a group that has been developing and using exactly the same capability deployed in the attack. This type of evidence is also not conclusive; it is, however, less misleading, because it bases the analysis on acquired information, and not merely on the flawed assumption that only states can engineer certain types of attack.

As mentioned in Chapter 1, the US Department of Defense revealed in 2011 that it was already working via 'foreign intelligence collection' 'to understand other nations' cyber capabilities in order to defend against them'.[80] Many organisations cannot acquire this type of intelligence, and non-state actors can certainly not compete with this type of capability. Regrettably, if the United States attributes an attack using this type of data, it is also unlikely to say so, because this would reveal its capabilities. This implies that the public must trust officials' claims of attribution without being able to verify the information behind the claims. Again, this would contribute to the tendency not to focus on the evidence behind attribution claims, and emphasises the shift from a process of information collection and analysis to a process of persuasion based on playing with public trust. Unless the intelligence community is ready to reveal more, the acquisition and cross-correlation of information about countries' capabilities is as prone to manipulation as other criteria.

The sixth commonly used criterion is the scale of an attack.[81] From the outset, it must be noted that the scale of an attack can be far from obvious, especially in cases of espionage or intellectual property theft. It is not easy to ascribe a value to a theft or to the reputational damage that can follow denial-of-service types of attack, because such theft does not have a direct effect on a company's balance sheet. Furthermore, the professionalisation of criminals means that it has become easier to coordinate large-scale attacks; states certainly do not have a monopoly on such attacks.[82]

These six criteria represent the pinnacle of disinterest in evidence and in twisting the chain of evidence behind attribution to make it fit hypotheses of state sponsorship. Analysts use them to formulate assessments, because the criteria are appealing when faced with the difficulty of obtaining evidence for attribution. The dangers are that the criteria can be misleading, and that government officials use their misleading nature to frame an attacker. Lack of scrutiny facilitates this. It transpires, therefore, that more important than the evidence itself is the political will of governmental leadership to attribute an attack, and the readiness of an audience to trust such leadership, and its judgement calls.

International norms regarding cyber attacks are still emerging, and this concerns the applicability of the current standards of evidence for attribution. However, regardless of the direction in which these norms will evolve, they will be set within a particular debate that has a long history and disputes the relevance of international norms. Realists tend to have a rather dismissive view of international law when it conflicts with the interests of states. States launching attacks generally seek to evade their responsibilities under international law and use various tricks to ensure that they can plausibly deny their involvement. On the other hand, victim states seeking to attribute attacks could be frustrated by the difficulty of gathering conclusive evidence to point fingers at instigators. Yet the empirical record shows that this frustration does not have to exist, because victim states can still attribute attacks when they believe this is appropriate.

Claims of attribution are rarely disputed, and the evidence on which they are based is often presented without being thoroughly examined. 'Experts' and unnamed intelligence officials are quoted as a way to give more legitimacy to evidence. Despite the fact that claims are only judgement-based opinions and lack conclusive proof, the readiness of the public to believe them makes the task easier for whoever is trying to convince an audience of attackers' identity. In more practical terms, this implies that political elites can overcome the deniability of cyber attacks and move on with the attribution process, provided that they are willing to do so.

More scrutiny for the evidence may come if the violence behind cyber attacks increases. Cyber attacks that are specifically targeted at industrial control systems could cause significant damage that would also potentially call for a military reaction. In this scenario, it is possible that each step of the attribution process would be more closely examined. At the moment, however, most cyber attacks remain at a sufficiently low threshold in terms of violence for the issue of attribution not to spark the interest of the public, and for administrative officials to stay removed from the public limelight.

Despite a lack of scrutiny of the evidence, there is, however, much discussion on the consequences of attribution. For cyber attacks, these consequences are rarely straightforward. With Mandiant's report, much of the debate was on how to respond to it so that Chinese attacks to steal US intellectual property would be curbed. For two years after the report, diplomatic relations between the US and China were strained by its revelations—until the end of September 2015, when a breakthrough occurred. The heads of the two governments agreed not to conduct espionage via cyber attacks. However, this agreement only concerned attacks aimed at gaining a 'commercial advantage', leaving open many options for further theft of intellectual property, for instance for military purposes or to improve the country's infrastructure.[83] According to US cyber security firm FireEye, by July 2016 the volume of cyber attacks attributable to the Chinese state had substantially decreased, a tentative indication that the agreement was holding.[84] However, a direct causal link is difficult to make: Chinese state-sponsored attacks may simply have become more difficult to detect; centralisation of the chain of command for directing cyber attacks, coupled with a thorough anti-corruption campaign, may also have deterred rogue military officers from launching attacks without hierarchical approval as 'favours' to local 'friends'.

Similarly, following Shamoon (2012), discussions also focused on how to respond to the threat from Iran—allegedly behind the virus—for instance by further tightening sanctions, by using a covert cyber attack or by engaging in diplomacy.[85] The appropriate reaction to cyber attacks is rarely clear because they transcend other political issues: the problem of espionage and of the economic rise of China, the problem of Iran's acquisition of the nuclear bomb, or the ongoing conflict between South and North Korea. The response is therefore complex and necessitates discussion. But this discussion can be dangerously misinformed if one neglects the evidence behind attribution for the sake of simplicity.

Blame games that try to play with the presentation of the evidence to seek, evade or shift accountability are still rather rare. They demonstrate, however, that contrary to a deterministic approach to attribution as technical and perfect, attribution is very much anchored within the sphere of politics. It follows that standards of evidence similarly present political traits, and, most of all, rely on discourse and presentation to shape public opinion. Actors can use this political aspect of attribution to significantly further their own political agendas. Acknowledging this aspect of attribution is essential to questioning any claims presenting the identification of a cyber attacker as certain, and to discerning what political motives may lie behind this particular attribution.

4

PRIVATE COMPANIES

Cyber attacks are unlike many other threats dealt with by intelligence services: private companies occupy a not negligible position as a provider of information to the intelligence community. The less legal clout an intelligence service has to broaden its view (for instance, the ability to force communication providers to provide data, or permission to tap cables), the more the service will rely on private companies to acquire intelligence on cyber attacks. Private companies have insight and expertise on what is occurring in networks around the world like no other entities. They can detect cyber attacks, defend against them, gather information and, of particular interest to this book, try to attribute them by sifting through the volume of collected traffic and malware. They can then market this intelligence, to intelligence services and governments, or even to other companies.

This shift in marketing is recent. Selling threat intelligence, or feeds, especially those detailing how state actors engineer attacks, has been a change in the cyber security model, from simply trying to block malware to considering who is behind the attacks. As a provider of information to governments and an important player in attribution, it is therefore natural that private companies be considered in this study.

The basic questions are therefore: What specific constraints do private companies face? What is the role of private companies in outing state-sponsored attacks? What are the consequences?

Private companies, as much as intelligence services, have to develop their sensors and sources if they want to be competitive in seriously investigating cyber attacks. The process of publishing reports, though, should be much easier than for a state: private companies do not need to discuss publication with half of an administration, and they are not bound by any specific standard for attribution. However, they also face constraints of their own. When a private company publishes a report pointing the finger at a state for sponsoring specific cyber attacks, its first aim is to disrupt and stop the attacks. The company seeks to achieve this with a combination of two methods. Firstly, it assumes that spreading the word on how the attackers behave technically (via the publication of so-called 'indicators of compromise') will enable other organisations to prevent future intrusions. Secondly, it further hopes to convince audiences—the domestic audience where the victims are located and the audience of the attacking state—that it has gathered conclusive evidence identifying the instigator of a state-sponsored attack.

States accused of cyber attacks use three commonly recurring arguments to try to undermine claims by private companies—but as with judgement inherent to attribution, these arguments are based on characteristics inherent to the functioning of cyber security companies. Accused states attempt to bring into question the companies' independence, and so to undermine the validity of their claims. To do so, they point out that many former government officials work for the company in question; that the timing of reports being published can appear to be in support of a government's policies; and that companies are not always keen on attributing any attacks at all, and are focused only on particular, official enemies of the state. This chapter will verify the strength of these arguments. It concludes that such critiques of private companies often lack an evidence base, exaggerate certain points, and can read at times closer to conspiracy theory than to serious counterarguments. Still, these counter-arguments highlight issues of authority for private companies, in comparison with the natural authority that states possess in the international arena, and seek to limit the otherwise influential role that they can play in reshaping the diplomatic agenda.

Despite these constraints that private companies face, there are advantages to their role in attribution. For instance, states can be reluctant to face criticism that their accusations of sponsorship lack conclusive evidence, but also to declassify intercepted intelligence. When companies take the risk of naming actors, states can utilise their findings to confront the seemingly attacking state, while protecting themselves against any critique that they are making baseless accusations. However, this new role of private companies has two major and mostly negative implications for cyber security at large: it implies that companies may not share information with other cyber security firms, because there is competition to reap the marketing benefits of uncovering a state-sponsored campaign; and critiques of companies' allegedly opaque relations with various states can be successful in undermining much-needed public trust in the companies' work to secure computer systems.

This chapter is divided into two parts, both of which rely primarily on empirical evidence drawn from the computer security companies Kaspersky Lab and Mandiant. First, it examines the reasons behind systematic suspicion of state involvement in companies' findings. Second, it presents the far reaching consequences of private companies' reports, analysing how such companies' role has become that of 'attributing authority'.

Three factors used to undermine companies' credibility

Private actors have always played a role in attributing incidents to criminals, but their share of attributing state-sponsored attacks has recently increased significantly. In the Zotob malware case presented in Chapter 1, Microsoft played a crucial role in identifying the connection with previous malware, which led to information enabling arrest of the criminals. Until recently, not many companies were in fact as ready to carry out attribution as Microsoft was in the Zotob case. The rationale was often that demand was quasi-non-existent, and the cost of operations too high to be profitable. In a 2010 US Congress hearing, for example, David Wheeler, author of one of the few articles on techniques for attribution, mentioned that:

> As of 2003, there is little evidence that the commercial sector was willing to shoulder the costs to develop attribution capabilities. Most commercial companies appeared to view identifying attackers as a law enforcement or military task, not a commercial one. If the government wants the ability to attribute attacks, in many cases the government may need to pay for it directly.[1]

Symantec also confirmed that 'attribution is non-important' for its customers, adding that 'generally our commercial customers are less interested in attribution, and more interested in the attack, its *modus operandi* and if it is linked to other attacks'.[2] Because of this low demand, Symantec, like many others, did not see any benefits in investing in human resources to carry out attribution. It kept its business focused on open-source intelligence and the analysis of technical systems. Statements by banks of their unwillingness to report attacks, much less have the attackers' identity investigated, confirmed this trend.[3]

But demand has slowly started to grow, from around the year 2010. Private companies could see the benefits of using technical intelligence describing the modus operandi of specific attacking groups; and other intelligence and law enforcement agencies were also keen on buying such information. This followed its logical course: as state actors increasingly conduct cyber attacks, other state actors are interested in identifying them. The question by Senator Lindsey Graham during a congressional hearing, and the response of Kevin Mandia, the then chief executive officer and founder of Mandiant (and now president at FireEye), are indicative of this interest in discovering the states behind cyber attacks:

> Senator Lindsey Graham: Who are the bad actors here? Would you say China is number one?
>
> Kevin Mandia: China is the number one reason my company grows and doubles in size every year. So yes, they are number one.[4]

Another indication of the demand for attribution, besides the extensive media coverage given to companies like Mandiant and FireEye (now merged under one roof) after making attribution claims, is the large funding received by several companies operating in the attribution business. The group of top contenders is rather small, with Mandiant/FireEye, iSight and CrowdStrike being the most vocal, and their worth on the market is clearly not insignificant.[5] In January 2016, FireEye bought iSight for $200 million. Two years earlier, even more spectacularly, FireEye acquired Mandiant in a deal worth $1 billion.[6] Prior to the acquisition, Mandiant was able to raise $70 million in investment funds from venture capital firms and to achieve a profit of roughly $160 million. CrowdStrike also managed to secure $56 million in investment funds over the course of 2012–13.[7]

Companies that do carry out attribution take the risk that their work will be scrutinised by the accused, and will come under attack when the latter tries to deny involvement.

As already noted, a first important argument that is used against several companies to try to undermine their claims about attribution is to point out the high number of employees who are former state officials. Critics can use this fact to portray the company as a 'puppet' of the government. Former state officials very often retain many contacts within the organisation they used to work for. This possibly allows them, amongst other things, to verify information about cyber attacks, or to obtain new information in an informal way. For cyber security companies, there is also an advantage in trying to replicate state services' well-established processes of intelligence production.

The employment of former state officials in private companies is a common trend in the United States, especially in cyber security, and had already started in the 1990s.[8] In 2013, *The Economist* published a brief table of seven senior directors who went on to work for private cyber security companies.[9] For example, Booz Allen Hamilton, a defence contractor that specialises in technology, hired John Michael McConnell, former director of the NSA and author of 'How to Win the Cyber-War We're Losing', as well as James Clapper, former director of the Defense Intelligence Agency from 1991 to 1995 (and, incidentally, director of National Intelligence since 2010).[10]

Two examples show how critics can use this synergy between companies and their government.[11] The first concerns Mandiant, which has hired several people, such as ex-intelligence officers, with a common background of working for governmental organisations.[12] For instance, in 2006, two years after the launch of the company, founder Kevin Mandia hired Trevis Reese, a former special agent with the Air Force Office of Special Investigations, as a director.[13] The nexus of the company with the US intelligence community notably led *The Global Times* to write that Mandia's background 'raise[s] doubts over the motives of the revelation'.[14] Mandia himself is a former cyber crime investigator for the US military.[15] At the time that Mandiant published its report, Mandia still had top-secret security clearance. According to the Chinese media, this could have helped him to obtain confirmatory information from former colleagues in the military.[16] However, in practice, the line is a lot more blurred. On the one hand, employees within the intelligence community are under obligation to respect the confidentiality of the information with which they deal. They are hence unlikely to be able to provide confirmation as to whether a whole report or just the assessment contained within a report is correct or not. On the other hand, the field of cyber security may be unlike any other intelligence business, with a large exchange of technical data flowing to and from entities external to the intelligence community. Mandiant may be obtaining such technical data from time to time, to better protect its clients, and potentially provide information back to the government, should the company gain some unique insight.

The second case in point concerns the Russian company Kaspersky Lab. Eugene Kaspersky was trained by, and started his career with, the Russian intelligence services, spending ten years within the intelligence community.[17] 'Mysteriously' discharged, as some critics argued, he founded the eponymous cyber security company with his then wife, Natalya Kaspersky, and a friend, Alexey De Mont De Rique.[18] They engineered and sold an antivirus programme, which constituted the core product of the company. The market for tackling malware at the time was very different from the market today. It involved countering the work of teenagers who were trying to disrupt networks, rather than the efforts of states to spy on companies professionally. As the years passed, many considered Kaspersky Lab to have retained its connections with the Russian intelligence services.[19] Eugene Kaspersky has vigorously defended the company against such accusations, pointing out in particular that all cyber security organisations work hand-in-hand with law enforcement agencies and intelligence services.[20] As a matter of fact, Kaspersky Lab also works very openly and intensely with other states' intelligence services. However, appearances do not always play in their favour. For example, President Dmitry Medvedev's choice of venue in 2009 for the launch of a governmental committee shows the significance of the company's influence: Medvedev visited Kaspersky Lab before making a speech about the role of 'strategic information technology' for innovation and development.[21]

The necessary work between companies and intelligence services naturally arouses suspicions, as very few details are known. On top of that, another element can help construct this potentially misleading narrative used to question companies' independent work: timing. Sequences of events do not indicate causality, but naysayers can easily manipulate such sequences as an argument against the companies—and they have done so in the past, in at least two cases.

The first case involves the January 2013 revelation by Kaspersky Lab regarding Red October, aka Rocra. The day after the release of Kaspersky Lab's report on Red October, on 15 January 2013, President Vladimir Putin issued a decree asking the Russian intelligence services, the FSB, 'to create a system to detect and prevent cyber attacks'.[22] Creating a new decree requires time for consultation and preparation. It is unlikely that the whole bureaucratic process could have started and ended within a day of the report's publication. Kaspersky Lab's report possibly helped justify the new legal measure taken by the Kremlin to the public (though the Kremlin did not comment on Red October). Therefore either the Russian president was lucky that Kaspersky Lab published its report at the same time, or the government somehow coordinated with Kaspersky on the publication of the report. Eugene Kaspersky vehemently refuted the latter claim, asking: 'Do you seriously believe that we coordinate our PR activities with the president's administration?'[23] Kaspersky's denial may be true, but the timing was unfortunate, because it could fuel potentially baseless theories.

Jeffrey Carr, an oft-quoted but controversial expert in cyber security, corroborated the hypothesis of a connection between the report and the Kremlin. According to him, the Russian intelligence services may have directly asked Kaspersky Lab to investigate the case, a situation that could have benefited both sides.[24] The interesting aspect is not whether Carr is correct, but rather that he is influential and that his opinion fuels theories undermining Kaspersky Lab's statements. The fact that the operation went on for five years without being detected, according to Carr, also adds to the mystery. Lastly, he also considered that the company gained publicity by releasing its report, and that the report gave more political weight to the decision to increase the capabilities of the Russian intelligence services.

The second case showing how easily a 'conspiracy theory' about private companies' roles in attribution can emerge concerns Mandiant's APT1 report, published in February 2013. The report directly pointed the finger at the Chinese military as instigators of several hundred attacks. Mandiant's report was one of the first to accuse the Chinese military outright of commonly practising espionage. Despite the importance of the claims, the release of Mandiant's report could have gone unnoticed, as so many other reports by private companies often do.[25]

However, Mandiant's report was not only unusual; it also came at a very specific time, and gained momentum probably for this reason. From October 2012, a series of attacks targeted journalists working for *The New York Times*. Investigators believed the attackers had ties to the Chinese government. A few months later, at the beginning of February 2013 and, importantly, two weeks before the publication of Mandiant's report, The Associated Press reported that the US administration was preparing a report 'to better understand and analyze the persistency of cyberattacks against America which come from China'.[26] The report came out a couple of days later but stayed confidential, although a leak indicated that the report mentioned China as the instigator of significant espionage operations via cyber attacks.[27] Then, on 10 February, a report from the different US intelligence agencies was released. Although confidential, its conclusions were leaked to various media outlets. *The Washington Post* wrote: 'The National Intelligence Estimate identifies China as the country most aggressively seeking to penetrate the computer systems of American businesses and institutions to gain access to data that could be used for economic gain.'[28]

Following the intelligence report, on 12 February the White House issued an executive order on cyber security to strengthen the exchange of information between private and public organisations.[29] The executive order came because Congress had repeatedly failed to pass any legislation on cyber security, despite recurring calls from the White House to do so. The same day, in President Barack Obama's annual State of the Union address, he made a veiled reference to Chinese espionage operations. He insisted that 'now, we know hackers steal people's identities and infiltrate private emails. We know foreign countries and companies swipe our corporate secrets'.[30] Two days after the release of the Mandiant report, on 20 February 2012, the White House released a new strategy to combat the theft of intellectual property, identifying China as a 'persistent collector'.[31]

From an analysis of the timing, therefore, it would be tempting but wrong to associate the sequence of events with causality. Mandiant confirmed that it had coordinated with the intelligence community before releasing the report.[32] It wanted above all to ensure that the publication would not hinder any ongoing investigation. This does not mean, however, that either the intelligence community or the White House directed any of its content, or even commented on it.[33]

The connections between Mandiant and the government, however, and the interest in releasing the report, did not go unnoticed. The Chinese news media commented that The Associated Press, a Western press agency, had also noted Mandiant's 'obvious commercial interest in releasing the information'.[34] Nonetheless, this commercial interest does not diminish the contribution the report makes, nor does it point to what the Chinese news agency was trying to imply: that Mandiant would have acted as a proxy for the government.

In fact, the release of the report did serve the interests of Mandiant as well as those of the public and the White House. Mandiant benefited from a large marketing campaign, making its name better-known— although the company did not expect that its report would get such coverage and become the watershed event that it did. Furthermore, Mandiant not only published the report, it also made available to the public a wide range of technical information so that companies could also defend themselves. The White House also benefited from the company's willingness to name China publicly. As the report was not official, it did not force either the government of the United States or that of China to react to it, even diplomatically. Lastly, in view of the difficulty of proving the involvement of the Chinese military, the United States' government insured itself against any criticisms about the report's level of standards, or its conclusion. As noted once more by The Associated Press, Mandiant had another advantage over the White House when it released its report: it did not 'have to consult with American diplomats in Beijing or declassify tactics to safely reveal government secrets'.[35] Although Mandia did not have to, he still ran the report past 'top intel officials, who, tellingly, didn't object to its release'.[36]

In an article published in the magazine *Fortune*, the journalist Nina Easton acknowledged that Mandia was 'meticulous and strategic in timing the publication of the report'.[37] But her portrait of Mandia aims at depicting him as an independent person who dislikes hierarchy. 'I don't deal with instructions well,' Mandia said to Easton.[38] Easton further explained that Mandia had decided to publish the report for two reasons. Firstly, she said that Mandia was 'moralistic' and 'patriotic', desirous to protect the US. Secondly, she said that Mandia was frustrated with Chinese officials' constant denial of China's involvement in hacking campaigns as well as their demand for 'solid proof'.[39] The report was certainly a step towards engaging with the Chinese.

The third and last possible critique that private companies face concerns their hyper-caution in naming state actors. Such caution can be justified, because companies understandably do not want to risk their reputations by blaming the wrong actor. However, caution can also at times be exaggerated, prompting critics to ask the reasons for it—to the point of companies making clear hints as to who they think is behind an attack, but without properly spelling it out. This has happened with many companies in the past.

Kaspersky Lab provides the first example. The company's position with regard to attribution is rather contradictory. On the one hand, it has repeatedly claimed it is not interested in attribution. Its chief executive officer stated in 2012 that: '[O]ur job is not to identify hackers or cyber-terrorists. Our firm is like an X-ray machine, meaning we can scan and identify a problem, but we cannot say who or what is behind it.'[40] A month after this statement, Kaspersky Lab re-emphasised the point by repeating, in front of an audience of students, that the company was not 'concerned about the "who" of attacks, but more about the "what" and "how" when it comes to understanding cyber-threats'.[41] On the other hand, Kaspersky Lab's reports give a great deal of information that helps to construct images of attackers' identities.[42] However, despite providing a wealth of details, the company can be extremely reluctant to name instigators. At times, this borders on the absurd.

On 14 October 2011, a small Hungarian laboratory, CrySys, linked with Budapest University, released a report about new malware it had received a few days earlier. The piece of malware was engineered to collect information, and was found to target very specific industries in Iran, the United States, the United Kingdom, Austria, Hungary and Indonesia.[43] CrySys named the malware 'Duqu' and noted in its report that 'at this point in time, we do not know more about their relationship, but we believe that the creator of Duqu had access to the source code of Stuxnet'.[44] Stuxnet was geared at destruction, but Duqu did not have this aim and was designed solely for espionage purposes—an important difference despite the similarities in the code. CrySys then forwarded the malware to other cyber security vendors. CrySys, Kaspersky Lab and McAfee were overly prudent, and none of them mentioned either the identity of Duqu's creator, or the hypothesis that Israel and the United States could be behind it.[45] Yet McAfee and Kaspersky Lab made strong suggestions as to who they thought was behind the malware, notably linking its sophistication to a state's capabilities.[46] On top of that, Kaspersky Lab noted that the working hours of the people logging onto the command-and-control server to which Duqu sent information corresponded to Jerusalem's working day, and to people respecting the Jewish Sabbath.[47] Putting these two observations together should have been enough to prompt the explicit mention of Israel, but the company refused to do so.

Also illustrative of this reluctance is a key Symantec report from February 2013 putting the creation date of Stuxnet as 2005, much earlier than previously thought.[48] At the time of the report's publication, the account in Sanger's book of US and Israeli involvement in Stuxnet had received plenty of support. However, again, the Symantec report did not make any mention of the United States or Israel. Symantec explained that the reason for this dismissal was mainly that the first goal of its research was to understand how the module functioned.[49] Furthermore, it claimed that it never had any evidence of who did it, despite the publication of the news report and of a book making mention of it. Kevin Hagan, vice president of Symantec Security Response, further explained:

> We could infer from circumstantial evidence in so far as the victim was Iran, and it was focused on their nuclear programme, we could infer a list of potential authors. But even that list, and we did this internally, even that list was somewhere between 6 and 10 different potential nation states and even within nation states when you're looking at various agencies within those governments, the list actually would have ended up being closer to 24–25 potential agencies. So it is hardly attribution, certainly not in my mind, certainly not enough to publish.[50]

Despite the reluctance of cyber security companies, several news organisations were much bolder about naming Duqu's authors.[51] The main issue that this dichotomy highlights is that cyber security companies do not provide a comprehensive analysis of the threat they deal with, while newspapers try to incorporate different elements—although, unfortunately, they can also disregard the evidence, as the previous chapter explored. Ideally, therefore, attribution would combine the sort of comprehensive reporting, including mention of hypotheses, conducted by the media, with the technical details contained in the analyses of private companies.

The mention of these three factors—presence of former intelligence officials, suspiciously beneficial timing and reluctance to name—attempts to push the analysis towards considering private companies as part of a covert state apparatus. It undermines the work of the company by calling its independence into question, and frames the company as having allegiance to a particular state. The following question, therefore, is a legitimate one: would cyber security companies be willing to attribute an attack to a government or law enforcement agency in the country where they have their headquarters, even if conclusive evidence came to light? Critics have sufficient material available to construct a negative answer to this question, even a very biased one.

Kaspersky Lab's official statement is that it has 'a very simple and straightforward policy as it relates to the detection of malware: [to] detect and remediate any malware attack, regardless of its origin or purpose'.[52] F-Secure's CEO, Christian Fredrikson, similarly stated that: 'To us, the source of the malware does not come into play when deciding whether to detect malware'.[53] But not all companies have made such statements. For instance, in 2001, news emerged of a keylogger called 'Magic Lantern', crafted by the FBI. Eric Chien, chief researcher at Symantec's antivirus research laboratory, was quick to react and to mention that 'Symantec would avoid updating its antivirus tools to detect' the malware.[54] McAfee's reaction was very similar. According to The Associated Press, the company quickly asserted that it would 'ensure its software wouldn't inadvertently detect the bureau's snooping software and alert a criminal suspect'.[55]

Since then, the scale of police use of such techniques has grown substantially; a 2009 policy document from the European Union 'encouraged' the police in its member states to use malware to infiltrate the computers of possible criminals.[56] A BBC report on the document even mentioned that the United Kingdom was already carrying out a 'small number' of such cyber attacks.[57] In 2011, confirmation came that the United Kingdom had set up regional units in Derbyshire, Leicestershire, Lincolnshire, Northamptonshire and Nottinghamshire, where police surveillance techniques included hacking techniques.[58] Germany also followed the European Union's brief.[59] Another case in point is the operation led by the FBI against the hosting company Freedom Hosting in 2013, which operated on Tor hidden services—a network of theoretically untraceable web pages where child pornography and drug sales have proliferated.[60] The attack by the FBI consisted of injecting codes on hidden services hosted by Freedom Hosting that contained child pornography. The malicious code could then identify the real location of the server. In the end, it led the FBI to arrest an individual who was behind several harmful websites.[61]

Hence, as many companies face fierce competition for lucrative contracts with the police, intelligence services and the military, it could be argued that these state organisations could pressure the companies into conceding to their requests and dismissing their own findings.[62] The veracity of this argument does not matter as much as its consequences, namely its potential to undermine trust in the work of the companies. As there is already much mistrust between governments and private security companies when these are foreign, this could be an unwelcome development.[63]

Nothing conclusively proves the extent of the relationship between state intelligence services and companies. The three criticisms outlined above can, however, explain a feeling of unease towards companies' publications, and the questions that follow. These questions weaken the companies' work because they offer opportunities for accused offenders to challenge their findings. The criticisms also highlight why private companies working on attribution are not without constraints. But even when working within these constraints, there is another political element that requires our attention. Although the companies examined above did not act in any official capacity, each publication of a report prompted the accused country to respond. In the case of Mandiant, it was also clear that there existed a political will to keep the focus of attention on its findings, rather than its sources of evidence. The power that Mandiant and other companies have acquired to reshape the diplomatic agenda is a political factor warranting careful consideration.

A significant role on the international scene

The Mandiant report was quite unusual in the way it bluntly pointed the finger at the Chinese military. For the previous ten years, state officials and cyber security companies had repeatedly exposed cyber attacks that they had traced to China. However, most official representatives were usually careful not to name the Chinese state directly. For example, in 2007 Germany, France and the United Kingdom all found traces of malware that had infected their ministries and whose connections they traced to China, but none said publicly that the Chinese state was responsible.[64] Likewise, in 2011 Canada's Department of National Defence, as well as its Finance Department and Treasury Board, were hacked, again with IP addresses originating from China.[65] However, no official agencies and no private companies formally attributed the attacks to the Chinese state.[66] In 2011, McAfee found a widespread espionage operation that it dubbed 'Operation ShadyRAT', which affected seventy-one organisations, including the International Olympic Committee, the World Anti-Doping Agency and the United Nations.[67] Once again, McAfee's official report was reserved, simply mentioning that there was 'potentially a state actor behind the intrusions'.[68] Unofficially, many commentators pointed at the Chinese state.[69] Even Mandiant, in a 2010 report about what it classified as an 'advanced persistent threat', wrote that 'the Chinese government may authorize this activity, but there's no way to determine the extent of its involvement'.[70] Three years later, when it published its report pointing to Chinese government involvement in cyber attacks, the company ironically reminded its readership of this 2010 conclusion.[71]

One of the direct consequences of the Mandiant report was to make companies and officials more comfortable with naming China as a sponsor of cyber attacks.[72] The Mandiant report aligned with the naming-and-shaming strategy started a few days earlier by the US government to incentivise China to curb its espionage activities. This change in approach was exemplified by the publication, a month after Mandiant's report, of a report by the communication service provider Verizon. In it, Verizon noted that 'state-affiliated actors tied to China are the biggest mover in 2012'.[73] The company then added that 'their efforts to steal IP comprise about one-fifth of all breaches in this dataset'.[74] President Obama was among officials who then pointed the finger at China, commenting in March 2013 that some, but not necessarily all, cyber attacks on US firms and infrastructure originating in China were 'state-sponsored'.[75] Following this approach, on 6 May 2013 the US Department of Defense published a report, in coordination with the White House, directly referring to the Chinese government and military being behind the attacks, and seemingly embracing the conclusions drawn by Mandiant.[76] Newspapers such as *The New York Times* and *The Guardian* said that this was the first time an official report had been so blunt in its accusations.[77] The report had been carefully vetted, and the naming of China was not accidental.[78] The report noted: 'In 2012, numerous computer systems around the world, including those owned by the U.S. government, continued to be targeted for intrusions, some of which appear to be attributable directly to the Chinese government and military.'[79]

US Senator Lindsey Graham also commented in a public hearing two days later that he would deliver the Chinese ambassador in the United States comments from experts showing that 'China, as a nation-state is actively involved in hacking into US databases, banks, stealing intellectual property', and that he would demand a response.[80] A Chinese Foreign Ministry spokeswoman responded to the Pentagon's report, as usual, by dismissing the claims, stating that the United States had repeatedly 'made irresponsible comments about China's normal and justified defence build-up and hyped up the so-called China military threat'.[81]

Hence, Mandiant's report eased the way for the US government to make public what intelligence services must have been expressing in confidence for a while: that the Chinese military was involved in cyber attacks for espionage purposes on a significant scale. Officials' repeated use of the Mandiant report can be seen as confirmation that they supported its conclusions. A further confirmation that their findings were spot-on came a year later: in May 2014, the Department of Justice indicted five Chinese hackers on counts of economic espionage, and the FBI released their pictures.[82] Amongst the five was notably Wang Dong, also known online as 'UglyGorilla', one of three individuals Mandiant had named in its report. In the indictment, some of the evidence used was different from that presented in Mandiant's reports, making the case against the hackers even stronger. For the FBI and the Department of Justice to take such a public step could also imply that they had even more evidence linking the individuals to these specific attacks, which they did not publish.

Proving sponsorship is difficult. Although the report by Mandiant did not provide conclusive evidence of Chinese sponsorship, it drew a strikingly convincing picture of it. The lack of definitive evidence did not escape the attention of Chinese officials. As we saw in Chapter 2, a Chinese Foreign Ministry spokesman responded to the report's accusations by claiming that 'making baseless accusations based on premature analysis is irresponsible and unprofessional'.[83] He added that 'the report, in only relying on linking IP address[es] to reach a conclusion [that] the hacking attacks originated from China, lacks technical proof'.[84] Although the report did not in fact use only IP addresses to attribute the attacks, the proof was indeed mostly technical, albeit comprehensive: proof was collected over the course of seven years and in relation to 141 cases.

Mandiant based its conclusions mainly on four elements: the attack methods were similar for 141 companies whose industries matched 'the seven strategic emerging industries that China identified in its 12th Five-Year Plan'; many IP addresses were traced back to China; the attackers used a Chinese simplified keyboard; and the exposed pseudonyms, and some personal information, suggested that three of the hackers worked for the military.[85]

These pieces of evidence are disputable when taken individually. The industries identified by China's 12th Five-Year Plan, such as health care, energy and technology, are broad. Almost any company could fit into one of these categories. Furthermore, there is no conclusive evidence that the people Mandiant seemingly identified were genuinely working for the military. In one case, for example, Mandiant noted that the individual 'publicly expressed his interest in China's "cyber troops" in January 2004'.[86] However, taken together over the course of seven years, the different pieces of evidence make it very unlikely that any other actor was behind this series of attacks. Otherwise, another actor masquerading as Chinese would have left a clue to his true identity at least once. There is little room for doubt, therefore, that the perpetrator is not criminal but a state: the large resources, the persistence, and the targets all indicate this.

The reliance on judgement for attribution means that such claims will never be incontestable, especially in the eyes of the accused party. However, improvements are foreseeable, and already in motion. To bring an even stronger case of Chinese military involvement would have required non-technical proof—as David Sanger provided for the Stuxnet case. Mandiant's resources at the time, however, were much more modest than they are now. Following the merger with FireEye, and FireEye's subsequent acquisition of iSight, a higher level of evidence can be expected, and notably more elements coming from human sources. This should allow Mandiant/FireEye's cases to stand up to criticism, whether from China or from another accused country.

A further important question to consider is whether Mandiant's report was effective in curbing the attacks, or even stopping them. Following its publication, the United States and China did not simply make accusatory statements, they also engaged in a constructive discussion. Thomas Donilon, national security advisor to the White House, made three demands of China on 'the issue of cyber-enabled theft' on 11 March 2013:

> First, we need a recognition of the urgency and scope of this problem and the risk it poses—to international trade, to the reputation of Chinese industry and to our overall relations. Second, Beijing should take serious steps to investigate and put a stop to these activities. Finally, we need China to engage with us in a constructive direct dialogue to establish acceptable norms of behavior in cyberspace.[87]

The next day, a spokesman for the Chinese Foreign Ministry, Hua Chunying, answered positively to Donilon's call for diplomatic discussions.[88] In June 2013, further news came out that the United States and China had agreed to hold regular high-level meetings on this subject, with the first in July 2013.[89] However, such diplomatic discussions did not aim to put China in an embarrassing situation: the United States still wanted to be able to discuss other important issues where it needed China's cooperation, such as the pressing threat of North Korea.[90] In fact, after trying to press his Chinese counterpart in an informal meeting about this issue, President Obama even backed down in his accusations and stated: 'Those are not issues that are unique to the US-China relationship. Those are issues that are of international concern. Oftentimes it's non-state actors who are engaging in these issues as well.'[91]

Obama's statement came as a surprise, especially after he had personally accused China. But understandably, it must have been difficult for the United States to try to reprimand China for launching cyber attacks when the United States had been doing the same with Stuxnet, Duqu and several others, although arguably not targeting companies for their intellectual property.[92]

Other revelations will have added to the feeling of unease when the United States wanted to reprimand China. Embarrassingly, *Foreign Policy* revealed in June 2013, just days after the meeting between the US and Chinese presidents, that the NSA 'has successfully penetrated Chinese computer and telecommunications systems for almost 15 years'.[93] This came as confirmation of a claim often repeated by Chinese officials, that they possessed 'mountains of data about U.S. cyber attacks', showing that the Chinese were not the only actors involved in cyber attacks for espionage purposes.[94] Just a few days later, Edward Snowden also revealed that the United States was specifically targeting China. Snowden alleged that the 'US had targeted Chinese phone companies as part of a widespread attempt to get its hands on a mass of data'.[95] He added that the NSA had attacked 'China's prestigious Tsinghua University, the hub of a major digital network from which data on millions of Chinese citizens could be harvested'.[96] In an ironic twist, revelations also emerged that the NSA had spied on the Chinese company Huawei, mainly to discover the nature of its relationship with the Chinese authorities. Thus, the tables were turned, and the Chinese called on the United States to rein in its espionage practices.[97]

For the United States to ask China not to commit the very act that it had also carried out—albeit for a different purpose—was therefore bold. The *Global Times*, a Chinese newspaper published in English and with strong ties to the Chinese government, ironically commented: 'Being the first known country to launch a cyber attack in peacetime and in the absence of any international treaty and protocol, the US has lost the moral high ground to define appropriate conduct in cyber space.'[98]

The revelations by Edward Snowden prompted China to speak publicly against the hypocrisy of the United States—it would have risked appearing 'weak' otherwise.[99] But the revelations also forced the United States to adapt its strategy slightly. Instead of 'naming and shaming' China for espionage in general, it tried to insist on the difference between economic espionage, as carried out by China, and espionage related to national security, as the United States was carrying out. But making this distinction was not nearly as strong a position for the United States, and on top of that, the argument was confusing to the Chinese, who consider that gaining economic advantage is part of their national security strategy.[100] Despite this, discussions went on—as did the attacks, at least at first.

Two months after Mandiant's revelations, in April, news re-emerged that the attacks on the same companies had resumed, using the same malware with only a few modifications.[101] According to Cyber Squared, a cyber security company, the hackers did not change their modus operandi in the slightest: they used the same tools and the same control-and-command servers, and targeted the same industries.[102] In September, FireEye also revealed that the same Chinese group identified in Mandiant's report had launched an important campaign targeting US defence contractors, to obtain drone technologies.[103]

However, the resumption of attacks did not discourage the United States from attributing them to the Chinese. In May 2014, the Department of Justice announced that it had filed charges of espionage using cyber attacks against individuals within the People's Liberation Army—a statement that highlighted once more the political nature of attribution, even when conducted via the judiciary, and even if it is still uncertain that the indictment will lead to prosecution.[104] The focus on the exact individuals behind the attacks is somewhat surprising, but circumvents the lack of international mechanism to indict and try states practising economic espionage. The indictment gave meticulous details of the operations that should help reach levels of standards sufficient for a US court, and help protect the accusations against the kind of argument Peter Sommer exposed in defence of Richard Pryce.[105] However, hardly any proof was made public showing that the individuals were officers within the People's Liberation Army; the public is therefore left to trust that the Department of Justice can indeed defend this fact.[106] The lack of evidence showing a connection with the Chinese state may also partially explain why the US government chose the rather bottom-up approach of targeting individuals rather than state institutions.[107]

The indictment turned out to be a key strategic move. It indicated strongly the US's readiness to escalate the issue even further. The next possible escalation could have included economic sanctions against China—something that could have been potentially very harmful to China. The fear of economic sanctions partially explains why China signed an agreement with the US in September 2015 not to conduct further economic espionage. It would seem that Chinese economic espionage perpetrated via cyber attacks towards US-based companies has decreased following the agreement. However, at the time of writing (February 2016), it is still too early to be able to draw comprehensive and conclusive lessons from it. If this really is the case, Mandiant could make the bold claim that its APT1 report has largely contributed to successful deterrence of Chinese cyber attacks against US companies.

While the outing of APT1 eventually had repercussions, this is not always so. The case of Duqu provides a contrast: revelations about it did not stop its authors, allegedly the United States and Israel, from continuing its development. In March 2012, six months after the exposure of the attacks, security researchers at Symantec discovered new variants of Duqu, engineered to evade the detecting mechanisms already in place.[108] Cyber security companies were quicker this time to respond to the incident (it had taken them four years to detect the previous version), because the new variant had only been compiled a month before its discovery, in February. It can only be assumed that the relation between US government organisations and Symantec, a global corporation headquartered in the United States, is complex. On the one hand, Symantec helps US law enforcement agencies to track criminals; on the other, the company's revelation of new Duqu variants must have thwarted US intelligence services' plans to keep Duqu alive.

Although cyber security companies do not have any official mandate to investigate and denunciate states that instigate attacks, the cases of APT1, Duqu and Red October demonstrate that such companies' work is not without political repercussions. In particular, APT1 has shown that if a state has the leverage to escalate attribution claims and threaten other measures, that state can be effective in deterring further attacks. Attribution alone is not enough, but it is a first step.

However, the value of attribution brought by cyber security companies could be further increased if the companies were willing to adapt their methods to the problem at hand—namely, in order to attribute attacks to corporate and state sponsors, companies need to look outside the realm of technical proof. For example, Information Warfare Monitor regularly carries out investigations of attacks, blending a mix of technical and carefully weighed political considerations, while also collecting further evidence 'in the field'.[109] This blend of analysis is exceptional in the circle of cyber security companies, but also very promising for attribution. To replicate such a model, other companies would probably have to hire, for example, investigative journalists and analysts that specialise in international relations and politics. Companies would have to start developing their expertise in human intelligence, recruiting human sources that they would have to protect at all costs, but who could yield them valuable input. A widely circulated article by Juan Andrés Guerrero-Saade of Kaspersky Lab has already gone in that direction in calling companies working on attributing cyber attacks to acknowledge that their role has evolved to be very close to that of an intelligence service in this field.[110] Recognising this change of role would mean developing the processes and expertise required to fit with it. As shown in Chapter 2, companies will never be able to make 'perfect' attribution claims, but minimising biases can be a step forward. Companies can change their methods, and they usually do so to adapt to the market.

For example, Mandiant did not always focus on attribution. It used to do a very different kind of work, focused on traditional blocking of attacks. In 2006 at Black Hat, the annual cyber security conference, CEO Kevin Mandia described the work his company was involved in, namely incident responses, by saying that it focused on answering the following questions: 'How do hackers hide backdoors? How can security researchers find the backdoors, and remove them? What other tools do the hackers use? What does the malware do? What does Mandiant do to know if a file is bad?'[111]

None of these questions pertain to attribution or to finding the instigator of attacks. The change in forensic analysis to find the instigator follows a change in the market: there was a need, especially from government, to know who the attackers were. For companies, which used to represent the bulk of Mandiant's clients, the answer to the question of 'who did it' was never prominent. It was more important to be able to secure the open breach, and assess the harm caused by the attack. As Mandiant had already changed its focus in the past, it could also change its method, especially if there was a demand for it. This seems now to be the case. Clients, be they companies seeking to protect their network or small intelligence services, now have higher expectations. The market appears to have responded to these expectations; FireEye's flamboyant acquisition of Mandiant and iSight has put many of the top candidates under one roof.

Despite the potential ineffectiveness in the short term of attributing attacks to state actors, attribution by private companies, and their ties with state agencies that grant them an almost authoritative status by pushing their conclusions forward, are unlikely to falter. The cyber security companies' interests converge with the states' interests in this situation in three ways.

First, cyber security companies offer states a means of sidestepping the frustration that comes from only attributing acts once high standards of proof have been achieved. Because attribution is mostly imperfect, high standards of proof are hardly ever met. Technical forensic elements are the easiest elements to obtain in an investigation. Unfortunately, these do not conclusively confirm a state's involvement in a string of cyber attacks. Instead, access to officials, to official documents or to whistle-blowers can be elements that support attribution. These resources are difficult to access. States must therefore form a hypothesis about the identity of the attackers on the basis of inconclusive information. A hypothesis is not, however, sound enough proof in most cases to enable attribution to be made public via state institutions, because the risks following misattribution are too high. These risks are much lower for companies, which do not have to adhere to high standards of proof. A private company naming a state actor is solely responsible for such attribution. When a state makes such an attribution, the implications can be far-reaching, leading to an escalation of tensions.

This brings us to the second, related convergence of interests: the opportunity to have a corporation attribute attacks to other state actors offers states a risk-shifting alternative to attribution, be it correct or incorrect. For the accusing state, such a model reduces the possibility of the accused state retaliating economically, or stifling diplomatic talks on other issues. The victim state can keep the upper hand if it wants to bring up a privately published report to pressurise the attacking state.

The company takes the risk of jeopardising its business opportunities in the denounced state, but the widespread publicity an attribution claim creates can balance this drawback by attracting many new domes tic clients. In the case of Mandiant, entering the 'business for attribution' was clearly an entrepreneurial opportunity, the risks of which must have been weighed carefully. If the company misattributed the attacks to China, it would not have to put up with the diplomatic inci dent that China could have created with an accusing state. On the other hand, misattribution could damage the company's reputation. At the moment, though, attribution has proved rather lucrative for Mandiant, attracting much attention from the press.

Third, companies' and states' interests are mutually served by the publication of new information without necessarily divulging confidential information. In many public-private partnerships where the state officially recognises and works with private companies, there is a two-way exchange between the state and the company. Exchanging information requires trust to be built between entities, which can be time-consuming. With the particular nature of cyber attacks still predominantly addressed by intelligence services, most incidents have been surrounded by secrecy and a lack of public details. Intelligence services traditionally do not share information with non-state actors, and they strive to keep this secret culture for cyber attacks too. But cyber security companies can seek acknowledgement of their suspicions by intelligence services, even though such contact may be informal. This acknowledgement does not mean that intelligence services have changed their secretive culture and are revealing information to non-state actors. In addition, this approach benefits the general public because more information finds its way into the public domain. Mandiant's manager expressed this idea very lucidly on the company's blog: 'Mandiant's report on APT1, which included actionable indicators, is a good example of how commercial (and unclassified) threat intelligence has been shared widely within the government space without the need to take classification and dissemination issues into account.'[112]

Attribution by cyber security companies, besides the problem of attributing state-sponsored attacks from specific states, does, however, have a few risks. First, a report gaining much momentum could come at a very unfortunate time. If two states were in the middle of productive exchanges, it could tip the balance and redefine the discussed agenda, but not always in the interest of the accusing state. As the government cannot control what the private sector publishes, at least in neo-liberal democracies, this is a risk, which can only be managed by maintaining good working relationships with private cyber security companies. Such a relationship should ensure that the company would, at the very least, have the politeness to warn the state of what was coming.

A second risk is for the cyber security companies themselves. After Mandiant published its report, it increasingly became a target for what the company believed were Chinese state-sponsored retaliatory cyber attacks. These involved 'very aggressive reconnaissance' of Mandiant's systems, and denial-of-service attacks to make the systems unresponsive.[113] Going forward, some companies may become concerned for the physical safety of their employees if they were to disclose the cyber operations of more aggressive intelligence services better versed in blackmailing, coercion methods, or even assassination.

The third risk of private companies playing this attribution role is probably more important when looking at improving cyber security as a whole: because companies seek to reap the benefits from publicity, they may fail to share threat information with other cyber security companies.

Normally, cyber security companies exchange information and pieces of malware in order to offer the public the best possible solutions for thwarting cyber attacks. They may even do so anonymously. For instance, when CrySys discovered Duqu, the company offered information and passed the malware to larger cyber security companies McAfee, Symantec and Kaspersky Lab, so that they could also analyse it and design appropriate responses against it; in return, CrySys specifically asked the other companies not to mention its name.[114] Subsequently, McAfee, Symantec and Kaspersky Lab all issued reports within six days.

However, the problem with information exchange may reside in larger campaigns. In the Mandiant case, and in the Red October campaign, collaboration between companies was in fact non-existent. This raises the issue of whether the cyber security companies' new role in the attribution of cyber attacks conflicts to a small degree with their goal of creating a more secure environment against cyber attacks. These campaigns are not the bulk of the companies' work, and in most cases, the latter take seriously their responsibility to defend computers on behalf of their customers. Although the reason for Mandiant and Kaspersky Lab not sharing information was probably to maximise the marketing benefits of the reports, delaying the announcement of the threat within the cyber security community may have exposed more victims to the risk of being infected by the malware. Furthermore, if a company suspects that another company has links with a government that it thinks engineered an attack, whether or not this is the case it is unlikely that the two companies will exchange information. Therefore, instead of helping to increase cyber security, companies working on attribution could actually damage traditionally functioning mechanisms.

In conclusion, the bulk of the cyber security companies' work with law enforcement agencies still does not concern cases of national security, and most of their cases are much less 'spectacular' than those looked into in this chapter. Disruptions by botnets, or forensic analysis of cyber criminals making money from fraud, are the main focus of their resources. Such attacks are also those that affect the greatest number of users. However, over the past few years, one particular dimension of cyber security companies' work has received increasing media attention: the detection of large state-sponsored operations and, at times, the naming of these attacking states in reports. Naming states is still the exception rather than the norm with cyber security companies. Moreover, media attention is not the only reaction that this work has provoked. Rather unusually, companies' reports, which politically attribute attacks, have also, in many instances, prompted officials of the accused country to respond. Cyber security companies have therefore entered a new business, where they play an important role in attributing attacks, and where governments accept their voices as authoritative. Consequently, this has attracted criticism, and critics have used three arguments, not always genuine, to undermine companies' work: their extreme caution, the high number of former officials they hire, and the timing of their reports.

The model of companies attributing attacks has advantages for state actors. For example, it can limit the escalation of conflict between states, because they do not accuse each other directly. A state accused of misbehaviour by a company can choose simply not to respond—a dismissal that would be much harder if the accusation came directly from a state actor. In addition, attribution by companies allows this to take place despite the limited evidence that may exist against a party. The formulation of a judgement, which is openly published, allows for a public debate to occur. The public can question the evidence and the conclusion of reports. This contributes to making the attribution process less secret than if it were only dealt with by intelligence services, and must also contribute to reaching sounder conclusions. With this new role, therefore, private companies have brought a fresh nuance to the meaning of attribution. Attribution used to be a political act solely conducted by actors with a political capacity. In carrying out attribution, cyber security companies have now embraced a political capacity as well, which they are yet to acknowledge.

As a political act, attribution cannot avoid being set within a particular time frame. Incidents and their attribution can only be used to leverage political actions within a specific period. The timing in which the incident takes place, and in which attribution also occurs, is decisive. This constraint is analysed in further depth in the next chapter.

5

TIME

The high speed at which cyber attacks are conducted has led many analysts to think that such attacks warrant a similarly rapid reaction. Richard Clarke, the former White House official and author of the seminal book *Cyber War*, wrote: 'As [the Pentagon's Defense Science Board] noted, cyberattacks can occur very quickly and without warning, requiring rapid decision-making by those responsible for protecting our country'.[1] Similarly, Jody Prescott, a senior fellow at the prestigious US military academy West Point noted that '[w]ith cyber operations conceivably moving at near light speed, commanders in cyber warfare will likely need to rely extensively upon autonomous decision-making processes (ADPs) to be effective'.[2] Prescott went on to suggest several methods that would ultimately short-circuit the political decision-making process and enable autonomous retaliatory action. Admittedly, a decision about the response, and hence about attributing the cyber attacks, needs to be taken rapidly by the government. But how rapidly? This question is not new, and surfaced during the 1960s in the context of the chain of command required to react to a nuclear attack.[3] The debate about cyber attacks, however, has recently moved to consider 'real-time' attribution, as if the sponsorship of an attack could systematically be openly exposed. Yet, following bomb attacks occurring at almost the same speed as cyber attacks, attribution rarely takes place quickly. The time constraint is tightly intertwined with two other components of attribution: the level of standards and the geopolitical context.

How important is the time constraint for attribution? How has the time constraint evolved? And what constitutes an appropriate time for attributing cyber attacks?

Whereas the standards of evidence were dismissed in Chapter 3 as being malleable and therefore of limited importance, timing, on the other hand, plays a significant role in attribution. The common assumption is that attribution is time-consuming, and warrants efforts to try to reduce the time it takes to identify instigators of cyber attacks. In the context of a national security incident, the rationale continues, this is problematic because fast reaction times are needed to ensure that any response will still be consistent with the fast-changing geopolitical context. Yet, counter-intuitively, focusing on time reduction can be misleading. In the national security context, timing matters, but not in terms of the measurable passage of time as much as in terms of external conjectures that influence the decision to attribute an act. Whether for a violent act of sabotage where the public expects a government reaction or for a less visible act of espionage, the time may not always be such that it is politically appropriate to attribute an attack. In this context, talking about reducing the time for attribution does not make much sense: such a proposal foregoes all the political elements that inform attribution, and over-emphasises the technical aspect of attribution over the context in which an attack takes place.

This chapter will introduce its argument in two parts. Firstly, it will show how time is approached in terms of measurability with the aim of reducing it. Secondly, it will show how this emphasis does not make sense, especially in national security cases, in which it is much more relevant to understand time in terms of context.

Measurable time: efforts to reduce it

As mentioned, time can have mainly two meanings. It can be understood in terms of the measurable unit that elapses between two moments, such as an attack and its attribution by an official authority. Time can also have a more general meaning: it relates to a succession of events, past, present and future, which are set into a specific space.

Taken as a whole, time is the context in which an event occurs, in relation to other events.[4] Temporality can be meaningful for the attribution of attacks under both definitions: either with regard to reducing time for attribution, or heeding the context when carrying out attribution. The current debate around attribution, however, has mainly revolved around shortening the attribution time. But the context for attribution may be more important than the repeated focus on time reduction, especially for attacks at the level of national security threats.

'Time and space are different in cyberspace. There is no "there" there, and humans are intolerably slow,' said Gary McGraw, the founder of a cyber security firm focusing on software flaws.[5] Such a stance, which states that the concept of time is different within cyberspace, is very common. It reflects a certain utopian ideal of cyberspace, which has imbued the concept from its very early usage in the 1990s, on the grounds that human beings live in another reality when they are 'in' cyberspace.[6] McGraw's comparison with the speed at which human beings interact is interesting. Communication happens much faster in 'cyberspace'. Nothing captures the vividness of this image of speed like the term 'information superhighway', attributed to the former US vice president Al Gore.[7] Because everything is accelerated, cyberspace 'contracts' time.[8] This speed of interaction also means that attacks are swift. As *The Huffington Post* wrote in 2013: 'Our foes now have the ability to deliver a disruptive or potentially destructive attack on American soil with previously unheard of speed'.[9] Likewise, according to Peter Feaver, professor of political science, and Kenneth Geers, a researcher at the Atlantic Council (and formerly at FireEye), 'malicious code travels across computer networks at lightning speed'.[10] A number of current and past officials have also repeated the analogy of cyber attacks going at the 'speed of light', including several working at the Pentagon such as Stewart Baker, former assistant secretary at the Department of Homeland Security, and former senator Mike J. Rogers.[11]

The comparison seems to be between cyber attacks travelling at the speed of light and the speed of a missile, a difference with an order of magnitude of 100,000. *A priori*, the difference is significant, but the comparison is disingenuous. Destructive attacks can take a long time to be effectively destructive.[12] Stuxnet did not instantly damage the centrifuges, but did so over the course of several months. Espionage attacks do not happen at the speed of light either, but, to quote McGraw, at a much slower human pace. Espionage campaigns can last months because the careful siphoning of information is nothing close to being instantaneous—an idea echoed by former NSA and CIA director Michael Hayden at the 2010 Black Hat conference.[13] Yet this powerful image of cyberspace activity as very quick is omnipresent, and has wider implications.

In comparison with the seemingly high speed at which attacks occur, the tracing of their instigators seems consequently to take a significant amount of time: attribution, in other words, is time-consuming. Shawn Henry, former executive assistant director at the FBI, bluntly stated that: 'It takes time. There is no simple fix'.[14] *The Business Insider* likewise noted that 'the high degree of anonymity of digital interactions makes identifying an attacker a time-consuming, if not impossible, task'.[15] Phil Meek, associate general counsel of the US Air Force, remarked that many factors make attribution 'much more time-consuming than you may normally have in an armed conflict scenario'.[16] Susan Brenner, an expert lawyer in questions of cyber security, not only stated that attribution 'can be difficult and time-consuming', but also explained that 'to gain access to the necessary information to trace an attack back through those computers, law enforcement will have to obtain assistance from government and civilian entities in the countries in which the computers were used'.[17] She then continued, 'the formal methods used to obtain assistance can take months or even years when digital evidence is fragile and can disappear by the time the investigators obtain the assistance they need'.[18] The issue of having to deal with foreign bureaucracies in order to produce a chain of evidence is especially relevant for the indictment of criminals, and when law enforcement agencies use 'formal' channels, as with the denial-of-service attacks on Estonia in 2007. On 10 May 2007, Estonia issued a formal request to Russia for information exchange, under the two countries' 'mutual legal assistance treaty'. Russia's negative response came a year later.[19] The process took an undeniably long time, even for a refusal.

When talking about the shutting down of a botnet's command-and-control server, Symantec's vice president of security response, Kevin Hogan, explained that the biggest challenge in the operation was the fact that the botnet's infrastructure was scattered over three different jurisdictions with victims all over the world.[20] After three years of active research, Symantec could not afford to spend more time trying to find the instigators: instead it chose to battle to shut down the infrastructure.

The time required by investigations is long, and not only in comparison with the high speed of cyber attacks. This represents a significant investment for companies that investigate cases, sometimes on a pro bono basis, but otherwise, especially for law enforcement agencies, the fact that attribution is time-consuming is nothing unusual: it is easily comparable with the investigations of other types of crime or attack. Murderers are never identified instantly, although their crimes can take place over a short period of time. It can take less than a second for a bullet to reach another human being, and months to discover who fired the weapon. Similarly, with a national security incident, the length of time for an investigation to identify a sponsor could certainly be described as 'time-consuming'. Hence, the problem of time is not unique to cyber attacks. But many overly technical solutions to improve attribution times have been proposed on that basis, even US officials exhorting companies to contribute toward this goal.[21] Steve Chabinsky, deputy assistant director of the cyber division at the FBI until 2012, told an audience at a cyber conflict conference that year that 'the owners and operators of an electric power grid in which all of the workers are cleared want to have perfect attribution of who's on the system at any given time'.[22] He then continued his presentation, saying:

> Right now, no systems, or very few systems, are designed to provide assurance and attribution. There are markets that are begging to be filled right now for these types of capabilities—that we really could sell globally if we're the ones here in this country that produce that—that are not being fulfilled.[23]

On the same panel as Chabinsky was CrowdStrike's president, Shawn Henry, also a former FBI director. As the president of CrowdStrike, one of the few companies marketing itself as a pioneer and leader in the field of attribution, Henry immediately recognised the market opportunity this represented. Just a year after Chabinsky's remark, CrowdStrike released a new product directly aimed at filling that gap: the CrowdStrike Falcon Platform. When presenting it, CrowdStrike's CEO, George Kurtz, reiterated that the company is 'shifting the discussion from defending against malware to defending against the adversary'.[24] According to the company's presentation of the product, the CrowdStrike Falcon Platform 'provides damage assessment and attacker attribution', while 'detect[ing] zero-day threats and prevent[ing] damage from targeted attacks in real time'.[25]

Beyond products released by a company such as CrowdStrike, many of the discussions on reducing attribution time have been heavily technology-focused. Before examining them, it would be informative to look briefly at how, over the past twenty years, attribution time actually has been reduced.

In 1986, in an incident dubbed the Cuckoo's Egg, a researcher named Clifford Stoll discovered that hackers had breached the network of Lawrence Berkeley Laboratory, which did work for the military. Stoll tried to alert the FBI and the NSA, but they did not really understand the extent of the breach; they only understood that the direct cost of the breach was less than a dollar, stemming from an accounting difference created by the attack. Stoll succeeded in convincing the police to obtain a warrant to follow up the origin of the attack, but it was valid in only one US state.[26] Because no traffic data were recorded, the attackers could only be pursued while they were online. But they were clever, and routed their traffic not only via different states within the United States, but also via different countries. This meant that Stoll had to keep the attackers connected on the networks long enough to be able to trace them, contacting each service provider one by one, while the hackers directed their traffic. To achieve this, Stoll and the other US investigators had to obtain several warrants in each state where the traffic was being routed. This turned out to be a problem once the investigators traced the attack to Germany, where cyber attacks were not yet criminalised. After long, back-and-forth negotiations between the United States and the German authorities, the German police finally arrested five individuals in the summer of 1987. Further investigation also showed that the hackers were selling the information to the KGB for money and drugs. In a dramatic twist of events, the police later found a suspect's corpse in a nearby forest. His body had been burnt, and was left next to a can of petrol and a borrowed car with the keys still in it. There was no suicide note.[27]

Three factors slowed down the identification of the five individuals involved in the breach: the difficulty of obtaining warrants to track down the telephone line, the lack of criminal law in Germany, and the lack of traffic data retention. In 1988, by contrast, when the Morris worm propagated and allegedly infected 60,000 computers, it took only two days for a journalist at *The New York Times*, John Markoff, to find its author, Robert Morris Jr.[28] However, Markoff was able to find Morris mainly because Morris phoned him anonymously to explain why he released the worm, and let slip that the perpetrator's login was 'rtm'—his own, in other words.[29] But in another case less than ten years after the Cuckoo's Egg, where similar cyber attacks were not yet criminalised and traffic data not retained, the time for attribution was halved from one year to six months. The first constraint of issuing warrants to follow traffic had mostly been overcome due to better recognition of cyber security issues.

This case started on 28 August 1995, when a system administrator at the US Naval Command, Control and Ocean Surveillance Center found a malicious programme intended to collect information about the network. The case was taken up by Peter Gaza, an investigator within the Naval Criminal Investigative Service, a law enforcement agency that can investigate breaches of law against the Department of Defense. All the attacks originated from computers at Harvard University. The attacker had compromised several Harvard accounts, and was using them to launch further attacks. From August to September, through the compromised accounts, the attacker accessed the NASA network, the NASA Jet Propulsion Laboratory and the Naval Research Laboratory. The number of accounts compromised at Harvard could have made investigation difficult for a law enforcement agency if it had had to monitor them one by one—but Gaza requested a warrant to tap the whole network at Harvard University, which was connected to 16,500 computers. The investigators intended to look for specific words to filter out packets that were likely to belong to the intruder. Gaza recalls ringing the US Attorney's office in Boston:

> [I] asked if we could have the court order in place by Monday. They laughed. Six months was considered the 'speed of light' for wiretap approval. But we started to put the affidavit together anyway, and got it okayed in only six weeks, which at that time was unheard of.[30]

The investigators started recording the connections from November. From his monitor, Gaza saw the attacker consecutively accessing an

Argentinian telephone company called DuPont and other institutions such as Telecom Argentina and the System Engineering Research Institute in Seoul.[31] Eventually, the hacker joined a chat room via the programme Internet Relay Chat (IRC), using the nickname Griton. Gaza soon found out that a couple of years earlier someone named Griton had left a telephone number, located in Argentina, for his own Bulletin Board System in a forum dedicated to hacking, cracking and phreaking. Although unauthorised access to computers was not illegal in Argentina at the time—similar to Germany at the time of Stoll's investigation—the Argentinian police cooperated. Gaza asked the Argentinian police to match the telephone number provided on the Bulletin Board System: it led to Julio Cesar Ardita, aged 21. On 28 December 1995, six months after the beginning of the operation, the Argentinian police seized Ardita's computer at his home. He had hacked into sixty-two US government networks, including the US Navy, NASA and the Department of Energy's National Laboratories, as well as 136 US academic networks and thirty-one US private company networks.[32]

The increase in the speed of dealing with warrants to tap lines, collaboration between different police forces, and the cooperation between telephone providers and law enforcement agencies helped to achieve this relatively quick attribution time of six months from the start to the end of the investigation. Despite all the suggestions that attribution is time-consuming, the case of Ardita is a salient counterexample, in comparison to murder investigations for instance, which can drag on for years.

Moreover, improvements to attribution time did not stop there. Following Ardita's case, cooperation between countries continued and became more effective, as policemen, prosecutors, judges and many other people involved in investigative work acquired greater knowledge of how to conduct this type of investigation. In the 2000s, several items of malware were attributed in a matter of days: the Love Bug, Zotob, Blaster.B and Blaster.F and Sasser are a few examples. On 1 May 2000, the Love Bug started propagating on the Internet. Once it infected a computer, the malware tried to download further malware from a website.[33] By tracing the email address provided to the hosting server of the website, the FBI was able to find the author in the Philippines by 11 May—ten days after the Love Bug's release.[34] It took the police exactly the same number of days to find and arrest the authors of the Zotob virus examined in Chapter 1. The virus was released on 15 August 2005, and its authors were arrested on 25 August.[35]

It took even less time to identify the authors of two variants of the Blaster worm, which infected more than 200,000 computers in two days, because the police used similar techniques to those employed against the Love Bug.[36] The Blaster.B authors released the worm on 12 August 2003; and when the worm attempted to download malware from a website, the FBI was able to trace the website's owner. The FBI arrested him on 19 August, seven days after the first infection.[37] Another version of the worm, released on 1 September 2003, mentioned the name of a Romanian lecturer against whom the worm's author had a grievance. After narrowing down the number of potential suspects, the police arrested the worm's author just two days later, on 3 September.[38] Finally, the Sasser worm was attributed in six days. It started spreading on the night of 30 April 2004, and on 5 May, Microsoft received a call from potential informants willing to provide information about the malware's author if Microsoft agreed to reward them with $250,000 from the fund set up the year earlier to catch the authors of two other malware (the Blaster and the Sobig worms) which had spread virally and very quickly in August 2003, roughly at the same time.[39] Microsoft accepted, and on 8 May 2004 the German police arrested the Sasser worm's author.

The shortness of the time frames within which these five authors were identified is rather uncommon. Furthermore, identifying the authors of five worms is only a modest achievement. The number of new items of malware treated by antivirus companies each day can average ten; and, of course, such companies cannot focus their energy on all of them.[40] Antivirus companies therefore tend to focus only on the most costly items of malware; and nowadays, the most costly are also the most professional and complex. In these cases, obvious attacker mistakes allow the police and intelligence services to collect evidence. Furthermore, the short time frame for attribution achieved in all the above cases was enabled by a common factor: a functioning legal system. The positive relations between countries where the investigations took place allowed for cooperation, even when no legal basis for it existed, as in the cases of the Cuckoo's Egg in Germany, Ardita in

Argentina, the Love Bug in the Philippines, and Zotob in Morocco and Turkey. Another important factor was that in each case the attack was discovered soon after its launch, allowing investigators to follow the trail 'while it was hot'. By contrast, many attacks discussed in earlier chapters, such as GhostNet, ShadyRAT and Red October, remained unknown for years. Notwithstanding the fact that these operations probably had sponsors behind them, an earlier discovery of the attacks would presumably have led to a more thorough collection of evidence, and better attribution.

Hence, there have been noticeable advances in attribution since the Cuckoo's Egg of 1986, but there is still room for improvement, particularly on the bureaucratic side.

First of all, many local law enforcement agencies are still struggling to get the measure of cyber attacks, and cyber crime more generally. A report published in the United Kingdom in April 2014 by Her Majesty's Inspectorate of Constabulary, an agency in charge of overseeing police forces, found that 'only three forces (Derbyshire, Lincolnshire and West Midlands) had developed comprehensive cybercrime strategies or plans and only fifteen forces had considered cybercrime threats in their STRAs [strategic threat and risk assessment].'[41] One obstacle identified by the report was that a 'large scale cyber incident' warranted a national response by the National Crime Unit or other law enforcement agencies, and that local forces were unable to tell when an attack had crossed this threshold—an issue already touched upon here in the model of attribution as two processes (see Chapter 1).[42] Clearing these two domestic bureaucratic hurdles can significantly help attribution.

In addition, internationally, it is still very difficult for investigators to juggle the different standards of proof in different jurisdictions, especially as the investigation of almost any criminal cyber attack will span multiple countries. Even within the European Union, where a 2000 law operational since 2005 is supposed to facilitate the exchange of criminal information between police forces, the procedure remains tedious and formal, and takes time because it 'often requires judicial authorization'.[43] The time spent by investigators obtaining warrants, or making their case to other law enforcement agencies in order to account for different standards of evidence, suggests the need for a more unified framework to deal with many issues throughout the judicial process. By simplifying legal processes, and potentially by lowering the standards of evidence required to shut down infrastructures used in illicit activities to support cyber attacks, attribution time could be further reduced. In line with this assessment, the Five Eyes countries of the 'Anglosphere' (the US, UK, Canada, New Zealand and Australia) started discussions in 2011 to foster information exchange on cyber attacks and to harmonise their laws, building on the 2001 Budapest Convention, by including a response to state-sponsored attacks.[44]

Current and former US officials have confirmed that attribution has become quicker. 'I think that we've gotten much, much better, I mean, within the FBI,' said Shawn Henry, former executive assistant director at the FBI.[45] He further explained that the FBI has improved its performance by centralising, as opposed to '56 field offices operating independently'.[46] Christopher M. Painter, coordinator for cyber issues at the US State Department, also said in 2012 that he had seen improvements. He attributed the change partly to the Love Bug case, which spurred efforts globally. Painter said:

> There was a ministerial meeting back in 1999 where this was pushed as a major agenda item that countries need to have better laws, better capabilities. Of the three legs of the stool you have to have good capacity to fight these crimes—law enforcement and others. You have to have good laws in place. And you have to have the ability to cooperate internationally.[47]

Painter highlighted the lesson already identified from the mid-1980s through to the early 2000s: that, to a large extent, sound legal practices account for the time reduction in attribution. But despite this lesson, the debate about time and attribution has strangely shifted towards technical means to reduce attribution time, and more specifically towards 'real-time' attribution.

James Clapper, director of national intelligence, considers 'definitive, real-time attribution of cyberattacks—that is, knowing who carried out such attacks and where perpetrators are located' as the foremost challenge that the United States is facing.[48] Similarly, the director of GCHQ, Iain Lobban, told a BBC journalist that 'attribution can be very hard'.[49] He then added: 'It's very difficult to do attribution *in real time*, [b]ut over a period, you can build up a pretty strong idea of where the attribution is' [emphasis added].[50] Going even further, Randall

Dipert, a philosophy professor at the University of Buffalo, emphasised the 'real-time' feature by putting it at the core of his definition of attribution. Dipert considers attribution 'the lack of certainty sufficient [to classify the incident] as a *casus belli* in real time, and by technical means alone'.[51] But the requirement that attribution come solely from technical sources is too stringent, unnecessary and unadapted. As seen in the previous attribution cases in this chapter, and, for instance, those of Stuxnet and Anonymous, technical elements play only a minor role in comparison with the collection of intelligence from other sources. Whistle-blowers, informants and traces of Internet activities (such as messages left on forums under specific pseudonyms) constitute essential aspects of attribution for cases falling within both the criminal and national security contexts.

The debate about 'real-time' attribution assumes that it is useful (and possible) to attribute 'in real time'. For instance, two very well-respected academics working on law and cyber security wrote that 'urgent actions' such as hacking back can be used 'to compel the responsible State' to stop the attack.[52] Yet, technically, this may not make sense, in either the criminal or the national security context (the latter will be examined in the next section of this chapter).

In the criminal context, one of the values of real-time attribution could be to stop attacks at an early point by incapacitating the attacker. However, this is only useful for a specific type of attack, such as a denial-of-service attack, that occurs when a person is sitting in front of his computer. For a denial-of-service attack, knowing the technical provenance of the source of malicious traffic can help in setting up a filter against the sources (the zombie computers) to stop the attack and mitigate the risk. Even better, if one can identify the source giving commands to the zombie computers, the command-and-control server, then it may be possible to shut it down. (Although this is not strictly necessary—from a technical perspective, simply increasing the target's bandwidth would be sufficient to stop the effect of such an attack.) But for other types of attack, such as a worm propagating on a network without requiring the assistance of a human being, incapacitating the attacker as soon as the worm started propagating would not stop the attack: the worm would continue its course as if the arrest of the instigator had not taken place.

Another potential value of real-time attribution in the criminal context relates to deterrence. One can argue that if criminals know that the police can quickly identify them, then they will not carry out cyber attacks. But it is hard to believe that such dissuasion would stem specifically from a policy that *quickly* identifies them, as opposed to identifying them at all. Jack Gibbs, an influential theorist on deterrence, distinguished three parameters to assess the effects of deterrence: the certainty, the severity and the celerity of punishment.[53] However, Gibbs goes on to dismiss celerity, the speed at which punishment will be administered to criminals. He writes that it is difficult to imagine a connection between a criminal act and either the objective or the perceived lapse between the time of the criminal offence and the time of the punishment.[54] This applies to criminal cyber attacks.

There is another, more practical potential benefit of quick, although not necessarily real-time, attribution in the criminal context: police forces cannot spend an indefinite amount of resources searching for one instigator of a cyber attack. The amount they spend will usually depend on the estimated extent of the damage caused, although there are also wider time limitations. For instance, Keith Roscoe, investigator for the Digital and Electronic Forensic Service of the UK Metropolitan Police, explains that twenty-eight days is usually the limit set by a judge to charge a criminal, and to gather and consolidate evidence on the suspect.[55] The Digital and Electronic Forensic Service must 'get the context of the evidence' for an investigator, who will then put the evidence together.[56] This means that if the police stumble upon encrypted traffic, the forensic unit within the Metropolitan Police has only twenty-eight days to try to decrypt it. After this, the police cannot afford to spend more time or resources on the issue, and will have to move on. If a prosecutor hopes to retrieve a crucial piece of evidence that is encrypted on a person's hard drive, the inability to decrypt the hard drive could turn problematic when it comes to convicting the individual.[57] However, if more evidence emerges later, the issue will not simply be dismissed—the police will still arrest the individual and try to charge him, even if the misdeed happened three years earlier.[58]

Lastly, quick—and mainly technically focused—attribution can only support 'hack back' in certain limited cases. 'Hack back', or penetrating the attacker's computer, first requires knowing from which computers an attack originates (or to which server data are then sent). Shane McGee, a legal counsellor working for Mandiant, compared 'hack back' with an immediate defence against an assault. If a pedestrian sees a thief mugging someone and running away with a stolen wallet, the pedestrian is legally allowed to try to restrain the thief until the police come, and will not be charged with assault and battery. McGee and two other authors wrote that:

> While immediacy is an important factor in weighing whether 'hot pursuit' to retake physical stolen property, perhaps the standard may be relaxed or redefined as to cyber detections and intrusions, which may occur simultaneously in real-time if a victim-company monitors leaked information being stolen or potentially after some reasonable amount of time after-the-fact that a victim-company realizes that company assets have been stolen.[59]

In other words, for Shane McGee and his co-authors, real-time attribution can help tackle intellectual property theft. (Interestingly, Mandiant is against hack back, writing that it 'does not endorse or support hacking back in any form'.)[60] But even real-time attribution would be unlikely to show who the sponsors of an attack are. At best, an entity hacking back will know the location of the server on which the attacker stores the stolen data. But this is very unlikely to have a positive effect against the systematic theft of intellectual property by a country like China. As the previous chapters have demonstrated, deterring China from engaging in this type of behaviour involves working with diplomats at a senior strategic level and is much more complex. Such diplomatic engagement requires the ability to pinpoint accurately that China sponsored specific attacks. Focusing on real-time attribution at a low technical level (and with claims that are easily refutable) will alert the attackers that the victim is trying to track them. Instead of desisting, the attackers may become more careful or stealthier and ultimately make the work of detecting their attack and finding their sponsors more difficult. These limits of real-time attribution for finding sponsors can be extended to all types of cyber attack. In general, real-time attribution, grounded in a technical approach, fails to establish the sponsorship of any attacks.

Thus, making attribution time shorter is not automatically warranted, and its value, for criminal cases at least, is questionable: it can only stop specific attacks while they are being carried out; it is unlikely to deter criminals; the police can still investigate cases long after they have been carried out; and its effect on limiting intellectual theft is doubtful. But the discussion on real-time attribution, and in general on reducing attribution time, is also misleading, especially for cases that reach the national security threshold. For national security incidents, timing is an important element, but not in the sense of reducing it—rather, in the sense of heeding the context in which attribution is being formulated.

Time in terms of context for national security incidents

Discussions about reducing attribution times make two assumptions. The first is that it is achievable. But to reduce the time frame for discovering an attack's sponsors is almost impossible because of the long process of finding sources willing to provide information. No technical system will ever be able to do this. Talking of 'real-time' attribution for finding sponsors is therefore nonsensical. The second assumption is that there is a trade-off between time and evidence: the more time analysts and investigators have to collect evidence, the better the evidence and the subsequent attribution claims. But, as a 2012 US submission to the UN stated: 'High-confidence attribution of identity to perpetrators cannot be achieved in a timely manner, if ever'.[61]

Time and evidence seem to balance each other. Pauline C. Reich, a scholar and lawyer, wrote with colleagues that there exists a 'tension between a policy need for rapid response and the *technical* reality that attribution is a time-consuming task' [emphasis added].[62] If investigators have more time, in other words, they can collect more intelligence and wait for the attackers to make a mistake, or wait for a whistle-blower to come forward—a time-consuming process and one that cannot rightly be called 'technical'. When facing tight time constraints, analysts are likely to make shaky assumptions based on the use of criteria (see Chapter 3). But is it really reasonable to think that a state will choose to retaliate against a cyber attack not because it is sure of the attacker, but because it has to answer quickly?

If it wished to do so, a state would probably have the ability to evade scrutiny of the evidence it can present, as highlighted in Chapter 3. But state action has inherently high stakes, and no state would want to retaliate against the wrong enemy. This implies that it would certainly prefer to carry out a diligent assessment of the situation before taking any action, including attributing attacks. 'The last thing we would want to do is misinterpret an attack and escalate to a real conflict,' said an official at the US Department of Defense.[63] Because the element of whom an attack benefits can be misleading, and because an attacker can hide under a false flag to trigger a specific response, carefully considering the identity of the attacker is far more sensible than simply seeking to attribute and retaliate as fast as possible 'in real time'.[64] With higher stakes comes a responsibility that attribution needs to be correct and cannot be traded for a shorter time-response.

The trade-off is therefore misleading. In light of too little information and too many uncertainties, any state looking at an incident rationally will prefer to have more evidence than to err by retaliating quickly—that is, if it does indeed consider the situation rationally. In the midst of events, it can be easy to misread an attack. The 1998 Solar Sunrise incident, when the US military networks were breached while the United States was preparing to deploy in Iraq, epitomised this willingness to see links between enemies and an attack where there was in fact none. When emotions overcome rationality, the evidence may be misinterpreted, and overwhelm any feeling of restraint. In fact, following the Solar Sunrise incident, the FBI deputy director Steve Chabinsky raised the following important question: '[W]ill our adversaries have the same restraint when they start seeing attacks against their infrastructure coming from us?'[65] Whether adversaries show restraint may in fact have more to do with other conjectural factors than merely considering if quick attribution and retaliation are in order.

Quick attribution followed by quick retaliation can have two purposes. One is to serve as a punishment, which the international community could regard as out of context if it were to come some time after the original attack. The other purpose is as deterrence to the attacking state and to other states. This could prove useful if it were the case, as many authors and US officials have put the question of attribution at the core of a possible deterrence strategy for cyber attacks and retaliation.[66] According to this rationale, quick attribution and retaliation would tell an attacking state and other states that it is not worth conducting an attack again, and that they should be wary of doing so. The crucial question about deterrence is the same as with celerity for the deterrence of criminals: would deterrence be effective even if retaliation comes long after the offence is committed?[67] The author of *Cyberdeterrence and Cyberwar*, Martin Libicki notes: 'By the time the opportunity for retaliation does come, it may be overtaken by events. The attacking state may be on better terms with the target'.[68]

Two other factors diminish the argument for the meaningfulness of timely attribution. Firstly, the attribution processes of many cyber attacks may start to become significant only years after the attacks, but without diminishing the pertinence of the claims, despite changes in the context. Mandiant's report on China appeared more than four years after the military had allegedly perpetrated the attacks. But this did not take any value from the report. The diplomatic dialogue that took place between the United States and China after the publication of the report shows that there is a value attached to attribution. On the other hand, the fact that China continued its operations for a while despite the publication suggests that deterrence failed, in the short term at least. But it would be far too simplistic to ascribe this failure to the time lapse between the attacks and their attribution.

The same was true of Stuxnet: the time between the discovery of the breach and its attribution was nowhere close to 'real time'. The discovery of the malware occurred in June 2010, but Sanger's revelations only came out in June 2012.[69] In the intervening two years, many incidents had happened, and the context had changed. The regime of sanctions against Iran had been tightened, and Iran had experienced even more cyber attacks: most notably Wiper in May 2012, which deleted the hard drive of the computers at the Iranian Oil Ministry and for which Iran sought technical help at the International Telecommunication Union, but also Flame, a very comprehensive espionage tool also probably developed by the United States and Israel.[70] But, as with the claim by Mandiant towards China, the attribution link remained pertinent despite being made two years after the discovery of the malware, and even despite several changes in the context. Notably, the baseline of the context did not dramatically change over the years: Iran and China were, and are still, adversaries of the United States with whom relations are difficult.

Secondly, more important than responding in a timely fashion is the decision to make attribution public by assessing, in context, the different outcomes of attributing the attacks. This point is central to attribution. Any discussion focused on reducing attribution time (and this includes 'real-time attribution') dismisses the possibility that a state may not want to attribute, or that it may choose not to attribute an attack for other, more complex reasons (e.g. because it does not want to confront the attacker, does not want to be drawn into an escalating conflict, or does not have the leverage to confront the attacker). In other words, a discussion about reducing attribution time does not recognise the fact that making claims of attribution public is strongly contingent upon the current geopolitical situation. A country may wish to use an attribution claim as an instrument for opening discussions with another country; or it may decide against using it, and not make any claim. The decision to attribute is taken by the political elite, and not merely by a technical system. In other words, attribution, as a political decision, is time-dependent in the contextual sense of the word, and 'real-time' attribution disregards the instrumental role of attribution. Attribution is political. As seen in Chapter 2, judgement is required to weigh the different cost-benefits of making attribution at a certain time. Unnamed officials at NATO hold a similar belief, according to a 2012 news report: 'NATO believes that in military battle, attribution will become more a political decision since technical and physical attribution is not feasible in [a] short time'.[71]

There is potentially a difference when taking account of context, depending on the type of attack. Scholars and policy-makers often distinguish between two types of cyber attack: those resulting in sabotage, and those resulting in espionage.[72] Sabotage operations are more visible than espionage operations, and so states cannot hide them; consequently, the public expects to see a government investigate and attribute such operations. Yet formal attribution and retaliation does not always take place, even in cases where attacks cause notable damage. No single cyber attack has yet killed anyone, and Stuxnet is one of very few attacks to have caused physical damage. But even in the case of Stuxnet, no clear retaliation seems to have followed—assumptions that Shamoon was of Iranian origin and was retaliation for Stuxnet remain publicly unsubstantiated. Attribution, therefore, does not systematically take place, and when it does, it does not systematically call for retaliation—these realities depend on political factors.

This also applies outside the realm of cyber attacks: Al Qaeda was eventually identified as the perpetrator of the *USS Cole* bombing, for instance, but no retaliation against the group followed. The *USS Cole* was a US Navy ship that came under a suicide bomb attack on 12 October 2000 while it was docked in Yemen, killing seventeen US sailors and two terrorists who drove the bomb up to the ship. Two days later, Osama Bin Laden and his organisation Al Qaeda were already the prime suspects of the investigation following Bin Laden's call, aired on Al Jazeera, "'to move forward" against American forces in the Persian Gulf'.[73] Bin Laden had also displayed a 'teasing' clue in a video, by wearing a 'distinctive curved Yemeni dagger in his belt'.[74] Furthermore, Richard Clarke, national security advisor at the time, drew parallels with Al Qaeda's bombings of US embassies in Kenya and Tanzania in 1998, in terms of the attack's 'sophistication' and the 'amount of planning'.[75] These similarities were highlighted once more when the police were able to draw a sketch of the two suicide bombers, and unnamed officials pointed out their resemblance to other suspects wanted for questioning over the embassy bombings.[76]

Gradually, the link became clearer. On 18 October, Yemeni authorities arrested two men in connection with the bombing because they found bomb-making material in their apartment.[77] A day later, a 12-year-old boy told investigators that 'a man paid him to watch his car, then took to sea in a small boat and never returned', and was able to give a description of the man; and on 25 October, the police detained a Yemeni carpenter who had helped modify the boat so that it could carry explosives.[78] Following several more arrests of suspects with ties to the terrorist organisation, there was little doubt of Al Qaeda's involvement. For instance, the Yemeni police arrested Fahd al-Quso, who was supposed to film the attack for propaganda purposes but had overslept. Al-Quso admitted giving money to a man called 'Khallad' whom US investigators were able to recognise as a confirmed member of Al Qaeda.[79] On 13 November, Al-Quso denied involvement with the attack in an interview with a Kuwaiti newspaper, although the week before he had stated that 'he was satisfied' with it.[80]

At the end of November, although doubts about Al Qaeda's role in the attack were few, the evidence supporting attribution to Al Qaeda was still inadequate. An unnamed official reported that US President

Bill Clinton had asked the US military 'to prepare detailed plans for a massive military strike against the network of reputed terrorist leader Osama bin Laden in Afghanistan and "against those parties who appear to have supported" that network'.[81] To the Clinton administration, Al Qaeda was therefore clearly responsible for the attack, but it did not make this view public. A few weeks later, from 11 December onwards, more senior officials started officially and publicly linking Al Qaeda to the bombing.[82] Yet no retaliation occurred. One of the explanations for this lack of reaction, albeit hypothetical, would be because of the context during which the attack took place, namely over the presidential election.

The attack happened in the midst of a presidential election campaign, with the vote taking place only three weeks after the attack, on 7 November 2000. President Clinton pledged that 'we will find out who is responsible and hold them accountable'.[83] The two presidential candidates, George W. Bush and Al Gore, made similar pledges, but none were fulfilled. Clinton was busy supporting Al Gore's election, and according to *The New York Times* journalist Philip Shenon, 'when Bush and his new team came to office three months later, they saw the *USS Cole* attack as old news; it had happened on Clinton's watch'.[84]

The time factor in the *USS Cole* incident highlights two elements. Firstly, quickly identifying an attacker does not necessarily mean that action will follow. Secondly, decisions about attribution and retaliation depend upon the political agenda at the time of the attack. Discussions about reducing attribution time completely—and wrongly—belittle the importance of the political agenda at the time when an attack takes place, and the impact of this context on whether or not the attack will be publicly attributed.

Context is not only able to explain a lack of response, it can also explain why officials refuse to publicly name actors behind attacks even though they have successfully attributed the attack to them. With cyber attacks, the context can explain a range of reasons for delaying or excluding attribution, from highly political elements, as in the *Cole* incident, to relatively trivial factors. For example, once attribution claims are made, the attackers know that they have been discovered and pull out of their operations. They switch off their command-and-control servers, and try to delete all of their traces quickly. It is then no longer possible for investigators to garner more evidence of their identities. Patiently waiting, and delaying attribution, can therefore be useful. When *The New York Times* found out that several of its computers had been hacked, most probably following a story published on 25 October 2012 about the wealth of then Chinese prime minister Wen Jiabao, they did not announce the matter straight away.[85] 'We had to wait until [the hackers] were out of [the] system, and [this] took months', according to *New York Times* journalist David Sanger.[86] Waiting to go public about an attack in order to track hackers for longer and more effectively is common sense. But with 'real-time' attribution, there is a sense that knowing who the attackers are implies making the claim public straight away—which is often not the case when the political stakes are high. Iain Lobban, director of GCHQ, reminded BBC journalist Gordon Corera of the difference between attribution and making attribution public during an interview. As Corera pressed Lobban on who was behind attacks aimed at stealing intellectual property, Lobban confirmed that 'we know who it is', but answered him 'I can't say who it is *to you*'.[87]

There are many political reasons for actively or openly refusing to name a party involved in an attack. They include the significant uncertainty that attribution will produce any change of behaviour, or the difficulty in assessing how a state will respond to an attribution claim. Even when this is known, a government may rationally weigh the pros and cons, and decide it would be more beneficial for the state to simply stay quiet. This is probably what happened with Australia in May 2013.

On 27 May, the Australian TV channel ABC broadcast that Chinese hackers had stolen blueprints for the new headquarters of the Australian intelligence services.[88] The blueprints included the 'building's floor plan, communications cabling layouts, server locations and security systems'.[89] Furthermore, ABC reported, the hackers had also breached the networks of the Department of Defence, the Department of Foreign Affairs and Trade, and of the prime minister. Despite the gravity of the breach, no officials confirmed it, while the Australian foreign minister declared: 'I won't comment on whether the Chinese have done what is being alleged or not'.[90] By not confirming the breach, the government also evaded any obligations it would have had to comment on the instigator of the attack, allegedly the Chinese. As duly noted by several media outlets a month prior to the attack, the then Australian prime minister, Julia Gillard, had struck an important deal with the Chinese. The Australian and Chinese prime ministers committed to annual meetings, a commitment that China has only accepted with three other countries.[91] This reinforced bilateral mechanisms between the two countries, especially in the area of economic partnership. It appears that Australia did not want cyber attacks to jeopardise this valued partnership with China. Following the May 2013 attacks, Bob Carr, the then Australian foreign minister, declared that 'it's got absolutely no implications for a strategic partnership. We have enormous areas of co-operation with China'.[92] It is unclear how much evidence the Australian authorities had against the Chinese. But it seems quite probable that Australia weighed the benefits of attributing the attacks against the cost that such attribution could have in the political sphere.

This book has repeatedly pointed out that attribution is political. Politics occurs both over time and within a specific context. It follows that time plays an important role in attribution. Moreover, as the *Cole* case demonstrates, context plays an important role in not only international, but also domestic, politics. Because attribution can be used to place blame on entities, the time at which attribution claims are made can have damaging results. This point is as valid for the attribution of cyber attacks as for the attribution of other types of attack. A specific event happening at a specific time can be used to leverage support for a specific action.

For example, depending on when a cyber attack is attributed, the political fallout can be damaging and reshape agendas. This was the case following a revelation that the NSA had breached the Brazilian president's communications.[93] More generally, following many of the revelations about NSA hacking operations, a direct consequence has been the re-emergence of a debate on privacy and the appropriate extent and oversight of states' surveillance capabilities. In the specific case of the United States and Brazil, the Brazilian president Dilma Rousseff called off a long-planned visit to the United States following the revelations that the NSA had breached her emails. There were also many more political ripple effects from Snowden's revelations of US intelligence services' role in cyber attacks, but we need not examine all of them. It will suffice to highlight that reducing attribution time would not make as much sense as heeding the domestic and international context of attacks.

Finally, in addition to the impact on national security cases, context also influences criminal cases, in two different ways. Firstly, time and the conjectures around an attack affect the evidence investigators can obtain. For example, if an attack takes place in the midst of a conflict between two states, there will not be any exchange of information, whereas if an attack takes place in the midst of a cooperative phase, information is likely to be exchanged.

Secondly, context can influence the outcome of trials. In the well-known case of the British hacker Gary McKinnon, who in 2000 hacked into several US governmental networks, there was a clear political prompt from the UK government to help McKinnon fight his extradition. The US wanted to trial McKinnon for his crimes, for which he could receive a maximum sentence of sixty years in prison, whilst the highest punishment he would face in the UK was a two-year sentence (under the Computer Misuse Act). After a ten-year legal battle, the UK Government acted to stop the defendant's extradition, on the grounds of his diagnosis with Asperger syndrome in 2008. Had the political class supported his extradition, it is likely that a full trial would have taken place in the United States, and that the court would have found him guilty. Similarly, in the case of the hacker Mathew Bevan, who had connections with DataStream Cowboy (Richard Pryce), the court dismissed his case because it would have been too costly to mount a trial with a maximum sentence of a £2,000 fine. This low maximum was heavily influenced by the context: six months before, a court had fined Pryce $1,200 for twelve similar charges brought against him. Bevan faced only five charges, and the case required US officials to fly to the United Kingdom to present evidence.

Hence, time in terms of context supersedes reducing time for attribution. The political saliency of a case determines the importance of this context and cannot be disregarded. The instrumentality and effects of attribution are important elements to factor into the decision about whether to publicise or officialise attribution, such as when a court chooses to pursue the prosecution of an accused person.

The time factor in the attribution of cyber attacks is a surprisingly similar constraint in the investigation of other incidents, be they criminal or threats to national security. Described as time-consuming, it is clear that the attribution process is nowhere close to 'the speed of light'. In both criminal and national security contexts, attribution can take years: either waiting for a criminal to make a mistake that will enable law enforcement agencies to track him down, or waiting for a whistle-blower to come forward. Understandably, this has prompted many people to seek shorter attribution times. These have been achieved over the years, with attribution times reduced from longer than the resolution of other types of crime to within the same range. But a desire to achieve even faster attribution times is unwarranted—or, more importantly, continuing to focus on time reduction is misplaced: it dismisses the important aspect of context, which is especially salient in national security cases. This context should always be considered.

Attribution is political and, as such, timing can play an instrumental role. Ultimately, attribution is inherently linked with blaming an entity. A decision to blame individuals, organisations or states can be used to achieve political objectives. These objectives are far-ranging: domestically, they include passing legislation or bringing down a political opponent; internationally, they include justifying or, conversely, masking the real reasons for a conflict with another state, or putting pressure on a state to strike a deal. Similarly, a decision not to attribute an attack can be made in order to preserve relations with other states; or, because decision-makers focus on other priorities, they may simply push attribution to the bottom of their task lists and then not carry it out later because the context has changed. Thus, it is not possible to talk about attribution without considering conjectural political elements to which it is linked.

In light of this political context, discussions to reduce attribution time do not make sense. They fail to take into account that attribution is not systematic, and that making attribution time shorter will not help in taking a decision about attribution that is based on many other factors. Addressing the question set at the beginning of the chapter, about an appropriate time for attribution, forces us to consider these political factors. Attribution is not automatic, but is bespoke for each incident. And yet, once again, the attribution of cyber attacks is not so different from the attribution of other national security incidents where decision-makers are involved.

It is not possible to shortcut the political process of deciding attribution. Discussions of real-time attribution, and in general any technical discussions about attribution, fail to grasp the political process behind it. Consequently, such discussions advocate the wrong solutions, such as re-engineering the Internet. Instead, approaches to attribution need to recognise that nothing can ensure systematic, perfect attribution. The same is true for the attribution of a terrorist bombing incident. In the end, there can still be a factor that prompts state actors not to attribute the attack, not because they have not found the group behind the attack, but because the political cost of attribution is not worthwhile. Therefore, timing can indeed explain why attribution sometimes does not take place, not only in the sense that the collection of evidence is very time-consuming, but mostly because of context.

Talking about attribution without putting it in its proper context is inappropriate. For example, attribution by courts for criminal incidents, while less political because decision-makers may not be directly involved, should not be disregarded too quickly on the grounds that such attribution has nothing to do with time. For instance, the conviction of a criminal may not happen because the criminal attacked foreign assets in a country with which the state is in conflict, and consequently the refusal to convict becomes a form of political statement. (This is a notably important aspect of attribution for states with weak rule of law.) All such possibilities, in which the concept of time is involved in one way or another, make it impossible to ensure attribution technically in all cases. This may come as a challenge to the well-established constraints on attribution; namely, forensic investigation techniques, and cooperation with other states to exchange information. While these are certainly significant constraints, this chapter has tried to emphasise that time, in the sense of context, should be considered alongside them.

6

PLAUSIBLE DENIABILITY

This final chapter is slightly different to its predecessors because it seeks to look at attribution from the perspective not of the investigators trying to achieve attribution, but of the instigators trying to evade it. When accused of misdeeds, states do not simply acquiesce or confirm the allegations. They not only deny claims, they also use a range of tactics to ensure that no evidence conclusively proves their involvement in attacks. In other words, these tactics provide states with the means to plausibly deny their sponsorship. Much of the literature on 'plausible deniability' can be found in relation to covert actions—actions taken by states to further political objectives, and which states seek to conceal from the public. This literature is richly informed by the numerous covert actions that the United States and the Soviet Union carried out during the years of the Cold War. In contrast, the number of cases that have emerged with accurate details about cyber attacks is still low, which makes it difficult to verify several of the assumptions in the literature. Yet the words 'plausible deniability' have appeared in many articles where cyber attacks and attribution are discussed, making it an unavoidable topic for research on attribution. With this in mind, several questions are relevant when discussing plausible deniability.

What does it mean for a cyber attack to be plausibly deniable? And, more to the point, how can states engineer plausible deniability?

Furthermore, do states have equal incentives to seek plausible deniability for all types of attack? If not, how is it possible to distinguish between their responses to attacks?

An initial, brief answer to the first question—how a cyber attack can be plausibly deniable or denied—is directly connected with an aforementioned argument: the reliance of attribution on judgement makes it relatively easy for the accused to brush off any claims. In addition, this chapter makes two related arguments that run against common assumptions in the literature. Firstly, states engineer plausible deniability by relying not on foreign and distant hacking groups, but usually on domestic proxies. Although this reliance increases the state's likelihood of being exposed, it also gives the state a greater ability to control the hired group. Secondly, connecting a state to an attack makes the state open to retaliation and largely accounts for why a state can be zealous in plausibly denying its involvement. Strategically, however, it does not make sense for states to seek plausible deniability for all types of attack. Espionage operations almost always prompt a backlash and can warrant special precautionary measures. But sabotage operations aimed at coercing an actor into a change of behaviour require clarity. The instigator needs to ensure that the victim is cognisant of the motive behind the attack so that the threat can inform their potential decision to change policy. By revealing its identity while leaving room for ambiguity, a state can simultaneously send this signal and avoid retaliation.

This chapter will first examine measures to achieve plausible deniability, and will especially focus on the use of proxy groups. Secondly, it will examine the conditions that must be in place in order for states to seek plausible deniability.

Sources of plausible deniability

Briefly defined, the term plausible deniability means that it is not possible for a victim to conclusively prove the involvement of the entity they suspect of having instigated an attack. The roots of this concept in US strategic thinking can be traced to the 1950s. In 1948, the CIA launched a covert action to influence the outcome of the election in Italy, fearing that a communist government would otherwise be instated. It was imperative that 'the hand of Washington' should not be revealed.[1] In light of the success of the operation, this became a dogma for future covert actions.[2] The 'hand of Washington' went on to mean first that the president himself, then that the whole US government, was not involved. Several systems existed to shun responsibility. For instance, a 'buddy system' existed until the Church Committee made recommendations against it in 1975 following the Watergate scandal.[3] This consisted of limiting any paper traces, and involved the director of the CIA simply engaging in informal exchanges with senior members of Congress.[4] Because of this informality, it is still difficult to know exactly who knew what about early covert actions engineered by the United States under the policy of keeping them plausibly deniable.[5]

Despite the original meaning of the term reflecting bureaucratic practices, many have thought of cyber attacks as being plausibly deniable because of their inherent technical nature. Mark Clayton wrote in *The Christian Science Monitor* that 'plausible deniability remains because attribution is so uncertain in cyberspace'.[6] 'The Internet is said to be the perfect platform for plausible deniability', explained Kamlesh Bajaj, the chief executive of the Data Security Council of India.[7] 'Cyberspace is made for plausible deniability,' said Ilan Berman, vice president at the American Foreign Policy Council.[8] With such comments in mind, what exactly makes cyberspace specifically suitable for deniability in comparison, for instance, with sponsoring an assassination?

A common tempting, but wrong, answer is to look for technical explanations. Cyber attacks can easily span many different countries, and with the use of computer proxies, it is possible to mask the real origins of malicious traffic. In fact, many states carrying out cyber attacks do use some form of proxies to hide their real origins. A US report from the Office of the National Counterintelligence Executive notes that 'many actors route operations through computers in third countries or physically operate from third countries to obscure the origin of their activity'.[9] The report then goes on to identify China specifically as 'increasingly us[ing] cyber tools to steal trade secrets and achieve plausible deniability'.[10] Unfortunately, however, the real locations of traffic cannot determine the sponsors of attacks. A lot more information is needed, and it is usually of a non-technical nature. In other words, knowing the genuine originating IP address behind an attack is not a conclusive indication of whether a specific government ordered, funded or even supported in any way the launching of the attack. In this sense, the structure of the Internet and the possibility of using computer proxies do not seem to add more layers to plausible deniability of cyber attacks than of other forms of covert operation.

Another answer, far more relevant, is that states can achieve plausible deniability by hiring proxy groups. According to a legal advisor to the US Department of State, Harold Koh, 'cyberspace significantly increases an actor's ability to engage in attacks with plausible deniability, by acting through proxies'.[11] Michele Markoff, also working at the State Department and overseeing the development and implementation of foreign policy on cyberspace issues, even considered that 'the potential to use skilled criminals as witting or unwitting proxies for cyberdisruption offers a state actor total plausible deniability'.[12]

However, although the evidence will show that use of proxy groups is indeed relevant in this context, this does not make plausible deniability of cyber attacks any different in comparison with other covert operations. In many other disruptions sponsored by the secret services (such as assassinations), the same capacity exists for covering one's tracks: the use of proxies, not keeping records of actions, and acting in countries other than the state commanding the operation. Even legal commentaries about the use of proxies by states are well developed, following several cases that emerged during the Cold War (see Chapter 3).[13] It is not, therefore, the nature of cyberspace that gives cyber attacks their particular layer of plausible deniability, but the nature of attack sponsorship. Instead of resorting to the use of their own domestic intelligence services, states can contract private individuals to carry out assassinations, and have done so in the past. And states 'will [inevitably] continue to work through non-State actors to achieve national security and foreign policy objectives'.[14] The ability for a state to contract groups to carry out covert actions is roughly the same, be it for cyber attacks or for any other more traditional covert operations.

Therefore, the argument is not about the uniqueness of using proxies to achieve plausible deniability, but about such deniability's inner working. In order to evade attribution, and for an attack to remain plausibly deniable, a state will hire a proxy group to which—counterintuitively—it is already close. In this regard, keeping control of the group and trusting it is considered more important than maximising plausible deniability.

Many reports have noted this use of proxy groups by states. A US publication from the Office of the National Counterintelligence Executive noted that '[foreign intelligence services] and other foreign entities have used independent hackers at times to augment their capabilities and act as proxies for intrusions, thereby providing plausible deniability'.[15] Likewise, the UK's annual report on intelligence and security for 2012–13 stated that: 'We [the Parliament] have been told that a number of countries are also using private groups to carry out state-sponsored attacks'.[16]

A statement by a senior advisor at the Estonian Ministry of Defence is a good illustration of one of the main assumptions about these hired groups: 'Nation states or state-sponsored institutions could use proxy attackers located in territories without proper law enforcement, places with weak government structures and non-existent national cyber monitoring systems.'[17] The former chief counterterrorism advisor of the National Security Council, Richard A. Clarke, made similar suggestions in his book.[18] But the empirical evidence gives a very different picture, namely that states would rather use proxies located within their own territory than look for ones located in remote countries without proper law enforcement.

Russia is a case in point. Firstly, the Russian authorities seem to have offered apprehended hackers the chance to work for them, instead of giving them a prison sentence, although few details are known.[19] In the United States, a similar practice seems to have emerged. The hacker discussed in Chapter 1, Xavier Hector Monsegur of the Anonymous group and the Lulzsec hacking group, not only became an FBI informant but also encouraged another hacker, Jeremy Hammond, to launch several attacks on various government websites (including those of Iran, Nigeria, Pakistan, Turkey and Brazil) while under FBI surveillance.[20] This strongly suggests that—as already suspected ever since Monsegur had been outed as a mole—the FBI directly ordered these attacks, and used Monsegur not only to inform on other hackers but also to collect intelligence of a national security nature.[21]

Secondly, and more notably in the case of Russia, rampant corruption sometimes blurs the line between criminal activities and the authorities' official position, criminals operating at times as proxies of the state. This was epitomised by the difficulty in bringing down the Russian Business Network, because of the Russian authorities' reluctance to get involved.[22] The Russian Business Network was connected with a great variety of online schemes such as phishing, denial-of-service attacks and child pornography. From 2007 to 2008, the Russian Business Network operated as a recognised Internet service provider, and acted as a hosting service under what is referred to as 'bulletproof hosting'. This meant that the company guaranteed to its clients the hosting of any content without fear of censure. It also meant that it was easier to launch denial-of-service attacks without being blocked.[23] Corruption in the Russian police allowed the service provider to evade law enforcement and quietly keep running.[24] The official police line was that they could not shut down the Russian Business Network because the organisation did not violate the law: it merely hosted websites, thereby facilitating misdeeds.[25]

But several analysts such as Andy Auld, head of intelligence for the e-crime unit at the UK Serious Organised Crime Agency, went further. Auld saw not only corruption behind the obstacles to prosecution, but also the involvement of the local police, local judiciary and local government.[26] Ron Deibert and Rafal Rohozinski, two Toronto-based academics, further alleged that the Russian state was using criminal organisations like the Russian Business Network to launch denial-of-service attacks against its adversaries.[27] Other academics have also noted that the Russian Business Network is likely to have played a role in cyber attacks launched against Georgia during the 2008 stand-off with Russia, further highlighting the link with the government in Moscow.[28]

Naturally, as with any argument, caveats also apply, and not all states necessarily turn to domestic groups for launching every attack on another state. It is also possible to discern—although not very clearly—a case where it seems that hiring capable hackers trumped keeping control of them. In September 2013, several US officials disclosed that hackers had infiltrated unclassified Navy computers.[29] The officials did not let many details come out, but felt very strongly about one point: they claimed the attacks came from Iran. James Lewis, a cyber security and oft-quoted expert at the Center for Strategic and International Studies, told *The Wall Street Journal* that the Iranians were 'getting help from the Russians'.[30] He then added that the Russian government probably authorised the criminals to support the Iranians. While this scenario is possible, Lewis did not give more information to support his claims. In fact, past attacks linked to Iran had also suggested that the Iranians hired domestic hackers, but it is quite possible that their strategy had evolved since then to include the use of proxy groups coming from both within (as the following case shows) and from outside the country (as Lewis was implying).

One of these past attacks was by the so-called Comodohacker. In March 2011, he infiltrated the international certificate authority Comodo and was then able to issue as many rogue certificates as he wanted. With a stolen certificate, it is possible for a hacker to make a user believe he is visiting a protected and secure website, when in fact, the website can inject malicious code into the user's computer. Alternatively, the hacker can simply act as a man-in-the-middle, and after redirecting users to a fake but authenticated webpage, read their encrypted traffic (such as email). The Iranian student behind the Comodo attack claimed it was revenge for Stuxnet, and said he intended to use the certificates to spy on opponents of the Iranian regime.[31] The two statements do not follow each other, however, as the American and Israeli governments were behind Stuxnet. Getting back at these two governments by means of the domestic Iranian population opposing the Iranian government makes little sense.

Then, on 19 July 2011, another certificate authority, DigiNotar, detected a similar attack.[32] DigiNotar did not make any public announcement until the consultancy company Fox-IT finished its investigation a month later. By then, on 27 July, a rogue certificate for google.com had already appeared for several Internet users based in Iran.[33] Comodohacker claimed this attack on the Google certificate a week later, on the website Pastebin.[34] It appeared that the two successful attacks on certificate authorities had allowed him to spy on Iranian citizens, as was his stated intention. Fox-IT thinks that, as a result of the operation, the hacker was able to access 300,000 Iranians' Google email accounts.[35]

Fox-IT's report confirmed that the same hacker was involved in the Comodo and DigiNotar incidents. In both cases, the hacker left the same message on the servers: 'Janam Fadaye Rahbar', meaning 'I will sacrifice my soul for my leader'.[36] The hacker used proxies to hide his real IP address, but he appeared to have forgotten to use the proxy in a couple of instances to reach the main web server. Each time, though, he corrected the mistake within seconds. After Fox-IT requested proxies to give the IP address that had passed through their services, and which the hacker had left in the clear, the company confirmed that the address was located in Iran.[37] If the hacker was in Iran and spying on Iranian citizens and companies, this does not prove or disprove any relation that he may have had with the Iranian government per se. But the assumption that the Iranian government sponsored the operation to some degree does not seem too far-fetched.[38]

Iran, and Russia, could have used many other, more distant groups to launch attacks; but interestingly, they did not do so. The Iranian and Russian authorities could have pursued two other main options. They could have contracted the services of professional companies specialising in finding zero-day exploits, writing malicious code, and selling it to states. Companies' official statements often mention that they sell such services only to non-rogue actors, although such a stance does not always match certain companies' records.[39] Vupen, a French company, recently came under the spotlight for selling its services to the NSA in this completely unregulated market.[40] However, the point here is that Vupen is not the only company to offer such a service: there is already a market for it.[41]

A second option for Iran and Russia could have been to hire groups via underground forums, where it is now possible to contract many different professionals to engage in tasks that lead to cyber attacks. A few hackers even offer a guarantee-of-service. For instance, when selling malware, the seller guarantees that if a large antivirus company updates its products to ban the malware, the hacker will strive to provide a new undetectable version as quickly as possible.[42] Other services on sale from hackers range from 'bulletproof' services, like that of the Russian Business Network, or simpler denial-of-service à la carte.[43] Such forums are well organised, but they must not be confused with mafias. Jonathan Lusthaus, a researcher at the University of Oxford, concluded after studying online organised crime that although 'cyber-criminal forums are like mafias', 'they are not mafias'.[44] According to Lusthaus, the problem with considering them as such is twofold: the forums are more of a marketplace than a criminal organisation with other goals; and because of anonymity, it is not possible to enforce rules within the criminal community. Furthermore, David Wall at the University of Durham contends that cybercriminals are not mafia-like because they divide the work horizontally by skill sets rather than in a hierarchical fashion as mafias do.[45]

The professionalisation of hacker services through companies such as Vupen and underground forums constitutes a challenge for attribution. These services make it more difficult to distinguish between the operator, 'the actual hacker' and the customer—the entity that 'stands to benefit from the activity conducted in the intrusion'.[46] Such confusion unquestionably benefits those trying to achieve plausible deniability. Creating ambiguity, and therefore introducing confusion about the role played by an entity, is central to establishing plausible deniability.

Two related reasons could explain why states prefer to choose local groups rather than more distant and less attributable ones. Firstly, once a state lends its support to a group, it can be difficult for the state to withdraw this support even after circumstances have changed.[47] Even if a state does withdraw its support, the group could speak out and make embarrassing revelations about the support it has already received, or blackmail the state by threatening such exposure. The sponsoring state needs to maintain a certain leverage against such a situation, particularly given that, because of the secret nature of the relationship between the state and the group, the state is in a weak negotiating position. Hiring local groups under the state's jurisdiction ensures that the state can always use its law enforcement agencies to threaten them, with jail terms for instance. This makes it much easier to control the hired group.

States have three more ways of building plausible deniability. The first and least effective method is simply to deny sponsorship. The Chinese government does this all the time. After each accusation of involvement in economic espionage, the Chinese government issues a statement along the lines of 'China is a victim of cyber attacks'.[48] Using one's own judgement can easily trump such statements—but there might be a more subtle explanation for why the Chinese have adopted this approach. One author has explained that Chinese denials, when they relate to security issues, are 'to allow the other side to save face when backing down'.[49] Further explaining this, he wrote: 'Even if everyone knows that there is a linkage, the idea that there isn't any linkage is something we might call "a polite fiction"'.[50] One example that gives credit to such an explanation is President Barack Obama's stance after meeting with his Chinese counterpart in June 2013, when Obama softened his attitude to Chinese espionage in the midst of the embarrassing revelations begun three days earlier by Edward Snowden. In a head-on competition for the public's trust, creating a credible political fiction can be an important factor in undermining the opposing government's claim—and so the trustworthiness of that government itself.

A second and more elaborate tactic for keeping an operation plausibly deniable is to stay below a certain threshold. Only large-scale attacks triggering important consequences are investigated. Small attacks, yielding small gains to attackers and where the damage is not considered a threat to national security, are not very likely to be detected, and even less likely to be attributed.[51] By infecting just a couple of carefully selected machines, a state's malware may remain under the radar for a long time. For example, the US-engineered espionage malware Duqu stayed undetected for four years probably because it infected fewer than 100 computers.[52] The Mask malware, supposedly of Spanish origin and characterised as 'one of the most advanced global cyber-espionage operations', similarly infected only 380 victims.[53] It stayed undetected for at least five years.

Lastly, a third tactic states can use is to masquerade their attacks. While many attacks attract a lot of attention from the media and government officials (for instance after Mandiant's 2013 report on the Chinese military), other attacks can make use of such distractions to ensure they will not be investigated with the same tenacity. This is a commonly used tactic among criminals. For instance, in August 2013, while the system administrators and various technicians at a bank were busy working against a denial-of-service attack, the attackers stole millions of dollars.[54] They targeted the 'wire payment switch', the system that manages the transfer of money at banks, although it is still unclear how they managed to gain access to this system. The attackers, still unfound, are by no means alone in using this tactic. Two months later, the Argentinian authorities arrested a 19-year-old boy who allegedly made $50,000 working alongside six other people using this exact modus operandi.[55] It is easy to imagine states similarly utilising other attacks to ensure that their own are successful and remain undetected, therefore preserving full plausible deniability.

It is, therefore, possible to engineer plausible deniability, or at least to put into place mechanisms that help undermine victim states' confidence in their knowledge of their attackers. But, from the instigator's standpoint, is it always an advantage to hide one's identity? When does hiding one's identity become more harmful than partially revealing it?

Strategic considerations for warranting plausible deniability

One argument against the use of any deception to hide the origin of attacks is that covert operations 'seldom remain secret; their broad contours and details seep into the public domain'.[56] Recent revelations by Wikileaks and Edward Snowden have demonstrated that it is very difficult to control sensitive information, not only about covert operations but also more generally about surveillance programmes. For cyber attacks, then, it should not be assumed that secrecy can prevail indefinitely. Launching cyber attacks therefore requires careful consideration, and weighing of the consequences, at home and abroad, that will follow once it emerges that a state actor was an active sponsor.

Looking at covert operations launched by the US since the 1950s, they have put forward four rationales for keeping operations plausibly deniable. First, a few operations have remained secret simply because of bureaucracy: they are launched by agencies that have been functioning with an element of secrecy for decades and no one questions their practices.[57] Second, many covert actions have been controversial. They include assassinations, and disputable recourse to violence to protect national interests. Therefore, the government in place could rightly be worried about the political backlash that might follow a public outing of its involvement in 'dirty tricks'. Third, again domestically, a policy of plausible deniability has shielded officials from prosecution—important in order to limit political fallout and retain the moral high ground. Fourth, keeping a covert action plausibly deniable heightens uncertainty about the identity of the instigator. Fostering such doubts directly lowers the likelihood of retaliation.

These rationales for keeping actions covert do not translate entirely or without nuance to cyber attacks. The general view is that all cyber attacks that the US government conducts are veiled in secrecy. *The New York Times* wrote in August 2013 about US officials' frustrating reluctance to discuss cyber attacks on the grounds that these were 'part of a secret arsenal'.[58] Is this secrecy warranted in every case? In fact, the need for plausible deniability depends on whether the cyber attacks take place at home or abroad, and whether the attack is aimed at espionage or sabotage.

Cyber attacks targeting entities located outside the United States are not so controversial. Sabotage operations are nowhere near as violent and fatal as deploying death squads or planting bombs.[59] The most violent example that exists to date is Stuxnet, which officially caused no deaths but only damage to physical infrastructure. Justifying non-violent action to the public is far easier than having to explain the use of assassinations. As for espionage operations, spying abroad is also accepted as common practice, be it targeted at states or individuals. This was shown in the Obama administration's repeated stance, following Edward Snowden's disclosure of NSA programmes, that 'only non-U.S. persons outside the U.S. are targeted'.[60]

A corollary is that operations conducted by law enforcement agencies and intelligence services at home, against US citizens, are much less accepted. Both the FBI and the NSA regularly use cyber attacks to identify criminals, a usage that triggers many privacy concerns. Yet until Snowden's revelations in the summer of 2013, these concerns were not, for the most part, publicly debated.[61] Following the revelations, Obama has had to take action to calm public opinion about the debate and assert that the government will restrict its surveillance capabilities.[62] Hence, from the US government's perspective, there are strong incentives to keep espionage cyber attacks secret when the target is on home ground: the government avoids political fallout and can keep the programmes up and running. Furthermore, the earlier argument about shielding officials from responsibility also applies in these cases. It is not entirely clear whether several of the programmes led by the NSA for information collection purposes, which can involve cyber attacks, are legal. Different judges have expressed differing opinions.[63] But it is worth noting that no high-level official seems to have lost their job either at the NSA or at Booz Allen Hamilton, Snowden's former employer, following the disclosures.[64] Keeping cyber attacks plausibly deniable allows this evasion of accountability.

The strong incentives for keeping attacks plausibly deniable must, however, be weighed against conducting the attacks in the first place, and putting in place significant legal and political machinery to hide them. When attacks come out, the revelation can be more damaging to policy-makers than the information derived from the attacks in the first place was useful. For instance, the NSA intercepted notes from the United Nations' secretary-general, Ban Ki-moon, ahead of a friendly discussion he was to have with President Obama. As *The New York Times* put it, 'it is hard to imagine what edge this could have given Mr. Obama in a friendly chat'.[65] It seems the NSA recklessly implemented the intercept simply because it could. Despite the secrecy with which intelligence services operate, it now appears very likely that their programmes will eventually come under public scrutiny This could force the NSA to rethink its policy on plausible deniability, and to ponder whether the costs are worth it. The CIA went through a very similar process a few decades ago. It suffered significant backlash when the public learnt about its involvement in the Iran-Contra affair and the programmes for the assassination of foreign leaders. Eventually, the CIA learned an important lesson: it being reasonable for the CIA to carry out an action was not sufficient implication that it should carry it out. The secrecy of the CIA's operations would not continue indefinitely, and could cost it dearly if it could not clearly articulate why it had pursued a particular course of action.

A more difficult point to address—and one that needs significant nuance—concerns the rationales behind seeking plausible deniability in order to avoid retaliation. Common strategic thinking is that a state conducting cyber attacks against another state ought to obfuscate its trail, whether the cyber attacks are for espionage or sabotage. This seems to make sense because 'if the identity of an attacker via cyberspace is unknown then retaliation is difficult'.[66] For instance, Chris Demchak, the prominent scholar on cyber security, has written that: 'Would-be cyber coercers must maintain both deception and opaqueness throughout their campaigns if they are to be successful... If identified, the would-be coercers could be punished by equally deceptive retribution campaigns or collective sanctions In other sectors.'[67]

Concerning cyber attacks, coercion can happen almost exclusively via sabotage operations. An unnamed former senior US official held a similar view that 'the United States is moving toward the use of tools short of traditional weapons that are unattributable—that cannot be easily tied to the attacker—to convince an adversary to change their behavior at a strategic level'.[68] Likewise, Michael N. Schmitt, a prolific scholar researching international law and cyber attacks, wrote with Liis Vihul that 'most [states] are understandably reticent to be identified' as the source of cyber attacks.[69] Yet two arguments stand against the belief that it is in a state's strategic interest to remain unknown if its cyber attacks are to be successfully coercive. One of these arguments is conceptual, while the other is grounded in practice.

As noted by Lawrence Freedman and Srinath Raghavan, 'military signals are notoriously ambiguous, [and] they need to be supplemented by some more direct forms of communication to ensure that the opponent receives the message sent without distortion'.[70] In the case of an assassination, or regime subversion, the signal sent by the instigating state is clear: a powerful and capable actor is supporting a regime change. With cyber attacks, however, it can be very difficult to interpret the motivation behind the attack without also knowing the identity of the instigators. The first question that attribution seeks to solve is whether a criminal or a state is behind the attack. If the victim assumes it was a criminal devoid of any political intent, they will not rethink any policy. But even if they assume it was a state, the breadth of political motives can be too great to pinpoint. For instance, several analysts interpreted the August 2012 cyber attack on oil giant Saudi Aramco as Iran retaliating against the United States for the latter's use of Stuxnet.[71] Conclusive evidence to back up such claims is hard to come by. From the instigator's perspective, the numerous possible misinterpretations undermine the attractiveness of using cyber attacks as a vector to force a policy change.

Empirically, the United States has therefore found a workaround. Instead of championing complete 'opaqueness', it has opted for a certain strategic ambiguity. Hypothetically, in the case of Stuxnet, for instance, the United States and Israel expected a change in Iranian policy on nuclear production. To achieve this, they needed to make sure that there were strong indications that they were responsible for the attack, so that the Iranians understood the sabotage operation correctly—in other words, that it was not an attack by a bored teenager. The leaking of documents, potentially coordinated by the White House, certainly helped the United States and Israel to frame their demand.[72] It is far from clear, however, whether the attack actually succeeded in achieving the set strategic goals—that is, forced any change of policy.[73]

This strategic ambiguity is not new, and follows a certain change in the United States' understanding of plausible deniability since the 1980s, after a report from the Chair Committee.[74] Under the Reagan administration, covert operations were 'overt' covert operations: the public knew or had strong suspicions of US involvement, but the government would not acknowledge this involvement in any official way. The main purpose of plausible deniability of covert actions was to avoid congressional committees indicting officials, rather than avoiding retaliation from an enemy.[75] One example is the support given to the Contras militia in Nicaragua, against the Sandinista regime. Reagan, very early in his presidency, saw the governing Sandinista party as a communist threat to the United States, and started orchestrating a coup d'état. From the start of the operation, the US government leaked details to journalists, confirmed by the then director of central intelligence, William Casey.[76] The decision to keep the Nicaragua operation less secret, according to Gregory F. Treverton, who worked on the first Senate Select Committee on Intelligence, was mainly due to the Reagan administration 'not being interested in secrecy'.[77] The policy was controversial enough for the government to have wanted to seek deniability—as in the government deception of Congress during the Iran-Contra affair—but it did not. One hypothesis is that the United States may have wanted to keep the covert operation 'overt' to put additional pressure on the Sandinista regime. By making its intentions known, the United States had greater leverage to threaten the regime and achieve its objective.

The empirical record of known sponsored espionage cyber attacks also challenges the assumption that a state needs to seek plausible deniability under any circumstances to avoid retaliation. Many reports, official and unofficial, have mentioned China systematically conducting espionage cyber attacks.[78] One of the most quoted reports was that of

Mandiant. As discussed in previous chapters, Mandiant published its findings on the group APT1 in February 2013, prompting various diplomatic discussions about the topic that even led President Obama to press President Xi Jinping about the matter in June 2013. Yet neither the revelation nor the diplomatic discussions sufficed to stop the attacks—only a political escalation of the issue led to an agreement. Less than two months after Mandiant's publication, China had resumed using exactly the same modus operandi to conduct its cyber attacks.[79] Hence, even for espionage cyber attacks, plausible deniability is not a primary requirement for evading retaliation if there is no political will on the other side to escalate the issue. For the attacking state not seeking plausible deniability, therefore, it is a matter of keeping the attack below the threshold of importance that would trigger a stronger political response.

It is also worth examining cases of sabotage cyber attacks where state sponsorship is rather unclear. A group such as the Syrian Electronic Army, where 'there are indications' that its operations are dependent on the Assad regime, seeks to voice its opinion openly and clearly.[80] It certainly does not seek to deny its actions per se, but keeps its relationship with the government purposely opaque in order to give more impetus to its attacks.

The Syrian Electronic Army (SEA) started its activity a few months after the beginning of the Syrian civil war in May 2011, a war that sought to topple the incumbent government of Bashar al-Assad.[81] The SEA has mainly targeted foreign websites, and far from seeking deniability, the group seeks acknowledgement of its capabilities. For instance, on 23 April 2013, The Associated Press Twitter account sent the following message to its 2 million followers: 'Breaking: Two Explosions in the White House and Barack Obama is injured'. Instantly, the New York Stock Exchange reacted, recording a drop in market value equivalent to $136 billion.[82] The drop lasted only three minutes, the time it took for people to realise that no explosion had occurred at the White House. An hour after the message was sent, a hacking group took credit for hijacking the Twitter account: the SEA. The group obtained the account's credentials by sending targeted spear-phishing emails to journalists.[83] But it did not only target The Associated Press. It also successfully hijacked the Twitter accounts of National Public Radio, the BBC, CBS's *60 Minutes* programme and Reuters News.[84] A few other news organisations also saw their social network accounts temporarily hijacked. For instance, the SEA hacked into *The Washington Post*, *Time* and CNN on 15 August via a third-party service that the three websites used to recommend stories to their readers.[85] Again, as soon as the attack was successful, the SEA claimed responsibility on Twitter.

A self-proclaimed leader interviewed by a journalist at *The Daily Beast* explained the reasons for the hack. 'We want to show the world the truth about what is happening in Syria,' he said, before clarifying that 'truth': 'there is no revolution in Syria, but terrorist groups killing people accusing the Syrian Arab Army'.[86] Although its motives and support for Assad are pretty clear, it is more difficult to distinguish the Syrian Electronic Army's precise relationship to his government.

There is, in fact, a minor but direct link to Assad. Presidency of the Syrian Computer Society, which hosts the SEA's website, was Assad's only public office before becoming president of Syria.[87] The SEA's choice of hosting company in May 2011 is unlikely to be completely anodyne. *The New York Times* noted that '[i]n speeches, Mr. Assad likened the S.E.A. to the government's own online security corps'.[88] For instance, during a speech on 20 June 2011, Assad mentioned the SEA as part of the army, seemingly endorsing its actions:

> The army consists of the brothers of every Syrian citizen, and the army always stands for honour and dignity. Young people have an important role to play at this stage, because they have proven themselves to be an active power. There is the electronic army which has been a real army in virtual reality.[89]

This endorsement is a form of (light) sponsorship, although it is unknown if the Syrian Electronic Army receives any other assistance, be it financial or in the form of intelligence, from Syrian governmental services.[90] Yet for Mikko Hyppönen, the chief research officer of the Finnish company F-Secure, 'the Syrian Electronic Army likes to portray [itself] as a government unit', but it is not: 'it's basically an online militia with no standing at all'.[91]

Furthermore, the identities of the individuals behind the Syrian Electronic Army are not completely unknown. In April 2013, the hacking group Anonymous managed to get inside the SEA's website and to download many usernames, passwords and email addresses.[92] By conducting a web search on the email addresses, Brian Krebs, a former journalist for *The Washington Post* and expert on researching cyber crime, found out that Mohammed Osman, a 23-year-old web designer, was part of the hacking team.[93] Osman, when contacted by the former journalist, denied being involved with the Syrian Electronic Army, and claimed that he registered the website for one of his clients. Similarly, using the same search techniques, *Vice* magazine was able to discover that Hatem Deeb was a member of the Syrian Electronic Army who went under the pseudonym of ThePro.[94] ThePro, when contacted, denied being Deeb, and claimed that Deeb was merely a friend who had contacts with the Syrian Computer Society, and had therefore registered the website.[95] In March 2016, the Department of Justice confirmed that ThePro was not Deeb. It then indicted three individuals as part of the Syrian Electronic Army: Ahmed al-Agha, 22 (ThePro), Firas Dardar, 27 ('The Shadow') and Peter Romar, 36, also a Syrian national but believed to be resident in Germany.[96]

This case vividly illustrates that when cyber attacks are conducted in order to influence events on an international scale, attribution is more likely to occur. Patriotic hackers, in general, seek as much exposure as possible, while confounding the public on their true ties to any state. Since the infamous 2007 denial-of-service attacks on Estonian infrastructures, there have been many more incidents by so-called 'patriotic hackers', enthusiastic individuals who join together against a common target to make a political point. For instance, mainland China and Taiwan have seen many of these attacks take place.[97] Commonly, attackers do not seek to specifically cover their traces, possibly because they trust that their government will not turn them in to the authorities of the victim state. They prefer a situation of ambiguity, where the role of the state in the attack is not clear. This ambiguity, of course, is a desired result for states that seek deniability.

Cyber attacks, despite the popular belief to the contrary, are not more 'plausibly deniable' than any other form of sponsored incident. Identifying the sponsorship of any incident, be it a bomb attack or an assassination, requires authorities to mount an investigation, or wait for enough information to emerge. The apparent veil of anonymity that permeates the Internet and other computer networks is just that: apparent. As with any other covert action, the sponsor of a cyber attack is likely to transpire eventually: a whistle-blower will talk, or more evidence will be found. Hence, the same techniques used to ensure plausible deniability in any other form of covert action are also applicable to cyber attacks. Mostly, these techniques are not inherently technical; they are bureaucratic trickeries designed to achieve one of two goals: to obfuscate the chain of command ordering the attack, or throw investigators off the scent. Such techniques need to be decided at the earliest stage of an operation's design in order to create a coherent alternative narrative of the event. Officials can then argue that there is more to the situation than meets the eye, and that the circumstances surrounding an incident are not as they seem. Such an understanding of plausible deniability leads to this chapter's first conclusion: that developing more forensic tools for cyber attacks is unlikely to reduce the potential for plausibly denying involvement in them.

Furthermore, it has been established that states do not always need to plausibly deny their involvement in cyber attacks. As in the 1980s, when covert actions meant 'unacknowledged overt actions', it can be strategically advantageous for countries to be in an ambiguous position. By making an attack slightly 'overt', an attacking state can make clear its purpose in attacking the victim, and what means it is prepared to use to achieve its goal. By divulging the instrumental role of the attack, therefore, an attacker can give greater encouragement to the victim to act in the desired way. On the other hand, by keeping the attack 'unacknowledged', a state retains the moral high ground at home and on the international scene, and may even avoid retaliation.

In the end, the reasons to keep an attack plausibly deniable, from the attacker's point of view, have more to do with domestic politics than international strategic considerations; from the victim's point of view, it may as well allow them to save face in case there is no political will to engage seriously with the attacker. This leads us to a second conclusion: it is not always in states' best interests to seek plausible deniability for attacks that they sponsor in the furtherance of political objectives. It is impossible to guarantee that an operation will remain secret indefinitely. Attribution will eventually occur, and the veil of deniability will fall at the same time. This implies that states may not need to go to great lengths to ensure deniability. For instance, choosing a trusted proxy hacking group is more important than choosing a remote and unconnected hacking group on which no pressure can be leveraged, even if it is better skilled or equipped. It also implies that many of the lies or cover-ups attempted by the state to ensure its deniability will most likely surface one day, creating political fallout. Plausible deniability, as appealing as it can at first appear, in fact has less to offer than promised.

CONCLUSION

The need for attribution stemming from the use of cyber attacks by criminals and states is not new, but dates back more than two decades. The Cuckoo's Egg incident of the mid-1980s was an early case of a state-sponsored cyber attack, in which the Russian secret service agency, the KGB, bought information from German hackers about US military research networks. Since then, the extent of state-sponsored attacks has largely increased, and with it the need for attribution has also been more pressing. Many more attacks have occurred and surfaced since the Cuckoo's Egg. For example, the United States has engineered the Stuxnet, Duqu and Flame malware; DarkSeoul has attacked South Korea; and the Chinese have initiated attacks that have been exposed by such companies as Mandiant and McAfee.

In each case, the question of who was behind the attacks was one of the first ones analysts needed to answer. There are several reasons for this. First of all, on a strategic level, analysts needed to consider if the attack called for a response, and if so, what type of response. Of course, states cannot respond to an attack against other states in the same way as they would against criminal groups. By not responding, states face the risk of showing that they are vulnerable to further attacks, and their inactivity would most likely be strongly criticised by their rightly concerned citizens. Second, addressing the question of the attacker's identity reflects a change of the cyber security threat landscape, wherein traditional defences are ineffective. Technical solutions, such as antivirus software or firewalls, cannot thwart these targeted and stealthy attacks. In fact, technical capabilities to engineer attacks progress at the same pace as technical capabilities to thwart these very attacks. On the technical level, when system administrators design and implement defensive solutions, attackers find new ways to circumvent them. This situation requires the implementation of solutions to find the attacker, and frustrate the attacks by restraining the attacker, whether a state or a criminal.

So attribution does matter. However, before trying to design policies to achieve the attribution of cyber attacks, which automatically hinge on matters of privacy, it is essential to understand what attribution is, how it functions, and what constraints policy-makers need to address. This book has aimed at filling those gaps.

The book has identified and examined five main constraints: the need for judgement underpinning the imperfection of attribution; the irrelevance of standards of proof in light of the will of officials to manipulate them; the role of private companies as attribution authorities; the significance of timing as a factor determining attribution; and the possibility of plausible deniability. The analysis of these five constraints has led to the rebutting of three commonly held views on the constraints for attribution: that the constraints are technical, unique and cannot be overcome. The analysis has also led to six conclusions, allowing us to see attribution in a much more nuanced way.

This concluding chapter will first revisit and bring together these six conclusions, consolidating the links between each chapter. It will then point out the limits of the research and draw a few policy lessons.

The book started by rejecting the idea that attribution is a single problem. It argued that instead of approaching it as a problem, it is much better to understand attribution as a process—as two processes, in fact. Problems have only two states: they can either have been solved, or remain unsolved. Looking at attribution as a problem does not explain how attribution changes from being 'unsolved' to being 'solved', and does not reflect the intermediary states in which attribution can lie. In contrast with problems, processes are in constant evolution, and by using them to approach attribution, it becomes possible to consider the chain of factors that turns an attacker's identity from 'unknown' to 'known'. It also becomes possible to consider more than the two states of 'unsolved' and 'solved'. In several cases, a number of important steps towards attributing attacks have already been reached before the final attribution takes place. Such nuance is important. Perceiving that an incident has been 'definitely' attributed to an entity, without any regard for this nuance, leads to action, and relegates to the background the importance of the evidence and methods used to assess the instigator's identity.

The first process identified in this book is closely linked to a judicial process whereby the police find criminals and a court judges them. The second process is linked with the collection and assessment of information by intelligence services while the executive branch acts upon the assessment. The model of separating attribution into a two-pronged process establishes differences and constraints on five levels: the authority responsible for attribution, the type of evidence the authority uses, the standard of evidence, the timing for attribution, and the issues at stake.

Distinguishing two attribution processes leads to the first conclusion: cases regarded as a threat to national security are more difficult to attribute conclusively than criminal cases, despite the mobilisation of outstanding capabilities and despite the use of lower standards of evidence to establish an entity as the instigator. For criminal attacks, uncovering an instigator's identity can be challenging, and requires the discovery of technical elements first—often an IP address, which investigators can then match to a name. With the identification of sponsors, the opposite is actually true. States are usually aware of their enemies, and can make an initial guess about instigators based on the biased criteria of the geopolitical context and the beneficiaries of the attacks. But obtaining conclusive evidence of sponsorship is then difficult. Technical elements, such as IP addresses, rarely identify sponsors. Instead, proof from leaked documents or whistle-blowers constitutes more relevant evidence. But even these do not constitute conclusive proof of sponsorship. Further, other political considerations hinder the attribution of cases that threaten national security: because attribution is likely to have political fallout with the accused state, the victim state needs to carefully weigh the benefits and disadvantages of withholding an attribution claim. The decision of whether to assign attribution is contingent upon timing: upon the current state of affairs between the victim and the accused state, in other words.

The second conclusion flows directly from the conundrum that judgement is both fallible and inescapable in attribution. It is commonly accepted that the outcome of the judicial process is a judgement. Similarly, but less well accepted, the attribution process for attacks threatening national security cannot escape the use of imperfect judgement. The attribution will therefore be similarly imperfect. This runs against one of the prevailing views on attribution: when attribution is approached as a technical problem, this implies that a technical solution exists that can provide perfect attribution. But no autonomous system is currently able to replace human judgement. This does not mean that attribution is unsolvable—quite the contrary. Approaching attribution as a process shows that in many cases, attribution has been achieved with certain caveats. For cases that threaten national security, because the stakes are political in the sense that they are linked to the public affairs of the state, the use of judgement reflects the instrumentality of attribution: decision-makers can use attribution to prompt an enemy to change behaviour, or they can decide to put attribution to one side if it will damage an already unstable relationship with a strategically important actor—for instance, by jeopardising trade relations.

The reliability of attribution with regard to judgement also has the significant effect of shifting the process towards one that depends on the trust and authority accorded to the entity making the claims. The use of judgement strongly contrasts with the standards of evidence used in legal proceedings. There are in fact a wealth of standards: 'beyond reasonable doubt' used in criminal courts, 'preponderance of the evidence' used in civil courts, or a government leader's conviction in cases of national security incidents. It is quickly apparent that there is no single, agreed standard of evidence for considering a case 'attributed'. But this does not matter. The third conclusion, following from the first and second, is that the standards of evidence and the correctness of the judgement are marginally relevant as long as attribution convinces the targeted audience of the correctness of the action that it leads to.

Attribution is rarely made for the sake of it. Attribution begets action. Attribution is therefore a precondition for taking action against an instigator. With regard to the existence of conflicting standards of evidence, governments and other investigators can easily use the standard that best fits their purpose, pushing the relevance of the standards per se into the background. Investigators can use inconclusive and misleading criteria, such as the sophistication of an attack, its geopolitical context, the political nature of the victim, the apparent origin of the instigator, the scale of the attack, and the actor it benefits, in order to frame the evidence to specifically support a desired conclusion. The focus is therefore rarely on the evidence pointing in the direction of the instigator, but essentially on the action it implies, and largely relies on the perceived authority of the accusing entity. In other words, once an organisation makes an attribution claim, the evidence can quickly become secondary to the trust accorded to the organisation making the claim. This can make the research of cases challenging, because the evidence against individuals or a state is rarely mentioned. Two reasons explain this lack of evidential scrutiny in the case of cyber security: the deep technicality of certain reports (which hinge on the difficulty of being judgemental about the case) and, more importantly, a readiness to believe in the correctness of an attribution claim. As shown by the experiments on expectation biases examined in Chapter 2, beliefs are constructed, and can easily and incorrectly influence attribution.

One of the issues raised by the reliance on judgement rather than strictly applicable legal criteria concerns the authority of entities to attribute attacks. In the national security context, the state is, theoretically, the only actor that can make authoritative and binding accusations against another state. But this does not mean that there is no space for private actors to play a role in attribution. Paradoxically, unlike the diminishing importance of the two factors discussed above, the third conclusion is that private companies have been playing an increasingly significant role with regard to the attribution of sponsors.

Private companies cannot compete with the resources of certain states for the attribution of national security incidents. Also, they do not possess the same experience in taking political factors into account to produce meaningful judgements about complex attacks. Because they focus mostly on technical elements for attribution, it is difficult for such companies to find compelling and conclusive evidence of sponsorship—which, again, is rarely technical. Yet private companies have demonstrated that they are highly capable of reshaping political agendas between countries. Their role, and this forms the fourth conclusion, has a political purpose, and is therefore not restricted to gathering technical forensics to make inconspicuous claims. And far from dismissing the attribution claims made by private companies, states react to them. Hence attribution is once again much more than a mere technical issue. Furthermore, the role of private companies in denouncing state actors as instigators is beneficial to both parties. For example, states can easily dismiss reports from companies if such reports do not match their own findings or purpose; or they can emphasise companies' findings and repeatedly cite them as evidence if need be. Reports by security companies such as Mandiant and Kaspersky Lab that expose long and ongoing espionage campaigns have also attracted a lot of media attention. In the case of Mandiant, its report has propelled the company from relative obscurity to the status of being quoted by senior officials. Therefore, because attribution by private companies benefits both company and state, the role of such companies as attributing authorities is unlikely to fade away.

The necessity of identifying attackers quickly, especially in national security contexts, also explains the use of appealing but inconclusive criteria for attribution (such as the sophistication of an attack or its geopolitical context). The time factor, therefore, appears to measure up against the certainty factor. The rationale goes as follows: the more time investigators have, the more high-standard evidence they can retrieve; consequently, the more robust the subsequent attribution claims. Yet in light of the third conclusion—that the standard of evidence is flexible and chosen on practical grounds to match the action following the attribution—the trade-off between time and certainty seems to be biased. Thus the fifth conclusion, again highlighting the political nature of attribution, is a consequence of the third: timing prevails over standards of evidence because the political elite can use attribution to advance their goals. Attribution, at the right time, can be important political leverage.

Once a judgement has been reached, a decision needs to be made whether or not to make the attribution public. A direct but misleading consequence of considering timing in terms of a measurable parameter is the impetus to work towards reducing attribution time. Yet, in this political context, time is understood in terms of external calculations rather than in terms of a measurable period between the attack and its attribution. The methods suggested to tackle the issue of timing therefore neglect the political and conjectural aspect of time, especially as they focus on 'real-time attribution'. The problems with the debate on real-time attribution are twofold. Firstly, the debate disregards an important lesson from history. Attribution times have been shortened over the past two decades mostly thanks to improvements in criminal procedures, and not thanks to technical innovations. Law enforcement agencies have become better at obtaining information and evidence via formal and informal channels. The issuing of paperwork, such as warrants, also takes less time, and communication between the different parties involved is smoother. Secondly, by putting the onus on technical devices, the concept of real-time attribution neglects the strong political dimension, and also ignores two important conclusions of this book: that attribution requires the exercise of judgement, something that no machine can automatically do, and that attribution is a political decision that needs to be taken—again, not by a machine, but by an entrusted official acting in a political capacity.

The last determining factor analysed in this book was the possibility of plausibly denying cyber attacks. As with the debate on timing, there were strong assumptions that 'plausible deniability' was a technical aspect of cyber attacks. But the sixth and final conclusion again reinforces the assumption laid out at the beginning of the book, that attribution is not a technical problem: plausible deniability relies not on technical prowess, but on bureaucratic manoeuvering, which helps create an alternative master-narrative of events. Again, therefore, the development of technical forensic apparatuses is of no avail in trying to counter the possibility of attackers plausibly denying their involvement. But a more important lesson was also that the sponsors of covert actions—the operations from which 'plausible deniability' originally drew its meaning—have almost always come out in the end. As with cyber attacks, sponsors are bound to emerge eventually, a conclusion that intersects with that on political judgement. This implies that any lies formulated in order to try to retain cover may quickly be overrun by their inconveniences. While operations remain covert, a government lacks enforcement measures to coerce the enemy towards whom the attack is targeted; it is in a weak political position to handle explanations about any hired third party; and it must lie to its electorate, thereby risking political fallout. Maintaining plausible deniability is therefore not in fact a very attractive option.

Working towards improving the process for the attribution of attacks, even if state-sponsored, should therefore not be a strategic problem for states, given its advantages.

These six conclusions show that attribution is not unique, technical or unsolvable. This is a deviation from the commonly held view, which can be explained by two factors. Firstly, many analysts working on the topic of cyber security come from a technical background. Naturally, this encourages them to look at the problem primarily from a technical standpoint. This situation is changing for the most part, with states setting cyber security strategies and looking at cyber security from a strategic angle. This leads us to the second factor informing the common understanding of attribution as a special and technical problem. When states allocate funding for cyber security, the technology-centred departments traditionally in charge of such security want to have their share of the budget. Consequently, these departments may rename several tools they use for network maintenance as 'cyber weapons', for instance, or may insist that attribution is a technical issue.[1]

So, though many scholars and policy-makers quoted want to highlight the unique nature of 'cyberspace', and therefore the unique 'problem' of attributing cyber attacks, this book contends the opposite. The similarities between the attribution of any other incident, violent or not, and the attribution of cyber attacks are striking, and more preponderant than the disparities. After a bomb explosion, there is significant uncertainty about whether it qualifies as an isolated criminal incident, or whether it should be categorised as a national security threat. Looking at the technical elements that composed the bomb (types of explosive used, delivery method) is a common start for the investigation, but this is unlikely to yield much information concerning who sponsored the bomb. Looking at the intelligence and intercepts available can reveal exchanges between suspected terrorist groups that discussed imminent attacks, and examining the pictures from surveillance cameras can help identify who placed the bomb. All such steps need to be taken in a timely fashion, and in parallel with one another. The process therefore requires good coordination between the different parties involved, and also access to the relevant material.

The non-technical aspects of attribution apply to its constraints, and also to what attribution inherently means in cases that threaten national security. All five constraints show a political component. Firstly, judgement is political. Secondly, the use of standards for attribution is mostly contingent upon the will to act rather than on the evidence per se. Thirdly, the impetus given to private companies' reports implicating other states as instigators depends on political will. Private companies do not have a mandate granting them authority to become involved in state-to-state relations—a government will have to decide if it wishes to use a company's report to confront an instigator in the hope of obtaining strategic advantages. Fourthly, the use of attribution in a timely fashion can allow the furthering of this strategic goal. Fifthly, plausible deniability is a concept with strong political resonance, used to move responsibility away from key political actors. Hence, especially in national security cases, attribution is a public statement that reflects a state's decision to pursue a case and its instigator—rarely for the sake of it, but to then act on the statement in an advantageous way.

One of the characteristics of politics is to work between the lines of what is impossible to make it possible. It is possible to relax some of the constraints that operate on the attribution process. Starting from the conclusion of this book, it is apparent that developing more technical tools is not the way to overcome the constraints of attribution. More broadly, two policy implications can henceforth be considered: one concerning the collection of evidence, and a second concerning its interpretation.

Firstly, any analysis requires evidence, and mostly non-circumstantial evidence, in order to apply a methodology that enables the analysts to use their judgement. The collection and processing of evidence, as has been shown, is strongly dependent domestically upon a sound criminal justice system, and internationally upon having a good formal and informal network of professionals working in cyber security. Fostering these relations is fundamental, as is finding ways to leverage pressure against non-cooperating Internet service providers abroad, or against the states where they are based.

For instance, concerning the exchange of information, agreements can be made between states with enforcement mechanisms. The Budapest Convention on Cybercrime already includes a few provisions in this regard, though its opponents argue that it is too eurocentric and therefore exclusive. The Budapest Convention facilitates the transfer of information from Internet service providers to a state, enabling the latter to identify the instigators of attacks. An enforcement mechanism can be crucial to ensure that such information transfers work effectively. For instance, if the information fails to reach the victim state, the latter could threaten to take action against the Internet service providers. The disincentives do not have to be restricted to cyber security-related issues. States can easily negotiate the use of other areas of state-to-state cooperation, such as those related to trade matters and aid programmes.

Domestically, the way for states to foster relations with cyber security professionals is for law enforcement agencies to work closely with private cyber security companies. This already happens to a large extent. Yet several issues have been identified and need to be resolved, most notably the issue of transparency. For example, businesses working very closely with specific governments should be clearly identified as such. Can these companies be trusted to disclose knowledge of US-sponsored cyber attacks, for example? In this regard, the competition between international companies is actually beneficial for discovering more information about cyber attacks, and makes it more likely that intelligence will eventually emerge. One of the issues that private companies face, however, is that they remain strongly focused on the technical aspects of attribution, although these are of secondary importance. Private cyber security companies need to be more innovative about setting up teams of investigative journalists and political experts who can combine the technical and political elements surrounding cyber attacks. This would help create attribution claims that are more robust, compared to the type of criticism Mandiant faced when it released its report pinpointing the Chinese military as the instigator of hundreds of attacks.

The second policy implication concerns the interpretation of collected information and the minimisation of bias. Discussions about setting legal standards of proof for attribution are hardly relevant on a national and international level. Attribution is not a matter solely for courts to decide. In fact, as we have seen, even in criminal cases, attribution can happen despite a court ruling in favour of the defendant. Hence, rather than fixing standards, it is more important to ensure that the methodologies used by various actors to interpret evidence and to make a judgement about a case are coherent, minimise bias and seriously consider various hypotheses. Cyber security companies, the media and government officials can mutually influence each other in the wrong direction by creating false expectations. In addition, following a cyber attack, it is common for different entities to play a blame game: the victim state will accuse another state of launching the attack, while the accused state will in turn accuse uncontrollable private actors within its borders. Creating a coherent methodological framework common to state officials, companies and news agencies could give more impetus to attribution claims and help overcome this blame game. Each of these three actors with a role in attribution speak a different language and use different techniques to draw conclusions. Bringing them together can surely add value to attribution claims.

This book's research has had two main limitations that future research could try to overcome. The first concerns its significant focus on political elements of attribution, which touches upon the political, but also the legal and the technical. The book has attempted to examine all three for each case study. However, mostly in order to keep the argument sharp, it has not examined much of the legal literature. The main legal constraints were discussed where relevant, but there is room for further research with a greater focus on the legal nuances.

There is an outright risk and challenge in approaching attribution from a politico-legal angle: it can be difficult to bridge the two cultures and languages.[2] Each field has its own concepts, interests and agendas, for instance. As noted by the international law expert Martti Koskenniemi, when given a task consisting of 75 per cent legal elements and 25 per cent political elements, a lawyer will adopt a legal approach from the beginning to the end.[3] 'People always visualise things as a whole,' he said.[4] In contrast to the framework used in this book, a legal approach tends to be more deterministic, working under the assumption that when specific 'preconditions are met, attribution results'.[5] Such an approach does not emphasise the role of political will and the decision-making process behind the act of making attribution public—a point central to this book. But putting the emphasis on legal issues can also provide more detail about the constraints of the process. For instance, Kevin Williams, an official with the recently founded UK National Crime Agency, mentioned that the 1990 Computer Misuse Act prevents the police from retrieving data hosted on a server abroad without the police committing a criminal act.[6] Such a hindrance makes retrieving information potentially important to courts for assessing guilt ineffective, and forces the police to rely on partnerships with other countries' law enforcement agencies to assist in their operations. Amendments to the Computer Misuse Act, and to its interpretation, have occurred gradually over the past decade and will surely need to continue.[7]

Therefore, at the international as much as at the domestic level, it is possible to compare many different approaches to attribution in terms of standards of proof used, but also in terms of the power given to law enforcement agencies to investigate or block attacks. The structure of intelligence services can also be significantly different in various countries, as can the power given them by the state and how states ensure the accountability of their services. Given that this book has relied heavily on the United States, legal scholars may regard attribution slightly differently, by examining and comparing the cases of other countries' legal systems, or even approaching the attribution-governance nexus of the Internet through the numerous norms regulating the establishment and usage of communication systems.[8] Widening the focus to the many cyber crime laws that look at accountability online (such as the United States' CAN-SPAM Act and the European Union's e-commerce directive) can provide a different understanding of several challenges that fall outside the scope of this book, but still very much pertain to the constraints of the attribution processes.[9]

This brings us to the second limitation of this book: reliance on many cases connected with the United States, which has a political and legal system different, to some extent, from those of other countries. China, for instance, may not approach attribution processes in the same way, especially as the distinction between intelligence services and law enforcement agencies may be more blurred than in the United States.

Moreover, several aspects of US involvement in cyber security may change in the future. For years, at least back to the World Summit on the Information Society first hosted in 2003, countries have expressed their desire for a more global way to govern the Internet.[11] The Internet Corporation for Assigned Names and Numbers, under the US Department of Commerce, holds a great deal of power to shape the Internet and the Web, for instance. However, many other stakeholders (private companies, civil societies and other nation-states) also have important roles in shaping the Internet, and want to have a greater say in decision-making. The outcome of the World Summit on the Information Society has never really changed anything, and many suggestions were rejected by the US State Department when the revision of a binding telecommunication treaty included references to the Internet at the 2012 World Conference on International Telecommunications. In fact, the United States did not even sign the treaty as a result.[12] But following Edward Snowden's revelations in the summer of 2013 that US intelligence services had extensive surveillance programmes involving telecommunication companies, many key operators of Internet governance started voicing their unease with the current model of such governance. The Internet Corporation for Assigned Names and Numbers and other core players such as the Internet Engineering Task Force, the Internet Architecture Board, the World Wide Web Consortium and the Internet Society, issued a joint statement for the 'acceleration of globalization' of their functions.[13] This call reflected the erosion of trust following the Snowden revelations, and a desire to move the Internet away from a US-centric model.

Internet governance, a very technical subject with large political stakes, plays a role in attribution, mainly at the technical level: it can be easier for a state other than the United States to twist the arm of an Internet service provider to obtain a match with a name if it can threaten the provider with revoking its operating licence, for instance. Slow modifications in the model of Internet governance may therefore come to mean that the United States plays a lesser role in the attribution of international cases. In the future, US agencies may not intervene to the same extent in cases where other domestic services are able to handle them. Their current involvement is predicated upon the fact that the incumbent responsibility to monitor, react and attribute attacks is still being defined. 'We are not, as a society, comfortable yet with a very active role of government in cyberspace', said Bruce McConnell, a former official in charge of cyber security at the Department of Homeland Security.[14] This applies to other governments as well, and to private actors' roles in attribution.

As these roles are still being defined, another factor may push the United States away from driving many facets of attribution. Along with the trend for the globalisation of Internet governance, it has emerged that different governments are fragmenting the Internet by imposing certain policy restrictions. Content deemed politically dangerous is not, for instance, accessible from China or Saudi Arabia. Similarly, certain content deemed to breach copyright laws is not available to a user located in the United Kingdom searching on Google. Ironically, the then UK foreign secretary William Hague spoke in 2013 against this 'balkanisation' of the Internet.[15]

The trend started a few years ago. In 2010, the political scientist Ian Bremmer wrote in *Foreign Affairs* that 'borders are about to become much more important. The result will be a world that has not one Internet but a set of interlinked intranets closely monitored by various governments'.[16] As governments closely monitor their own networks, they will increasingly have the authority and the capacity to trace attacks within their own jurisdiction. This means that attacks may have greater difficulty reaching a certain country from outside its borders, depending on the level of filtering in place. For instance, as a reaction to Snowden's revelation that US intelligence services captured much of the metadata traffic passing through US nodes, German telecommunication providers, including Deutsche Telekom, joined the German interior minister Hans-Peter Friedrich in calling for attempts to keep German emails within the country's borders in order to limit the chance of interception by any foreign entity.[17] In fact, Friedrich even called for such a limitation to be enshrined in law.[18] This is more than a simple request: the project is already under way under the name 'Internetz', a compound word combining 'Internet' and the German word for network.[19] A similar reaction to the revelations was the Brazilian president Dilma Rousseff's call for the country to set up its own e-national email service, and to legally require information about Brazilians to be stored within the country.[20] This would prevent other countries such as the United States from easily intruding into Brazilians' lives, while it would also make it easier for Brazilian security services to access the data. In a way, this could make attribution easier. However, a new law known as the Marco Civil Law (April 2014) did not contain such requirements.[21]

Switzerland has also registered an increase of interest in its main data centre—located in a former Second World War bunker—now that users are moving away from US companies.[22] Banks, pharmaceutical companies and insurance companies are storing their confidential data in the Swiss centre, where they are more confident that the NSA will not be able to access their details—although the United States could always legally request an information exchange, with which the data centre would likely comply. One of the companies using the bunker and offering secure storage of companies' data, SecureSafe, claimed in 2014 that it had been attracting 1,000 new clients every day since the Snowden revelations.[23]

Following the 'balkanisation' of the Internet, also called the 'fragmentation of the world wide web' by Eugene Kaspersky, the international tracing of attacks may become more difficult, because it will involve governments exchanging closely guarded data monitored by their own intelligence services on their own networks.[24] At the same time, networks will be more secure—or so the rationale goes—as the new networks will be 'air gapped' from the Internet.[25] How far governments are willing to trade this information will depend on what they can negotiate in return for it, and how much they trust the other government.

This book could also be a springboard for further research on attribution policies. Attribution has many implications for privacy, and much of the debate on retention of communication data is applicable to the debate on attribution. There is a real need for discussion of the extent to which it is useful to retain data, for what purposes and by whom. In the US, Keith Alexander, at the head of the NSA, reportedly told government officials: 'I can't defend the country until I'm into all the networks'.[26] Although the acquisition of all data by intelligence services may not be quite so warranted, Alexander's remark raises the important question of how much data should be kept, and what resources are required.

In fact, at least two arguments stand against the efficacy of collecting all possible data. Firstly, empirical evidence from the Czech Republic suggests that having 'too much' communication data can hinder investigations. In 2011, the Constitutional Court of the Czech Republic declared unconstitutional the law imposed by a European Union directive on data retention. Following the scratching of the law, the police could no longer use communications data as they had been accustomed to doing. But the statistics did not show case resolution being impeded. The clearance rate increased from 37.55 per cent to 38.54 per cent between 2010 and 2011.[27] In general, the more information the police obtain, the more they have to wade through, and the more difficult and complex their task becomes. Supporting this argument, the researcher Ian Brown has noted that 'data retention could raise the crime clearance rate by 0.002 per cent at best'.[28] By significantly augmenting the amount of data available, it becomes more difficult to find relevant information, if it is even there. The former head of the NSA General Keith Alexander has argued that 'you need the haystack to find the needle'.[29] But a possible line of reply is that 'if you are looking for a needle in a haystack, it doesn't help to throw more hay on the stack'.[30]

The withdrawal of laws on retention of communication data may in the future expand well beyond the Czech Republic. Many other European countries have run into problems of one sort or another with implementing the directive.[31] Moreover, in December 2013, a non-binding legal report from the European Court of Justice opined that requiring the storage of communication data for two years 'is a serious interference with citizens' right to privacy'.[32] And in April 2014, the umbrella Court of Justice of the European Union declared the data retention directive invalid.[33] A change in the law would have important policy implications for the ways in which police are forced to use other methods to carry out their investigations—which may not necessarily lead to reduced efficacy.

This brings us to the second argument against the efficacy of mass data collection: many other investigation methods exist. The empirical records presented in this book show that these not only exist for attribution, but are already in use. These include open-source searches to link a pseudonym to personal information, and informants and human sources such as officials. Other dubious methods examined include 'hack back', the infection of criminals' computers with malware to gather evidence (such as the German *Bundestrojaner*). A 2014 New America Foundation study of 225 cases of terrorism also pointed in this direction, finding that the bulk collection of metadata had 'had no discernible impact on preventing acts of terrorism'.[34] The Foundation discovered that, in most cases, conventional investigative techniques such as those cited above helped initiate the investigation into cases, a similar conclusion to that reached by a White House-appointed panel the previous month, which had concluded that asking for a court warrant for specific cases would be just as effective.[35] These studies question the necessity of collecting meta-data not just for the attribution of cyber attacks, but also for wider criminal and terrorism-related cases. They also contradict, perhaps unsurprisingly, the intelligence communities' claims. For instance, a 2005 NSA statement disclosed in the Snowden files noted that the use of communication metadata 'has been a contribution to virtually every successful rendition of suspects and often, the deciding factor'.[36] It is unclear whether the NSA can genuinely substantiate such claims, or if this is merely a form of wishful thinking.

A policy for attribution not only needs to walk the fine line of allowing users to be at times anonymous and at others identifiable, but also needs to provide mechanisms to ensure people can prove their identities in a reliable fashion. The identification of human beings in society is a difficult problem, even in situations of direct interaction between individuals.[37] Criminals can forge national documents, passports included, and this can create problems online as well. But the greatest difficulty may not lie where expected— in designing a resilient system of identification—but rather in overcoming people's unwillingness to accept such a system in the first place. A few states, Belgium and Germany for instance, have attempted to create a means of identification that is also usable online.[39] But the public has largely shunned these schemes, seemingly showing a preference for anonymity. This rejection by the public may partly stem from fear that the state would start exploiting such systems, a fear also present in the United States.[39] For instance, South Korea, via its 2007 Real Name Verification Law, created a system that identified its citizens, and forced them to be identifiable online when posting comments on websites. The law had positive effects in reducing the amount of unethical behaviour occurring under the protection of anonymity.[40] However, in August 2012, a court declared the law unconstitutional because it impeded freedom of speech.[41] Finding the right balance for attribution in general, and not only of cyber attacks, is not easy.

In a similar fashion to the way that citizens shun online national identification systems, programmes that enable people to be anonymous online are only used by a very small portion of Internet users. The users of Tor, by far the most famous such programme, represent 0.015 per cent of the global Internet population.[42] This figure demonstrates that users may not be ready to go to great lengths to be more anonymous online. Users may therefore be satisfied with the status quo: they are not completely anonymous, and their IP address does not immediately give away their real names, but they are identifiable by law enforcement agencies if the need arises. The lack of enthusiasm for anonymous services guaranteeing authentication may also be explained by people's trust in the Internet, or their lack of knowledge and understanding of cyber security—the two not being completely dissociated. Notably, however, users are increasingly technology-savvy, and are also aware of the risks they face online. This could help with engaging users in the future, and creating a safer environment.

Yet, as this book has shown, individuals are not the sole actors interacting online. Companies and states also play a preponderant role, not only in designing laws and policies, but also in instigating cyber attacks. A stronger policy focus on attribution will therefore hopefully create a deterrent effect against the use of cyber attacks by not only criminals, but also corporations and states. Focusing on a policy of deterrence via attribution, rather than the development of offensive strategies, could ensure the prevention of escalating tensions.[43] With the number of connected devices increasing, and the range of possibilities that they offer for exploitation also rising, the topics of cyber security and attribution can only become increasingly prominent. Therefore, shaping 'appropriate' policy for attribution now will influence cyber security for years to come and should not be dismissed lightly. The responsibility of policy-makers, and also corporate executives and individuals, to understand attribution correctly and act accordingly will have repercussions for the way they seek to shape our society in terms of privacy, surveillance and Internet governance. This book is only the first step in studying attribution. Many more challenges remain to be studied and overcome in order to refine our understanding of how to achieve it, and one such challenge concerns the appropriate balance between privacy, anonymity, and the powers given to the security apparatus when implementing attribution mechanisms.

NOTES

INTRODUCTION

1. Sean Sullivan, 'Trojan:Android/Pincer.A', *F-Secure*, 5 April 2013. Fortunately, despite all the fears provoked by the idea of mobile phone malware, until now there have been only a few incidens, and the infection rates have been low. *The Economist*, 'The threat in the pocket', 18 October 2013.

2. Brian Krebs, 'Who Wrote the Pincer Android Trojan?', *KrebsOnSecurity*, 27 August 2013.

3. Regarding the professionalisation and specialisation of cyber attacks, see for instance Jonathan Lusthaus, 'How organised is organised cyber-crime?', *Global Crime* 14, 1 (2013).

4. Jonathan Watts and Adam Gabbatt, 'China denies Gmail hacking accusations', *The Guardian*, 2 June 2011.

5. For a more detailed review of the possible different meanings of a state-sponsored attack, see Healey, 'Beyond Attribution: Seeking National Responsibility for Cyber Attacks'.

6. Sergio Caltagirone, Andrew Pendergast and Christopher Betz, *The Diamond Model of Intrusion Analysis* (Arlington, VA: Threat Connect, 2013), pp. 1–61.

7. Ibid.

8. Atlantic Council, 'Lessons from Our Cyber Past: The First Cyber Cops', 16 May 2012.

9. NATO Parliamentary Assembly, 'Information and National Security' (Brussels: NATO, 2011), p. 22.

10. Jane Holl Lute, 'Cyber Security: A Mission Impossible?' (paper presented at the Lennart Meri Conference, Tallinn, 2014).

11. William J. Lynn, 'Roundtable on Cyber Security with Australian Business and Civic Leaders', US Department of Defense, http://

archive.defense.gov/speeches/speech.aspx?speechid=1422, accessed 30 June 2016.

12. Jared Serbu, 'DoD cyber strategy aims at deterrence', *Federal News Radio*, 15 July 2011.

13. Joel Brenner, *America the Vulnerable* (New York: Penguin Press, 2011), pp. 13–14.

14. Richard A. Clarke and Steven Andreasen, 'Cyberwar's threat does not justify a new policy of nuclear deterrence', *The Washington Post*, 15 June 2013; Tim Stevens, 'A Cyberwar of Ideas? Deterrence and Norms in Cyberspace', *Contemporary Security Policy* 33, 1 (2012); Dmitri Alperovitch, 'Towards Establishment of Cyberspace Deterrence Strategy' (paper presented at the International Conference on Cyber Conflict, Tallinn, 2011); Martin C. Libicki, *Cyberdeterrence and Cyberwar* (Santa Monica, CA: RAND, 2009); Clement Guitton, 'Criminals and Cyber Attacks: The Missing Link Between Attribution and Deterrence', *International Journal of Cyber Criminology* 6, 2 (2012).

15. Atlantic Council, 'International Engagement on Cyber Conference', http://www.atlanticcouncil.org/news/transcripts/international-engagement-on-cyber-conference-panel-1-3-29-11-transcript, accessed 30 June 2016.

16. The White House, 'International Strategy for Cyberspace', ed. President of the United States (Washington, DC: 2011), p. 13.

17. Robert K. Knake, 'Untangling Attribution: Moving to Accountability in Cyberspace' (Washington, DC: Subcommittee on Technology and Innovation, 2010).

18. W. Earl Boebert, 'A Survey of Challenges in Attribution' (paper presented at the Workshop on Deterring Cyber Attacks: Informing Strategies and Developing Options for U.S. Policy, Washington, DC: 2010), p. 51; Joe Pato et al., 'Aintno: Demonstration of Information Accountability on the Web' (paper presented at the International Conference on Privacy, Security, Risk, and Trust, Boston, MA: 2011), p. 1072; Richard Clayton, 'Anonymity and traceability in cyberspace' (doctoral dissertation, University of Cambridge, 2005), p. 36.

19. Anthony Loyd, 'Army of hackers takes on the world', *The Times*, 8 March 2010.

20. One exception is a peer-reviewed article by two scholars at King's College London and with whom the author worked closely: Thomas Rid and Ben Buchanan, 'Attributing Cyber Attacks', *Journal of Strategic Studies* 38, 1–2 (2015), pp. 4–37.

21. By 'technical', this book means the activities encompassing the automatic recording or processing of data by a system.

22. 'Blueprint for a Secure Cyber Future' (Washington, DC: 2011).

23. The White House, 'Cyberspace Policy Review' (Washington, DC: 2009); 'Department of Defense Cyberspace Policy Report: A Report to Congress Pursuant to the National Defense Authorization Act for Fiscal Year 2011, Section 934' (Washington, DC: 2011).

24. US Congress, 'Cybersecurity Act of 2012' (Washington, DC: 2012).

25. Dan Kaplan, 'Offensive line: Fighting back against hackers', *SC Magazine* (2012).

26. Steven Chabinsky, 'Cyber Warfare', talk at American Center for Democracy (New York, 2013), https://www.youtube.com/watch?v=Uiz2R_f1Lxo, accessed 29 July 2016.

27. Ibid.

28. Ibid.

29. Ian Brown, David D. Clark and Dirk Trossen, 'Should Specific Values Be Embedded In The Internet Architecture?' (paper presented at the Re-Architecting the Internet workshop, New York, 2011); Sophie Stalla-Bourdillon, 'The flip side of ISP's liability regimes: The ambiguous protection of fundamental rights and liberties in private digital spaces', *Computer Law & Security Review* 26 (2010).

30. Jeffrey Hunker, Bob Hutchinson and Jonathan Marguiles, 'Role and Challenges for Sufficient Cyber-Attack Attribution', in *Institute for Information Infrastructure Protection* (Hanover, NH: Dartmouth College, 2008).

31. Bruce Schneier, 'Anonymity and the Internet', 25 March 2005, https://www.schneier.com/blog/archives/2005/03/anonymity_and_t.html, accessed 30 June 2016.

32. Peter Sommer and Ian Brown, 'Reducing Systemic Cybersecurity Risks', in *Future Global Shocks*, ed. OECD (Paris: OECD, 2011).

33. Jack Goldsmith, 'The pervasive cyberthreat that goes unchallenged', *The Washington Post*, 25 November 2011.

34. Sandro Gaycken, Thilo Marauhn and Paul Cornish, 'Attribution—How to live without it?', in German Council on Foreign Relations, *Cyber Security* (Berlin: German Council on Foreign Relations, 2012).

35. Julian Richards, *A Guide to National Security* (Oxford: Oxford University Press, 2011), pp. 42–3.

36. David D. Clark and Susan Landau, 'Untangling Attribution' (paper presented at the Workshop on Deterring CyberAttacks: Informing Strategies and Developing Options for U.S. Policy, Washington, DC: 2010), p. 28; Kenneth Rapoza, 'War Drums Beat Louder For "World War C"', *Forbes*, 6 October 2013; InfoSec Island, 'Attribution Problems Hinder U.S. Cyberwar Strategy', 7 June 2011; Ben Bain, 'Tracking a cyberattack', *FCW*, 15 August 2008; Marcus J. Ranum, 'Cyberwar: About Attribution (identifying your attacker)', *Fabius Maxim*, 21 October

2011; ForexTV, 'The US at Cyber War? Chinese Hacking Debate Intensifies', *ForexTV*, 14 March 2013; Marie Harbo Dahle, 'Cyberattacks: A short guide', *Atlantic Voices* 2, 5 (2012).

37. Mike McConnell, 'Mike McConnell on how to win the cyber-war we're losing', *The Washington Post*, 28 February 2010.

38. US Department of Defense, 'DOD, Partners Better Prepared for Cyber Attacks', 18 October 2011, http://archive.defense.gov/news/newsarticle.aspx?id=65709, accessed 1 July 2016.

39. Sheldon Whitehouse, 'At West Point, Whitehouse Calls for Greater Awareness of Cyber Threats', 4 June 2012, http://www.whitehouse.senate.gov/news/release/at-west-point-whitehouse-calls-for-greater-awareness-of-cyber-threats, accessed 1 July 2016.

40. Atlantic Council, 'International Engagement'.

41. The scholar of international law Marco Roscini also contends that 'difficulties in identification and attribution are not unique to cyber-operations, as they are a well-known problem also with regard to international terrorism and asymmetric warfare in general. Marco Roscini, *Cyber Operations and the Use of Force in International Law* (New York: Oxford University Press, 2014), p. 33, p. 281.

42. For instance, two researchers on cyber security wrote: 'From a technical perspective, it is theoretically possible to solve the attribution problem. It is, however, difficult to see how technical devices could ever directly determine who sponsored an attack (e.g. states and the level of their sponsorship, from financing to ordering the attack), a question embedded within the topic of attribution.' Peter Feaver and Kenneth Geers, '"When the Urgency of Time and Circumstances Clearly Does Not Permit…": Predelegation in Nuclear and Cyber Scenarios', in *Cyber Analogies*, ed. Emily O. Goldman and John Arquilla (Monterey, CA: Naval Postgraduate School, 2014), p. 39.

43. William J. Broad, John Markoff and David E. Sanger, 'Israeli Test on Worm Called Crucial in Iran Nuclear Delay', *The New York Times*, 15 January 2011; Josh Halliday, 'Stuxnet worm is the "work of a national government agency"', *The Guardian*, 24 September 2010.

44. David E. Sanger, 'Obama Order Sped Up Wave of Cyberattacks Against Iran', *The New York Times*, 1 June 2012.

45. *The Guardian*, 'Former US general James Cartwright named in Stuxnet leak inquiry', 28 June 2013. Julia Harte, 'Retired US general pleads guilty to lying to FBI in Stuxnet leak case', *Reuters*, 17 October 2016.

46. *Der Spiegel*, '"Als Zielobjekt markiert": Der Enthüller Edward Snowden über die geheime Macht der NSA', 8 July 2013.

47. House of Commons, 'Defence and Cyber Security' (London: UK Parliament, 2012).

48. Charlotte Krol, AP and APTN, 'Barack Obama explains US sanctions on North Korea over Sony attack', *The Telegraph*, 2 January 2015.

49. Andrew Bennett and Alexander L. George, *Case Studies and Theory Development in the Social Sciences* (London: MIT Press, 2004), p. 5.

50. Kathleen M. Eisenhardt and Melissa E. Graebner, 'Theory Building from Cases: Opportunities and Challenges', *Academy of Management Journal* 50, 1 (2007), p. 27.

51. Kathleen M. Eisenhardt, 'Building Theories from Case Study Research', *The Academy of Management Review* 14, 4 (1989), p. 533.

52. Rolf Johansson, 'Case Study Methodology' (paper presented at the Methodologies in Housing Research conference, Stockholm, 2003).

53. Richard A. Clarke and Robert K. Knake, *Cyber War: The Next Threat to National Security and What to Do About It* (New York: Ecco, 2010).

54. Philip Shenon, *The Commission: The Uncensored History of the 9/11 Investigation* (New York: Twelve, 2008).

55. Mark E. Russinovich, *Zero Day* (New York: Thomas Dunne Books, 2011); Dan Verton, *Black Ice: The Invisible Threat of Cyber-Terrorism* (Emeryville, CA: McGraw Hill Osborne Media, 2003); International Group of Experts, *Tallinn Manual on the International Law Applicable to Cyber Warfare*, ed. Michael N. Schmitt (Cambridge: Cambridge University Press, 2013). Noticeably, other works equivalently base their conceptual analysis on imagining how the field of cyber security might develop in the future. See for instance: Chris C. Demchak, 'Economic and Political Coercion and a Rising Cyber Westphalia', in *Peacetime Regime for State Activities in Cyberspace*, ed. Katharina Ziolkowski (Tallinn: NATO CCD COE Publication, 2013), pp. 612–17; Randall R. Dipert, 'Other-Than-Internet (OTI) Cyberwarfare: Challenges for Ethics, Law, and Policy', *Journal of Military Ethics* 12, 1 (2013).

56. International Group of Experts, *Tallinn Manual*, p. 106.

57. Ibid.

58. Ibid., p. 109.

59. Roscini, *Cyber Operations and the Use of Force*, p. 284.

60. Whether the purposes were really malicious and intentional can only emerge following attribution. For a breach to count as an attack, the assumption that it is not of accidental nature is sufficient.

61. John D. Howard and Thomas A. Longstaff, 'A Common Language for Computer Security Incidents' (New Mexico and Livermore, CA: Sandia National Laboratories, 1998).

62. Annalee Newitz, 'The Bizarre Evolution of the Word "Cyber"', *io9*, 16 September 2013.

63. Michael N. Schmitt and Liis Vihul, 'The International Law of Attribution During Proxy "Wars" in Cyberspace', *Fletcher Security Review* 1

(2014); Scott J. Shackelford, 'State Responsibility for Cyber Attacks: Competing Standards for a Growing Problem' (paper presented at the Conference on Cyber Conflict, Tallinn, 2010); Ian Walden, *Computer Crimes and Digital Investigation* (New York: Oxford University Press, 2007); Roscini, *Cyber Operations and the Use of Force*.

64. Roscini, *Cyber Operations and the Use of Force*, p. 34.
65. ITU-T, 'Overview of cybersecurity', in *X.1205* 64 (Geneva: ITU, 2008).
66. This categorisation of cyber crime into crimes targeting computers and crimes facilitated by the use of a computer is common in the literature. United Nations Office on Drugs and Crime, 'Comprehensive Study on Cybercrime' (New York: United Nations, 2013).
67. Ian Brown and Christopher T. Marsden, *Regulating Code* (Cambridge, MA: MIT Press, 2014), p. x.
68. Ibid., p. 60.
69. Alan Travis, 'Surveillance society soon a reality, report suggests', *The Guardian*, 11 November 2014.
70. P.W. Singer and Allan Friedman, *Cybersecurity and Cyberwar: What Everyone Needs to Know* (New York: Oxford University Press, 2014), p. 74.
71. Neelie Kroes, 'Towards more confidence and more value for European Digital Citizens' (paper presented at the European Roundtable on the Benefits of Online Advertising for Consumers, Brussels, 17 September 2010).
72. Brown and Marsden, *Regulating Code*, p. 53.
73. David A. Wheeler and Gregory N. Larsen, 'Techniques for Cyber Attack Attribution' (Alexandria, VA: Institute for Defense Analyses, 2003).
74. Isaac Ben Israel and Lior Tabansky, 'An Interdisciplinary Look at Security Challenges in the Information Age', *Military and Strategic Affairs* 3, 3 (2011).
75. Valerie Manusov and Brian Spitzberg, 'Attribution Theory—Finding Good Cause in the Search for Theory', in *Engaging Theories in Interpersonal Communication*, ed. D. O. Braithwaite & L. A. Baxter (Thousand Oaks, CA: Sage Publications, 2008).
76. Sanford Sherizen, 'Criminological concepts and research findings relevant for improving computer crime control', *Computer & Security* 9, 3 (1990), p. 219.
77. Harry Rubin, Leigh Fraser and Monica Smith, 'US and International Law Aspects of the Internet: Fitting Square Pegs Into Round Holes', *International Journal of Law and Information Technology* 3, 2 (1995), p. 133.
78. William Bechtel, 'Attributing Responsibility to Computer Systems', *Metaphilosophy* 16, 4 (1985).

79. Joachim J. Savelsberg and Peter Brühl, *Constructing white-collar crime: rationalities, communication, power* (Philadelphia, PA: University of Pennsylvania Press, 1994), p. 34. James Backhouse and Gurpreet Dhillon, 'Managing computer crime: a research outlook', *Computer & Security* 14 (2013), p. 650.

80. Concerning nuclear weapons, see Tom R. Tyler and Kathleen M. McGraw, 'The Threat of Nuclear War: Risk Interpretation and Behavioral Response', *Journal of Social Issues* 39, 1 (1983).

81. None of the following works mention the word 'attribution', although they deal with it: Bruce Sterling, *The Hacker Crackdown: Law and Disorder on the Electronic Frontier* (New York: Bantam Books, 1992); Eugene H. Spafford and Stephen A. Weeber, 'Software forensics: Can we track code to its authors?', *Computer & Security* 12, 6 (1993); Winn Schwartau, *Information Warfare: Chaos on the Electronic Superhighway* (New York: Thunder's Mouth Press, 1994), p. 74.

82. Federal News Service, 'Prepared statement of Michael A. Vatis, Director, National Infrastructure Portection Center, Federal Bureau of Investigation before the Senate Judiciary Committee, Subcommittee on Technology and Terrorism', Federal News Service, 6 October 1999; The White House, 'The National Strategy to Secure Cyberspace' (2003), p. 50. Concerning the usage of 'attribution' in the nuclear threat literature, see for instance: Wendell B. McKeown, 'Information Operations: Countering the Asymmetric Threat to the United States' (Carlisle Barracks, PA: US Army War College, 1999); E. Anders Eriksson, 'Viewpoint: Information Warfare—Hype or reality?', *The Nonproliferation Review* 6, 3 (1999), p. 63; National Research Council, 'Making the Nation Safer: The Role of Science and Technology in Countering Terrorism' (Washington, DC: 2002).

83. Another similar but opposite policy change came two years later. While in December 1999 the government chose to potentially restrict its access to intercepts, the policies after 9/11 ensured that it could have as much access as possible to all data transiting via the United States. This will be examined further in the next chapter.

84. Timothy C. May, 'The Crypto Anarchist Manifesto', 22 November 1992, http://www.activism.net/cypherpunk/crypto-anarchy.html, accessed 29 July 2016 (Aptos, CA: 1992).

85. See for instance Chaum's design to allow users to stay anonymous in online exchanges. D. Chaum, 'Untraceable electronic mail return addresses and digital pseudonyms', *Communications of the ACM* 24, 2 (1981).

86. Steven Levy, *Crypto: How the Code Rebels Beat the Government Saving Privacy in the Digital Age* (New York: Penguin Books, 2001), p. 207

87. Ibid.

88. May, 'The Crypto Anarchist Manifesto'.
89. This argument can be found again concerning the debate on meta-data conservation. For instance, in 2012 the government of the United Kingdom tried for the second time to introduce a Communications Data Bill, which aimed at increasing police access to all telecommunication metadata. 'There has been a degradation in [the police's] monitoring ability,' said Michael Ellis, a member of parliament who spoke during the debate on the 'Draft Communications Data Bill (17 July 2012)' (London: 2012). The final report of the committee later concluded, however, that there was not enough evidence supporting such a stance. Joint Committee on the Draft Communications Data Bill, 'Draft Communications Data Bill' (London: House of Lords, House of Commons, 2012).
90. Levy, *Crypto*, p. 284.
91. Ibid.
92. This argument appeared again when discussing the UK Draft Communications Data Bill. For instance: 'It would be difficult, for reasons you would understand, to be hugely specific about the precise type of data, or indeed the companies in some cases, because that is something that we, sitting here, do not want to tell all the criminals right now,' said Cressida Dick, assistant commissioner at the Metropolitan Police, 'Draft Communications Data Bill (12 July)', (London: 2012).
93. Levy, *Crypto*, pp. 235–6.
94. Steven Levy, 'Battle of the Clipper Chip', *The New York Times*, 12 June 1994.
95. Levy, *Crypto*, p. 258.
96. Ibid., p. 250.
97. John Markoff, 'Flaw discovered in federal plan for wiretapping', *The New York Times*, 2 June 1994.
98. Levy, *Crypto*, p. 263.
99. National Research Council, 'Cryptography's Role in Securing the Information Society', ed. Kenneth W. Dam and Herbert S. Lin (Washington, DC: National Academy Press, 1996).
100. Ibid., p. 251.
101. Levy, *Crypto*, p. 6296.
102. Ibid., p. 6297.
103. Ibid., p. 7301.
104. Robert S. Mueller III, 'The Future of Cyber Security from the FBI's Perspective', in Fordham University, *International Conference on Cyber Security 2013* (New York: Fordham University, 2013).
105. Ibid.

106. Clark and Landau, 'Untangling Attribution', p. 25.
107. Boebert, 'A Survey of Challenges in Attribution', p. 41.
108. Debra K. Decker, 'Before the First Bomb Goes Off: Developing Nuclear Attribution Standards and Policies', (Cambridge, MA: Harvard Kennedy School, 2011).

1. MODELLING ATTRIBUTION

1. Part of this chapter is taken from Clement Guitton, 'Modelling Attribution' (paper presented at the 12th European Conference on Information Warfare and Security, Jyväskylä, 11–12 July 2013).
2. Sam Jones, 'Cyber warfare: Iran opens a new front', Financial Times, 26 April 2016.
3. Ibid.
4. Leon Panetta, 'Text of Speech by Secretary of Defense Leon Panetta' (New York: Business Executives for National Security, 2012); Leon Panetta and Martin Dempsey, 'News Briefing', US Department of Defense, 25 October 2012.
5. Associated Press, 'Official: US blames Iran hackers for cyberattacks', The Washington Post, 11 October 2012.
6. Anick Jesdanun, 'New virus snarls hundreds of thousands of machines worldwide', The Associated Press, 3 May 2004.
7. Robert Lemos, 'Microsoft to reward informants after Sasser conviction', SecurityFocus, 8 July 2005.
8. The separation of powers between the executive and the judiciary is set in the US Constitution. This is also the case for many other democracies around the world, where a similar definition is taken. John A. Fairlie, 'The Separation of Powers', Michigan Law Review 21, 4 (1923), p. 393.
9. Tom Parker et al., Cyber Adversary Characterisation (Rockland, MA Syngress Publishing, 2004).
10. It was notably used in the following works: Van Nguyen, 'Attribution of Spear Phishing Attacks: A Literature Survey' (Edinburgh, South Australia: Government of Australia, 2013). Eric M. Hutchins, Michael J. Cloppert and Rohan M. Amin, 'Intelligence-Driven Computer Network Defense Informed by Analysis of Adversary Campaigns and Intrusion Kill Chains' (paper presented at the 6th Annual International Conference on Information Warfare and Security, Washington, DC: 2011); Jeff Carr, 'The Cyber Kill Chain: Trademarked by Lockheed Martin?', Digital Dao, 18 August 2013; Sergio Caltagirone, Andrew Pendergast and Christopher Betz, The Diamond Model of Intrusion Analysis (Arlington, VA: Threat Connect, 2013), pp. 1–61.

11. In comparison, explaining the motives that rationally led to the deviant act is of primary importance for Japanese courts. Mariko Oi, 'Japan crime: Why do innocent people confess?', *BBC News*, 2 January 2013.

12. Brian N. Cox, 'International Police Officer Criminal Investigation Training Manual' (Windsor, ON: Criminal Investigation Training Bureau, 2011).

13. Andrea Lelli, 'Zeusbot/Spyeye P2P Updated, Fortifying the Botnet', Symantec Connect, http://www.symantec.com/connect/blogs/zeus-botspyeye-p2p-updated-fortifying-botnet, accessed 4 July 2016.

14. Caltagirone, Pendergast and Betz, 'The Diamond Model of Intrusion Analysis', p. 12; Don Cohen and K. Narayanaswamy, 'Survey/Analysis of Levels l II, IIII—Attack Attribution Techniques' (Los Angeles, CA: CS3 Inc., 2004).

15. Kyle Dobitz et al., 'The Characterization and Measurement of Cyber Warfare' (Omaha, NE: Global Innovation and Strategy Center, 2008); Jason Healey, 'Beyond Attribution: Seeking National Responsibility for Cyber Attacks' (Washington, DC: Atlantic Council, 2012).

16. Susanne W. Brenner, *Cyber Threats: The Emerging Fault Lines of the Nation State* (Oxford: Oxford University Press, 2009), p. 96.

17. David D. Clark and Susan Landau, 'Untangling Attribution' (paper presented at the Workshop on Deterring CyberAttacks: Informing Strategies and Developing Options for U.S. Policy, Washington, DC: 2010), p. 37; W. Earl Boebert, 'A Survey of Challenges in Attribution' (paper presented at the Workshop on Deterring Cyber Attacks: Informing Strategies and Developing Options for U.S. Policy, Washington, DC: 2010).

18. David A. Wheeler and Gregory N. Larsen, 'Techniques for Cyber Attack Attribution' (Alexandria, VA: Institute for Defense Analyses, 2003); Richard Clayton, 'Anonymity and traceability in cyberspace' (doctoral dissertation, University of Cambridge, 2005); Jeffrey Hunker, Bob Hutchinson and Jonathan Margulies, 'Role and Challenges for Sufficient Cyber-Attack Attribution', in *Institute for Information Infrastructure Protection* (Hanover, NH: Dartmouth College, 2008), p. 10; Clark and Landau, 'Untangling Attribution', p. 39; Olivier Thonnard, Wim Mees and Marc Dacier, 'On a Multi-criteria Clustering Approach for Attack Attribution', *ACM Special Interest Group on Knowledge Discovery and Data Mining Explorations* 12, 1 (2010); Olivier Thonnard, 'Vers un regroupement multicritères comme outil d'aide à l'attribution d'attaque dans le cyber-espace' (École Nationale Supérieure des Télécommunications, 2010); Paulo Shakarian et al., 'An Argumentation-Based Framework to Address the Attribution Problem in Cyber-Warfare', Academy of Science and Engineering, 27 April 2014.

19. Thomas Rid and Ben Buchanan, 'Attributing Cyber Attacks', *Journal of Strategic Studies* 38, 1–2 (2015), pp. 4–37.
20. Ibid., p. 13.
21. Tess Owen, 'The US Has Indicted Three Alleged Syrian Electronic Army Hackers for Cyber Crimes', *Vice*, 23 March 2016; Dustin Volz and Jim Finkle, 'U.S. indicts Iranians for hacking dozens of banks, New York dam', Reuters, 25 March 2016; Ellen Nakashima, 'Syrian hacker extradited to the United States from Germany', *The Washington Post*, 9 May 2016.
22. Several authors refer to attribution as a process, although without elaborating on what it entails or what they mean by it. See for instance: Josephine Charlotte Paulina Wolff, 'Unraveling Internet Identities: Accountability & Anonymity at the Application Layer' (Massachusetts Institute of Technology, 2012), pp. 48, 141; Brenner, *Cyber Threats*, p. 74; Andrew Nicholson, Helge Janicke and Tim Watson, 'An Initial Investigation into Attribution in SCADA Systems' (paper presented at the International Symposium for ICS & SCADA Cyber Security Research, Leicester, 2013).
23. Jason Healey, 'Beyond Attribution: Seeking National Responsibility for Cyber Attacks' (Washington, DC: Atlantic Council, 2012), pp. 1–7; Martin Libicki, 'The Specter of Non-Obvious Warfare', *Strategic Studies Quarterly* 6, 3 (Fall 2012).
24. In brief, and in the words of the famous international relations theorist Hans Morgenthau, 'the executive and legislative functions' are 'political functions'. Hans J. Morgenthau, *The Concept of the Political*, ed. Hatmut Behr and Felix Rösch, trans. Maeva Vidal (New York: Palgrave Macmillan, 2012), p. 103.
25. Carl Schmitt, *The Concept of the Political* (New Brunswick, NJ: Rutgers University Press, 1976), p. 19; Andrew Heywood, *Political theory: an introduction* (New York: Palgrave Macmillan, 2004), p. 53. In fact, for Carl Schmitt, this is not too helpful, because the concept of the state relies on the concept of the political. Schmitt, *The Concept of the Political*, p. 19.
26. Ibid., p. 30. Such a definition of the political has attracted much criticism, notably from Hans Morgenthau, who has argued that Schmitt's division is metaphysical and that he does not indicate what the political sphere comprises. Morgenthau defines the political as an activity, which is the expression of a group's will to power (i.e. to maintain, increase or assert its power). When the parliament, an organ of the state, passes a law, it gives other embodiments of the state, often the police, the capacity to enforce the authority of the law. By doing so, it increases the power of the state to assert its authority. Morgenthau, *The Concept of the Political*.

27. Levy, *Crypto*, p. 286.

28. Daniel Akst, 'Postcard from Cyberspace: The Helsinki Incident and the Right to Anonymity', *Los Angeles Times*, 22 February 1995.

29. Dan Garvin, 'What Really Happened in INCOMM-Part 2', https://groups.google.com/forum/?fromgroups#!msg/alt.religion.scientology/zpp3nfabhQI/f2WEdA6clLAJ, accessed 4 July 2016.

30. Assange et al., *Cypherpunks: Freedom and the Future of the Internet* (New York: OR Books, 2009), p. 7.

31. Morgenthau, *The Concept of the Political*, p. 120.

32. Márton Szabo, 'Review Article: The Conceptual History of Politics as the History of Political Conceptualizations: Kari Palonen, The Struggle with Time: A Conceptual History of 'Politics' as an Activity, LIT Verlag: Hamburg, London and Münster, 2006', *European Journal of Political Theory* 8 (2009), p. 277.

33. The OED mentions that political activities are 'typically considered to be devious or divisive'; J. A. Simpson and E. S. C. Weiner, *The Oxford English Dictionary* (Oxford: Oxford University Press, 1989), p. 361; Niccolò Machiavelli, *The Prince*, ed. Quentin Skinner and Russell Price (Cambridge: Cambridge University Press, 1988); Heywood, *Political theory: an introduction*, p. 54.

34. Committee on Armed Servies, 'US Cyber Command: Organizing for Cyberspace Operations', (Washington, DC: US Government Printing Office, 2010).

35. Arnold Wolfers, '"National Security" as an Ambiguous Symbol', *Political Science Quarterly* 67, 4 (1952), p. 483.

36. David A. Baldwin, 'The Concept of Security', *Review of International Studies* 23 (1997), p. 9.

37. Certain scholars such as Ian Walden have also recognised that 'advantage may be taken of the consensus present around the issue of child abuse images to promote broader content-control strategies'. Ian Walden, *Computer Crimes and Digital Investigation* (New York: Oxford University Press, 2007), p. 394. Concerning the Cypherpunk movement, see for instance Levy, *Crypto*, p. 295; Assange et al., *Cypherpunks*, pp. 69–70.

38. Richard A. Clarke and Robert K. Knake, *Cyber War: The Next Threat to National Security and What to Do About It* (New York: Ecco, 2010); Dan Verton, *Black Ice: The Invisible Threat of Cyber-Terrorism* (Emeryville, CA: McGraw-Hill Osborne Media, 2003).

39. Myriam Dunn Cavelty, 'The Militarisation of Cyberspace: Why Less May Be Better' (paper presented at the 4th International Conference on Cyber Conflict, Tallinn, 2012); Ronald J. Deibert, 'Black Code: Censorship, Surveillance, and the Militarisation of Cyberspace', *Journal*

of International Studies 32 (2003); Jerry Brito and Tate Watkins, 'Loving the Cyberbomb? The Danger of Threat Inflation in Cybersecurity Policy' (Arlington, VA: Mercatus Center, George Mason University, 2011).

40. Clarke and Knake, *Cyber War;* Lene Hansen and Helen Nissenbaum, 'Digital Disaster, Cyber Security, and the Copenhagen School', *International Studies Quarterly* 53, 4 (2009), p. 1162.

41. Daniel E. Geer, 'Cybersecurity and National Policy', *National Security Journal*, http://harvardnsj.com/2011/01/cybersecurity-and-national-policy/, accessed 4 July 2016.

42. See, for instance, Benjamin Miller, 'The Concept of Security: Should it be Redefined?', *Journal of Strategic Studies* 24, 2 (2001); Baldwin, 'The Concept of Security'; Julian Richards, *A Guide to National Security* (Oxford: Oxford University Press, 2011).

43. Most notably, see Myriam Dunn Cavelty, *Cyber-Security and Threat Politics: US efforts to secure the information age* (New York: Routledge, 2008).

44. Richards, *A Guide to National Security*, p. 17.

45. See, for instance, several criminal cases that happened solely within the boundaries of one country, and did not involve any steps taken by the instigators to hide their traces. Drew Cullen, 'Computer dealer fined for sending virus to rival', *The Register*, 11 April 2001; *Philipe P. v. Lyonnaise Communications* (24 May 2012), 0207090006, Tribunal de Grande Instance, Paris; John Oates, 'Kid who crashed email server gets tagged', *The Register*, 23 August 2006; *Amen v. Michel M.* (8 June 2006), Tribunal de Grande Instance, Nanterre.

46. For a more detailed review of the procedure, see Walden, *Computer Crimes and Digital Investigation*, pp. 210–11.

47. Thomas Rid, *Cyber War Will Not Take Place* (London: Hurst & Company, 2013), p. 161.

48. See, for instance, the 2007 denial-of-service attacks against Estonia. The damage was fairly limited, although various senior officials still discussed the attacks, notably the Estonian foreign minister Urmas Paet, the Estonian prime minister Andrus Ansip, and the Estonian president Toomas Hendrik Ilves. Rain Ottis, 'Analysis of the 2007 Cyber Attacks Against Estonia from the Information Warfare Perspective' (paper presented at the 7th European Conference on Information Warfare and Security, Plymouth, 2008). The case of the attack 'against the world's largest gambling company' is another example of a non-critical infrastructure being targeted by a state, and of an ensuing response from high-level officials. The director of national intelligence, James Clapper, publicly attributed the campaign to Iran. Tony Capaccio,

David Lerman and Chris Strohm, 'Iran Behind Cyber-Attack on Adelson's Sands Corp., Clapper Says', *Bloomberg*, 26 February 2015.

49. Michael Cieply and Brooks Barnes, 'Sony Cyberattack, First a Nuisance, Swiftly Grew Into a Firestorm', *The New York Times*, 30 December 2014.

50. Ibid.

51. Charlotte Krol, AP, APTN, 'Barack Obama explains US sanctions on North Korea over Sony attack', *The Telegraph*, 2 January 2015.

52. David E. Sanger and Martin Fackler, 'N.S.A. Breached North Korean Networks Before Sony Attack, Officials Say', *The New York Times*, 18 January 2015.

53. Kim Zetter, 'Critics say new evidence linking North Korea to the Sony hack is still flimsy', *Wired*, 1 August 2015.

54. David E. Sanger and Martin Fackler, 'N.S.A. Breached North Korean Networks Before Sony Attack, Officials Say', *The New York Times*, 18 January 2015.

55. *The Guardian*, 'Obama: North Korea Sony hack 'not an act of war', 21 December 2014.

56. Dan Robert, 'Obama imposes new sanctions against North Korea in response to Sony hack', *The Guardian*, 2 January 2015.

57. The first objective of the United Kingdom's cyber security strategy is to establish the country as 'one of the most secure places in the world to do business in cyberspace'. Cabinet Office, 'The UK Cyber Security Strategy—Protecting and promoting the UK in a digital world', (London: Cabinet Office, 2011), p. 8. Similarly, see the United States' repeated stances against China: Committee on Foreign Affairs, 'China's Approach to Cyber Operations: Implications for the United States' (Washington, DC: U.S.-China Economic and Security Review Commission, 2010); Office of the National Counterintelligence Executive, 'Foreign spies stealing US economic secrets in cyberspace: Report to Congress on Foreign Economic Collection and Industrial Espionage, 2009–2011' (Washington, DC: ONCIX, 2011).

58. Yao Chung Chang, 'Combating cybercrime across the Taiwan Strait: investigation and prosecution issues', *Australian Journal of Forensic Sciences* 44, 1 (2012).

59. Ibid., p. 11.

60. Josh Halliday, 'Stuxnet worm is the "work of a national government agency"', *The Guardian*, 24 September 2010.

61. Arab Youth Group, 'Arab Youth Group', Pastebin, http://pastebin.com/PUHqDQnd; Guest, 'Saudi Aramco, once again...', Pastebin, http://pastebin.com/WKSk3pmp; Cutting Sword of Justice, 'Untitled', Pastebin, http://pastebin.com/HqAgaQRj, all accessed 6 July 2016.

62. Cutting Sword of Justice, 'Untitled'.

63. Lucian Constantin, 'Kill timer found in Shamoon malware suggests possible connection to Saudi Aramco attack', *Computer World*, 23 August 2012.

64. Associated Press, 'Official: US blames Iran hackers for cyberattacks', *The Washington Post*, 11 October 2012.

65. Panetta, 'Text of Speech'.

66. Lolita C. Baldor, 'US warning reflects fears of Iranian cyberattack', Associated Press, 12 October 2012; Nicole Perlroth, David E. Sanger and Michael S. Schmidt, 'As Hacking Against U.S. Rises, Experts Try to Pin Down Motive', *The New York Times*, 3 March 2013.

67. Andrea Shalal-Esa, 'Top general says U.S. under constant cyber attack threat', Reuters, 14 May 2013.

68. Susan W. Brenner, 'Cyber-threats and the Limits of Bureaucratic Control', *Minnesota Journal of Law, Science, and Technology* 14, 137–258 (2013).

69. Of particular interest are a series of hacks into US military networks in the 1990s that turned out to be criminal cases, and for most of which law enforcement agencies were able to collect not only information but also evidence. See In 1991 and in 1998, Peter Jennings, 'World News Tonight with Peter Jennings', *ABC News*, 25 April 1991; National Counterintelligence Center, Federal Bureau of Investigation, and National Infrastructure Protection Center, 'Solar Sunrise', http://www.youtube.com/watch?v=bOr5CtqYnsA&nofeather=True, accessed 6 July 2016.

70. The White House, 'National Security Presidential Directive /NSPD-54' (Washington, DC: 2008).

71. Lennon Yao-chung Chang, *Cybercrime in the Greater China Region: Regulatory Responses and Crime Prevention Across the Taiwan Strait* (Cheltenham and Northampton, MA: Edward Elgar Publishing Limited, 2013), pp. 7–8.

72. David Barboza, 'China's President Will Lead a New Effort on Cybersecurity', *The New York Times*, 27 February 2014.

73. Walden, *Computer Crimes and Digital Investigation*, p. 393.

74. Ibid., p. 391.

75. Three separate statements from state officials can illustrate these fears. Firstly, Larry Wortzel, the commissioner for the U.S.-China Economic and Security Review Commission, testified before Congress in March 2010 that 'if one describes how attribution is achieved, it tells the intruder how to modify its operations and make them more effective': Committee on Foreign Affairs, 'China's Approach to Cyber Operations: Implications for the United States' (Washington, DC: U.S.-China Economic and Security Review Commission, 2010). Secondly, follow-

ing a denial-of-service attack on the website of the Australian prime minister Julia Gillard in 2011, a spokesperson from the Ministry of Defence stated, 'public discussion of the attribution of specific cyber incidents could jeopardise on-going investigations, monitoring of cyber incidents and the ability to protect information and networks': Jeanne-Vida Douglas, 'Hacktivist link to PM attack', *Australian Financial Review*, 28 October 2011. Lastly, Michael Chertoff, former US Homeland Security secretary under George W. Bush (2005–9), also refused to give more information about attribution techniques even when asked by a House Judiciary Committee on the subject. He answered: 'Some of the ways we might prove [attribution] make reference to sophisticated and secret sources and methods that we're not going to want to reveal': Hearing of the Crime, Terrorism and Homeland Security Subcommittee of the House Judiciary Committee, 'Cyber Security: Protecting America's New Frontier' (Washington, D.C.: Crime, Terrorism and Homeland Security Subcommittee, 2011).

76. Joseph Menn, 'FBI says more cooperation with banks key to probe of cyber attacks', Reuters, 13 May 2013.

77. The legal scholar Ian Walden divides techniques into two other categories: coercive (e.g. search and seizure) and covert (e.g. interception and surveillance). However, investigators can use these techniques only after they know the identity of suspects. In order to draw up a list of suspects, it is argued that law enforcement will mostly use forensics and informants. Walden, *Computer Crimes and Digital Investigation*, p. 203.

78. On the other hand, private actors such as Microsoft have in the past successfully offered monetary rewards, leading for instance to the capture in 2004 of Sven Jaschan, author of a variant of the Blaster worm. Robert Lemos, 'Microsoft to reward informants after Sasser conviction', *SecurityFocus*, 8 July 2005.

79. The Melissa virus had infected 200,000 computers, spreading via a Word document masquerading as a list of passwords to access paywall-protected pornographic websites, and was posted on a forum using a hijacked email address. But the email service provider was able to give the police a list of IP addresses that had last accessed the email address, and the last such address was Smith's. John Markoff, 'Digital Fingerprints Leave Clues to Creator of Internet Virus', *The New York Times*, 30 March 1999; Matt Richtel, 'U.S. Agents Seeking Clues To Who Made E-Mail Virus', *The New York Times*, 2 April 1999.

80. Martha Mendoza, 'Virus sender helped FBI bust hackers, court records say', Associated Press, 17 September 2003.

81. Steven Morris, 'Computer virus creator jailed as "global menace"', *The Guardian*, 22 January 2003.

82. Ibid.

83. Parmy Olson, *We Are Anonymous* (London: William Heinemann, 2012), p. 406.

84. Ibid., p. 95.

85. Ibid., p. 211.

86. Ibid., p. 307.

87. Ibid., p. 392.

88. FBI, 'Six Hackers in the United States and Abroad Charged for Crimes Affecting Over One Million Victims', 6 March 2012; Jeremy Kirk, 'LulzSec Leader "Sabu" Granted Six-Month Sentencing Delay', *PCWorld*, 23 August 2012.

89. Mark Mazzetti, 'F.B.I. Informant Is Tied to Cyberattacks Abroad', *The New York Times*, 23 April 2014.

90. See for instance the Comment Group, a group of hackers allegedly within the Chinese military who encrypt malicious code in the comments line of webpage source codes; this has become their 'signature'. Nicole Perlroth, 'Hackers in China Attacked The Times for Last 4 Months', *The New York Times*, 30 January 2013.

91. Tom Parker et al., *Cyber Adversary Characterisation* (Rockland, MA Syngress Publishing, 2004); Cameron H. Malin, Eoghan Casey and James M. Aquilina, *Malware Forensics Field Guide for Windows Systems: Digital Forensics Field Guides* (Waltham: Elsevier, 2012).

92. For a review of the problems that arise with tracing IP addresses abroad through formal channels, see Susan W. Brenner and Joseph J. Schwerha, 'Transnational evidence gathering and local prosecution of international cybercrime', *The John Marshall Journal of Computer & Information Law* 20 (2002).

93. A new ruling by the European Court of Justice may soon make it more difficult to find information linked to hackers. Implementing a version of a 'right to be forgotten' online, the court ruled on 12 May 2014 that search engines should give users the opportunity to call for the removal of search results on information that concerns them. It is still unclear how search engines will implement this ruling, and how it will be enforced. Jonathan Zittrain, 'Don't Force Google to "Forget"', *The New York Times*, 14 May 2014; Viktor Mayer-Schönberger, 'Omission of search results is not a "right to be forgotten" or the end of Google', *The Guardian*, 13 May 2014.

94. Kevin Hagan, Interview, 18 October 2013; Chris W. Johnson, 'Anti-social networking: crowdsourcing and the cyber defence of national critical infrastructures', *Ergonomics* 57, 3 (2014), pp. 419–33.

95. David Omand, Jamie Bartlett and Carl Miller, 'Introducing Social Media Intelligence (SOCMINT)', *Intelligence and National Security* 27, 6 (2012).

96. Charles Arthur, 'Jake Davis, aka LulzSec's "Topiary", on how the group formed—and broke up', *The Guardian*, 9 September 2013.

97. Lawrence Wright, 'The Spymaster', *The New Yorker*, 21 January 2008.

98. Ibid.

99. Ryan Singel, 'NSA Must Examine All Internet Traffic to Prevent Cyber Nine-Eleven, Top Spy Says', *Wired*, 15 January 2008.

100. Lolita C. Baldor, 'Officials: US better at finding cyber attackers', Associated Press, 28 January 2011.

101. Committee on Intelligence, 'Cyber threats and ongoing efforts to protect the nation', (Washington, DC: US House of Representatives, 2011). A recent revelation by Edward Snowden about a programme called MonsterMind also builds on that figure. James Bamford, 'Edward Snowden: The Untold Story', *Wired*, 22 August 2014.

102. Panetta, 'Text of Speech'.

103. US Department of Defense, 'Cyberspace Policy Report: A Report to Congress Pursuant to the National Defense Authorization Act for Fiscal Year 2011, Section 934' (Washington, DC: Department of Defense, 2011).

104. Ibid., p. 3.

105. David E. Sanger, 'N.S.A. Nominee Promotes Cyberwar Units', *The New York Times*, 11 March 2014.

106. Mark Mazzetti, 'F.B.I. Informant Is Tied to Cyberattacks Abroad', *The New York Times*, 23 April 2014. For instance, Israel's intelligence services also closely monitor activities of Internet groups planning to launch cyber attacks: see Tova Dvorin, 'Secret Shin Bet Unit at The Front Lines of Israel's Cyber-War', *Arutz Sheva*, 25 April 2014.

107. David E. Sanger and Thom Shanker, 'Broad Powers Seen for Obama in Cyberstrikes', *The New York Times*, 3 February 2013. A pre-emptive strike would, however, raise many issues, nicely summarised by the Rand scholar Martin Libicki in these words: '[T]he many ambiguities of who is doing what to whom in cyberspace suggest that understanding who is preparing to do what to whom is even harder to discern. Grave mistakes are possible—particularly if the decision to preempt attacks is delegated from the president, as many have suggested it might be'. Martin C. Libicki, 'Why Cyber War Will Not and Should Not Have Its Grand Strategist', *Strategic Studies Quarterly* (Spring 2014), p. 36.

108. Bamford, 'Edward Snowden'.

109. At home, the NSA was able to obtain data from Verizon, while abroad it targeted Brazilian and Belgian telecommunication providers, for instance. Glenn Greenwald, 'NSA collecting phone records of millions of Verizon customers daily', *The Guardian*, 6 June 2013;

BBC News, 'US allies Mexico, Chile and Brazil seek spying answers', 11 July 2013.

110. James Risen and Laura Poitras, 'N.S.A. Gathers Data on Social Connections of U.S. Citizens', *The New York Times*, 28 September 2013.

111. Ibid.

112. Jacques Follorou and Glenn Greenwald, 'France in the NSA's cross-hair: phone networks under surveillance', *Le Monde*, 25 October 2013. 'La NSA rastreó 60 millones de llamadas en España en un mes', *El País*, 28 October 2013.

113. Matthew M. Aid, 'NSA can't break into your computer, these guys break into your house', *Foreign Policy*, 17 July 2013.

114. Barton Gellman and Ellen Nakashima, 'U.S. spy agencies mounted 231 offensive cyber-operations in 2011, documents show', *The Washington Post*, 31 August 2013.

115. James Ball, Julian Borger and Glenn Greenwald, 'Revealed: how US and UK spy agencies defeat internet privacy and security', *The Guardian*, 6 September 2013.

116. Ibid.

117. There is some controversy about whether the NSA intentionally weakened the encryption algorithm, or if it just pushed for its implementation in this form. Kim Zetter, 'How a Crypto "Backdoor" Pitted the Tech World Against the NSA', *Wired*, 24 September 2013; Lily Hay Newman, 'Can You Trust NIST?', *IEEE Spectrum*, 9 October 2013.

118. Jennifer Valentino-DeVries and Siobhan Gorman, 'What You Need to Know on New Details of NSA Spying', *The Wall Street Journal*, 20 August 2013.

119. Ibid.

120. Dominic Rushe and James Ball, 'PRISM scandal: tech giants flatly deny allowing NSA direct access to servers', *The Guardian*, 7 June 2013.

121. James Risen and Laura Poitras, 'N.S.A. Report Outlined Goals for More Power', *The New York Times*, 22 November 2013.

122. Laurent Borredon and Jacques Follorou, 'En France, la DGSE au cœur d'un programme de surveillance d'Internet', *Le Monde*, 11 June 2013.

123. Jean-Marc Leclerc, 'Téléphone, Internet: l'État pourra bientôt tout espionner', *Le Figaro*, 26 November 2013; *The New York Times*, 'Domestic Spying, French Style', 13 December 2013.

124. Ewen MacAskill et al., 'GCHQ taps fibre-optic cables for secret access to world's communications', *The Guardian*, 21 June 2013.

125. Ibid.

126. GCHQ, 'Our Intelligence and Security mission in the Internet age', press release, 3 May 2009.

127. Ian Brown, 'Communications Data Retention in an Evolving Internet', *International Journal of Law and Information Technology* 19, 2 (2010), p. 101.

128. Glenn Greenwald, 'XKeyscore: NSA tool collects "nearly everything a user does on the internet"', *The Guardian*, 31 July 2013.

129. Ibid.

130. David Francis, 'Noted Hacker Edward Snowden Has Some Thoughts on the DNC Hack', *Foreign Policy*, 25 July 2016.

131. Eric Lichtblau, 'In Secret, Court Vastly Broadens Powers of N.S.A.', *The New York Times*, 6 July 2013.

132. James Risen and Laura Poitras, 'N.S.A. Gathers Data on Social Connections of U.S. Citizens', *The New York Times*, 28 September 2013.

133. Laura Poitras, Marcel Rosenbach and Holger Stark, '"Follow the Money": NSA Monitors Financial World', *Der Spiegel*, 16 September 2013.

134. Police Central e-Crime Unit, 'Financial Harm Reduction & Performance Report', (London: Association of Chief Police Officers, PCeU, 2013).

135. Ian Brown, Lilian Edwards and Christopher Marsden, 'Information Security and Cybercrime', in *Law and the Internet*, ed. Lilian Edwards and Charlotte Waelde (Oxford: Hart Publishing, 2009), p. 675.

136. Risen and Poitras, 'N.S.A. Report'.

137. Barack Obama, 'Remarks by the President on Review of Signals Intelligence', The White House, 17 January 2014.

138. Ibid.

139. Charlie Savage and Laura Pointras, 'How a Court Secretly Evolved, Extending U.S. Spies' Reach', *The New York Times*, 11 March 2014.

140. Eric Lichtblau and Michael S. Schmidt, 'Other Agencies Clamor for Data N.S.A. Compiles', *The New York Times*, 3 August 2013.

141. Ibid.

142. Ryan Gallagher, 'The Surveillance Engine: How the NSA Built Its Own Secret Google', *The Intercept*, 25 August 2014.

143. Intelligence and Security Committee of Parliament, 'Open Evidence Session', (London: UK Parliament, 7 November 2013).

144. Ibid.

145. Russia's capabilities, while not widely known, seem to be very similar to those of the US. See for instance: Andrei Soldatov and Irina Borogan, 'Russia's Surveillance State', *World Policy Journal* (Fall 2013).

146. Walden, *Computer Crimes and Digital Investigation*, p. 375.

147. Assange et al., *Cypherpunks*, p. 43.
148. Harold C. Relyea, 'The Coming of Secret Law', *Government Information Quarterly* 5, 2 (1998), p. 111.
149. Obama, 'Remarks by the President'.
150. Nick Hopkins, 'Huge swath of GCHQ mass surveillance is illegal, says top lawyer', *The Guardian*, 28 January 2014. Alan Travis, 'UK security agencies unlawfully collected data for 17 years, court rules', *The Guardian*, 17 October 2016.
151. Ibid., p. 110.
152. Ryan Lizza, 'State of Deception', *The New Yorker*, 16 December 2013.
153. Ibid.
154. Ibid.
155. Ibid.
156. Charlie Savage, 'Judge Questions Legality of N.S.A. Phone Records', *The New York Times*, 16 December 2013; *Klayman et al. v. Obama et al.*, [16 December 2013], D.D.C., 13–0851; Charlie Savage, 'Watchdog Report Says N.S.A. Program Is Illegal and Should End', *The New York Times*, 23 January 2014.
157. Laurie Thomas Lee, 'Can Police Track Your Wireless Calls—Call Location Information and Privacy Law', *Cardozo Arts & Entertainment Law Journal* 21(2003).
158. Savage, 'Judge Questions Legality'.
159. Catherine Crump, 'Data Retention: Privacy, Anonymity, and Accountability Online', *Stanford Law Review* 56, 1 (2003).
160. Adam Liptak and Michael S. Schmidt, 'Judge Upholds N.S.A.'s Bulk Collection of Data on Calls', *The New York Times*, 27 December 2013.
161. Lizza, 'State of Deception'.
162. Cassel Bryan-Low, 'To catch crooks in cyberspace, FBI goes global', Associated Press, 21 November 2006.
163. Andrew Brandt, 'Stupid hacker tricks, part two: The folly of youth', *InfoWorld Daily News*, 5 May 2005.
164. Risha Gotlieb, 'Cybercop Fights Organized Internet Crime', *Pacific Standard*, 14 March 2011.
165. Bryan-Low, 'To catch crooks in cyberspace'.
166. Damien Bancal, 'La traque de Zotob comme si vous y étiez', Zataz, http://archives.zataz.com/reportage-virus/9056/zotob-hunter.html.
167. Brandt, 'Stupid hacker tricks'.
168. Mark Sherman, 'Two Arrested in U.S. Computer Worm Probe', Associated Press, 26 August 2005; Brian Krebs, 'Suspected Worm Creators Arrested', *The Washington Post*, 27 August 2005.
169. Brian Krebs, 'Conversation With a Worm Author', *The Washington Post*, 29 August 2005.
170. Bryan-Low, 'To catch crooks in cyberspace'.

2. RELIANCE ON JUDGEMENT

1. Siobhan Gorman, Devlin Barrett and Danny Yadron, 'Chinese Hackers Hit U.S. Media', *The Wall Street Journal*, 31 January 2013.
2. Charlie Osborne, 'US government debates action over alleged Chinese cyberattacks', *ZDNet*, 1 February 2013.
3. Ellen Nakashima, 'U.S. said to be target of massive cyber-espionage campaign', *The Washington Post*, 11 February 2013.
4. Bryan Krekel et al., 'Occupying the Information High Ground: Chinese Capabilities for Computer Network Operations and Cyber Espionage', ed. U.S.-China Economic and Security Review Commission (Washington, DC: 2012); Mike Rogers and Dutch Ruppersberger, 'Investigative Report on the U.S. National Security Issues Posed by Chinese Telecommunications Companies Huawei and ZTE' (Washington, DC: US House of Representatives, 2012), p. 60.
5. Mandiant, 'APT1: Exposing One of China's Cyber Espionage Units' (Alexandria, VA: Mandiant, 2013).
6. Oliver Joy, 'Mandiant: China is sponsoring cyber-espionage', *CNN*, 20 February 2013.
7. Reuters, 'China says U.S. hacking accusations lack technical proof', 20 February 2013.
8. Richard J. Heuer, *Psychology of Intelligence Analysis* (Washington, DC: Center for the Study of Intelligence, 1999), p. 86.
9. Randall R. Dipert, 'Other-Than-Internet (OTI) Cyberwarfare: Challenges for Ethics, Law, and Policy', *Journal of Military Ethics* 12, 1 (2013), p. 38.
10. Christopher J. Eberle, 'Just War and Cyberwar', *Journal of Military Ethics* 12, 1 (2013), p. 57.
11. Myriam Dunn Cavelty, 'Breaking the Cyber-Security Dilemma: Aligning Security Needs and Removing Vulnerabilities', *Science and Engineering Ethics* (April 2014), p. 9.
12. US Department of State, 'Cybersecurity Update', 18 October 2011, http://fpc.state.gov/175773.htm, accessed 7 July 2016.
13. Mike McConnell, 'Mike McConnell on how to win the cyber-war we're losing', *The Washington Post*, 28 February 2010.
14. Libicki, 'The Specter of Non-Obvious Warfare', *Strategic Studies Quarterly* 6, 3 (Fall 2012), p. 95.
15. Jason Healey, *A Fierce Domain: Conflict in Cyberspace, 1986 to 2012* (Washington, DC: CCSA; The Atlantic Council, 2013), p. 21.
16. The incident involved a US Air Force base coming under a cyber attack while the United States was mounting a military intervention in Iraq. In the opinion of many analysts at the time, the attack had come from Iraqi intelligence services trying to gather information. In

the end, however, it turned out only to be three teenagers with no connections to any form of sponsorship. National Counterintelligence Center, Federal Bureau of Investigation, and National Infrastructure Protection Center, 'Solar Sunrise', http://www.youtube.com/watch?v=bOr5CtqYnsA&nofeather=True, accessed 20 July 2016.

17. James Andrew Lewis, *The Cyber War Has Not Begun* (Washington, DC: Center for Strategic & International Studies, 2010).

18. Perri 6, *Explaining Political Judgement* (Cambridge: Cambridge University Press, 2011).

19. Raymond Geuss, 'What is political judgement?', in *Political Judgement: Essays for John Dunn*, ed. Richard Bourke and Raymond Geuss (Cambridge: Cambridge University Press, 2009), p. 40.

20. Ibid.

21. The next chapter will look with further nuance at the role of judgement for attribution within the judicial context.

22. Jim Finkle, 'Mandiant goes viral after China hacking report', *Reuters*, 23 February 2013.

23. 6, *Explaining Political Judgement*, p. 1.

24. Nart Villeneuve and Masashi Crete-Nishihata, 'Control and Resistance: Attacks on Burmese Opposition Media', in *Access Contested: Security, Identity, and Resistance in Asian Cyberspace*, ed. Ronald Deibert, et al. (Cambridge, MA: MIT Press, 2012), p. 158; Ronald Deibert et al., 'Access Contested: Toward the Fourth Phase of Cyberspace Controls', in ibid., p. 13; Adam Segal, 'Hacking Back, Signaling, and State-Society Relations', *Cyber Dialogue 2013*, 1 March 2013.

25. Charles Nesson, 'The Evidence or the Event? On Judicial Proof and the Acceptability of Verdicts', *Harvard Law Review* 98, 7 (1985), p. 1362.

26. Ian Walden, *Computer Crimes and Digital Investigation* (New York: Oxford University Press, 2007), p. 383.

27. Peter J. Steinberger, *The Concept of Political Judgement* (Chicago, IL: University of Chicago Press, 1993), p. 282.

28. 6, *Explaining Political Judgement*, p. 281.

29. Ronald Beiner, *Political Judgement* (Chicago, IL: University of Chicago Press, 1984), p. 148.

30. Richards J. Heuer, 'Limits of Intelligence Analysis', *Orbis* 49, 1 (2005), p. 79.

31. Ibid.

32. Paul R. Pillar, 'Intelligence, Policy, and the War in Iraq', *Foreign Affairs* 85, 2 (2006), p. 21.

33. Peter C. Wason, 'On the Failure to Eliminate Hypotheses in a Conceptual Task', *The Quarterly Journal of Experimental Psychology* XII, 3 (1960).

34. Karl R. Popper, *Conjectures and Refutations: The Growth of Scientific Knowledge* (London: Routledge, 1996), p. 36; Stéphane Lefebvre, 'A Look at Intelligence Analysis', *International Journal of Intelligence and CounterIntelligence* 17, 2 (2004), p. 237.

35. Leon Festinger, *A Theory of Cognitive Dissonance* (Stanford, CA: Stanford University Press, 1957).

36. Simon A. Herbert, 'Theories of Bounded Rationality', in *Decision and Organization*, ed. C. B. McGuire and Roy Radner (Minneapolis, MN: University of Minnesota Press, 1972), p. 163.

37. Ibid., p. 170.

38. Sam Kim, 'South Korea misidentifies China as cyberattack origin', Associated Press, 22 March 2013.

39. Kim Zetter, 'Logic Bomb Set Off South Korea Cyberattack', *Wired*, 21 March 2013.

40. Tania Branigan, 'South Korea on alert for cyber-attacks after major network goes down', *The Guardian*, 20 March 2013.

41. Choe Sang-Hun, 'North Korea Declares 1953 War Truce Nullified', *The New York Times*, 11 March 2013.

42. John Doody, 'Introductory remarks' (paper presented at the Future of Cyber Security conference, London, 21 March 2013).

43. Thomas Rid, *Cyber War Will Not Take Place* (London: Hurst & Company, 2013).

44. Associated Press, 'South Korea Says North Korea Behind Computer Crash in March', *The New York Times*, 10 April 2013.

45. Kim Kwang-tae, 'N. Korea's hacking capabilities advance', *Yonhap News Agency*, 11 April 2013; Associated Press, 'South Korea says North Korean spy agency behind March cyberattack', 10 April 2013.

46. Kwang-tae, 'N. Korea's hacking capabilities'; Associated Press, 'South Korea says'.

47. Sherman Kent, 'Words of Estimative Probability', *Studies in Intelligence* 8, 4 (1964).

48. Heuer (*Psychology of Intelligence Analysis*, p. 33) uses the wording 'principal strategies' instead of 'tools'. They are arguably a mix of both—the quotation marks here are thus merely an indicator of this slight imprecision. Scholars are also trying to develop mathematical models that acknowledge the need for different hypotheses while trying to avoid the many systematic logical fallacies that can spoil a reasoning. Technical solutions can help, but can never be sufficient to address attribution and notably its political components. Paulo Shakarian et al., 'An Argumentation-Based Framework to Address the Attribution Problem in Cyber-Warfare', *[submitted on 27 April]* (2014).

49. Heuer, *Psychology of Intelligence Analysis*, p. 33.

50. Jeffrey Carr, 'Mandiant APT1 Report Has Critical Analytic Flaws', *Digital Dao*, 19 February 2013; Sergio Caltagirone, Andrew Pendergast and Christopher Betz, *The Diamond Model of Intrusion Analysis* (Arlington, VA: Threat Connect, 2013), p. 36.

51. Heuer, *Psychology of Intelligence Analysis*, p. 98.

52. Ibid., p. 109.

53. Ibid.

54. Steinberger, *The Concept of Political Judgement*, p. 283.

55. Francis Fukuyama, *Trust: The Social Virtues and the Creation of Prosperity* (New York: The Free Press, 1995), p. 25; Bruce Schneier, *Liars and Outliers: enabling the trust that society needs to thrive* (Indianapolis, IN: Wiley, 2012).

56. Beiner, *Political Judgement*, p. 133.

57. Carl Schmitt, *The Concept of the Political* (New Brunswick, NJ: Rutgers University Press, 1976).

58. Richard J. Aldrich, 'Whitehall and the Iraq War: the UK's Four Intelligence Enquiries', *Irish Studies in International Affairs* 16 (2005), p. 76.

59. Department of Homeland Security, 'Joint Statement from the Department Of Homeland Security and Office of the Director of National Intelligence on Election Security', *DHS Press Office*, 7 October 2016.

60. Pillar, 'Intelligence, Policy, and the War in Iraq', p. 21.

61. Ibid.

62. Michael V. Hayden, *Playing to the Edge: American Intelligence in the Age of Terror* (New York: Penguin Press, 2016, p. 50).

63. Richard J. Aldrich, *GCHQ* (London: HarperPress, 2010), p. 521.

64. Robert David Steele, 'The Evolving Craft of Intelligence', in *Routledge Companion to Intelligence Studies*, ed. Robert Dover, Michael Goodman and Claudia Hillebrand (Oxford: Routledge, 2013), p. 71.

65. International Group of Experts, *Tallinn Manual on the International Law Applicable to Cyber Warfare*, ed. Michael N. Schmitt (Cambridge: Cambridge University Press, 2013), p. 54.

66. Joel Brenner, *America the Vulnerable* (New York: Penguin Press, 2011), p. 61.

67. William Lynn, 'The Cyber Security Challenge: Defending a New Domain', (Washington, DC: US Department of Defense, 2012).

68. Ellen Nakashima and Matt Zapotsky, 'U.S. charges Iran-linked hackers with targeting banks, N.Y. dam', *The Washington Post*, 24 March 2016.

3. STANDARDS OF PROOF

1. Jason Healey, 'Beyond Attribution: Seeking National Responsibility for Cyber Attacks' (Washington, DC: Atlantic Council, 2012), pp. 1–7; Shane McGee, Randy V. Sabet and Anand Shah, 'Adequate Attribution: A Framework for Developing a National Policy for Private Sector Use of Active Defense', *Journal of Business & Technology Law* 8, 1 (2013); Nicholas Tsagourias, 'Cyber attacks, self-defence and the problem of attribution', *Journal of Conflict & Security Law* 17, 2 (2013).
2. Healey, 'Beyond Attribution'.
3. Such a standard notably falls short of showing 'direct' or 'overall' control, two common standards used in international law.
4. Other standards relevant to criminal cyber attacks include the 'preponderance of the evidence' used in civil courts, for instance. These standards of proof are applicable mostly in countries following a common law system; in civil law systems, judges 'evaluate the evidence produced according to their personal convictions'. Marco Roscini, *Cyber Operations and the Use of Force in International Law* (New York: Oxford University Press, 2014), p. 98. In contrast, at the level of national security, different types of standards exist, such as 'probable cause finding'—used, for instance, when applying to the Foreign Intelligence Surveillance Court in order to be granted access to information on US citizens—or 'sufficiently certain', as mentioned in an official Dutch policy report on the standards needed for retaliating to a cyber attack. Advisory Council on International Affairs, and Advisory Committee on Issues of Public International Law, 'Cyber Warfare' (The Hague: AIV/CAVV, 2011).
5. Interview with Mark D. Rasch, 16 July 2013.
6. See also the US case in which the police accused Aaron Caffrey of hacking into the Port of Houston's networks in 2003, but he evaded conviction mostly by arguing that a Trojan had infected his computer. BBC News, 'Questions cloud cyber crime cases', 17 October 2003. Concerning trials in Hong Kong, see Richard E. Overill and Jantje A. M. Silomon, 'A Complexity Based Forensic Analysis of the Trojan Horse Defence' (paper presented at the 4th International Workshop on Digital Forensics, Vienna, 2011).
7. Permanent Subcommittee on Investigations of the Committee on Governmental Affairs, 'Security in Cyberspace' (Washington, DC: 1996).
8. Ibid.
9. Peter Sommer, 'Intrusion detection systems as evidence', *Journal Computer Networks: The International Journal of Computer and Telecommunications Networking* 31, 23–4 (1999).

10. Ian Walden, *Computer Crimes and Digital Investigation* (New York: Oxford University Press, 2007), p. 372.

11. Adam Fresco, 'Schoolboy hacker was "No 1 threat" to US security', *The Times*, 22 March 1997.

12. Keith Roscoe, 16 July 2012.

13. See for example the case of attribution of the infamous Love Bug, which was traced back to Onel Guzman in the Philippines. Associated Press, 'Saying they lack evidence, Philippine investigators release suspect', *The Associated Press*, 10 May 2000; *The New York Times*, 'Computer Virus Charges Sought', *The New York Times*, 6 September 2000.

14. See for instance the cases of Mathew Bevan and Gary McKinnon. Kuji Media Corporation, 'History', http://www.kujimedia.com/articles/, accessed 8 July 2016; *Gary McKinnon v. Government of the USA* (3 March 2007), EWHC 762, High Court of Justice Queen's Bench Division.

15. See for instance *Greenpeace and others vs. EDF and others* (10 November 2011), Correctional Tribunal of Nanterre.

16. Jennifer Arlen and Reinier Kraakman, 'Controlling Corporate Misconduct: An Analysis of Corporate Liability Regimes', *New York Univeristy Law Review* 72, 1 (1997).

17. European Parliament, 'Directive 2013/40/EU of the European Parliament and of the Council of 12 August 2013 on attacks against information systems and replacing Council Framework Decision 2005/222/JHA', in *P7_TA(2013)0321*, ed. European Parliament (Strasbourg: European Parliament, 2013).

18. The common and different standards of evidence highlighted above also apply. On top of that, there exist two different and controversial 'standards of attribution': 'overall control' and 'direct control'. For an overview of the general principles guiding the attribution of acts to states, see International Law Commission, 'Draft Articles on the Responsibility of States for Internationally Wrongful Acts', in *Yearbook of the International Law Commission*, ed. International Law Commission (New York and Geneva: United Nations, 2001).

19. In June 2013, a group of experts from the United Nations reached the important conclusion that certain cyber attacks do fall within international law, although many details are still ambivalent. It is still unclear, for instance, which cyber attacks constitute an 'armed attack', a 'use of force' or how self-defence can apply. See Michael N. Schmitt, 'Computer Network Attack and the Use of Force in International Law: Thoughts on a Normative Framework', *Columbia Journal of Transnational Law* 37 (1998); Harold Hongju Koh, 'International Law in Cyberspace', in *USCYBERCOM Inter-Agency Legal Conference* (Fort Meade, MD: 2012); Matthew C. Waxman, 'Cyber-Attacks and the Use of Force: Back to the Future of Article 2(4)', *Yale Journal of International Law* 36, 2

(2011); Harry Rubin, Leigh Fraser and Monica Smith, 'US and International Law Aspects of the Internet: Fitting Square Pegs Into Round Holes', *International Journal of Law and Information Technology* 3, 2 (1995), pp. 117–43; Jack Goldsmith, 'How Cyber Changes the Laws of War', *The European Journal of International Law* 24, 1 (2013).

20. The bombing of Libya was notably based on an intercept by the NSA, later made public in an exceptional gesture by President Reagan. The intercept came from the head of the Libyan secret services, who had ordered the West Germany attack. Richard J. Aldrich, *GCHQ* (London: HarperPress, 2010), p. 457. Concerning 9/11, on 23 September 2001, US Secretary of State Colin Powell confirmed that Al Qaeda was behind the attack. This confirmation was based on just two intercepts by the NSA, which read, 'The match is about to begin' and 'Tomorrow is zero hour'. Agence France-Presse, 'US to present evidence of bin Laden link to terror attacks: Powell', 23 September 2001; Walter Pincus and Dana Priest, 'NSA Intercepts On Eve of 9/11 Sent a Warning', *The Washington Post*, 20 June 2002.

21. Jason Healey, 'The Spectrum of National Responsibility for Cyberattacks', *Brown Journal of World Affairs* 18, 1 (2011).

22. The use of standards for political goals is exemplified by Saudi Arabia's role in 9/11. The first commission investigating the attacks deemed the evidence sufficient to make the claims in its report, whereas the second commission did not. Members of the second investigative team felt that the director, Dieter Snell, demanded such a high level of proof that this could only 'exonerate the guilty'. The policy implications for US-Saudi relations of applying this standard were substantial. See Philip Shenon, *The Commission: The Uncensored History of the 9/11 Investigation* (New York: Twelve, 2008), p. 398.

23. Martti Koskenniemi, 'The Politics of International Law', *Journal of International Law* 1 (1990), p. 5.

24. Ibid., p. 8.

25. Michael S. Schmidt, 'U.S. to Charge Chinese Army Personnel With Cyberspying', *The New York Times*, 19 May 2014; Tom Donilon, 'Remarks By Tom Donilon, National Security Advisory to the President: "The United States and the Asia-Pacific in 2013"', *The White House*, 11 March 2013.

26. Mrt. Izz ad-Din al-Qassam Cyber Fighters, 'Bank of America and New York Stock Exchange under attack unt', Pastebin, 18 September 2012, http://pastebin.com/mCHia4W5, accessed 8 July 2016.

27. Michael Rogers, 'Rebooting Trust? Freedom vs. Security in Cyberspace', in Munich Security Conference (Munich, 2014).

28. Joseph Menn, 'Cyber attacks against banks more severe than most realize', *Reuters*, 18 May 2013.

29. C-Span, 'Newsmakers with Senator Joe Lieberman', 21 September 2012.
30. Eduard Kovacs, 'Hackers of Izz ad-Din al-Qassam Cyber Fighters', *Softpedia*, 7 November 2012.
31. Jim Finkle and Rick Rothacker, 'Exclusive: Iranian hackers target Bank of America, JPMorgan, Citi', *Reuters*, 21 September 2012.
32. Fars News Agency, 'Iran Rejects Media Reports on Hacking US Banks', *Fars News Agency*, 23 September 2012.
33. Richard Ledgett, 'The NSA responds to Edward Snowden's TED Talk' (talk at TED2014, Vancouver).
34. Ellen Nakashima and Matt Zapotsky, 'U.S. charges Iran-linked hackers with targeting banks, N.Y. dam', *The Washington Post*, 24 March 2016.
35. Cutting Sword of Justice, 'Untitled', Pastebin, http://pastebin.com/HqAgaQRj, all accessed 6 July 2016; Lucian Constantin, 'Kill timer found in Shamoon malware suggests possible connection to Saudi Aramco attack', *Computer World*, 23 August 2012.
36. Associated Press, 'Official: US blames Iran hackers for cyberattacks', *The Washington Post*, 11 October 2012.
37. Nicole Perlroth, David E. Sanger and Michael S. Schmidt, 'As Hacking Against U.S. Rises, Experts Try to Pin Down Motive', *The New York Times*, 3 March 2013; Thom Shanker and David E. Sanger, 'U.S. Helps Allies Trying to Battle Iranian Hackers', *The New York Times*, 8 June 2013.
38. Thomas E. Ricks, *Fiasco: The Amercian Military Adventure in Iraq* (London: Penguin Books, 2006), pp. 380–5.
39. Ibid., pp. 92–3.
40. James Hider, 'Iran attacked by 'Israeli computer virus'', *The Times*, 29 May 2012.
41. Kaspersky Lab, 'Kaspersky Lab and ITU Research Reveals New Advanced Cyber Threat', 28 May 2012, http://www.kaspersky.com/about/news/virus/2012/Kaspersky_Lab_and_ITU_Research_Reveals_New_Advanced_Cyber_Threat, accessed 8 July 2016.
42. Kaspersky Lab, 'Resource 207: Kaspersky Lab Research Proves that Stuxnet and Flame Developers are Connected', 11 June 2012, http://www.kaspersky.com/about/news/virus/2012/Resource_207_Kaspersky_Lab_Research_Proves_that_Stuxnet_and_Flame_Developers_are_Connected, 8 July 2016.
43. Ellen Nakashima, 'Iran blamed for cyberattacks on U.S. banks and companies', *The Washington Post*, 22 September 2012.
44. There are, however, a few notable exceptions. See for instance Del Quentin Wilber, 'U.S. Agent Lures Romanian Hackers in Subway Data Heist', *Bloomberg*, 17 April 2014.

45. Government of France, 'Synthèse nationale de renseignement déclassifié: Programme chimique syrien—Cas d'emploi passés d'agents chimiques par le régime. Attaque chimique conduite par le régime le 21 août 2013', (Paris: Government of France, 2013); 'JIC Assessment of 27 August on Reported Chemical Weapons Use in Damascus', (London: 2013).

46. Ian Black and Ian Sample, 'UK report on chemical attack in Syria adds nothing to informed speculation', *The Guardian*, 29 August 2013.

47. Tucker Reals, 'Syria chemical weapons attack blamed on Assad, but where's the evidence?', *CBS News*, 30 August 2013; Kimberly Dozier and Matt Apuzzo, 'Intelligence on weapons no "slam dunk"', *Associated Press*, 29 August 2013.

48. United Nations Mission to Investigate Allegations of the Use of Chemical Weapons in the Syrian Arab Republic, 'Report on the Alleged Use of Chemical Weapons in the Ghouta Area of Damascus on 21 August 2013' (The Hague, 2013).

49. C. J. Chivers, 'U.N. Data on Gas Attack Point to Assad's Top Forces', *The New York Times*, 19 September 2013.

50. Ibid.

51. Vladimir Putin, 'What Putin Has to Say to Americans About Syria', *The New York Times*, 11 September 2013.

52. Center for Strategic and International Studies, 'The Economic Impact of Cybercrime and Cyber Espionage', (Santa Clara, CA: McAfee, 2013).

53. Aldrich, *GCHQ*, p. 388.

54. United Nations, 'Group of Governmental Experts on Developments in the Field of Information and Telecommunications in the Context of International Security' (New York: United Nations, 2010).

55. Walden, *Computer Crimes and Digital Investigation*, p. 393.

56. Jason Healey, *A Fierce Domain: Conflict in Cyberspace, 1986 to 2012* (Washington, DC: CCSA; The Atlantic Council, 2013), p. 21.

57. CNN, 'Israel sets up Patriot missiles amid Iraq tensions', *CNN*, 2 February 1998.

58. National Counterintelligence Center, Federal Bureau of Investigation, and National Infrastructure Protection Center, 'Solar Sunrise', http://www.youtube.com/watch?v=bOr5CtqYnsA&nofeather=True, accessed 20 July 2016.

59. Agence France-Presse, 'Iraq says its army is ready to thwart US attack', 9 February 1998.

60. Atlantic Council, 'Lessons from Our Cyber Past: The First Cyber Cops', 16 May 2012.

61. National Counterintelligence Center, Federal Bureau of Investigation, and National Infrastructure Protection Center, 'Solar Sunrise'.

62. Gerald Butt, 'Iraqi deal: winners and losers', *BBC News*, 25 February 1998.

63. Kevin Poulsen, 'Solar Sunrise hacker "Analyzer" escapes jail', *The Register*, 15 June 2001.

64. Ibid.

65. Kim Zetter, '"The Analyzer" Gets Time Served for Million Dollar Bank Heist', *Wired*, 5 July 2012.

66. See for instance the infamous distributed denial-of-service attacks against Estonia in 2007, a clear case of sabotage where evidence of connections to state actors and to Russia in particular is scant. Deibert et al., *Access Contested: Toward the Fourth Phase of Cyberspace Controls* (Cambridge, MA: MIT Press, 2011), p. 13; Ronald Deibert and Rafal Rohozinski, 'Control and Subversion in Russian Cyberspace', in *Access Controlled: The Shaping of Power, Rights, and Rule in Cyberspace*, ed. Ronald Deibert, et al. (Cambridge, MA: MIT Press, 2010).

67. This logic can be found for instance in Dmitri Alperovitch, 'Revealed: Operation Shady RAT' (Santa Clara, CA: McAfee, 2011).

68. Healey, *A Fierce Domain*.

69. For instance, in the case of the cyber attacks during the 2008 conflict between Georgia and Russia, researchers noted that: 'Although we could find no definitive evidence linking the Russian government to the computer network operations during the Russia–Georgia conflict, the Russian government benefited from DDoS and other measures degrading cyberspace'. Ronald J. Deibert, Rafal Rohozinski and Masashi Crete-Nishihata, 'Cyclones in cyberspace: Information shaping and denial in the 2008 Russia-Georgia war', *Security Dialogue* 43, 3 (2013), p. 17.

70. 'An Assessment of International Legal Issues in Information Operations' (Washington DC: 1999), p. 21.

71. Mandiant, 'APT1: Exposing One of China's Cyber Espionage Units' (Alexandria, VA: Mandiant, 2013), p. 76.

72. Brian Bartholomew and Juan Andres Guerrero-Saade, 'Wave your false flags! Deception tactics muddying attribution in targeted attacks', Kasperky Lab, October 2016, p. 6.

73. George W. Bush, 'Transcript of President Bush's address', *CNN*, 21 September 2001.

74. Richard A. Clarke and Robert K. Knake, *Cyber War: The Next Threat to National Security and What to Do About It* (New York: Ecco, 2010), p. 178.

75. Catherine Lotrionte, 'Introduction: Strengthening the Norms of State Responsibility', *Georgetown Journal of International Affairs* 11 (2010), p. 105; Healey, 'Beyond Attribution'.

76. Sergio Caltagirone, Andrew Pendergast and Christopher Betz, *The Diamond Model of Intrusion Analysis* (Arlington, VA: Threat Connect, 2013), p. 28.

77. Josh Halliday, 'Stuxnet worm is the "work of a national government agency"', *The Guardian*, 24 September 2010.

78. Clement Guitton and Elaine Korzak, 'The Sophistication Criterion for Attribution', *The RUSI Journal* 158, 4 (2013).

79. Ibid.

80. US Department of Defense, 'Department of Defense Cyberspace Policy Report: A Report to Congress Pursuant to the National Defense Authorization Act for Fiscal Year 2011, Section 934' (Washington, DC: Department of Defense, 2011), p. 3.

81. See for instance the case of Estonia, in which this claim was made by several US and Estonian officials. BBC News, 'Russian daily views Estonian efforts to enlist EU support in row with Moscow', 13 May 2007; Baltic News Wire, 'US Congressman rises to defend Estonia's sovereignty', *Baltic News Wire*, 4 June 2007.

82. Jonathan Lusthaus, 'How organised is organised cybercrime?', *Global Crime* 14, 1 (2013).

83. A further loophole in the joint agreement is that most of the cyber attacks are currently conducted by units within the People Liberation Army, which falls organisationally under the Communist Party, not under the government. The Chinese government could use this as an excuse if the topic was to come back between the two heads of governments.

84. FireEye, 'Redline drawn: China recalculates its use of cyber espionage', June 2016.

85. Associated Press, 'Official: US blames Iran hackers for cyberattacks', *The Washington Post*, 11 October 2012; Nicole Perlroth, 'In Cyberattack on Saudi Firm, U.S. Sees Iran Firing Back', *The New York Times*, 23 October 2012; Michael Lipin, 'Saudi Cyber Attack Seen as Work of Amateur Hackers Backed by Iran', *Voice of America*, 25 October 2012.

4. PRIVATE COMPANIES

1. Subcommittee on Technology and Innovation of the House of Committee of Science and Technology, 'Planning for the Future of Cyber Attack Attribution', (Washington, DC: Federal News Service, 2010).

2. Interview with Kevin Hagan, 18 October 2013.

3. Sam Jones, 'Groups face the conundrum of cyber crime', *Financial Times*, 24 February 2014.

4. Judiciary Subcommittee on Crime & Terrorism, 'Cybersecurity Threats', (Washington, DC: C-Span, 2013).

5. Many other companies now offer threat intelligence services, but the quality of their intelligence on state-sponsored attacks can also greatly vary. These include Dell SecureWork, BAE and PwC, for instance.

6. Nicole Perlroth and David E. Sanger, 'FireEye Computer Security Firm Acquires Mandiant', *The New York Times*, 2 January 2014.

7. George Kurtz, 'CrowdStrike launches in stealth-mode with $26 million Series A round led by Warburg Pincus', CrowdStrike blog, 22 February 2012, https://www.crowdstrike.com/blog/crowdstrike-launch/, accessed 11 July 2016; Alex Williams, 'CrowdStrike Raises $30M For Data Security Platform Built To Put Adversaries On The Defensive', *TechCrunch*, 8 September 2013.

8. Tim Shorrock, *Spies for Hire: The Secret World of Intelligence Outsourcing* (New York: Simon and Schuster, 2008).

9. *The Economist*, 'Hiring digital 007s', 15 June 2013.

10. Mike McConnell, 'Mike McConnell on how to win the cyber-war we're losing', *The Washington Post*, 28 February 2010; *The Economist*, 'Hiring digital 007s'.

11. A third interesting example would be the case of Microsoft, especially in light of the Snowden revelations. Duqu targeted primarily Microsoft systems, and although it targeted fewer than 100 computers, the time it took for security vendors to discover it is remarkable. Far from suggesting that Microsoft actually played a role either in keeping the malware hidden or in crafting it, the Snowden documents highlighted that the company has very close relations to the NSA. Notably, the documents showed that Microsoft's companies Outlook, Skype and Hotmail helped law enforcement agents intercept data, although the company vehemently denied it. The journalist Tim Shorrock has also commented, as early as 2008, about the nexus between the NSA and the company. Angela Moscaritolo, 'Duqu underscores trouble AV industry has in stopping threats', *SC Magazine*, 2011; James Ball, 'NSA's Prism surveillance program: how it works and what it can do', *The Guardian*, 8 June 2013; Glenn Greenwald et al., 'How Microsoft handed the NSA access to encrypted messages', *The Guardian*, 11 July 2013; Shorrock, *Spies for Hire*, p. 26.

12. Ibid., p. 85.

13. *Business Wire*, 'Mandiant Hires Travis Reese as Vice President of Federal Services; Travis Reese, the Former Vice President of ManTech International's Computer Forensics & Intrusion Analysis Group Will Drive Mandiant's Government Business', 25 April 2006.

14. Yang Jinghao and Duan Wuning, 'Regular cyber attacks from US: China', *Global Times*, 21 February 2013.

15. Nina Easton, 'The CEO Who Caught the Chinese Spies Red-Handed', *Fortune*, 22 July 2013, p. 86.

16. Ibid., p. 83.

17. Noah Shachtman, 'Russia's Top Cyber Sleuth Foils US Spies, Helps Kremlin Pals', *Wired*, 23 July 2012.

18. Ibid.

19. Ibid.

20. Eugene Kaspersky, 'What Wired Is Not Telling You—A Response to Noah Shachtman's Article in Wired Magazine', *Nota Bene*, 25 July 2012.

21. *Russia Today*, 'Russia steps into tech competition', 18 June 2009.

22. Government of the Russian Federation, "Указ Президента Российской Федерации от 15.01.2013 N° 31c (выписка) "О создании государственной системы обнаружения, предупреждения и ликвидации последствий компьютерных атак на информационные ресурсы Российской Федерации' ['Decree of the President of the Russian Federation from 15.01.2013 extract n°31c "about an initiative to create a state system of tracking, preventing and removing the outcomes of cyber attacks on informational resources of the russian federation"'], Official Website of the Government of the Russian Federation, http://pravo.gov.ru:8080/page.aspx?35023, accessed 11 July 2016; BBC News, 'Summary of Russian press for Tuesday 22 January 2013', *BBC Monitoring Former Soviet Union*, 22 January 2013.

23. Vladislav Noviy, 'Kaspersky Lab Wants to Save Digital World', *RusData Dialine—BizEkon News*, 4 April 2013.

24. Sergei L. Loiko, 'Russian cyber-security firm reports major malware find', *Los Angeles Times*, 17 January 2013.

25. One publication containing an attribution that did not gain momentum was a December 2012 report by Conflict Armament Research, a small private research group based in the UK. They had investigated for seven years the origin of ammunition manufactured without factory codes and found in several conflicts around the globe. They found out that Iran was a state sponsor behind it. Beside a report in *The New York Times*, and a few states that 'noted' the report, no official statements ever emerged. Conflict Armament Research, 'The distribution of Iranian ammunition in Africa: evidence from a nine-country investigation', (London: Conflict Armament Research, 2012), p. 50. C. J. Chivers, 'A Trail of Bullet Casings Leads From Africa's Wars Back to Iran', *The New York Times*, 11 January 2013. Communication with James Bevan, 17 May 2013.

26. Charlie Osborne, 'US government debates action over alleged Chinese cyberattacks', *ZDNet*, 1 February 2013.

27. Ellen Nakashima, 'U.S. said to be target of massive cyber-espionage campaign', *The Washington Post*, 11 February 2013.

28. *The Washington Post*, 'Cyber-spying said to target U.S. business', 11 February 2013.

29. The White House, 'Improving Critical Infrastructure Cybersecurity' (Washington, DC: 2013).

30. Barack Obama, 'Remarks by the President in the State of the Union Address', The White House, 12 February 2013.

31. The White House, 'Administration Strategy on Mitigating the Theft of U.S. Trade Secrets', (Washington, DC: 2013), p. 141.

32. Discussion with the author on 10 February 2016.

33. Adam Segal, 'Hacking Back, Signaling, and State-Society Relations', *Cyber Dialogue 2013*, 1 March 2013.

34. Anne Flaherty, 'A look at Mandiant, allegations on China hacking', *The Associated Press*, 20 February 2013.

35. 'Private US firms take major role vs. cyberattacks', *The Associated Press*, 21 February 2013.

36. Easton, 'The CEO Who Caught the Chinese Spies Red-Handed', p. 83.

37. Ibid., p. 84.

38. Ibid., p. 88.

39. Ibid., p. 83.

40. *RT*, 'Global cyber war: New Flame-linked malware detected', 16 October 2012.

41. Fahmida Y. Rashid, 'Eugene Kaspersky: Definition Of "Cyberwar" In Flux, Threat Of Cyber Weapons Underestimated', *SecurityWeek*, 21 November 2012.

42. See for instance the numerous details for attribution that Kaspersky Lab provided in its reports on Rocra in 2013, or on The Mask in 2014. Kaspersky Lab, 'The "Red October" Campaign—An Advanced Cyber Espionage Network Targeting Diplomatic and Government Agencies', *SecureList*, 14 January 2013; Kaspersky Lab, 'Kaspersky Lab Uncovers "The Mask": One of the Most Advanced Global Cyber-espionage Operations to Date Due to the Complexity of the Toolset Used by the Attackers', 11 February 2014.

43. Peter Szor, 'Duqu—Threat Research and Analysis', (Santa Clara, CA: McAfee, 2011); McAfee Labs, 'McAfee Labs Consolidated Threat Report: Duqu', (Santa Clara, CA: McAfee, 2012).

44. Boldizsar Bencsath et al., 'Duqu: A Stuxnet-like malware found in the wild' (Budapest: Laboratory of Cryptography and System Security 2011).

45. McAfee Labs, 'McAfee Labs Consolidated Threat Report: Duqu', p. 14; Vitaly Kamluk, 'The Mystery of Duqu: Part Six (The Command and Control servers)', *SecureList*, 30 November 2011.

46. Kenneth Rapoza, '"Duqu" Virus Likely Handiwork Of Sophisticated Government, Kaspersky Lab Says', *Forbes*, 21 October 2011; Tom Espiner, 'McAfee: Why Duqu is a big deal', *ZDNet*, 26 October 2011.

47. Nicole Perlroth, 'Researchers Find Clues in Malware', *The New York Times*, 30 May 2012.

48. Symantec, 'Stuxnet 0.5: The Missing Link' (Mountain View, CA: Symantec, 2013).

49. Interview with Kevin Hagan, 18 October 2013.

50. Ibid.

51. See in Reuters and CBS in the United States and Fars in Iran: Tabassum Zakaria, 'First came Stuxnet computer virus: now there's Duqu', *Reuters*, 18 October 2011; Charlie Rose et al., 'For March 5, 2012, CBS', *CBS News Transcripts*, 5 March 2012; FARS News Agency, 'Iran Stops Israeli Duqu Virus Attack', 15 November 2011.

52. Alyssa Ames, 'Kaspersky Lab's Policy on the Use of Software for the Purpose of State Surveillance', Kaspersky Lab, 11 June 2013.

53. Dan Goodin, 'Kaspersky: "We detect and remediate any malware attack," even by NSA (Updated)', *ArsTechnica*, 6 November 2013.

54. John Leyden, 'AV vendors split over FBI Trojan snoops', *The Register*, 27 November 2001.

55. Ted Bridis, 'FBI Is Building a "Magic Lantern"', *The Washington Post*, 23 November 2001.

56. Flora Graham, 'Police "encouraged" to hack more', BBC News, 5 January 2009.

57. Ibid.

58. Tom Espiner, 'Police set up regional hacking units', *ZDNet*, 26 July 2011.

59. *Der Spiegel*, 'CCC findet Sicherheitslücken in Bundestrojaner [CCC finds security breach in the Bundestrojaner]', 8 October 2011.

60. Clement Guitton, 'A Review of the Available Content on Tor Hidden Services: The Case Against Further Development', *Computers in Human Behavior* 29, 6 (2013).

61. Steven J. Vaughan-Nichols, 'Inside the Tor exploit', *ZDNet*, 5 August 2013; Larry Seltzer, 'The professionalization of malware', *ZDNet*, 19 August 2013.

62. Eli Dourado, 'Put trust back in the Internet', *The New York Times*, 10 October 2013.

63. An example of this mistrust is the US government's avoidance of purchasing Russian cyber security products, 'out of concern they could have hidden functions that might allow Moscow to penetrate U.S. networks'. Jim Finkle, 'Kaspersky plans push for sales to U.S. government', *Reuters*, 15 May 2014.

64. *Der Spiegel*, 'Computerspionage: Chinesische Trojaner auf PCs im Kanzleramt', http://www.spiegel.de/netzwelt/tech/0,1518,501954,00.html, accessed 11 July 2016; Richard Norton-Taylor, 'Titan Rain—how Chinese hackers targeted Whitehall', *The Guardian*, 5 September 2007, http://www.guardian.co.uk/technology/2007/sep/04/news.internet, accessed 11 July 2016; Agence France-Presse, 'La France victime de cyber-attaques avec "passage" par la Chine', AFP, http://www.ladepeche.fr/article/2007/09/08/9369-la-france-victime-de-cyber-attaques-chinoises.html, accessed 11 July 2016.

65. Greg Watson, 'Foreign hackers attack Canadian government', *CBCNews*, 16 February 2011.

66. Ibid.

67. Dmitri Alperovitch, 'Revealed: Operation Shady RAT' (Santa Clara, CA: McAfee, 2011).

68. Ibid., p. 6.

69. Mathew J. Schwartz and J. Nicolas Hoover, 'China Suspected Of Shady RAT Attacks', *InformationWeek*, 3 August 2011; Richi Jennings, 'Operation Shady RAT smells like Chinese hacking', *Computerworld*, 3 August 2011; Michael Joseph Gross, 'Exclusive: Operation Shady Rat—Unprecedented Cyber-espionage Campaign and Intellectual-Property Bonanza', *Vanity Fair*, 2 August 2011.

70. 'M Trends: The advanced persistent threat' (Alexandria, VA: 2013).

71. Mandiant, 'APT1: Exposing One of China's Cyber Espionage Units' (Alexandria, VA: Mandiant, 2013), p. 2.

72. Prior to Mandiant's report, official references to China as an instigator were rare but not non-existent. For instance, General Keith Alexander, the director of the NSA and head of the US Cyber Command made such a reference in March 2012 in front of the Senate Armed Services Committee. Colin Clark, 'China Attacked Internet Security Company RSA, Cyber Commander Tells SASC', *Breaking Defense*, 27 March 2014.

73. Verizon, '2013 Data Breach Investigation Report' (New York: Verizon, 2013), p. 63.

74. Ibid.

75. Agence France-Presse, 'Obama says some Chinese cyber attacks state sponsored', 13 March 2013.

76. David E. Sanger, 'U.S. Directly Blames China's Military for Cyber-attacks', *The New York Times*, 6 May 2013.

77. Ibid.; Reuters, 'Pentagon accuses China of trying to hack US defence networks', *The Guardian*, 7 May 2013.

78. David E. Sanger, 'As Chinese Leader's Visit Nears, U.S. Is Urged to Allow Counterattacks on Hackers', *The New York Times*, 21 May 2013.

79. US Department of Defense, 'Annual Report to Congress: Military and Security Developments Involving the People's Republic of China 2013' (Washington, DC: Department of Defense 2013).

80. Judiciary Subcommitee on Crime & Terrorism, 'Cybersecurity Threats'.

81. Reuters, 'Pentagon accuses China of trying to hack US defence networks', *The Guardian*, 7 May 2013.

82. Indicting alleged state-sponsored hackers then became a new US policy. In 2016 it went alongside indicting further hackers acting on behalf of the Syrian and Iranian governments.

83. Oliver Joy, 'Mandiant: China is sponsoring cyber-espionage', *CNN*, 20 February 2013.

84. Reuters, 'China says U.S. hacking accusations lack technical proof', 20 February 2013.

85. Mandiant, 'APT1'.

86. Ibid., p. 7. The individual was found while monitoring a command-and-control server the group was using, so his link with the group is strong.

87. Tom Donilon, 'Remarks By Tom Donilon, National Security Advisory to the President: "The United States and the Asia-Pacific in 2013"' (Washington, DC: The White House, 11 March 2013).

88. China Business News, 'Ministry of Foreign Affairs of the People's Republic of China: Foreign Ministry Spokesperson Hua Chunying's Regular Press Conference on March 12, 2013', *China Business News*, 13 March 2013.

89. David E. Sanger and Mark Landler, 'U.S. and China Agree to Hold Regular Talks on Hacking', *The New York Times*, 1 June 2013.

90. Tony Romm, 'President Obama likely to talk softly with China on cyber-snooping', *Politico*, 2 June 2013.

91. Jackie Calmes and Steven Lee Myers, 'Hit and miss for Obama and Xi', *The New York Times*, 10 June 2013.

92. Two other cases sponsored by the United States are also worth mentioning: Flame (discovered by Kaspersky Lab as they investigated Wiper in Iran, a malware which deleted everything even itself), and Gauss. Ellen Nakashima, Greg Miller and Julie Tate, 'U.S., Israel developed Flame computer virus to slow Iranian nuclear efforts, officials say', *The Washington Post*, 19 June 2012; Kaspersky Lab, 'Gauss: Nation-state cyber-surveillance meets banking Trojan', SecureList, https://securelist.com/blog/incidents/33854/gauss-nation-state-cyber-surveillance-meets-banking-trojan-54/, accessed 13 July 2016.

93. Matthew M. Aid, 'Inside the NSA's Ultra-Secret China Hacking Group', *Foreign Policy*, 10 June 2013.

94. Reuters, 'China has "mountains of data" about U.S. cyber attacks: official', 5 June 2013.

95. Toby Helm, Daniel Boffey and Nick Hopkins, 'Snowden spy row grows as US is accused of hacking China', *The Guardian*, 22 June 2013.

96. Ibid.

97. Andrew Jacobs, 'After Reports on N.S.A., China Urges End to Spying', *The New York Times*, 24 March 2014.

98. George Koo and Ling-chi Wang, 'Shoddy evidence and past hypocrisy weaken US cyber-spying charges', *Global Times*, 6 March 2012.

99. Henry Farrell and Martha Finnemore, 'The End of Hypocrisy', *Foreign Affairs* 92, 6 (2013).

100. David E. Sanger and Thom Shanker, 'N.S.A. Devises Radio Pathway Into Computers', *The New York Times*, 14 January 2014.

101. David E. Sanger and Nicole Perlroth, 'Chinese Hackers Resume Attacks on U.S. Targets', *The New York Times*, 19 May 2013.

102. John Leyden, 'Chinese cyber-spook crew back in business, say security watchers', *The Register*, 29 April 2013; David E. Sanger and Nicole Perlroth, 'Hackers From China Resume Attacks on U.S. Targets', *The New York Times*, 19 May 2013.

103. Edward Wong, 'Hacking U.S. Secrets, China Pushes for Drones', *The New York Times*, 20 September 2013.

104. Michael S. Schmidt, 'U.S. to Charge Chinese Army Personnel With Cyberspying', *The New York Times*, 19 May 2014; Ellen Nakashima, 'U.S. to announce first criminal charges against China for cyberspying', *The Washington Post*, 19 May 2014.

105. *United States of America v. Wang Dong, Sun Kailiang, Wen Xinyu, Huang Zhenyu, Gu Chunhui*, [1 May 2014], W.D. Pa., 14–118.

106. FBI, 'Cyber's Most Wanted', https://www.fbi.gov/wanted/cyber, accessed 13 July 2016.

107. This (legal) thinking is also contrary to the prevalent practice of the International Criminal Court, for instance, where the emphasis has traditionally been top-down, bringing charges against leaders but not against mere 'executioners'. Phil Clark, 'All Justice Is Local', *The New York Times*, 11 June 2014.

108. Ryan Naraine, 'New variant shows Duqu attackers still in operation', *ZDNet*, 20 March 2012.

109. Nart Villeneuve and Masashi Crete-Nishihata, 'Control and Resistance: Attacks on Burmese Opposition Media', in *Access Contested: Security, Identity, and Resistance in Asian Cyberspace*, ed. Ronald Deibert, et al. (Cambridge, MA: MIT Press, 2012); The SecDev Group and The Citizen Lab, 'Tracking GhostNet: Investigating a Cyber Espionage Network', (Toronto: Munk Centre for International Studies, 2009).

110. Juan Andrés Guerrero-Saade, 'The Ethics and Perils of APT Research:

An Unexpected Transition into Intelligence Brokerage', *Virus Bulletin Conference*, September 2015.

111. Kevin Mandia, 'The State of Incident Response', talk at the BlackHat Conference (Las Vegas, NV: 2006), http://www.youtube.com/watch?v=Jqv93DcZdDE, accessed 6 October 2016.

112. Jen Weedon, 'No Clearance Required: Using Commercial Threat Intelligence in the Federal Space' (Alexandria, VA: Mandiant, 2 May 2013).

113. Eamon Javers, 'Cybersecurity Firm Says It Is Under Attack', *CNBC*, 20 March 2013.

114. The reason for this request is still unclear, but it is common enough for information to be provided on such a condition when it could reveal secret techniques used by the informant, or when the informant has, embarrassingly, already been a victim of the attack. Interview with Kevin Hagan, 18 October 2013.

5. TIME

1. Richard A. Clarke and Steven Andreasen, 'Cyberwar's threat does not justify a new policy of nuclear deterrence', *The Washington Post*, 15 June 2013.

2. Jody M. Prescott, 'Autonomous Decision-Making Processes and the Responsible Cyber Commander' (paper presented at the 5th International Conference on Cyber Conflict, Tallinn, 2013).

3. Peter Feaver and Kenneth Geers, '"When the Urgency of Time and Circumstances Clearly Does Not Permit...": Predelegation in Nuclear and Cyber Scenarios', in *Cyber Analogies*, ed. Emily O. Goldman and John Arquilla (Monterey, CA: Naval Postgraduate School, 2014), p. 34.

4. Paul Pierson, *Politics in Time: History, institutions, and social analysis* (Princeton, NJ: Princeton University Press, 2004), p. 54.

5. Gary McGraw, 'Cyber War is Inevitable (Unless We Build Security In)', *Journal of Strategic Studies* 36, 1 (2012), p. 114.

6. Stephen Graham, 'The end of geography or the explosion of place? Conceptualizing space, place and information technology', *Human Geography* 22, 2 (1998).

7. Jill Lawrence, 'Gore Denounces Bush Jobs Plan As Ploy for Votes', *The Associated Press*, 25 August 1992.

8. Marisa Gomez, 'Cyberspace and real time: The virtual beyond the screen', *Interartive*, June 2009.

9. Brian E. Finch, 'Forget The Red Line, Worry About the Digital Line', *The Huffington Post*, 26 September 2013.

10. Feaver and Geers, '"When the Urgency of Time"', p. 38.

11. The Associated Press, 'Pentagon still grappling with rules of cyber-

war', 25 July 2012; Committee on Homeland Security and Governmental Affairs, 'The Department of Homeland Security At 10 Years: Examining Challenges and Achievements and Addressing Emerging Threats' (Washington, DC: 2013); CBS, 'Face the Nation', *Federal News Service*, 10 February 2013.

12. Michael S. Goodman, 'Applying the Historical Lessons of Surprise Attack to the Cyber Domain: The Example of the United Kingdom', in *Cyber Analogies*, ed. Emily O. Goldman and John Arquilla (Monterey, CA: Naval Postgraduate School, 2014), p. 18.

13. Feaver and Geers, '"When the Urgency of Time"', p. 39; Michael Hayden, 'Keynote' (paper presented at the Black Hat conference, Las Vegas, NV, 2010).

14. William Jackson, 'Former FBI cyber cop: Hunt the hacker, not the hack', *Government Computer News*, 19 April 2012.

15. Jonathan Masters, 'Here's How The U.S. Plans To Plug The Holes In Its Cybersecurity Policy', *The Business Insider*, 24 May 2011.

16. US-China Economic and Security Review Commission, 'China's Views of Sovereignty and Methods of Access Control', (Washington, DC: Federal News Service, 2008).

17. Susan W. Brenner, '"At Light Speed": Attribution and Response to Cybercrime/Terrorism/Warfare', *The Journal of Criminal Law & Criminology* 97, 2 (2007), p. 420.

18. Ibid.

19. Eneken Tikk and Kadri Kaska, 'Legal Cooperation to Investigate Cyber Incidents: Estonian Case Study and Lessons' (paper presented at the 9th European Conference on Information Warfare and Security, Thessaloniki, 2010).

20. Interview with Kevin Hagan, 18 October 2013.

21. Similarly, studies on the timing for reacting to cyber attacks have attracted technical experts who apply technical understanding to political questions: a mathematical model cannot reflect the chain of decisions taking place within the executive to reach a conclusion. See Robert Axelrod and Rumen Iliev, 'Timing of cyber conflict', *PNAS* (2014).

22. Atlantic Council, 'Lessons from Our Cyber Past: The First Cyber Cops', 16 May 2012.

23. Ibid.

24. Wireless News, 'CrowdStrike Unveils Big Data Active Defense Platform', 29 June 2013.

25. Ibid.

26. Clifford Stoll, *The Cuckoo's Egg: Tracking a Spy Through the Maze of Computer Espionage* (New York: Doubleday, 1989).

27. Ibid.
28. John Markoff, 'Author of Computer 'Virus' Is Son Of N.S.A. Expert on Data Security', *The New York Times*, 5 November 1988.
29. Katie Hafner and John Markoff, *Cyberpunk: Outlaws and Hackers on the Computer Frontier* (New York: Simon & Schuster, 1995).
30. Richard Power, 'Joy Riders: Mischief That Leads to Mayhem', *informIT*, 30 October 2000.
31. Ibid.
32. US Department of Agriculture, 'Hacking U.S. Government Computers from Overseas', US Department of Agriculture, http://www.sri-hq.com/SRI-NET/Security/Spystory/Hacking.htm#hacking, accessed 6 October 2016.
33. Seth Mydans, 'Student Sought In Virus Case In Philippines', *The New York Times*, 11 May 2000.
34. Ibid.
35. Andrew Brandt, 'Stupid hacker tricks, part two: The folly of youth', *InfoWorld Daily News*, 5 May 2005.
36. *Business Wire*, 'Symantec Sees Decrease in New W32.Blaster.Worm Infections; Systems in the United States, United Kingdom, Canada, Australia and Ireland Most Affected', 13 August 2003.
37. *United States of America v. Jeffrey Lee Parson*, [August 2003], W.D. Wash., 03–457M.
38. John Leyden, 'Blaster-F suspect charged with cybercrime', *The Register*, 11 September 2003.
39. Dan Verton and Andrew Brandt, 'Biography of a Worm', PCWorld, http://www.networkworld.com/article/2326282/cloud-computing/biography-of-a-worm.html, accessed 15 July 2016. Both Blaster and Sobig infected at least half a million computers within less than a week, forcing institutions to close for a few days to clean up their machines. Victims of Blaster included for instance: the Maryland Motor Vehicle Administration, the financial group Nordea, the US Senate, and the Federal Reserve Bank of Atlanta. See: ZDNet, 5 November 2003.
40. Interview with Kevin Hagan, 18 October 2013.
41. HMIC, 'The Strategic Policing Requirement: An inspection of the arrangements that police forces have in place to meet the Strategic Policing Requirement' (London: HMIC, 2014).
42. Ibid.
43. Ian Brown and Douwe Korff, 'Terrorism and the Proportionality of Internet Surveillance', *European Journal of Criminology* 6 (2009), p. 125.
44. One of the differences between the United States and the United Kingdom concerns how they view the need for a warrant to access

information. In the United States, a warrant is required for US citizens, but the law is much more flexible for non-US citizens. In the United Kingdom, citizenship does not matter, only geographical boundaries do: if an individual is communicating from the United Kingdom, strict regulations apply; if they are outside the country, then law enforcement agencies have more options. Avner Levin and Paul Goodrick, 'From cybercrime to cyberwar? The international policy shift and its implications for Canada', *Canadian Foreign Policy Journal* 19, 2 (2013), p. 133.

45. Atlantic Council, 'Lessons from Our Cyber Past'.
46. Ibid.
47. Ibid.
48. Senate Armed Services Committee, 'Current and Future Worldwide Threats to the National Security of the United States', (Washington, DC: Federal News Service, 2012).
49. Gordon Corera, 'Under Attack: The Threat from Cyberspace', *BBC Radio 4*, 1 July 2013.
50. Ibid.
51. Randall Dipert, 'Response to Cyber Attacks: The Attribution Problem', USNA 2012 McCain Conference (Annapolis, MD, 2012).
52. Michael N. Schmitt and Liis Vihul, 'The International Law of Attribution During Proxy "Wars" in Cyberspace', *Fletcher Security Review* 1 (2014).
53. Jack P. Gibbs, 'Deterrence Theory and Research', in ed. Gary B. Melton, *Nebraska Symposium on Motivation: The Law as a Behavioral Instrument* (Lincoln, NE: University of Nebraska Press, 1985), p. 89.
54. Ibid., p. 101.
55. Interview with Keith Roscoe, 16 July 2012.
56. Ibid.
57. BBC News, 'Man jailed over computer password refusal', 5 October 2010.
58. See for instance the case of Mathew Bevan, where evidence appeared three years after the misdeeds: Kuji Media Corporation, 'History', http://www.kujimedia.com/articles/, accessed 8 July 2016.
59. McGee, Sabet and Shah, 'Adequate Attribution', p. 33.
60. Helena Brito, 'Q&A Follow-up—Tools of Engagement: The Mechanics of Threat Intelligence', *Mandiant*, 30 April 2013.
61. Government of the United States, 'United States Submission to the UN Group of Governmental Experts on Developments in the Field of Information and Telecommunications in the Context of International Security' (Washington, DC: Government of the United States, 2012).
62. Pauline C. Reich et al., 'Cyber Warfare: A Review of Theories, Law,

Policies, Actual Incidents—and the Dilemma of Anonymity', *European Journal of Law and Technology* 1, 2 (2010), p. 20.

63. David E. Sanger, 'U.S. Tries Candor to Assure China on Cyberattacks', *The New York Times*, 6 April 2014.

64. Martin C. Libicki, *Cyberdeterrence and Cyberwar* (Santa Monica, CA: RAND, 2009).

65. Atlantic Council, 'Lessons from Our Cyber Past'.

66. Tim Stevens, 'A Cyberwar of Ideas? Deterrence and Norms in Cyberspace', *Contemporary Security Policy* 33, 1 (2012); Sheldon Whitehouse, 'At West Point, Whitehouse Calls for Greater Awareness of Cyber Threats', 4 June 2012, http://www.whitehouse.senate.gov/news/release/at-west-point-whitehouse-calls-for-greater-awareness-of-cyber-threats, accessed 1 July 2016.

67. Libicki, *Cyberdeterrence and Cyberwar*, p. 97.

68. Ibid.

69. Eugene Kaspersky, 'The Man Who Found Stuxnet—Sergey Ulasen in the Spotlight', 2 November 2011, https://eugenekaspersky.com/2011/11/02/the-man-who-found-stuxnet-sergey-ulasen-in-the-spotlight/, accessed 6 October 2016.

70. Ellen Nakashima, Greg Miller and Julie Tate, 'U.S., Israel developed Flame computer virus to slow Iranian nuclear efforts, officials say', *The Washington Post*, 19 June 2012.

71. Dataquest, 'Cyberspace as Global Commons: The Challenges', *Dataquest*, 15 April 2012.

72. Dmitri Alperovitch, 'Offence as the Best Defence' (Brisbane: AusCERT, 2013); McAfee, 'In the Dark—Crucial Industries Confront Cyberattacks', (Santa Clara, CA: McAfee, 2011); Thomas Rid, *Cyber War Will Not Take Place* (London: Hurst & Company, 2013).

73. Niles Lathem, 'Bin Laden Made Tape Vowing Attack', *The New York Post*, 14 October 2013; Brian Nelson and Peter Bergen, 'Osama Bin Laden No. 1 Suspect in U.S.S. Cole Bombing', *CNN*, 14 October 2000.

74. Lawrence Wright, *The Looming Tower: Al-Qaeda's Road to 9/11* (London: Penguin Books, 2006), p. 318.

75. The Associated Press, 'U.S. official draws similarities to embassy bombings', 22 October 2000.

76. Ahmed Al-Haj, 'Investigators find link between Cole, African embassy bombings', *Associated Press International*, 23 November 2000.

77. Bill Hutchinson, 'Two busted in Cole blast: Investigators find bomb factory in Yemen apartment', *Daily News*, 18 October 2000.

78. Donna Abu-Nasr, 'One of suspected Cole bombers was Egyptian, Yemen's president says', *The Associated Press*, 25 October 2000.

79. Wright, *The Looming Tower: Al-Qaeda's Road to 9/11*, p. 329.

80. Deutsche Presse Agentur, 'Bin Laden denies links to USS Cole bomb-

ing, Kuwait group', 13 November 2000; Agence France-Presse, 'Bin Laden Is Reported "Satisfied" By Cole Hit', *The New York Times*, 5 November 2000.

81. Richard Sale, 'Clinton Administration considers strike options', *United Press International*, 28 November 2000.

82. The White House Bulletin, 'Investigators Close To Tying USS Cole Bombing To Bin Laden', *The White House Bulletin*, 11 December 2000; Corky Siemaszko, 'Bin Laden Linked to Bombing of Cole', *Daily News*, 11 December 2000.

83. Jim Mannion, 'US officials point to terrorism in navy destroyer blast', Agence France-Presse, 12 October 2000.

84. Philip Shenon, *The Commission: The Uncensored History of the 9/11 Investigation* (New York: Twelve, 2008), p. 315.

85. Nicole Perlroth, 'Hackers in China Attacked The Times for Last 4 Months', *The New York Times*, 30 January 2013.

86. Nina Easton, 'The CEO Who Caught the Chinese Spies Red-Handed', *Fortune*, 22 July 2013, p. 84.

87. Corera, 'Under Attack: The Threat from Cyberspace'.

88. ABC News, 'China blamed after ASIO blueprints stolen in major cyber attack on Canberra HQ', 28 May 2013.

89. *The Guardian*, 'Asio hacking claim won't hurt Australia—China ties, says Carr', 28 May 2013.

90. Ibid.

91. Mark Kenny, 'Gillard scores coup with China agreement', *The Sydney Morning Herald*, 10 April 2013.

92. *The Guardian*, 'Asio hacking claim won't hurt Australia'.

93. John Lyons and Paulo Trevisani, 'Brazil President Halts Planning for U.S. Visit Over NSA Spying Rift', *The Wall Street Journal*, 5 September 2013.

6. PLAUSIBLE DENIABILITY

1. Gregory F. Treverton, *Covert Actions: The limits of intervention in the post-war world* (New York: Basic Books, 1987), p. 73.

2. Ibid.

3. Select Committee to Study Governmental Operations with Respect to Intelligence Activities, 'Alleged assassination plots involving foreign leaders: an interim report of the Select Committee to Study Governmental Operations with Respect to Intelligence Activities, United States Senate: together with additional, supplemental and separate views', (Washington, DC: US Government Printing Office, 1975).

4. Treverton, *Covert Actions*, p. 229.

5. Ibid., p. 230.

6. Mark Clayton, 'Stealing US business secrets: Experts ID two huge cyber "gangs" in China', *The Christian Science Monitor*, 14 September 2012.

7. Agence France-Presse, 'Cybersecurity summit kicks off with calls to action', 4 May 2010.

8. Cybersecurity, Infrastructure Protection, and Security Technologies, 'Iranian Cyber Threat to the U.S. Homeland', (Washington, DC: 2012).

9. Office of the National Counterintelligence Executive, 'Foreign spies stealing US economic secrets in cyberspace: Report to Congress on Foreign Economic Collection and Industrial Espionage, 2009–2011' (Washington, DC: ONCIX, 2011), p. 1.

10. Ibid., p. 20.

11. Harold Hongju Koh, 'International Law in Cyberspace', in *USCYBER-COM Inter-Agency Legal Conference* (Fort Meade, MD: 2012).

12. Atlantic Council of the United States, 'International Engagement on Cyber: Establishing Norms and Improved Security', in *National and Global Strategies for Managing Cyberspace and Security* (Washington, DC: 2011).

13. For a review of how these legal rulings apply to cyber attacks, see Michael N. Schmitt and Liis Vihul, 'The International Law of Attribution During Proxy "Wars" in Cyberspace', *Fletcher Security Review* 1 (2014).

14. Ibid., p. 12.

15. Office of the National Counterintelligence Executive, 'Foreign spies stealing US economic secrets in cyberspace'.

16. Intelligence and Security Committee of Parliament, 'Annual Report 2012–2013' (London: UK Parliament, 2013).

17. Heli Tiirmaa-Klaar, 'Protecting cyberspace at different levels: Vulnerabilities and responses' (Tallinn: Estonian Ministry of Foreign Affairs, 2009).

18. Richard A. Clarke and Robert K. Knake, *Cyber War: The Next Threat to National Security and What to Do About It* (New York: Ecco, 2010), p. 177.

19. Timothy Thomas, 'Russia's Information Warfare Strategy: Can the Nation Cope in Future Conflicts?', *The Journal of Slavic Military Studies* 27, 1 (2014), p. 107.

20. Mark Mazzetti, 'F.B.I. Informant Is Tied to Cyberattacks Abroad', *The New York Times*, 23 April 2014.

21. On suspicions that were still unconfirmed before the aforementioned article in *The New York Times*, see Parmy Olson, *We Are Anonymous* (London: William Heinemann, 2012), p. 406.

22. Brian Krebs, 'Shadowy Russian Firm Seen as Conduit for Cybercrime', *The Washington Post*, 13 October 2007.

23. Andrew Donoghue, 'Russian Police And Internet Registry Accused Of Aiding Cybercrime', *TechWeek Europe*, 21 October 2009; Jeffrey Carr, *Inside Cyber Warfare* (Sebastopol, CA: O'Reilly, 2010), p. 122; David Bizeul, 'Russian Business Network study', 20 November 2007, http://www.bizeul.org/files/RBN_study.pdf, accessed 20 July 2016.

24. Donoghue, 'Russian Police And Internet Registry'.

25. Krebs, 'Shadowy Russian Firm Seen as Conduit for Cybercrime'.

26. Donoghue, 'Russian Police And Internet Registry'.

27. Ronald J. Deibert and Rafal Rohozinski, 'Risking Security: Policies and Paradoxes of Cyberspace Security', *International Political Sociology* 4 (2010), p. 21.

28. Eneken Tikk et al., 'Cyber Attacks Against Georgia: Legal Lessons Identified', (Tallinn: CCDCOE, 2008); Marco Roscini, *Cyber Operations and the Use of Force in International Law* (New York: Oxford University Press, 2014), p. 36; John Markoff, 'Before the Gunfire, Cyberattacks', *The New York Times*, 12 August 2008.

29. Julian E. Barnes and Siobhan Gorman, 'U.S. Says Iran Hacked Navy Computers', *The Wall Street Journal*, 27 September 2013; Siobhan Gorman and Julian E. Barnes, 'Iranian Hacking to Test NSA Nominee Michael Rogers', *The Wall Street Journal*, 18 February 2014.

30. Barnes and Gorman, 'U.S. Says Iran Hacked Navy Computers'.

31. Riva Richmond, 'An Attack Sheds Light on Internet Security Holes', *The New York Times*, 6 April 2011.

32. John Leyden, 'Inside "Operation Black Tulip": DigiNotar hack analysed', *The Register*, 6 September 2011.

33. Somini Sengupta, 'In Latest Breach, Hackers Impersonate Google to Snoop on Users in Iran', *The New York Times*, 30 August 2011.

34. Comodohacker, 'Striking back…', Pastebin, http://pastebin.com/1AxH30em, accessed 18 July 2016.

35. Fox-IT, 'Interim Report: DigiNotar Certificate Authority breach "Operation Black Tulip"', (Delft: Fox-IT, 2011).

36. Ibid., p. 6.

37. Fox-IT, 'Black Tulip: Report of the investigation into the DigiNotar Certificate Authority breach ', (Delft: Fox-IT, 2012).

38. Rid, *Cyber War Will Not Take Place*, p. 30.

39. Matthew Rice, 'Exploiting privacy: Surveillance companies pushing zero-day exploits', *Privacy International*, 11 March 2014.

40. Danielle Walker, 'NSA sought services of French security firm, zero-day seller Vupen', *SC Magazine*, 18 September 2014.

41. Nicole Perlroth and David E. Sanger, 'Nations Buying as Hackers Sell Flaws in Computer Code', *The New York Times*, 13 July 2013.

42. Cristinano Lincoln Mattos, interview with the author, 20 June 2013.

43. Jonathan Lusthaus, 'How organised is organised cybercrime?', *Global Crime* 14, 1 (2013), p. 59.

44. Ibid., p. 57.

45. David S. Wall, 'Internet Mafias? The Dis-Organisation of Crime on the Internet', in *Organized Crime, Corruption and Crime Prevention*, ed. Stefano Caneppele and Francesco Calderoni (Cham: Springer, 2014).

46. Sergio Caltagirone, Andrew Pendergast and Christopher Betz, *The Diamond Model of Intrusion Analysis* (Arlington, VA: Threat Connect, 2013), p. 12.

47. Treverton, *Covert Actions*, p. 124.

48. Agence France-Presse, 'China "gravely concerned" over US cyber attacks', 23 June 2013.

49. Robert Axelrod, 'A Repertory of Cyber Analogies', in *Cyber Analogies*, ed. Emily O. Goldman and John Arquilla (Monterey, CA: Naval Postgraduate School, 2014), p. 114.

50. Ibid.

51. The same conclusions have been reached concerning terrorist attacks. The political scientists Keir Lieber and Daryl Press came to the conclusion that there is a 'strong positive relationship between the number of fatalities stemming from an attack and the rate of attribution'. Keir A. Lieber and Daryl G. Press, 'Why States Won't Give Nuclear Weapons to Terrorists', *International Security* 38, 1 (2013), p. 83.

52. Alexander Gostev and Igor Soumenkov, 'Stuxnet/Duqu: The Evolution of Drivers', *SecureList*, 28 December 2011.

53. Kaspersky Lab, 'Kaspersky Lab Uncovers "The Mask": One of the Most Advanced Global Cyber-espionage Operations to Date Due to the Complexity of the Toolset Used by the Attackers', 11 February 2014.

54. Danielle Walker, 'Millions stolen from US banks after "wire payment switch" targeted', *SC Magazine*, 21 August 2013.

55. Alastair Stevenson, 'Police arrest teenage hacker behind $50,000-per-month cyber ring', *V3*, 16 September 2013; The Associated Press, 'Teen "super-hacker" in Argentina arrested in mass raid', *CBC*, 14 September 2013.

56. Treverton, *Covert Actions*, p. viii.

57. The oldest non-declassified document is an example of such bureaucracy: a 1917 ink recipe, made public in a 1931 book. Despite the 'secret' recipe not being quite so secret anymore, and despite the important changes in communication since that time, the CIA still refuses to declassify it because it is apparently still in use. Mark S. Zaid, 'Central Intelligence Agency Refuses to Release Oldest US Classified Documents Sought in Litigation', *Federation of American*

Scientists, 30 March 1999. Also, about secrecy in bureaucracies, see Max Weber, *Essays in sociology*, ed. H. H. Gerth and C. Wright Mills, trans. H. H. Gerth and C. Wright Mills (New York: Oxford University Press, 1946), pp. 233–4.

58. David E. Sanger, 'Budget Documents Detail Extent of U.S. Cyber-operations', *The New York Times*, 31 August 2013.

59. Rid, *Cyber War Will Not Take Place*.

60. James R. Clapper, 'DNI Statement on Activities Authorized Under Section 702 of FISA', Washington, DC: Office of the Director of National Intelligence, 6 June 2013.

61. A recent example of such techniques was the FBI's use of a 'sink hole' attack, whereby the agency planted malware on a server hosting many child pornography websites on Tor, in order to identify the authors and visitors of these websites. The FBI was ultimately successful in arresting one of the leaders of the ring. Kevin Poulsen, 'FBI Admits It Controlled Tor Servers Behind Mass Malware Attack', 13 September 2013; Steven J. Vaughan-Nichols, 'Inside the Tor exploit', *ZDNet*, 5 August 2013.

62. Barack Obama, 'Remarks by the President on Review of Signals Intelligence', Washington, DC: The White House, 17 January 2014.

63. Charlie Savage, 'Judge Questions Legality of N.S.A. Phone Records', *The New York Times*, 16 December 2013.

64. Tabassum Zakaria and Warren Strobel, 'After "cataclysmic" Snowden affair, NSA faces winds of change', *Reuters*, 13 December 2013. 'Snowden gained access to some of the documents he took by per-suading 20 to 25 of his colleagues to give him their logins and pass-words, saying he needed the information to check on some technical problems. Most of these officials were subsequently fired for their careless trust', Fred Kaplan, 'The Leaky Myth of Snowden', *Slate*, 16 September 2016. http://www.slate.com/articles/news_and_politics/war_stories/2016/09/what_snowden_gets_wrong_about_its_hero.html?wpsrc=sh_all_dt_tw_bot, accessed 7 October 2016.

65. Scott Shane, 'No Morsel Too Minuscule for All-Consuming N.S.A.', *The New York Times*, 2 November 2013.

66. David Betz and Tim Stevens, *Cyberspace and the state: toward a strategy for cyber-power* (Abingdon and New York: International Institute for Strategic Studies, 2011), p. 67.

67. Chris C. Demchak, 'Economic and Political Coercion and a Rising Cyber Westphalia', in *Peacetime Regime for State Activities in Cyberspace*, ed. Katharina Ziolkowski (Tallinn: NATO CCD COE Publication, 2013), pp. 595–6.

68. Barton Gellman and Ellen Nakashima, 'U.S. spy agencies mounted 231

offensive cyber-operations in 2011, documents show', *The Washington Post*, 31 August 2013.

69. Schmitt and Vihul, 'The International Law of Attribution', p. 1.
70. Lawrence Freedman and Srinath Raghavan, 'Coercion', in *Security Studies*, ed. Paul D. Williams (Abingdon and New York: Routledge, 2008), p. 219.
71. Christopher Bronk and Eneken Tikk-Ringas, 'The Cyber Attack on Saudi Aramco', *Survival* 55, 2 (2013).
72. *The Guardian*, 'Former US general James Cartwright named in Stuxnet leak inquiry', 28 June 2013.
73. Ivanka Barzashka, 'Are Cyber-Weapons Effective?', *The RUSI Journal* 158, 2 (2013); Colin S. Gray, *Making Strategic Sense of Cyber Power: Why the Sky Is Not Falling* (Carliste Barracks, PA: Strategic Studies Institute, U.S. Army War College Press, 2013), p. 45.
74. The Chair Committee investigated US intelligence agencies in 1975, after the Watergate affair and a series of allegations against the CIA assassination programme. Following the report, which strongly criticised the way in which the intelligence apparatus conducted itself based on unverifiable oral exchanges, many more controls were added to ensure the responsibility of intelligence units.
75. John Jacob Nutter, *The CIA's Black Ops: Covert Action, Foreign Policy, and Democracy* (New York: Prometheus Books, 2000), p. 37.
76. Treverton, *Covert Actions*, p. 179.
77. Ibid.
78. Mandiant, 'APT1: Exposing One of China's Cyber Espionage Units' (Alexandria, VA: Mandiant, 2013), p. 76; Agence France-Presse, 'Obama says some Chinese cyber attacks state sponsored', 13 March 2013; Perlroth and Sanger, 'Nations Buying as Hackers Sell Flaws in Computer Code'.
79. John Leyden, 'Chinese cyber-spook crew back in business, say security watchers', *The Register*, 29 April 2013; David E. Sanger and Nicole Perlroth, 'Hackers From China Resume Attacks on U.S. Targets', *The New York Times*, 19 May 2013.
80. Schmitt and Vihul, 'The International Law of Attribution During Proxy "Wars" in Cyberspace', p. 8; Nicole Perlroth, 'Hunting for Syrian Hackers' Chain of Command', *The New York Times*, 17 May 2013.
81. Jennifer Preston, 'Seeking to Disrupt Protesters, Syria Cracks Down on Social Media', ibid., 23 May 2011.
82. Max Fisher, 'Syrian hackers claim AP hack that tipped stock market by $136 billion. Is it terrorism?', *Washington Post*, 23 April 2013.
83. Will Oremus, 'Would You Click the Link in This Email That Apparently Tricked the AP?', *Slate*, 23 April 2013.

84. Alina Selyukh, 'Hackers send fake market-moving AP tweet on White House explosions', *Reuters*, 23 April 2013.
85. Will Oremus, 'The Syrian Hackers Are Winning. Here's Why', *Slate*, 15 August 2013.
86. Brian Ries, 'Syrian Electronic Army Leader Says the Hacks Won't Stop', *The Daily Beast*, 14 August 2013.
87. Kenneth Geers and Ayed Alqartah, 'Syrian Electronic Army Hacks Major Communications Websites', *FireEye*, 30 July 2013.
88. Perlroth, 'Hunting for Syrian Hackers' Chain of Command'.
89. Bashar al-Assad, 'Speech by President Bashar al-Assad at Damascus University, 20 June 2011. This is a translation issued by the official Syrian news agency, Sana', *Al Bab*, 20 June 2011.
90. The form of sponsorship would also be in adequacy with international law. A state can be held responsible for conducts of private actors if it 'acknowledges and adopts the conduct in question as its own' International Law Commission, 'Draft Articles on the Responsability of States for Internationally Wrongful Acts', art. 11. For instance, although the initial attack on the United States embassy in Teheran in 1979 was not attributable to Iran, the subsequent endorsement of the Iranian authorities turned the occupation of the embassy into acts of the Iranian state. *Case Concerning United States Diplomatic and Consular Staff in Tehran*, para. 74 (1980).
91. Hyppönen, 'Cyber Security: A Mission Impossible?'.
92. Tom Brewster, 'How Anonymous Plans To Expose Syrian Electronic Army Leaders', *TechWeek*, 3 September 2013.
93. Brian Krebs, 'Who Built the Syrian Electronic Army?', *KrebsOnSecurity*, 28 August 2013.
94. Brian Merchant, 'Is This the Leader of the Syrian Electronic Army?', *Vice*, 28 August 2013.
95. Ibid.
96. Tess Owen, 'The US Has Indicted Three Alleged Syrian Electronic Army Hackers for Cyber Crimes', *Vice*, 23 March 2016.
97. Chang, 'Combating cybercrime across the Taiwan Strait: investigation and prosecution issues'.

CONCLUSION

1. Andrea Shalal-Esa, 'Six U.S. Air Force cyber capabilities designated "weapons"', *Reuters*, 8 April 2013.
2. Martti Koskenniemi, 'The Politics of International Law', in *LCIL International Law Seminar Series 2011–2012* (Cambridge, 2012).
3. Ibid.

4. Ibid.

5. Michael N. Schmitt and Liis Vihul, 'The International Law of Attribution During Proxy "Wars" in Cyberspace', *Fletcher Security Review* 1 (2014), p. 10.

6. Kevin Williams, 'Cybercrime' (paper presented at the Information Security & Cyber Crime Summit, London, 18–19 February 2014).

7. Ian Brown, Lilian Edwards and Christopher Marsden, 'Information Security and Cybercrime', in *Law and the Internet*, ed. Lilian Edwards and Charlotte Waelde (Oxford: Hart Publishing, 2009), p. 678.

8. For a legal approach to the Internet governance issue, see for instance Ian Walden, 'International Telecommunication Law, the Internet and the Regulation of Cyberspace', in *Peacetime Regime for State Activities in Cyberspace*, ed. Katharina Ziolkowski (Tallinn: NATO CCD COE, 2013).

9. Josephine Charlotte Paulina Wolff, 'Unraveling Internet Identities: Accountability & Anonymity at the Application Layer' (Massachusetts Institute of Technology, 2012), p. 125.

10. A cursory look at the new legislation voted through the Swiss Parliament in September 2015 highlight the limits of the existing legislation regulating the power of the Federal Intelligence Service. See VBS, 'Beispiele Nachrichtendienstgesetz (NDG) [Examples of the new law on the intelligence service]', (Bern: VBS 2014).

11. United Nations Economic and Social Council, 'Assessment of the progress made in the implementation of and follow-up to the outcomes of the World Summit on the Information Society' (New York, 2011).

12. Danielle Kehl and Tim Maurer, 'Did the U.N. Internet Governance Summit Actually Accomplish Anything?', *Slate*, 14 December 2012.

13. Arik Hesseldahl, 'What Last Week's Anti-U.S. Shift in Internet Governance Means to You', *All Things D*, 14 October 2013.

14. EWI Communications, 'EastWest Direct: Bruce McConnell on Cyber Challenges', *EastWest Institute*, 7 October 2013.

15. William Hague, 'Foreign Secretary calls for open internet that spurs economic growth' (London: Foreign & Commonwealth Office, 16 October 2013).

16. Ian Bremmer, 'Democracy in Cyberspace', *Foreign Affairs* (November/December 2010), p. 92.

17. *Der Spiegel*, 'E-Mail-Sicherheit: Telekom will E-Mail an USA und Großbritannien vorbeileiten', 12 October 2013; Michael Bröcker, 'Interview mit Hans-Peter Friedrich: "Notfalls müssen wir Diplomaten ausweisen"', *RP*, 30 October 2013; Alison Smale and David E. Sanger, 'Spying Scandal Alters U.S. Ties With Allies and Raises Talk of Policy Shift', *The New York Times*, 11 November 2013.

18. *Die Welt*, 'Friedrich fordert IT-Sicherheitsgesetz', 3 November 2013.

19. David Charter, 'German-only internet is planned to beat spies who monitored Merkel', *The Times*, 14 November 2013.
20. *Financial Times*, 'Brazil going too far on internet security', 12 November 2013.
21. *NewsBites*, 'Brazilian Government pulls local storage obligation from internet bill', 22 March 2014.
22. Mehdi Atmani, 'Sous la roche d'Uri, le bunker numérique suisse', *Le Temps*, 13 March 2014.
23. Ibid.
24. Eugene Kaspersky, 'What will happen if countries carve up the internet?', *The Guardian*, 17 December 2013.
25. Ibid.
26. Jack Goldsmith, 'We Need an Invasive NSA', *New Republic*, 10 October 2013.
27. UN Watched, 'Tschechien: Neuer Anlauf zur Wiedereinführung der Vorratsdatenspeicherung', https://edri.org/edrigramnumber10-11data-retention-back-czech-republic/, accessed 6 October 2016.
28. Ian Brown, 'Communications Data Retention in an Evolving Internet', *International Journal of Law and Information Technology* 19, 2 (2010), p. 107.
29. Barton Gellman and Ashkan Soltani, 'NSA collects millions of e-mail address books globally', *The Washington Post*, 14 October 2013.
30. Ian Brown and Douwe Korff, 'Terrorism and the Proportionality of Internet Surveillance', *European Journal of Criminology* 6 (2009), p. 125.
31. Brown, 'Communications Data Retention in an Evolving Internet', p. 96.
32. Ruadhan Mac Cormaic, 'Data retention interferes with privacy—European Court opinion', *The Irish Times*, 13 December 2013.
33. Court of Justice of the European Union, 'The Court of Justice declares the Data Retention Directive to be invalid', (Luxembourg: CJEU, 2014).
34. Ellen Nakashima, 'NSA phone record collection does little to prevent terrorist attacks, group says', *The Washington Post*, 12 January 2014; Peter Bergen et al., 'Do NSA's Bulk Surveillance Programs Stop Terrorists?', (Washington, DC: New America Foundation, 2014).
35. Ellen Nakashima and Ashkan Soltani, 'Panel urges new curbs on surveillance by U.S.', *The Washington Post*, 18 December 2013; Richard A. Clarke et al., 'Liberty and Security in a Changing World: Report and Recommendations of The President's Review Group on Intelligence and Communications Technologies', (Washington, DC: The White House, 2013).
36. Ryan Gallagher, 'The Surveillance Engine: How the NSA Built Its Own Secret Google', *The Intercept*, 25 August 2014.

37. See for instance the impersonation case of Martin Guerre in the 17th century, which far predates any computer technology. Natalie Zemon Davis, *The Return of Martin Guerre* (Cambridge, MA: Harvard University Press, 1983).
38. OECD, 'Digital Identity Management: Enabling Innovation and Trust in the Internet Economy' (Paris: OECD, 2011).
39. For a further analysis of the legal problem that an electronic identification document would pose in the United States, see for instance adjunct law professor Marc Rotenberg's statement to the US Congress: 'Planning for the Future of Cyber Attack Attribution' (Washington, DC: US House of Representatives, 2010).
40. Daegon Cho, 'Real Name Verification Law on the Internet: A Poison or Cure for Privacy?' (paper presented at the Workshop on the Economics of Information Security, George Mason University, VA, 2011).
41. Emily Alpert, 'Court deals blow to South Korean law outing Internet users', *Los Angeles Times*, 23 August 2012.
42. Clement Guitton, 'A Review of the Available Content on Tor Hidden Services: The Case Against Further Development', *Computers in Human Behavior* 29, 6 (2013)., p. 2813.
43. Richard Norton-Taylor and Nick Hopkins, 'Britain plans cyber strike force—with help from GCHQ', *The Guardian*, 30 September 2013.

Bibliography

6, Perri. *Explaining Political Judgement*. Cambridge: Cambridge University Press, 2011.

ABC News. 'China blamed after ASIO blueprints stolen in major cyber attack on Canberra HQ'. *ABC News*, 28 May 2013.

Abu Nasr, Donna. 'One of suspected Cole bombers was Egyptian, Yemen's president says'. *The Associated Press*, 25 October 2000.

Advisory Council on International Affairs, and Advisory Committee on Issues of Public International Law. 'Cyber Warfare'. The Hague: AIV/CAVV, 2011.

Agence France-Presse. 'Iraq says its army is ready to thwart US attack'. *Agence France-Presse*, 9 February 1998.

———. 'Bin Laden Is Reported "Satisfied" By Cole Hit'. *The New York Times*, 5 November 2000.

———. 'US to present evidence of bin Laden link to terror attacks: Powell'. *Agence France-Presse*, 23 September 2001.

———. 'La France victime de cyber-attaques avec "passage" par la Chine'. *Agence France-Presse*, 8 September 2007, http://www.ladepeche.fr/article/2007/09/08/9369-la-france-victime-de-cyber-attaques-chinoises.html, accessed 11 July 2016.

———. 'Cybersecurity summit kicks off with calls to action'. *Agence France-Presse*, 4 May 2010.

———. 'Obama says some Chinese cyber attacks state sponsored'. *Agence France-Presse*, 13 March 2013.

———. 'China "gravely concerned" over US cyber attacks'. *Agence France-Presse*, 23 June 2013.

Aid, Matthew M. 'Inside the NSA's Ultra-Secret China Hacking Group'. *Foreign Policy*, 10 June 2013.

———. 'NSA can't break into your computer, these guys break into your house' *Foreign Policy*, 17 July 2013.

BIBLIOGRAPHY

Akst, Daniel. 'Postcard from Cyberspace: The Helsinki Incident and the Right to Anonymity'. *Los Angeles Times*, 22 February 1995.

al-Assad, Bashar. 'Speech by President Bashar al-Assad at Damascus University, 20 June 2011. This is a translation issued by the official Syrian news agency, Sana'. *Al-Bab*, 20 June 2011.

Al-Haj, Ahmed. 'Investigators find link between Cole, African embassy bombings'. *Associated Press International*, 23 November 2000.

Aldrich, Richard J. *GCHQ*. London: HarperPress, 2010.

————. 'Whitehall and the Iraq War: the UK's Four Intelligence Enquiries'. *Irish Studies in International Affairs* 16 (2005): 73–88.

Alperovitch, Dmitri. 'Offence as the Best Defence'. Brisbane: AusCERT, 2013.

————. 'Revealed: Operation Shady RAT'. Santa Clara, CA: McAfee, 2011.

————. 'Towards Establishment of Cyberspace Deterrence Strategy'. Paper presented at the International Conference on Cyber Conflict, Tallinn, 2011.

Alpert, Emily. 'Court deals blow to South Korean law outing Internet users'. *Los Angeles Times*, 23 August 2012.

Amen v. Michel M. (8 June 2006), Tribunal de Grande Instance, Nanterre.

Ames, Alyssa. 'Kaspersky Lab's Policy on the Use of Software for the Purpose of State Surveillance'. *Kaspersky Lab*, 11 June 2013.

Arab Youth Group. 'Arab Youth Group'. Pastebin, http://pastebin.com/PUHqDQnd, accessed 6 July 2016.

Arlen, Jennifer, and Reinier Kraakman. 'Controlling Corporate Misconduct: An Analysis of Corporate Liability Regimes'. *New York Univeristy Law Review* 72, no. 4 (1997): 687–779.

Arthur, Charles. 'Jake Davis, aka LulzSec's "Topiary", on how the group formed—and broke up'. *The Guardian*, 9 September 2013.

Assange, Julian, Jacob Appelbaum, Andy Müller-Magnum, and Jérémie Zimmermann. *Cypherpunks: Freedom and the Future of the Internet*. New York: OR Books, 2012.

Associated Press. 'South Korea says North Korean spy agency behind March cyberattack'. *Associated Press*, 10 April 2013.

Atlantic Council. 'International Engagement on Cyber Conference'. Atlantic Council, http://www.atlanticcouncil.org/news/transcripts/international-engagement-on-cyber-conference-panel-1-3-29-11-transcript, accessed 30 June 2016.

————. 'Lessons from Our Cyber Past: The First Cyber Cops'. *Atlantic Council*, 16 May 2012.

Atlantic Council of the United States. 'International Engagement on Cyber: Establishing Norms and Improved Security'. In *National and Global Strategies for Managing Cyberspace and Security*. Washington, DC, 2011.

BIBLIOGRAPHY

Atmani, Mehdi. 'Sous la roche d'Uri, le bunker numérique suisse'. *Le Temps*, 13 March 2014.

Axelrod, Robert. 'A Repertory of Cyber Analogies'. In *Cyber Analogies*, edited by Emily O. Goldman and John Arquilla, 108–17. Monterey, CA: Naval Postgraduate School, 2014.

Axelrod, Robert, and Rumen Iliev. 'Timing of cyber conflict'. *PNAS* (2014): 1–6.

Backhouse, James, and Gurpreet Dhillon. 'Managing computer crime: a research outlook'. *Computer & Security* 14 (2013): 645–51.

Bain, Ben. 'Tracking a cyberattack'. *FCW*, 15 August 2008.

Baldor, Lolita C. 'Officials: US better at finding cyber attackers'. *Associated Press*, 28 January 2011.

————. 'US warning reflects fears of Iranian cyberattack'. *AP*, 12 October 2012.

Baldwin, David A. 'The Concept of Security'. *Review of International Studies* 23 (1997): 5–26.

Ball, James. 'NSA's Prism surveillance program: how it works and what it can do'. *The Guardian*, 8 June 2013.

Ball, James, Julian Borger, and Glenn Greenwald. 'Revealed: how US and UK spy agencies defeat internet privacy and security'. *The Guardian*, 6 September 2013.

Baltic News Wire. 'US Congressman rises to defend Estonia's sovereignty'. *Baltic News Wire*, 4 June 2007.

Bamford, James. 'Edward Snowden: The Untold Story'. *Wired*, 22 August 2014.

Bancal, Damien. 'La traque de Zotob comme si vous y étiez'. Zataz, http://archives.zataz.com/reportage-virus/9065/zotob-hunter.html, accessed 6 October 2016.

Barboza, David. 'China's President Will Lead a New Effort on Cybersecurity'. *The New York Times*, 27 February 2014.

Barnes, Julian E., and Siobhan Gorman. 'U.S. Says Iran Hacked Navy Computers'. *The Wall Street Journal*, 27 September 2013.

Barzashka, Ivanka. 'Are Cyber-Weapons Effective?'. *The RUSI Journal* 158, no. 2 (2013): 48–56.

BBC News. 'Iraqi deal: winners and losers'. *BBC News*, 25 February 1998.

————. 'Questions cloud cyber crime cases'. *BBC News*, 17 October 2003.

————. 'Russian daily views Estonian efforts to enlist EU support in row with Moscow'. *BBC News*, 13 May 2007.

————. 'Man jailed over computer password refusal'. *BBC News*, 5 October 2010.

————. 'Summary of Russian press for Tuesday 22 January 2013'. *BBC Monitoring Former Soviet Union*, 22 January 2013.

BIBLIOGRAPHY

————. 'US allies Mexico, Chile and Brazil seek spying answers'. *BBC News*, 11 July 2013.

Bechtel, William. 'Attributing Responsibility to Computer Systems'. *Metaphilosophy* 16, no. 4 (1985): 296–306.

Beiner, Ronald. *Political Judgement*. Chicago, IL: Univeristy of Chicago Press, 1984.

Ben-Israel, Isaac, and Lior Tabansky. 'An Interdisciplinary Look at Security Challenges in the Information Age'. *Military and Strategic Affairs* 3, no. 3 (2011): 21–38.

Bencsath, Boldizsar, Gabor Pek, Levente Buttyan, and Mark Félegyházi. 'Duqu: A Stuxnet-like malware found in the wild'. Budapest: Laboratory of Cryptography and System Security (CrySyS), 2011.

Bennett, Andrew, and Alexander L. George *Case Studies and Theory Development in the Social Sciences*. London: MIT Press, 2004.

Bergen, Peter, David Sterman, Emily Schneider, and Bailey Cahall. 'Do NSA's Bulk Surveillance Programs Stop Terrorists?'. Washington, DC: New America Foundation, 2014.

Betz, David, and Tim Stevens. *Cyberspace and the state: toward a strategy for cyber-power* [in English]. Abingdon and New York: International Institute for Strategic Studies, 2011.

Bevan, James, Communication on 17 May 2013.

Bizeul, David. 'Russian Business Network study'. 20 November 2007, http://www.bizeul.org/files/RBN_study.pdf, accessed 20 July 2016.

Black, Ian, and Ian Sample. 'UK report on chemical attack in Syria adds nothing to informed speculation'. *The Guardian*, 29 August 2013.

Boebert, W. Earl. 'A Survey of Challenges in Attribution'. Paper presented at the Workshop on Deterring Cyber Attacks: Informing Strategies and Developing Options for U.S. Policy, Washington DC, 2010.

Borredon, Laurent, and Jacques Follorou. 'En France, la DGSE au cœur d'un programme de surveillance d'Internet'. *Le Monde*, 11 June 2013.

Brandt, Andrew. 'Stupid hacker tricks, part two: The folly of youth'. *InfoWorld Daily News*, 5 May 2005.

Branigan, Tania. 'South Korea on alert for cyber-attacks after major network goes down'. *The Guardian*, 20 March 2013.

Bremmer, Ian. 'Democracy in Cyberspace'. *Foreign Affairs*, November/December 2010: 86–92.

Brenner, Joel. *America the Vulnerable*. New York: The Penguin Press, 2011.

Brenner, Susan W. '"At Light Speed": Attribution and Response to Cybercrime/Terrorism/Warfare'. *The Journal of Criminal Law & Criminology* 97, no. 2 (2007): 379–476.

————. *Cyber Threats: The Emerging Fault Lines of the Nation State*. Oxford: Oxford Scholarship Online, 2009.

BIBLIOGRAPHY

————. 'Cyber-threats and the Limits of Bureaucratic Control'. *Minnesota Journal of Law, Science, and Technology* 14, no. 137–258 (2013).

Brenner, Susan W., and Joseph J. Schwerha. 'Transnational evidence gathering and local prosecution of international cybercrime'. *The John Marshall Journal of Computer & Information Law* 20 (2002): 347–96.

Brewster, Tom. 'How Anonymous Plans To Expose Syrian Electronic Army Leaders'. *TechWeek*, 3 September 2013.

Bridis, Ted. 'FBI Is Building a 'Magic Lantern''. *The Washington Post*, 23 November 2001.

Brito, Helena. 'Q&A Follow-up—Tools of Engagement: The Mechanics of Threat Intelligence'. *Mandiant*, 30 April 2013.

Brito, Jerry, and Tate Watkins. 'Loving the Cyberbomb? The Danger of Threat Inflation in Cybersecurity Policy'. Mercatus Center—George Mason University (2011).

Broad, William J., John Markoff, and David E. Sanger. 'Israeli Test on Worm Called Crucial in Iran Nuclear Delay'. *The New York Times*, 15 January 2011.

Bröcker, Michael. 'Interview mit Hans-Peter Friedrich: "Notfalls müssen wir Diplomaten ausweisen"'. *RP*, 30 October 2013.

Bronk, Christopher, and Eneken Tikk-Ringas. 'The Cyber Attack on Saudi Aramco'. *Survival* 55, no. 2 (2013): 81–96.

Brown, Ian. 'Communications Data Retention in an Evolving Internet'. *International Journal of Law and Information Technology* 19, no. 2 (2010): 95–109.

————. David D. Clark, and Dirk Trossen. 'Should Specific Values Be Embedded In The Internet Architecture?'. Paper presented at the Re-Architecting the Internet workshop, New York, 2011.

————. Lilian Edwards, and Christopher Marsden. 'Information Security and Cybercrime'. In *Law and the Internet*, edited by Lilian Edwards and Charlotte Waelde, 671–92. Oxford: Hart Publishing, 2009.

————. and Douwe Korff. 'Terrorism and the Proportionality of Internet Surveillance'. *European Journal of Criminology* 6 (2009): 119–35.

————. and Christopher T. Marsden. *Regulating Code*. Cambridge, MA: MIT Press, 2014.

Bryan-Low, Cassel. 'To catch crooks in cyberspace, FBI goes global'. *The Associated Press*, 21 November 2006.

Bush, George W. 'Transcript of President Bush's address'. *CNN*, 21 September 2001.

Business Wire. 'Symantec Sees Decrease in New W32.Blaster.Worm Infections; Systems in the United States, United Kingdom, Canada, Australia and Ireland Most Affected'. *Business Wire*, 13 August 2003.

————. 'Mandiant Hires Travis Reese as Vice President of Federal Services; Travis Reese, the Former Vice President of ManTech International's

Computer Forensics & Intrusion Analysis Group Will Drive Mandiant's Government Business'. *Business Wire*, 25 April 2006.

C-Span. 'Newsmakers with Senator Joe Lieberman'. 21 September 2012.

Cabinet Office. 'The UK Cyber Security Strategy—Protecting and promoting the UK in a digital world'. London: Cabinet Office, 2011.

Calmes, Jackie, and Steven Lee Myers. 'Hit and miss for Obama and Xi'. *The New York Times*, 10 June 2013.

Caltagirone, Sergio, Andrew Pendergast, and Christopher Betz. 'The Diamond Model of Intrusion Analysis'. 1–61. Arlington, VA: Threat Connect, 2013.

Capaccio, Tony, David Lerman and Chris Strohm. 'Iran Behind Cyber-Attack on Adelson's Sands Corp., Clapper Says'. *Bloomberg*, 26 February 2015.

Carr, Jeffrey. *Inside Cyber Warfare* [in English]. Sebastopol, CA: O'Reilly, 2010.

———. 'Stuxnet's Finnish-Chinese Connection'. *Forbes*, 14 December 2010.

———. 'Mandiant APT1 Report Has Critical Analytic Flaws'. *Digital Dao*, 19 February 2013.

———. 'The Cyber Kill Chain: Trademarked by Lockheed Martin?'. *Digital Dao*, 18 August 2013.

Case Concerning United States Diplomatic and Consular Staff in Tehran, International Court of Justice: Netherlands (1980).

Cavelty, Myriam Dunn. 'The Militarisation of Cyberspace: Why Less May Be Better'. Paper presented at the 4th International Conference on Cyber Conflict, Tallinn, 2012.

———. 'Breaking the Cyber-Security Dilemma: Aligning Security Needs and Removing Vulnerabilities'. *Science and Engineering Ethics* (April 2014).

CBS. 'Face the Nation'. *Federal News Service*, 10 February 2013.

Center for Strategic and International Studies. 'The Economic Impact of Cybercrime and Cyber Espionage'. Santa Clara, CA: McAfee, 2013.

Chabinsky, Steven, 'Cyber Warfare', talk at American Center for Democracy (New York, 2013), https://www.youtube.com/watch?v=Uiz2R_f1Lxo, accessed 29 July 2016.

Chang, Lennon Yao-chung. *Cybercrime in the Greater China Region: Regulatory Responses and Crime Prevention Across the Taiwan Strait*. Cheltenham, Northampton, MA: Edward Elgar Publishing Limited, 2013.

Chang, Yao Chung. 'Combating cybercrime across the Taiwan Strait: investigation and prosecution issues'. *Australian Journal of Forensic Sciences* 44, no. 1 (2012): 5–14.

Charter, David. 'German-only internet is planned to beat spies who monitored Merkel'. *The Times*, 14 November 2013.

Chaum, D. 'Untraceable electronic mail return addresses and digital pseudonyms'. *Communications of the ACM* 24, no. 2 (1981): 84–8.

China Business News. 'Ministry of Foreign Affairs of the People's Republic of

China: Foreign Ministry Spokesperson Hua Chunying's Regular Press Conference on March 12, 2013'. *China Business News*, 13 March 2013.

Chivers, C. J. 'A Trail of Bullet Casings Leads From Africa's Wars Back to Iran'. *The New York Times*, 11 January 2013.

————. 'U.N. Data on Gas Attack Point to Assad's Top Forces', *The New York Times*, 19 September 2013.

Cho, Daegon. 'Real Name Verification Law on the Internet: A Poison or Cure for Privacy?'. Paper presented at the Workshop on the Economics of Information Security, George Mason University, 2011.

Cieply, Michael and Brooks Barnes. 'Sony Cyberattack, First a Nuisance, Swiftly Grew Into a Firestorm'. *The New York Times*, 30 December 2014.

Clapper, James R. 'DNI Statement on Activities Authorized Under Section 702 of FISA'. Office of the Director of National Intelligence, 6 June 2013.

Clark, Colin. 'China Attacked Internet Security Company RSA, Cyber Commander Tells SASC'. *Breaking Defense*, 27 March 2014.

Clark, David D., and Susan Landau. 'Untangling Attribution'. Paper presented at the Workshop on Deterring CyberAttacks: Informing Strategies and Developing Options for U.S Policy, Washington, DC, 2010.

Clark, Phil. 'All Justice Is Local'. *The New York Times*, 11 June 2014.

Clarke, Richard A., and Steven Andreasen. 'Cyberwar's threat does not justify a new policy of nuclear deterrence'. *The Washington Post*, 15 June 2013.

Clarke, Richard A., and Robert K. Knake. *CyberWar: the next threat to national security and what to do about it*. New York: Ecco, 2010.

Clarke, Richard A., Michael J. Morell, Geoffrey R. Stone, Cass R. Sunstein, and Peter Swire. 'Liberty and Security in a Changing World: Report and Recommendations of The President's Review Group on Intelligence and Communications Technologies'. Washington, DC: The White House, 2013.

Clayton, Mark. 'Stealing US business secrets: Experts ID two huge cyber "gangs" in China'. *The Christian Science Monitor*, 14 September 2012.

Clayton, Richard. 'Anonymity and traceability in cyberspace'. University of Cambridge, 2005.

CNN. 'Israel sets up Patriot missiles amid Iraq tensions'. *CNN*, 2 February 1998.

Cohen, Don, and K. Narayanaswamy. 'Survey/Analysis of Levels l II, IIII—Attack Attribution Techniques'. Los Angeles, CA: CS3 Inc., 2004.

Committee on Armed Services. 'US Cyber Command: Organizing for Cyberspace Operations'. Washington, DC: US Government Printing Office, 2010.

Committee on Foreign Affairs. 'China's Approach to Cyber Operations: Implications for the United States'. Washington, DC: U.S.-China Economic and Security Review Commission, 2010.

Committee on Homeland Security and Governmental Affairs. 'The

BIBLIOGRAPHY

Department of Homeland Security At 10 Years: Examining Challenges and Achievements and Addressing Emerging Threats'. Washington, DC, 2013.

Committee on Intelligence. 'Cyber threats and ongoing efforts to protect the nation'. 7. Washington, D.C.: US House of Representatives, 2011.

Comodohacker. 'Striking back…'. Pastebin, http://pastebin.com/1AxH30em, accessed 6 July 2016.

Conflict Armament Research. 'The distribution of Iranian ammunition in Africa: evidence from a nine-country invetsigation'. 50. London: Conflict Armament Research, 2012.

Constantin, Lucian. 'Kill timer found in Shamoon malware suggests possible connection to Saudi Aramco attack'. ComputerWorld, 23 August 2012.

Corera, Gordon. 'Under Attack: The Threat from Cyberspace'. BBC Radio 4, 1 July 2013.

Cormaic, Ruadhan Mac. 'Data retention interferes with privacy—European Court opinion'. The Irish Times, 13 December 2013.

Court of Justice of the European Union. 'The Court of Justice declares the Data Retention Directive to be invalid'. Luxembourg: Court of Justice of the European Union, 2014.

Cox, Brian N. 'International Police Officer Criminal Investigation Training Manual'. Windsor, ON: Criminal Investigation Training Bureau, 2011.

Crump, Catherine. 'Data Retention: Privacy, Anonymity, and Accountability Online'. Stanford Law Review 56, no. 1 (2003): 191–229.

Cullen, Drew. 'Computer dealer fined for sending virus to rival'. The Register, 11 April 2001.

Cutting Sword of Justice. 'Untitled'. Pastebin, http://pastebin.com/HqAgaQRj, accessed 6 July 2016.

Cybersecurity, Infrastructure Protection, and Security Technologies, 'Iranian Cyber Threat to the U.S. Homeland'. Washington, DC, 2012.

Dahle, Marie Harbo. 'Cyber-attacks: A short guide'. Atlantic Voices 2, no. 5 (2012): 2–3.

Dataquest. 'Cyberspace as Global Commons: The Challenges'. Dataquest, 15 April 2012.

Davis, Natalie Zemon. The Return of Martin Guerre [in English]. Cambridge, MA: Harvard University Press, 1983.

de Zayas, Alfred. 'The Practice of Naming and Shaming'. Alfred de Zayas, 10 September 2013.

Decker, Debra K. 'Before the First Bomb Goes Off: Developing Nuclear Attribution Standards and Policies'. Cambridge, MA: Harvard Kennedy School, 2011.

Deibert, Ronald J. 'Black Code: Censorship, Surveillance, and the Militarisation of Cyberspace'. Journal of International Studies 32 (2003): 501–30.

BIBLIOGRAPHY

Deibert, Ronald, John Palfrey, Rafal Rohonzinski, and Jonathan Zittrain. 'Access Contested: Toward the Fourth Phase of Cyberspace Controls'. In *Access Contested: Security, Identity, and Resistance in Asian Cyberspace*, edited by Ronald Deibert, John Palfrey, Rafal Rohonzinski and Jonathan Zittrain. Cambridge, MA: MIT Press, 2012.

Deibert, Ronald J., and Rafal Rohozinski. 'Risking Security: Policies and Paradoxes of Cyberspace Security'. *International Political Sociology* 4 (2010): 15–32.

———. 'Control and Subversion in Russian Cyberspace'. In *Access Controlled: The Shaping of Power, Rights, and Rule in Cyberspace*, edited by Ronald Deibert, John Palfrey, Rafal Rohozinski and Jonathan Zittrain. Cambridge, MA: The MIT Press, 2010.

Deibert, Ronald J., Rafal Rohozinski, and Masashi Crete-Nishihata. 'Cyclones in cyberspace: Information shaping and denial in the 2008 Russia-Georgia war'. *Security Dialogue* 43, no. 3 (2013): 3–24.

Demchak, Chris C. 'Economic and Political Coercion and a Rising Cyber Westphalia'. In *Peacetime Regime for State Activities in Cyberspace*, edited by Katharina Ziolkowski, 595–619. Tallinn: NATO CCD COE Publication, 2013.

Der Spiegel. 'Chinesische Trojaner auf PCs im Kanzleramt'. *Der Spiegel*, 25 August 2007, http://www.spiegel.de/netzwelt/tech/0,1518,501 954,00.html, accessed 20 July 2016.

———. 'CCC findet Sicherheitslücken in Bundestrojaner [CCC finds security breach in the Bundestrojaner]'. *Der Spiegel*, 8 October 2011.

———. '"Als Zielobject markiert": Der Enthüller Edward Snowden über die geheime Macht der NSA'. *Der Spiegel*, 2013, 22–4.

———. 'E-Mail-Sicherheit: Telekom will E-Mail an USA und Großbritannien vorbeileiten'. *Der Spiegel*, 12 October 2013.

Deutsche Presse Agentur. 'Bin Laden denies links to USS Cole bombing, Kuwait group'. *Deutsche Presse Agentur*, 13 November 2000.

Die Welt. 'Friedrich fordert IT-Sicherheitsgesetz'. *Die Welt*, 3 November 2013.

Dipert, Randal. 'Response to Cyber Attacks: The Attribution Problem'. In *USNA 2012 McCain Conference*. Annapolis, MD, 2012.

Dipert, Randall R. 'Other-Than-Internet (OTI) Cyberwarfare: Challenges for Ethics, Law, and Policy'. *Journal of Military Ethics* 12, no. 1 (2013): 34–53.

Dobitz, Kyle, Brad Haas, Michael Holtje, Amanda Jokerst, Geoff Ochsner, and Stephanie Silva. 'The Characterization and Measurement of Cyber Warfare'. Omaha, NE: Global Innovation and Strategy Center, 2008.

Donilon, Tom. 'Remarks By Tom Donilon, National Security Advisory to the President: "The United States and the Asia-Pacific in 2013"'. *The White House*, 11 March 2013.

BIBLIOGRAPHY

Donoghue, Andrew. 'Russian Police And Internet Registry Accused Of Aiding Cybercrime'. *TechWeek Europe*, 21 October 2009.

Doody, John. 'Introductory remarks'. Paper presented at the Future of Cyber Security conference, London, 21 March 2013.

Douglas, Jeanne-Vida. 'Hacktivist link to PM attack'. *Australian Financial Review*, 28 October 2011.

Dourado, Eli. 'Put trust back in the Internet'. *The New York Times*, 10 October 2013.

Downier, Leonard. 'In Obama's war on leaks, reporters fight back'. *The Washington Post*, 6 October 2013.

Dozier, Kimberly, and Matt Apuzzo. 'Intelligence on weapons no "slam dunk"'. *AP*, 29 August 2013.

Dunn Cavelty, Myriam. *Cyber-security and threat politics: US efforts to secure the information age*. New York: Routledge, 2008.

Dvorin, Tova. 'Secret Shin Bet Unit At The Front Lines of Israel's Cyber-War'. *Arutz Sheva*, 25 April 2014.

Easton, Nina. 'The CEO Who Caught the Chinese Spies Red-Handed'. *Fortune*, 22 July 2013, 80–8.

Eberle, Christopher J. 'Just War and Cyberwar'. *Journal of Military Ethics* 12, no. 1 (2013): 54–67.

Eisenhardt, Kathleen M. 'Building Theories from Case Study Research'. *The Academy of Management Review* 14, no. 4 (1989): 532–50.

Eisenhardt, Kathleen M., and Melissa E. Graebner. 'Theory Building from Cases: Opportunities and Challenges'. *Academy of Management Journal* 50, no. 1 (2007): 25–32.

El País. 'La NSA rastreó 60 millones de llamadas en España en un mes'. *El País*, 28 October 2013.

Eriksson, E. Anders. 'Viewpoint: Information warfare: Hype or reality?'. *The Nonproliferation Review* 6, no. 3 (1999): 57–64.

Espiner, Tom. 'Police set up regional hacking units'. *ZDNet*, 26 July 2011.

———. 'McAfee: Why Duqu is a big deal'. *ZDNet*, 26 October 2011.

European Parliament. 'Directive 2013/40/EU of the European Parliament and of the Council of 12 August 2013 on attacks against information systems and replacing Council Framework Decision 2005/222/JHA'. In *P7_TA(2013)0321*, edited by European Parliament. Strasbourg: European Parliament, 2013.

EWI Communications. 'EastWest Direct: Bruce McConnell on Cyber Challenges'. *EastWest Institute*, 7 October 2013.

Fairlie, John A. 'The Separation of Powers'. *Michigan Law Review* 21, no. 4 (1923): 393–436.

Farrell, Henry, and Martha Finnemore. 'The End of Hypocrisy'. *Foreign Affairs* 92, no. 6 (2013): 22–6.

BIBLIOGRAPHY

Fars News Agency. 'Iran Stops Israeli Duqu Virus Attack'. *Fars News Agency*, 15 November 2011.

———. 'Iran Rejects Media Reports on Hacking US Banks'. *Fars News Agency*, 23 September 2012.

FBI. 'Cyber's Most Wanted'. FBI, https://www.fbi.gov/wanted/cyber, accessed 13 July 2016.

———. 'Six Hackers in the United States and Abroad Charged for Crimes Affecting Over One Million Victims'. *FBI*, 6 March 2012.

Feaver, Peter, and Kenneth Geers. '"When the Urgency of Time and Circumstances Clearly Does Not Permit...": Predelegation in Nuclear and Cyber Scenarios'. In *Cyber Analogies*, edited by Emily O. Goldman and John Arquilla, 33–45. Monterey, CA: Naval Postgraduate School, 2014.

Federal News Service. 'Prepared statement of Michael A Vatis, Director, National Infrastructure Protection Center, Federal Bureau of Investigation before the Senate Judiciary Committee, Subcommittee on Technology and Terrorism'. *Federal News Service*, 6 October 1999.

———. 'Press Conference with President Barack Obama'. *Federal News Service*, 8 June 2012.

Festinger, Leon. *A Theory of Cognitive Dissonance*. Stanford, CA: Stanford University Press, 1957.

Financial Times. 'Brazil going too far on internet security'. *FT*, 12 November 2013.

Finkle, Jim. 'Kaspersky plans push for sales to u.s. government'. *Reuters*, 15 May 2014.

———. 'Mandiant goes viral after China hacking report'. *Reuters*, 23 February 2013.

Finkle, Jim, and Rick Rothacker. 'Exclusive: Iranian hackers target Bank of America, JPMorgan, Citi'. *Reuters*, 21 September 2012.

Fisher, Max. 'Syrian hackers claim AP hack that tipped stock market by $136 billion. Is it terrorism?'. *Washington Post*, 23 April 2013.

Flaherty, Anne. 'A look at Mandiant, allegations on China hacking'. *The Associated Press*, 20 February 2013.

———. 'Private US firms take major role vs. cyberattacks'. *The Associated Press*, 21 February 2013.

Follorou, Jacques, and Glenn Greenwald. 'France in the NSA's crosshair: phone networks under surveillance'. *Le Monde*, 25 October 2013.

ForexTV. 'The US at Cyber War? Chinese Hacking Debate Intensifies'. *ForexTV*, 14 March 2013.

Fox-IT. 'Interim Report: DigiNotar Certificate Authority Breach "Operation Black Tulip"'. 13. Delft: Fox-IT, 2011.

———. 'Black Tulip: Report of the investigation into the DigiNotar Certificate Authority breach'. Delft: Fox-IT, 2012.

BIBLIOGRAPHY

Freedman, Lawrence, and Srinath Raghavan. 'Coercion'. In *Security Studies*, edited by Paul D. Williams. Abingdon and New York: Routledge, 2008.

Fresco, Adam. 'Schoolboy hacker was "No 1 threat" to US security'. *The Times*, 22 March 1997.

Froomkin, Michael. 'Wrong Turn in Cyberspace: Using ICANN to Route Around the APA and the Constitution'. *Duke Law Journal* 50, no. 1 (2000): 17–186.

Fukuyama, Francis. *Trust: The Social Virtues and the Creation of Prosperity*. New York: The Free Press, 1995.

Gallagher, Ryan. 'The Surveillance Engine: How the NSA Built Its Own Secret Google'. *The Intercept*, 25 August 2014.

Garvin, Dan. 'What Really Happened in INCOMM-Part 2'. https://groups. google.com/forum/?fromgroups#!msg/alt.religion.scientology/ zpp3nfabhQI/f2WEdA6clLAJ, accessed 4 July 2016.

Gary McKinnon v. Government of the USA (3 March 2007) EWHC 762, High Court of Justice Queen's Bench Division.

Gaycken, Sandro, Thilo Marauhn, and Paul Cornish. 'Attribution—How to live without it?'. In *Cyber Security*. Berlin: German Council on Foreign Relations, 2012.

GCHQ. 'Our Intelligence and Security mission in the Internet age'. Press release, 3 May 2009.

Geer, Daniel E. 'Cybersecurity and National Policy'. *National Security Journal*, http://harvardnsj.com/2011/01/cybersecurity-and-national-policy/, accessed 4 July 2016.

Geers, Kenneth, and Ayed Alqartah. 'Syrian Electronic Army Hacks Major Communications Websites'. *FireEye*, 30 July 2013.

Gellman, Barton, and Ellen Nakashima. 'U.S. spy agencies mounted 231 offensive cyber-operations in 2011, documents show'. *The Washington Post*, 31 August 2013.

Gellman, Barton, and Ashkan Soltani. 'NSA collects millions of e-mail address books globally'. *The Washington Post*, 14 October 2013.

Geuss, Raymond. 'What is political judgement?'. In *Political Judgement: Essays for John Dunn*, edited by Richard Bourke and Raymond Geuss, 29–46. Cambridge: Cambridge University Press, 2009.

Gibbs, Jack P. 'Deterrence Theory and Research'. In *Nebraska Symposium on Motivation: The Law as a Behavioral Instrument*. Lincoln, NE: University of Nebraska Press, 1985.

Goldsmith, Jack. 'The pervasive cyberthreat that goes unchallenged'. *The Washington Post*, 25 November 2011.

———. 'How Cyber Changes the Laws of War'. *The European Journal of International Law* 24, no. 1 (2013): 129–38.

———. 'We Need an Invasive NSA'. *New Republic*, 10 October 2013.

BIBLIOGRAPHY

Gomez, Marisa. 'Cyberspace and real time: The virtual beyond the screen'. *Interartive*, June 2009.

Goodin, Dan. 'Kaspersky: "We detect and remediate any malware attack," even by NSA (Updated)'. *ArsTechnica*, 6 November 2013.

Goodman, Michael S. 'Applying the Historical Lessons of Surprise Attack to the Cyber Domain: The Example of the United Kingdom'. In *Cyber Analogies*, edited by Emily O. Goldman and John Arquilla, 15–25. Monterey, CA: Naval Postgraduate School, 2014.

Gorman, Siobhan, and Julian E. Barnes. 'Iranian Hacking to Test NSA Nominee Michael Rogers'. *The Wall Street Journal*, 18 February 2014.

Gorman, Siobhan, Devlin Barrett, and Danny Yadron. 'Chinese Hackers Hit U.S. Media'. *The Wall Street Journal*, 31 January 2013.

Gostev, Alexander, and Igor Soumenkov. 'Stuxnet/Duqu: The Evolution of Drivers'. *SecureList*, 28 December 2011.

Gotlieb, Risha. 'Cybercop Fights Organized Internet Crime'. *Pacific Standard*, 14 March 2011.

Government of France. 'Synthèse nationale de renseignement déclassifié : Programme chimique syrien Cas d'emploi passés d'agents chimiques par le régime Attaque chimique conduite par le régime le 21 août 2013'. Paris: Government of France, 2013.

Government of the Russian Federation. "Указ Президента Российской Федерации от 15.01.2013 N° 31с (выписка) "О создании государственной системы обнаружения, предупреждения и ликвидации последствий компьютерных атак на информационные ресурсы Российской Федерации"" ['Decree of the President of the Russian Federation from 15.01.2013 extract n°31c "about an initiative to create a state system of tracking, preventing and removing the outcomes of cyber attacks on informational resources of the russian federation"']. Official Website of the Government of the Russian Federation, http://pravo.gov.ru:8080/page.aspx?35023, accessed 11 July 2016.

Government of the United States. 'United States Submission to the UN Group of Governmental Experts on Developments in the Field of Information and Telecommunications in the Context of International Security'. 2012.

Graham, Flora. 'Police "encouraged' to hack more". *BBC News*, 5 January 2009.

Graham, Stephen. 'The end of geography or the explosion of place? Conceptualizing space, place and information technology'. *Human Geography* 22, no. 2 (1998): 165–85.

Gray, Colin S. *Making Strategic Sense of Cyber Power: Why the Sky Is Not Falling*. Carlisle Barracks, PA: Strategic Studies Institute, U.S. Army War College Press, 2013.

BIBLIOGRAPHY

Greenpeace and others vs. EDF and others (10 November 2011), Correctional Tribunal of Nanterre.

Greenwald, Glenn. 'NSA collecting phone records of millions of Verizon customers daily'. *The Guardian*, 6 June 2013.

————. 'XKeyscore: NSA tool collects "nearly everything a user does on the internet"'. *The Guardian*, 31 July 2013.

Greenwald, Glenn, Ewen MacAskill, Laura Poitras, Spencer Ackerman, and Dominic Rushe. 'How Microsoft handed the NSA access to encrypted messages'. *The Guardian*, 11 July 2013.

Gross, Michael Joseph. 'Exclusive: Operation Shady Rat—Unprecedented Cyber-espionage Campaign and Intellectual-Property Bonanza'. *Vanity Fair*, 2 August 2011.

Guerrero-Saade, Juan Andrés. 'The Ethics and Perils of APT Research: An Unexpected Transition into Intelligence Brokerage'. *Virus Bulletin Conference*, September 2015.

Guest. 'Saudi Aramco, once again…'. Pastebin, http://pastebin.com/WKSk3pmp, accessed 6 July 2016.

Guitton, Clement. 'Criminals and Cyber Attacks: The Missing Link Between Attribution and Deterrence'. *International Journal of Cyber Criminology* 6, no. 2 (2012): 1030–43.

————. 'Modelling Attribution'. Paper presented at the 12th European Conference on Information Warfare and Security, Jyväskylä, 11–12 July 2013.

————. 'A Review of the Available Content on Tor Hidden Services: The Case Against Further Development'. *Computers in Human Behavior* 29, no. 6 (2013): 2805–15.

Guitton, Clement, and Elaine Korzak. 'The Sophistication Criterion for Attribution'. *The RUSI Journal* 158, no. 4 (2013).

Hafner, Katie, and John Markoff. *Cyberpunk: Outlaws and Hackers on the Computer Frontier*. New York: Simon & Schuster, 1995.

Hagan, Kevin, Interview, 18 October 2013.

Hague, William. 'Foreign Secretary calls for open internet that spurs economic growth'. Foreign & Commonwealth Office, 16 October 2013.

Hallam-Baker, Phillip. 'Nobody Has Proposed a Sustainable Model for Internet Governance Yet'. *CircleID*, 27 October 2013.

Halliday, Josh. 'Stuxnet worm is the "work of a national government agency"'. *The Guardian*, 24 September 2010.

Hansen, Lene, and Helen Nissenbaum. 'Digital Disaster, Cyber Security, and the Copenhagen School'. *International Studies Quarterly* 53, no. 4 (2009): 1155–75.

Hayden, Michael. 'Keynote'. Paper presented at the Black Hat conference, Las Vegas, 2010.

————. *Playing to the Edge: American Intelligence in the Age of Terror*. New York: Penguin Press, 2016.

Healey, Jason. 'The Spectrum of National Responsibility for Cyberattacks'. *Brown Journal of World Affairs* 18, no. 1 (2011): 57–70.

————. *A Fierce Domain: Conflict in Cyberspace, 1986 to 2012*. Washington, DC: CCSA and The Atlantic Council, 2013.

————. 'Beyond Attribution: Seeking National Responsibility for Cyber Attacks'. 1–7. Washington, DC: Atlantic Council, 2012.

Hearing of the Crime, Terrorism and Homeland Security Subcommittee of the House Judiciary Committee. 'Cyber Security: Protecting America's New Frontier'. Washington, D.C, 2011.

Helm, Toby, Daniel Boffey, and Nick Hopkins. 'Snowden spy row grows as US is accused of hacking China'. *The Guardian*, 22 June 2013.

Herbert, Simon A. 'Theories of Bounded Rationality'. Chap. 8 In *Decision and Organization*, edited by C. B. McGuire and Roy Radner, 161–76. Minneapolis, MN: University of Minnesota Press, 1972.

Hesseldahl, Arik. 'What Last Week's Anti-U.S. Shift in Internet Governance Means to You'. *All Things D*, 14 October 2013.

Heuer, Richard J. *Psychology of Intelligence Analysis*. Washington, D.C.: Center for the Study of Intelligence, 1999.

————. 'Limits of Intelligence Analysis'. *Orbis* 49, no. 1 (2005): 75–94.

Heywood, Andrew. *Political Theory: an introduction*. New York: Palgrave Macmillan, 2004.

Hider, James. 'Iran attacked by 'Israeli computer virus"'. *The Times*, 29 May 2012.

HMIC. 'The Strategic Policing Requirement: An inspection of the arrangements that police forces have in place to meet the Strategic Policing Requirement'. London: HMIC, 2014.

Hopkins, Nick. 'Huge swath of GCHQ mass surveillance is illegal, says top lawyer'. *The Guardian*, 28 January 2014.

House of Commons. 'Defence and Cyber Security'. London: UK Parliament, 2012.

Howard, John D., and Thomas A. Longstaff. 'A Common Language for Computer Security Incidents'. New Mexico and Livermore, CA: Sandia National Laboratories, 1998.

Hughes, Eric. 'A Cypherpunk's Manifesto'. In *Activism.net*, edited by Cypherpunks, 1993.

Hunker, Jeffrey, Bob Hutchinson, and Jonathan Marguiles. 'Role and Challenges for Sufficient Cyber-Attack Attribution'. In *Institute for Information Infrastructure Protection*. Hanover, NH: Dartmouth College, 2008.

Hutchins, Eric M., Michael J Cloppert, and Rohan M. Amin. 'Intelligence-

Driven Computer Network Defense Informed by Analysis of Adversary Campaigns and Intrusion Kill Chains'. Paper presented at the 6th Annual International Conference on Information Warfare and Security, Washington, DC, 2011.

Hutchinson, Bill. 'Two busted in Cole blast: Investigators find bomb factory in Yemen apartment'. *Daily News*, 18 October 2000.

Hyppönen, Mikko. 'Cyber Security: A Mission Impossible?'. Paper presented at the Lennart Meri Conference, Tallinn, 2014.

InfoSec Island. 'Attribution Problems Hinder U.S. Cyberwar Strategy'. *InfoSec Island*, 7 June 2011.

Intelligence and Security Committee of Parliament. 'Annual Report 2012–2013'. London: Parliament, 2013.

————. 'Open Evidence Session'. London: UK Parliament, 2013.

International Group of Experts. *Tallinn Manual on the International Law Applicable to Cyber Warfare*. edited by Michael N. Schmitt. Cambridge: Cambridge University Press, 2013.

International Law Commission. 'Draft Articles on the Responsibility of States for Internationally Wrongful Acts'. In *Yearbook of the International Law Commission*, edited by International Law Commission. New York and Geneva: United Nations, 2001.

ITU-T. 'Overview of cybersecurity'. In *X.1205*, 64. Geneva: ITU, 2008.

Jackson, William. 'Former FBI cyber cop: Hunt the hacker, not the hack'. *Government Computer News*, 19 April 2012.

Jacobs, Andrew. 'After Reports on N.S.A., China Urges End to Spying'. *The New York Times*, 24 March 2014.

Javers, Eamon. Cybersecurity Firm Says It Is Under Attack'. *CNBC*, 20 March 2013.

Jennings, Peter. 'World News Tonight with Peter Jennings'. *ABC News*, 25 April 1991.

Jennings, Richi. 'Operation Shady RAT smells like Chinese hacking'. *Computerworld*, 3 August 2011.

Jesdanun, Anick. 'New virus snarls hundreds of thousands of machines worldwide'. *The Associated Press*, 3 May 2004.

Jinghao, Yang, and Duan Wuning. 'Regular cyber attacks from US: China'. *Global Times*, 21 February 2013.

Johansson, Rolf. 'Case Study Methodology'. Paper presented at the Methodologies in Housing Research, Stockholm, 2003.

Johnson, Chris W. 'Anti-social networking: crowdsourcing and the cyber defence of national critical infrastructures'. *Ergonomics* (2013): 1–16.

Joint Committee on the Draft Communication Data Bill. 'Draft Communication Data Bill (12 July)'. London: UK Parliament, 2012.

————. 'Draft Communication Data Bill (17 July)'. London: UK Parliament, 2012.

BIBLIOGRAPHY

Joint Intelligence Organisation. 'JIC assessment of 27 August on Reported Chemical Weapons Use in Damascus '. London: Cabinet Office, 2013.

Jones, Sam. 'Groups face the conundrum of cyber crime'. *Financial Times*, 24 February 2014.

———. 'Cyber warfare: Iran opens a new front'. *Financial Times*, 26 April 2016.

Joy, Oliver. 'Mandiant: China is sponsoring cyber-espionage'. *CNN*, 20 February 2013.

Judiciary Subcommittee on Crime & Terrorism. 'Cybersecurity Threats'. Washington, DC: C-Span, 2013.

Kamluk, Vitaly. 'The Mystery of Duqu: Part Six (The Command and Control servers)'. *SecureList*, 30 November 2011.

Kaplan, Dan. 'Offensive line: Fighting back against hackers'. *SC Magazine* (1 June 2012).

Kaspersky, Eugene. 'The Man Who Found Stuxnet—Sergey Ulasen in the Spotlight'. 2 November 2011.

———. 'What Wired Is Not Telling You –a Response to Noah Shachtman's Article in Wired Magazine'. *Nota Bene*, 25 July 2012.

——— -. 'What will happen if countries carve up the internet?'. *The Guardian*, 17 December 2013.

Kaspersky Lab. 'Gauss: Nation-state cyber-surveillance meets banking Trojan'. SecureList, https://securelist.com/blog/incidents/33854/gauss-nation-state-cyber-surveillance-meets-banking-trojan-54/, accessed 13 July 2016.

———. 'Kaspersky Lab and ITU Research Reveals New Advanced Cyber Threat'. Kaspersky Lab, 28 May 2012, http://www.kaspersky.com/about/news/virus/2012/Kaspersky_Lab_and_ITU_Research_Reveals_New_Advanced_Cyber_Threat, accessed 8 July 2016.

———. 'Resource 207: Kaspersky Lab Research Proves that Stuxnet and Flame Developers are Connected'. *Kaspersky Lab*, 11 June 2012.

———. 'The "Red October" Campaign—An Advanced Cyber Espionage Network Targeting Diplomatic and Government Agencies'. *SecureList*, 14 January 2013.

———. 'Kaspersky Lab Uncovers "The Mask": One of the Most Advanced Global Cyber-espionage Operations to Date Due to the Complexity of the Toolset Used by the Attackers'. *Kaspersky Lab*, 11 February 2014.

Kehl, Danielle, and Tim Maurer. 'Did the U.N. Internet Governance Summit Actually Accomplish Anything?'. *Slate*, 14 December 2012.

Kenny, Mark. 'Gillard scores coup with China agreement'. *The Sydney Morning Herlad*, 10 April 2013.

Kent, Sherman. 'Words of Estimative Probability'. *Studies in Intelligence 8*, no. 4 (1964): 49–65.

BIBLIOGRAPHY

Kim, Sam. 'SKorea misidentifies China as cyberattack origin'. *The Associated Press*, 22 March 2013.

Kirk, Jeremy. 'LulzSec Leader "Sabu" Granted Six-Month Sentencing Delay'. *PCWorld*, 23 August 2012.

Klayman et al. v. Obama et al., (16 December 2013), D.D.C., 13–0851.

Knake, Robert K. 'Untangling Attribution: Moving to Accountability in Cyberspace'. 12. Washington, DC: Subcommittee on Technology and Innovation, 2010.

Koh, Harold Hongju. 'International Law in Cyberspace'. In *USCYBERCOM Inter-Agency Legal Conference*. Fort Meade, MD, 2012.

Koo, George, and Ling-chi Wang. 'Shoddy evidence and past hypocrisy weaken US cyber-spying charges'. *Global Times*, 6 March 2012.

Koskenniemi, Martti. 'The Politics of International Law'. *Journal of International Law* 1 (1990): 5–32.

———. 'The Politics of International Law'. In *LCIL International Law Seminar Series 2011–2012*. Cambridge, 2012.

Kovacs, Eduard. 'Hackers of Izz ad-Din al-Qassam Cyber Fighters'. *Softpedia*, 7 November 2012.

Krebs, Brian. 'Conversation With a Worm Author'. *The Washington Post*, 29 August 2005.

———. 'Suspected Worm Creators Arrested'. *The Washington Post*, 27 August 2005.

———. 'Shadowy Russian Firm Seen as Conduit for Cybercrime'. *The Washington Post*, 13 October 2007.

———. 'Who Wrote the Pincer Android Trojan?'. *KrebsOnSecurity*, 27 August 2013.

———. 'Who Built the Syrian Electronic Army?'. *KrebsOnSecurity*, 28 August 2013.

Krekel, Bryan, Patton Adams, George Bakos, and Northrop Grumman Corp. 'Occupying the Information High Ground: Chinese Capabilities for Computer Network Operations and Cyber Espionage'. edited by U.S.-China Economic and Security Review Commission. Washington, DC, 2012.

Kroes, Neelie. 'Towards more confidence and more value for European Digital Citizens'. Paper presented at the European Roundtable on the Benefits of Online Advertising for Consumers, Brussels, 17 September 2010.

Krol, Charlotte, AP and APTN, 'Barack Obama explains US sanctions on North Korea over Sony attack'. *The Telegraph*, 2 January 2015.

Kuji Media Corporation, 'History', http://www.kujimedia.com/articles/, accessed 8 July 2016.

Kurtz, George. 'CrowdStrike launches in stealth-mode with $26 million Series A round led by Warburg Pincus'. *George Kurtz*, 22 February 2012.

BIBLIOGRAPHY

Kwang-tae, Kim. 'N. Korea's hacking capabilities advance'. *Yonhap News Agency*, 11 April 2013.

Lathem, Niles. 'Bin Laden Made Tape Vowing Attack'. *The New York Post*, 14 October 2013.

Lawrence, Jill. 'Gore Denounces Bush Jobs Plan As Ploy for Votes'. *The Associated Press*, 25 August 1992.

Leclerc, Jean-Marc. 'Téléphone, Internet: l'État pourra bientôt tout espionner'. *Le Figaro*, 26 November 2013.

Ledgett, Richard. 'The NSA responds to Edward Snowden's TED Talk'. In *TED*. Vancouver: TED, 2014.

Lee, Laurie Thomas. 'Can Police Track Your Wireless Calls—Call Location Information and Privacy Law'. *Cardozo Arts & Entertainment Law Journal* 21 (2003): 381–407.

Lefebvre, Stéphane. 'A Look at Intelligence Analysis'. *International Journal of Intelligence and CounterIntelligence* 17, no. 2 (2004): 231–64.

Lelli, Andrea. 'Zeusbot/Spyeye P2P Updated, Fortifying the Botnet'. Symantec Connect, http://www.symantec.com/connect/blogs/zeusbotspyeye-p2p-updated-fortifying-botnet, accessed 4 July 2016.

Lemos, Robert. 'Microsoft to reward informants after Sasser conviction'. *SecurityFocus*, 8 July 2005.

Lennon, Mike. 'Kaspersky Unveils "The Mask"—Most Advanced Cyber Espionage Operation Seen To Date'. *SecurityWeek*, 10 February 2014.

Levin, Avner, and Paul Goodrick. 'From cybercrime to cyberwar? The international policy shift and its implications for Canada'. *Canadian Foreign Policy Journal* 19, no. 2 (2013): 127–43.

Levy, Steven. 'Battle of the Clipper Chip'. *The New York Times*, 12 June 1994.

———. *Crypto: How the Code Rebels Beat the Government Saving Privacy in the Digital Age*. New York: Penguin Books, 2001.

Lewis, James Andrew. 'The Cyber War Has Not Begun'. Washington, DC: Center for Strategic & International Studies, 2010.

Leyden, John. 'AV vendors split over FBI Trojan snoops'. *The Register*, 27 November 2001.

———. 'Blaster-F suspect charged with cybercrime'. *The Register*, 11 September 2003.

———. 'Inside "Operation Black Tulip": DigiNotar hack analysed'. *The Register*, 6 September 2011.

———. 'Chinese cyber-spook crew back in business, say security watchers'. *The Register*, 29 April 2013.

Libicki, Martin C. *Cyberdeterrence and Cyberwar*. Santa Monica, CA: RAND, 2009.

———. 'The Specter of Non-Obvious Warfare'. *Strategic Studies Quarterly* (Fall 2012): 88–101.

BIBLIOGRAPHY

————. 'Why Cyber War Will Not and Should Not Have Its Grand Strategist'. *Strategic Studies Quarterly* Spring (2014): 23–39.

Lichtblau, Eric. 'In Secret, Court Vastly Broadens Powers of N.S.A.'. *The New York Times*, 6 July 2013.

Lichtblau, Eric, and Michael S. Schmidt. 'Other Agencies Clamor for Data N.S.A. Compiles'. *The New York Times*, 3 August 2013.

Lieber, Keir A., and Daryl G. Press. 'Why States Won't Give Nuclear Weapons to Terrorists'. *International Security* 38, no. 1 (2013): 80–104.

Lipin, Michael. 'Saudi Cyber Attack Seen as Work of Amateur Hackers Backed by Iran'. *Voice of America*, 25 October 2012.

Liptak, Adam, and Michael S. Schmidt. 'Judge Upholds N.S.A.'s Bulk Collection of Data on Calls'. *The New York Times*, 27 December 2013.

Lizza, Ryan. 'State of Deception'. *The New Yorker*, 16 December 2013.

Loiko, Sergei L. 'Russian cyber-security firm reports major malware find'. *Los Angeles Times*, 17 January 2013.

Lotrionte, Catherine. 'Introduction: Strengthening the Norms of State Responsibilty'. *Georgetown Journal of International Affairs* 11 (2010): 101–9.

Loyd, Anthony. 'Army of hackers takes on the world'. *The Times*, 8 March 2010.

Lusthaus, Jonathan. 'How organised is organised cybercrime?'. *Global Crime* 14, no. 1 (2013): 52–60.

Lute, Jane Holl. 'Cyber Security: A Mission Impossible?'. Paper presented at the Lennart Meri Conference, Tallinn, 2014.

Lynn, William J. 'The Cyber Security Challenge: Defending a New Domain'. Washington, DC: US Department of Defense, 2012.

————. 'Roundtable on Cyber Security with Australian Business and Civic Leaders'. US Department of Defense, http://archive.defense.gov/speeches/speech.aspx?speechid=1422, accessed 30 June 2016.

Lyons, John, and Paulo Trevisani. 'Brazil President Halts Planning for U.S. Visit Over NSA Spying Rift'. *The Wall Street Journal*, 5 September 2013.

MacAskill, Ewen, Julian Borger, Nick Hopkins, Nick Davies, and James Ball. 'GCHQ taps fibre-optic cables for secret access to world's communications'. *The Guardian*, 21 June 2013.

Machiavelli, Niccolò. *The Prince*. Edited by Quentin Skinner and Russell Price. Cambridge: Cambridge University Press, 1988.

Malin, Cameron H., Eoghan Casey, and James M. Aquilina. *Malware Forensics Field Guide for Windows Systems: Digital Forensics Field Guides*. Waltham: Elsevier, 2012.

Mandia, Kevin. 'The State of Incident Response'. BlackHat conference. Las Vegas, NV, 2006, available at: http://www.youtube.com/watch?v=Jqv93DcZdDE.

BIBLIOGRAPHY

Mandiant. 'APT1: Exposing One of China's Cyber Espionage Units'. 76. Alexandria, VA: Mandiant, 2013.

————. 'M Trends: The advanced persistent threat'. Alexandria, VA: Mandiant, 2013.

Mannion, Jim. 'US officials point to terrorism in navy destroyer blast'. *Agence France-Presse*, 12 October 2000.

Manusov, Valerie, and Brian Spitzberg. 'Attribution Theory—Finding Good Cause in the Search for Theory'. In *Engaging theories in interpersonal communication*, edited by D. O. Braithwaite & L. A. Baxter. Thousand Oaks, CA: Sage Publications, 2008.

Markoff, John. 'Author of Computer "Virus" Is Son Of N.S.A. Expert on Data Security'. *The New York Times*, 5 November 1988.

————. 'Flaw discovered in federal plan for wiretapping'. *The New York Times*, 2 June 1994.

————. 'Digital Fingerprints Leave Clues to Creator of Internet Virus'. *The New York Times*, 30 March 1999.

————. 'Before the Gunfire, Cyberattacks'. *The New York Times*, 12 August 2008.

Masters, Jonathan. 'Here's How The U.S. Plans To Plug The Holes In Its Cybersecurity Policy'. *The Business Insider*, 24 May 2011.

Mattos, Cristinano Lincoln. Interview with author, 20 June 2013.

May, Timothy C. 'The Crypto Anarchist Manifesto', 22 November 1992, http://www.activism.net/cypherpunk/crypto-anarchy.html, accessed 29 July 2016 (Aptos, CA, 1992).

Mayer-Schönberger, Viktor. 'Omission of search results is not a "right to be forgotten" or the end of Google'. *The Guardian*, 13 May 2014.

Mazzetti, Mark. 'F.B.I. Informant Is Tied to Cyberattacks Abroad'. *The New York Times*, 23 April 2014.

McAfee. 'In the Dark—Crucial Industries Confront Cyberattacks'. Santa Clara, CA, 2011.

McAfee Labs. 'McAfee Labs Consolidated Threat Report: Duqu'. Santa Clara, CA, 2012.

McConnell, Mike. 'Mike McConnell on how to win the cyber-war we're losing'. *The Washington Post*, 28 February 2010.

McGee, Shane, Randy V. Sabet, and Anand Shah. 'Adequate Attribution: A Framework for Developing a National Policy for Private Sector Use of Active Defense'. *Journal of Business & Technology Law* 8, no. 1 (2013): 1–47.

McGraw, Gary. 'Cyber War is Inevitable (Unless We Build Security In)'. *Journal of Strategic Studies* 36, no. 1 (2012): 109–19.

McKeown, Wendell B. 'Information Operations: Countering the Asymmetric Threat to the United States'. Carlisle Barracks, PA: US Army War College, 1999.

Mendoza, Martha. 'Virus sender helped FBI bust hackers, court records say'. *The Associated Press*, 17 September 2003.

Menn, Joseph. 'FBI says more cooperation with banks key to probe of cyber attacks'. *Reuters*, 13 May 2013.

————. 'Cyber attacks against banks more severe than most realize'. *Reuters*, 18 May 2013.

Merchant, Brian. 'Is This the Leader of the Syrian Electronic Army?'. *Vice*, 28 August 2013.

Miller, Benjamin. 'The Concept of Security: Should it be Redefined?'. *Journal of Strategic Studies* 24, no. 2 (2001).

Morgenthau, Hans J. *The Concept of the Political*. Translated by Maeva Vidal, edited by Hatmut Behr and Felix Rösch. New York: Palgrave Macmillan, 2012.

Morris, Steven. 'Computer virus creator jailed as "global menace"'. *The Guardian*, 22 January 2003.

Moscaritolo, Angela. 'Duqu underscores trouble AV industry has in stopping threats'. *SC Magazine*, 2011.

Mrt. Izz ad-Din al-Qassam Cyber Fighters. 'Bank of America and New York Stock Exchange under attack unit'. http://pastebin.com/mCHia4W5, accessed 6 July 2016.

Mueller, Milton. 'Why ICANN can't '. *IEEE Spectrum* July (2002): 15–16.

————. 'Meltdown IV: How ICANN Resists Accountability'. *Internet Governance Project*, 18 September 2013.

Mueller, Robert S. III. 'The Future of Cyber Security from the FBI's Perspective'. In *International Conference on Cyber Security 2013*. Fordham University, New York, 2013.

Mydans, Seth. 'Student Sought In Virus Case In Philippines'. *The New York Times*, 11 May 2000.

Nakashima, Ellen. 'Iran blamed for cyberattacks on U.S. banks and companies'. *The Washington Post*, 22 September 2012.

————. 'Cyber-spying said to target U.S. business'. *The Washington Post*, 11 February 2013.

————. 'U.S. said to be target of massive cyber-espionage campaign'. *The Washington Post*, 11 February 2013.

————. 'NSA phone record collection does little to prevent terrorist attacks, group says'. *The Washington Post*, 12 January 2014.

————. 'U.S. to announce first criminal charges against China for cyberspying'. *The Washington Post*, 19 May 2014.

————. 'Syrian hacker extradited to the United States from Germany'. *The Washington Post*, 9 May 2016.

Nakashima, Ellen, Greg Miller, and Julie Tate. 'U.S., Israel developed Flame computer virus to slow Iranian nuclear efforts, officials say'. *The Washington Post*, 19 June 2012.

BIBLIOGRAPHY

Nakashima, Ellen, and Ashkan Soltani. 'Panel urges new curbs on surveillance by U.S.'. *The Washington Post*, 18 December 2013.

Nakashima, Ellen, and Matt Zapotsky. 'U.S. charges Iran-linked hackers with targeting banks, N.Y. dam'. *The Washington Post*, 24 March 2016.

Naraine, Ryan. 'New variant shows Duqu attackers still in operation'. *ZDNet*, 20 March 2012.

National Counterintelligence Center, Federal Bureau of Investigation, and National Infrastructure Protection Center. 'Solar Sunrise'. http://www. youtube.com/watch?v=bOr5CtqYnsA&nofeather=True, accessed 20 July 2016.

National Research Council. 'Cryptography's Role in Securing the Information Society'. edited by Kenneth W. Dam and Herbert S. Lin. Washington, DC: National Academy Press, 1996.

————. 'Making the Nation Safer: The Role of Science and Technology in Countering Terrorism'. Washington, DC: National Academy Press, 2002.

NATO Parliamentary Assembly. 'Information and National Security'. 22. Brussels: NATO, 2011.

Nelson, Brian, and Peter Bergen. 'Osama Bin Laden No. 1 Suspect in U.S.S. Cole Bombing'. *CNN*, 14 October 2000.

Nesson, Charles. 'The Evidence or the Event? On Judicial Proof and the Acceptability of Verdicts'. *Harvard Law Review* 98, no. 7 (1985): 1357–92.

Newitz, Annalee. 'The Bizarre Evolution of the Word "Cyber"'. *io9*, 16 September 2013.

Newman, Lily Hay. 'Can You Trust NIST?'. *IEEE Spectrum*, 9 October 2013.

NewsBites. 'Brazilian Government pulls local storage obligation from internet bill'. *NewsBites*, 22 March 2014.

Nguyen, Van. 'Attribution of Spear Phishing Attacks: A Literature Survey'. Edinburgh, South Australia: Government of Australia, 2013.

Nicholson, Andrew, Helge Janicke, and Tim Watson. 'An Initial Investigation into Attribution in SCADA Systems'. Paper presented at the International Symposium for ICS & SCADA Cyber Security Research, Leicester, 2013.

Norton-Taylor, Richard. 'Titan Rain—how Chinese hackers targeted Whitehall'. *The Guardian*, 5 September 2007, http://www.guardian.co. uk/technology/2007/sep/04/news.internet, accessed 11 July 2016.

Norton-Taylor, Richard, and Nick Hopkins. 'Britain plans cyber strike force—with help from GCHQ'. *The Guardian*, 30 September 2013.

Noviy, Vladislav. 'Kaspersky Lab Wants to Save Digital World'. *RusData Dialine—BizEkon News*, 4 April 2013.

Nutter, John Jacob. *The CIA's Black Ops: Covert Action, Foreign Policy, and Democracy*. New York: Prometheus Books, 2000.

Oates, John. 'Kid who crashed email server gets tagged'. *The Register*, 23 August 2006.

BIBLIOGRAPHY

Obama, Barack. 'Remarks by the President in the State of the Union Address'. Washington, DC: The White House, 12 February 2013.

————. 'Remarks by the President on Review of Signals Intelligence'. Washington, DC: The White House, 17 January 2014.

OECD. 'Digital Identity Management: Enabling Innovation and Trust in the Internet Economy'. Paris: OECD, 2011.

Office of the National Counterintelligence Executive. 'Foreign spies stealing US economic secrets in cyberspace: Report to Congress on Foreign Economic Collection and Industrial Espionage, 2009–2011'. Washington, DC: ONCIX, 2011.

Oi, Mariko. 'Japan crime: Why do innocent people confess?'. *BBC News*, 2 January 2013.

Olson, Parmy. *We are anonymous*. London: William Heinemann, 2012.

Omand, David, Jamie Bartlett, and Carl Miller. 'Introducing Social Media Intelligence (SOCMINT)'. *Intelligence and National Security* 27, no. 6 (2012): 801–23.

Oremus, Will. 'Would You Click the Link in This Email That Apparently Tricked the AP?'. *Slate*, 23 April 2013.

————. 'The Syrian Hackers Are Winning. Here's Why.'. *Slate*, 15 August 2013.

Osborne, Charlie. 'US government debates action over alleged Chinese cyberattacks'. *ZDNet*, 1 February 2013.

Ottis, Rain. 'Analysis of the 2007 Cyber Attacks Against Estonia from the Information Warfare Perspective'. Paper presented at the 7th European Conference on Information Warfare and Security, Plymouth, 2008.

Overill, Richard E., and Jantje A. M. Silomon. 'A Complexity Based Forensic Analysis of the Trojan Horse Defence'. Paper presented at the 4th International Workshop on Digital Forensics, Vienna, 2011.

Owen, Tess. 'The US Has Indicted Three Alleged Syrian Electronic Army Hackers for Cyber Crimes'. *Vice*, 23 March 2016.

Panetta, Leon. 'Text of Speech by Secretary of Defense Leon Panetta'. New York: Business Executives for National Security, 2012.

Panetta, Leon, and Martin Dempsey. 'News Briefing'. Washington, DC: US Department of Defense, 25 October 2012.

Parker, Tom, Matthew G. Devost, Marcus H. Sach, Eric Shaw, and Ed Stroz. *Cyber Adversary Characterisation*. Rockland: Syngress Publishing, 2004.

Pato, Joe, Sharon Paradesi, Ian Jacobi, Fuming Shih, and Sam Wang. 'Aintno: Demonstration of Information Accountability on the Web'. Paper presented at the International Conference on Privacy, Security, Risk, and Trust, Boston, 2011.

Perlroth, Nicole. 'Researchers Find Clues in Malware'. *The New York Times*, 30 May 2012.

BIBLIOGRAPHY

————. 'In Cyberattack on Saudi Firm, U.S. Sees Iran Firing Back'. *The New York Times*, 23 October 2012.

————. 'Hackers in China Attacked The Times for Last 4 Months'. *The New York Times*, 30 January 2013.

————. 'Hunting for Syrian Hackers' Chain of Command'. *The New York Times*, 17 May 2013.

Perlroth, Nicole, and David E. Sanger. 'Nations Buying as Hackers Sell Flaws in Computer Code'. *The New York Times*, 13 July 2013.

————. 'FireEye Computer Security Firm Acquires Mandiant'. *The New York Times*, 2 January 2014.

Perlroth, Nicole, David E. Sanger, and Michael S. Schmidt. 'As Hacking Against U.S. Rises, Experts Try to Pin Down Motive'. *The New York Times*, 3 March 2013.

Permanent subcommittee on investigations of the Committee on Governmental Affairs. 'Security in Cyberspace'. Washington, DC, 1996.

Philipe P. v. Lyonnaise Communications (24 May 2002), 0207090006, Tribunal de Grande Instance, Paris,

Pierson, Paul. *Politics in time: history, institutions, and social analysis.* Princeton, NJ: Princeton University Press, 2004.

Pillar, Paul R. 'Intelligence, Policy, and the War in Iraq'. *Foreign Affairs* 85, no. 2 (2006): 15–27.

Pincus, Walter, and Dana Priest. 'NSA Intercepts On Eve of 9/11 Sent a Warning'. *The Washington Post*, 20 June 2002.

Poitras, Laura, Marcel Rosenbach, and Holger Stark. '"Follow the Money": NSA Monitors Financial World'. *Der Spiegel*, 16 September 2013.

Police Central e-Crime Unit. 'Financial Harm Reduction & Performance Report'. London: Association of Chief Police Officers, PCeU, 2013.

Popper, Karl R. *Conjectures and Refutations: The Growth of Scientific Knowledge.* 1963. London: Routledge, 1996.

Poulsen, Kevin. 'Solar Sunrise hacker "Analyzer" escapes jail'. *The Register*, 15 June 2001.

————. 'FBI Admits It Controlled Tor Servers Behind Mass Malware Attack'. 13 September 2013.

Power, Richard. 'Joy Riders: Mischief That Leads to Mayhem'. *informIT*, 30 October 2000.

Prescott, Jody M. 'Autonomous Decision-Making Processes and the Responsible Cyber Commander'. Paper presented at the 5th International Conference on Cyber Conflict, Tallinn, 2013.

Preston, Jennifer. 'Seeking to Disrupt Protesters, Syria Cracks Down on Social Media'. *The New York Times*, 23 May 2011.

Putin, Vladimir. 'What Putin Has to Say to Americans About Syria'. *The New York Times*, 11 September 2013.

BIBLIOGRAPHY

Ranum, Marcus J. 'Cyberwar: About Attribution (identifying your attacker)'. *Fabius Maxim*, 21 October 2011.

Rapoza, Kenneth. '"Duqu" Virus Likely Handiwork Of Sophisticated Government, Kaspersky Lab Says'. *Forbes*, 21 October 2011.

———. 'War Drums Beat Louder For "World War C"'. *Forbes*, 6 October 2013.

Rasch, Mark D., Interview, 16 July 2013.

Rashid, Fahmida Y. 'Eugene Kaspersky: Definition Of "Cyberwar" In Flux, Threat Of Cyber Weapons Underestimated'. *SecurityWeek*, 21 November 2012.

Reals, Tucker. 'Syria chemical weapons attack blamed on Assad, but where's the evidence?'. *CBS News*, 30 August 2013.

Reich, Pauline C., Stuart Weinstein, Charles Wild, and Allan S. Cabanlong. 'Cyber Warfare: A Review of Theories, Law, Policies, Actual Incidents—and the Dilemma of Anonymity'. *European Journal of Law and Technology* 1, no. 2 (2010): 1–58.

Relyea, Harold C. 'The Coming of Secret Law'. *Government Information Quarterly* 5, no. 2 (1998): 97–116.

Reuters. 'China says U.S. hacking accusations lack technical proof'. *Reuters*, 20 February 2013.

———. 'Pentagon accuses China of trying to hack US defence networks'. *The Guardian*, 7 May 2013.

———. 'China has "mountains of data" about U.S. cyber attacks: official'. *Reuters*, 5 June 2013.

———. 'In cyber spying row, Chinese media call U.S. a "mincing rascal"'. *Reuters*, 20 May 2014.

Rice, Matthew. 'Exploiting privacy: Surveillance companies pushing zero-day exploits'. *Privacy International*, 11 March 2014.

Richards, Julian. *A Guide to National Security*. Oxford: Oxford University Press, 2011.

Richmond, Riva. 'An Attack Sheds Light on Internet Security Holes'. *New York Times*, 6 April 2011.

Richtel, Matt. 'U.S. Agents Seeking Clues To Who Made E-Mail Virus'. *The New York Times*, 2 April 1999.

Ricks, Thomas E. *Fiasco: The Amercian Military Adventure in Iraq*. London: Penguin Books, 2006.

Rid, Thomas. *Cyber War Will Not Take Place*. London: Hurst & Company, 2013.

Rid, Thomas and Ben Buchanan. '"Attributing Cyber Attacks"'. *Journal of Strategic Studies* 38, no. 1–2 (2015): 4–37.

Ries, Brian. 'Syrian Electronic Army Leader Says the Hacks Won't Stop'. *The Daily Beast*, 14 August 2013.

Risen, James, and Laura Poitras. 'N.S.A. Gathers Data on Social Connections of U.S. Citizens'. *The New York Times*, 28 September 2013.

BIBLIOGRAPHY

————. 'N.S.A. Report Outlined Goals for More Power'. *The New York Times*, 22 November 2013.

Roberts, Dan. 'Obama imposes new sanctions against North Korea in response to Sony hack'. *The Guardian*, 2 January 2015.

Rogers, Michael. 'Rebooting Trust? Freedom vs. Security in Cyberspace'. In *Munich Security Conference*. Munich, 2014.

Rogers, Mike, and Dutch Ruppersberger. 'Investigative Report on the U.S. National Security Issues Posed by Chinese Telecommunications Companies Huawei and ZTE '. 60. Washington, DC: US House of Representatives, 2012.

Romm, Tony. 'President Obama likely to talk softly with China on cyber-snooping'. *Politico*, 2 June 2013.

Roscini, Marco. *Cyber Operations and the Use of Force in International Law*. New York: Oxford University Press, 2014.

Roscoe, Keith, Interview, 16 July 2012.

Rose, Charlie, Gayle King, Erica Hill, John Blackstone, and Steve Kroft. 'For March 5, 2012, CBS'. *CBS News Transcripts*, 5 March 2012.

Rotenberg, Marc. 'Planning for the Future of Cyber Attack Attribution'. In *House Committee on Science and Technology*. Washington, DC: US House of Representatives, 2010.

RT. 'Global cyber war: New Flame-linked malware detected'. *RT*, 16 October 2012.

————. 'Russia won't disconnect from global internet, works on cyber security—Kremlin'. *RT*, 19 September 2014.

Rubin, Harry, Leigh Fraser, and Monica Smith. 'US and International Law Aspects of the Internet: Fitting Square Pegs Into Round Holes'. *International Journal of Law and Information Technology* 3, no. 2 (1995): 117–43.

Rushe, Dominic, and James Ball. 'PRISM scandal: tech giants flatly deny allowing NSA direct access to servers'. *The Guardian*, 7 June 2013.

Russia Today. 'Russia steps into tech competition'. *Russia Today*, 18 June 2009.

Russinovich, Mark E. *Zero Day*. New York: Thomas Dunne Books, 2011.

Sale, Richard. 'Clinton Administration considers strike options'. *United Press International*, 28 November 2000.

Sang-Hun, Choe. 'North Korea Declares 1953 War Truce Nullified'. *The New York Times*, 11 March 2013.

Sanger, David E. 'Obama Order Sped Up Wave of Cyberattacks Against Iran'. *The New York Times*, 1 June 2012.

————. 'U.S. Blames China's Military Directly for Cyberattacks'. *The New York Times*, 6 May 2013.

————. 'As Chinese Leader's Visit Nears, U.S. Is Urged to Allow Counterattacks on Hackers'. *The New York Times*, 21 May 2013. 'N S A. Nominee Promotes Cyberwar Units'. *The New York Times*, 11 March 2014.

BIBLIOGRAPHY

————. 'Budget Documents Detail Extent of U.S. Cyberoperations'. *The New York Times*, 31 August 2013.

————. 'U.S. Tries Candor to Assure China on Cyberattacks'. *The New York Times*, 6 April 2014.

Sanger, David E. and Martin Fackler. 'N.S.A. Breached North Korean Networks Before Sony Attack, Officials Say'. *The New York Times*, 18 January 2015.

Sanger, David E., and Mark Landler. 'U.S. and China Agree to Hold Regular Talks on Hacking'. *The New York Times*, 1 June 2013.

Sanger, David E., and Nicole Perlroth. 'Chinese Hackers Resume Attacks on U.S. Targets'. *The New York Times*, 19 May 2013.

————. 'Hackers From China Resume Attacks on U.S. Targets'. *The New York Times*, 19 May 2013.

Sanger, David E., and Thom Shanker. 'Broad Powers Seen for Obama in Cyberstrikes'. *The New York Times*, 3 February 2013.

————. 'N.S.A. Devises Radio Pathway Into Computers'. *The New York Times*, 14 January 2014.

Savage, Charlie. 'Judge Questions Legality of N.S.A. Phone Records'. *The New York Times*, 16 December 2013.

————. 'Watchdog Report Says N.S.A. Program Is Illegal and Should End'. *The New York Times*, 23 January 2014.

Savage, Charlie, and Laura Pointras. 'How a Court Secretly Evolved, Extending U.S. Spies' Reach'. *The New York Times*, 11 March 2014.

Savelsberg, Joachim J., and Peter Brühl. *Constructing white-collar crime: rationalities, communication, power*. Philadelphia, PA: University of Pennsylvania Press, 1994.

Schmidt, Michael S. 'U.S. to Charge Chinese Army Personnel With Cyberspying'. *The New York Times*, 19 May 2014.

Schmitt, Carl. *The Concept of the Political*. New Brunswick, NJ: Rutgers University Press, 1976.

Schmitt, Michael N. 'Computer Network Attack and the Use of Force in International Law: Thoughts on a Normative Framework'. *Columbia Journal of Transnational Law* 37 (1998).

Schmitt, Michael N., and Liis Vihul. 'The International Law of Attribution During Proxy "Wars" in Cyberspace'. *Fletcher Security Review* 1 (2014).

Schneier, Bruce. 'Anonymity and the Internet'. Schneier.com, 25 March 2005, https://www.schneier.com/blog/archives/2005/03/anonymity_and_t.html, accessed 30 June 2016.

————. *Liars and outliers: enabling the trust that society needs to thrive* [in English]. Indianapolis, IN: Wiley, 2012.

Schwartau, Winn. *Information Warfare: Chaos on the Electronic Superhighway*. New York: Thunder's Mouth Press, 1994.

BIBLIOGRAPHY

Schwartz, Mathew J., and J. Nicolas Hoover. 'China Suspected Of Shady RAT Attacks'. *InformationWeek*, 3 August 2011.

Segal, Adam. 'Hacking Back, Signaling, and State-Society Relations'. *Cyber Dialogue 2013*, 1 March 2013.

Select Committee to Study Governmental Operations with Respect to Intelligence Activities. 'Alleged assassination plots involving foreign leaders: an interim report of the Select Committee to Study Governmental Operations with Respect to Intelligence Activities, United States Senate: together with additional, supplemental and separate views'. Washington, DC: US Government Printing Office, 1975.

Seltzer, Larry. 'The professionalization of malware'. *ZDNet*, 19 August 2013.

Selyukh, Alina. 'Hackers send fake market-moving AP tweet on White House explosions'. *Reuters*, 23 April 2013.

Senate Armed Services Committee. 'Current and Future Worldwide Threats to the National Security of the United States'. Washington, DC: Federal News Service, 2012.

Sengupta, Somini. 'In Latest Breach, Hackers Impersonate Google to Snoop on Users in Iran'. *NewYork Times*, 30 August 2011.

Serbu, Jared. 'DoD cyber strategy aims at deterrence'. *Federal News Radio*, 15 July 2011.

Shachtman, Noah. 'Russia's Top Cyber Sleuth Foils US Spies, Helps Kremlin Pals'. *Wired*, 23 July 2012.

Shackelford, Scott J. 'State Responsibility for Cyber Attacks: Competing Standards for a Growing Problem'. Paper presented at the Conference on Cyber Conflict, Tallinn, 2010.

Shafer, Jack. 'The State of Secrecy in America'. *Reuters*, 6 May 2014.

Shakarian, Paulo, Gerardo I. Simari, Geoffrey Moores, Simon Parsons, and Marcelo A. Falappa, 'An Argumentation-Based Framework to Address the Attribution Problem in Cyber-Warfare', Academy of Science and Engineering, 27 April 2014.

Shalal-Esa, Andrea. 'Six U.S. Air Force cyber capabilities designated "weapons"'. *Reuters*, 8 April 2013.

————. 'Top general says U.S. under constant cyber attack threat'. *Reuters*, 14 May 2013.

Shane, Scott. 'No Morsel Too Minuscule for All-Consuming N.S.A.'. *The New York Times*, 2 November 2013.

Shanker, Thom, and David E. Sanger. 'U.S. Helps Allies Trying to Battle Iranian Hackers'. *The NewYork Times*, 8 June 2013.

Shenon, Philip. *The Commission:The Uncensored History of the 9/11 Investigation*. NewYork:Twelve, 2008.

Sherizen, Sanford. 'Criminological concepts and research findings relevant for improving computer crime control'. *Computer & Security* 9, no. 3 (1990): 215–22.

BIBLIOGRAPHY

Sherman, Mark. 'Two Arrested in U.S. Computer Worm Probe'. *The Associated Press*, 26 August 2005.

Shorrock, Tim. *Spies for Hire: The Secret World of Intelligence Outsourcing*. New York: Simon and Schuster, 2008.

Siemaszko, Corky. 'Bin Laden Linked to Bombing of Cole'. *Daily News*, 11 December 2000.

Simpson, J. A., and E. S. C. Weiner. *The Oxford English Dictionary*. Oxford: Oxford University Press, 1989.

Singel, Ryan. 'NSA Must Examine All Internet Traffic to Prevent Cyber Nine-Eleven, Top Spy Says'. *Wired*, 15 January 2008.

Singer, P. W., and Allan Friedman. *Cybersecurity and Cyberwar: What Everyone Needs to Know*. New York: Oxford University Press, 2014.

Smale, Alison, and David E. Sanger. 'Spying Scandal Alters U.S. Ties With Allies and Raises Talk of Policy Shift'. *The New York Times*, 11 November 2013.

Soldatov, Andrei, and Irina Borogan. 'Russia's Surveillance State'. *World Policy Journal* (Fall 2013).

Sommer, Peter. 'Intrusion detection systems as evidence'. *Journal Computer Networks: The International Journal of Computer and Telecommunications Networking* 31, no. 23–4 (1999): 2477–87.

Sommer, Peter, and Ian Brown. 'Reducing Systemic Cybersecurity Risks'. In *Future Global Shocks*, edited by Organization for European Cooperation and Development. Paris: OECD, 2011.

Spafford, Eugene H., and Stephen A. Weeber. 'Software forensics: Can we track code to its authors?'. *Computer & Security* 12, no. 6 (1993): 585–95.

Stalla-Bourdillon, Sophie. 'The flip side of ISP's liability regimes: The ambiguous protection of fundamental rights and liberties in private digital spaces'. *Computer Law & Security Review* 26 (2010): 492–501.

Steele, Robert David. 'The Evolving Craft of Intelligence'. In *Routledge Companion to Intelligence Studies*, edited by Robert Dover, Michael Goodman and Claudia Hillebrand, 71–83. Oxford: Routledge, 2013.

Steinberger, Peter J. *The Concept of Political Judgement*. Chicago, IL: The University of Chicago Press, 1993.

Sterling, Bruce. *The Hacker Crackdown: Law and Disorder on the Electronic Frontier*. New York: Bantam Books, 1992.

Stevens, Tim. 'A Cyberwar of Ideas? Deterrence and Norms in Cyberspace'. *Contemporary Security Policy* 33, no. 1 (2012): 148–70.

Stevenson, Alastair. 'Police arrest teenage hacker behind $50,000-per-month cyber ring'. *V3*, 16 September 2013.

Stoll, Clifford. *The Cuckoo's Egg: tracking a spy through the maze of computer espionage* [in English]. New York: Doubleday, 1989.

Subcommittee on Technology and Innovation of the House of Committee of

BIBLIOGRAPHY

Science and Technology. 'Planning for the Future of Cyber Attack Attribution'. Washington, DC: Federal News Service, 2010.

Sullivan, Sean. 'Trojan:Android/Pincer.A'. *F-Secure*, 5 April 2013.

Symantec. 'Stuxnet 0.5: The Missing Link'. Mountain View, CA: Symantec, 2013.

Szabo, Márton. 'Review Article: The Conceptual History of Politics as the History of Political Conceptualizations: Kari Palonen The Struggle with Time: A Conceptual History of "Politics" as an Activity', LIT Verlag: Hamburg, London and Münster, 2006. *European Journal of Political Theory* 8 (2009): 275–84.

Szor, Peter. 'Duqu—Threat Research and Analysis'. Santa Clara, CA: McAfee, 2011.

The Associated Press. 'Saying they lack evidence, Philippine investigators release suspect in'. *The Associated Press*, 10 May 2000.

———. 'U.S. official draws similarities to embassy bombings'. *The Associated Press*, 22 October 2000.

———. 'Pentagon still grappling with rules of cyberwar'. *The Associated Press*, 25 July 2012.

———. 'Official: US blames Iran hackers for cyberattacks'. *The Washington Post*, 11 October 2012.

———. 'South Korea Says North Korea Behind Computer Crash in March'. *The New York Times*, 10 April 2013.

———. 'Teen "super-hacker" in Argentina arrested in mass raid'. *CBC*, 14 September 2013.

The Economist. 'Hiring digital 007s'. *The Economist*, 15 June 2013.

———. 'The threat in the pocket'. *The Economist*, 18 October 2013.

The Guardian. 'Asio hacking claim won't hurt Australia—China ties, says Carr'. *The Guardian*, 28 May 2013.

———. 'Former US general James Cartwright named in Stuxnet leak inquiry'. *The Guardian*, 28 June 2013.

———. 'Obama: North Korea Sony hack "not an act of war"'. *The Guardian*, 21 December 2014.

The Huffington Post. 'Forget The Red Line, Worry About the Digital Line'. *The Huffington Post*, 26 September 2013.

The New York Times. 'Computer Virus Charges Sought'. *The New York Times*, 6 September 2000.

———. 'Domestic Spying, French Style'. *The New York Times*, 13 December 2013.

The SecDev Group, and The Citizen Lab. 'Tracking GhostNet: Investigating a Cyber Espionage Network'. In *Information Warfare Monitor*. Ottowa and Toronto: Munk Centre for International Studies, 2009.

The White House. 'The National Strategy to Secure Cyberspace'. 76. Washington, DC, 2003.

BIBLIOGRAPHY

————. 'National Security Presidential Directive /NSPD-54'. Washington, DC, 2008.

————. 'Cyberspace Policy Review'. Washington, DC, 2009.

————. 'International Strategy for Cyberspace'. edited by President of the United States. Washington, DC, 2011.

————. 'Administration Strategy on Mitigating the Theft of U.S. Trade Secrets'. 141. Washington, DC: The White House, 2013.

————. 'Improving Critical Infrastructure Cybersecurity'. Washington, DC, 2013.

The White House Bulletin. 'Investigators Close To Tying USS Cole Bombing To Bin Laden'. The White House Bulletin, 11 December 2000.

Thomas, Timothy. 'Russia's Information Warfare Strategy: Can the Nation Cope in Future Conflicts?'. The Journal of Slavic Military Studies 27, no. 1 (2014): 101–30.

Thonnard, Olivier. 'Vers un regroupement multicritères comme outil d'aide à l'attribution d'attaque dans le cyber-espace'. École Nationale Supérieure des Télécommunications, 2010.

Thonnard, Olivier, Wim Mees, and Marc Dacier. 'On a Multi-criteria Clustering Approach for Attack Attribution'. ACM Special Interest Group on Knowledge Discovery and Data Mining Explorations 12, no. 1 (2010): 11–21.

Tiirmaa-Klaar, Heli. 'Protecting cyberspace at different levels: Vulnerabilities and responses'. Tallinn: Estonian Ministry of Foreign Affairs, 2009.

Tikk, Eneken, and Kadri Kaska. 'Legal Cooperation to Investigate Cyber Incidents: Estonian Case Study and Lessons'. Paper presented at the 9th European Conference on Information Warfare and Security, Thessaloniki, 2010.

Tikk, Eneken, Kadri Kaska, Kristel Rünnimeri, Mari Kert, Anna-Maria Talihärm, and Liis Vihul. 'Cyber Attacks Against Georgia: Legal Lessons Identified'. Tallinn: CCDCOE, 2008.

Travis, Alan. 'Surveillance society soon a reality, report suggests'. The Guardian, 11 November 2014.

Treverton, Gregory F. Covert Actions: The limits of intervention in the postwar world. New York: Basic Books, 1987.

Tsagourias, Nicholas. 'Cyber attacks, self-defence and the problem of attribution'. Journal of Conflict & Security Law 17, no. 2 (2013): 229–44.

Tyler, Tom R., and Kathleen M. McGraw. 'The Threat of Nuclear War: Risk Interpretation and Behavioral Response'. Journal of Social Issues 39, no. 1 (1983): 25–40.

UN Watched. 'Tschechien: Neuer Anlauf zur Wiedereinführung der Vorratsdatenspeicherung'. UN Watched, https://http://www.unwatched.org/EDRigram_10.11_Tschechien_Neuer_Anlauf_zur_Wiedereinfuehrung_der_Vorratsdatenspeicherung?pk_campaign=edri&pk_kwd=20120606.

United Nations. 'Group of Governmental Experts on Developments in the

BIBLIOGRAPHY

Field of Information and Telecommunications in the Context of International Security'. New York: United Nations, 2010.

————. 'Report on the Alleged Use of Chemical Weapons in the Ghouta Area of Damascus on 21 August 2013'. The Hague: United Nations Mission to Investigate Allegations of the Use of Chemical Weapons in the Syrian Arab Republic, 2013.

United Nations Economic and Social Council. 'Assessment of the progress made in the implementation of and follow-up to the outcomes of the World Summit on the Information Society'. New York: United Nations, 2011.

United Nations Office on Drugs and Crime. 'Comprehensive Study on Cybercrime'. New York: United Nations, 2013.

United States Congress. *Cybersecurity Act of 2012*.

United States of America v. Jeffrey Lee Parson, (August 2003), W.D Wash., 03–457M.

United States of America v. Wang Dong, Sun Kailiang, Wen Xinyu, Huang Zhenyu, Gu Chunhui, (1 May 2014), W.D. Pa., 14–118.

US Department of Agriculture. 'Hacking U.S. Government Computers from Overseas'. US Department of Agriculture, http://www.dm.usda.gov/ocpm/Security Guide/Spystory/Hacking.htm.

US Department of Defense. 'An Assessment of International Legal Issues in Information Operations', edited by Michael N. Schmitt and Brian T. O'Donnell. Washington, DC, 1999.

————. 'Department of Defense Cyberspace Policy Report: A Report to Congress Pursuant to the National Defense Authorization Act for Fiscal Year 2011, Section 934'. Washington, DC: Department of Defense, 2011.

————. 'DOD, Partners Better Prepared for Cyber Attacks'. Washington, DC: Department of Defense, 18 October 2011, http://archive.defense.gov/news/newsarticle.aspx?id=65709, accessed 1 July 2016.

————. 'Annual Report to Congress: Military and Security Developments Involving the People's Republic of China 2013'. Washington, DC: Department of Defense, 2013.

US Department of Homeland Security. 'Blueprint for a Secure Cyber Future'. 50. Washington, DC: US Department of Homeland Security, 2011.

US Department of State. 'Cybersecurity Update'. US Department of State, 18 October 2011, http://fpc.state.gov/175773.htm, accessed 7 July 2016.

US-China Economic and Security Review Commission. 'China's Views of Sovereignty and Methods of Access Control'. Washington, DC: Federal News Service, 2008.

Valentino-DeVries, Jennifer, and Siobhan Gorman. 'What You Need to Know on New Details of NSA Spying'. *The Wall Street Journal*, 20 August 2013.

Vaughan-Nichols, Steven J 'Inside the Tor exploit'. *ZDNet*, 5 August 2013.

287

BIBLIOGRAPHY

VBS. 'Beispiele Nachrichtendienstgesetz (NDG) [Examples of the new law on the intelligence service]'. Bern: VBS, 2014.

Verizon. '2013 Data Breach Investigation Report'. 63. New York: Verizon, 2013.

Verton, Dan. *Black Ice: The Invisible Threat of Cyber-Terrorism*. Emeryville, CA: McGraw-Hill Osborne Media, 2003.

Verton, Dan, and Andrew Brandt. 'Biography of a Worm'. PCWorld, http://www.networkworld.com/article/2326282/cloud-computing/biography-of-a-worm.html, accessed 15 July 2016.

Villeneuve, Nart, and Masashi Crete-Nishihata. 'Control and Resistance: Attacks on Burmese Opposition Media'. In *Access Contested: Security, Identity, and Resistance in Asian Cyberspace*, edited by Ronald Deibert, John Palfrey, Rafal Rohonzinski and Jonathan Zittrain. Cambridge, MA: MIT Press, 2012.

Volz, Dustin, and Jim Finkle. 'U.S. indicts Iranians for hacking dozens of banks, New York dam'. *Reuters*, 25 March 2016.

Walden, Ian. *Computer Crimes and Digital Investigation*. New York: Oxford University Press, 2007.

————. 'International Telecommunication Law, the Internet and the Regulation of Cyberspace'. In *Peacetime Regime for State Activities in Cyberspace*, edited by Katharina Ziolkowski, 261–89. Tallinn: NATO CCD COE Publication, 2013.

Walker, Danielle. 'Millions stolen from US banks after "wire payment switch" targeted'. *SC Magazine*, 21 August 2013.

————. 'NSA sought services of French security firm, zero-day seller Vupen'. *SC Magazine*, 18 September 2014.

Wall, David S. 'Internet Mafias? The Dis-Organisation of Crime on the Internet'. In *Organized Crime, Corruption and Crime Prevention*, edited by Stefano Caneppele and Francesco Calderoni, 227–38. Cham: Springer, 2014.

Wason, Peter C. 'On the Failure to Eliminate Hypotheses in a Conceptual Task'. *The Quarterly Journal of Experimental Psychology* XII, no. 3. 129–140. (1960).

Watson, Greg. 'Foreign hackers attack Canadian government'. *CBCNews*, 16 February 2011.

Watts, Jonathan, and Adam Gabbatt. 'China denies Gmail hacking accusations'. *The Guardian*, 2 June 2011.

Waxman, Matthew C. 'Cyber-Attacks and the Use of Force: Back to the Future of Article 2(4)'. *Yale Journal of International Law* 36, no. 2 (2011): 421–59.

Weber, Max. *Essays in Sociology*. Translated by H. H. Gerth and C. Wright Mills, edited by H. H. Gerth and C. Wright Mills. New York: Oxford University Press, 1946.

BIBLIOGRAPHY

Weedon, Jen. 'No Clearance Required: Using Commercial Threat Intelligence in the Federal Space'. *Mandiant*, 2 May 2013.

Wheeler, David A., and Gregory N. Larsen. 'Techniques for Cyber Attack Attribution'. Alexandria, VA: Institute for Defense Analyses, 2003.

Whitehouse, Sheldon. 'At West Point, Whitehouse Calls for Greater Awareness of Cyber Threats'. Whitehouse, 4 June 2012, http://www.whitehouse.senate.gov/news/release/at-west-point-whitehouse-calls-for-greater-awareness-of-cyber-threats, accessed 1 July 2016.

Wilber, Del Quentin. 'U.S. Agent Lures Romanian Hackers in Subway Data Heist'. *Bloomberg*, 17 April 2014.

Williams, Alex. 'CrowdStrike Raises $30M For Data Security Platform Built To Put Adversaries On The Defensive'. *TechCrunch*, 8 September 2013.

Williams, Kevin. 'Cybercrime'. Paper presented at the Information Security & Cyber Crime Summit, London, 18–19 February 2014.

Wireless News. 'CrowdStrike Unveils Big Data Active Defense Platform'. *Wireless News*, 29 June 2013.

Wolfers, Arnold. '"National Security" as an Ambiguous Symbol'. *Political Science Quarterly* 67, no. 4 (1952): 481–502.

Wolff, Josephine Charlotte Paulina. 'Unraveling Internet Identities: Accountability & Anonymity at the Application Layer'. Massachusetts Institute of Technology, 2012.

Wong, Edward. 'Hacking U.S. Secrets, China Pushes for Drones'. *The New York Times*, 20 September 2013.

Wright, Lawrence. *The Looming Tower: Al-Qaeda's Road to 9/11*. London: Penguin Books, 2006.

———. 'The Spymaster'. *The New Yorker*, 21 January 2008.

Zaid, Mark S. 'Central Intelligence Agency Refuses to Release Oldest US Classified Documents Sought in Litigation'. *Federation of American Scientists*, 30 March 1999.

Zakaria, Tabassum. 'First came Stuxnet computer virus: now there's Duqu'. *Reuters*, 18 October 2011.

Zakaria, Tabassum, and Warren Strobel. 'After "cataclysmic" Snowden affair, NSA faces winds of change'. *Reuters*, 13 December 2013.

Zetter, Kim. '"The Analyzer" Gets Time Served for Million-Dollar Bank Heist'. *Wired*, 5 July 2012.

———. 'Logic Bomb Set Off South Korea Cyberattack'. *Wired*, 21 March 2013.

———. 'How a Crypto "Backdoor" Pitted the Tech World Against the NSA'. *Wired*, 24 September 2013.

———. 'Critics say new evidence linking North Korea to the Sony hack is still flimsy'. *Wired*, 1 August 2015.

Zittrain, Jonathan. 'Don't Force Google to "Forget"'. *The New York Times*, 14 May 2014.

INDEX

INDEX

INDEX

legal standards, 86–91, 192
and plausible deniability,
167–73, 176
political context, 159
political nature of, 34–5
time factor, 146, 148–51
Croom, Charles, 8
CrowdStrike, 114, 141–2
Crypto Anarchist Manifesto (May), 22
cryptography, 21–4, 34–5, 53
CrySys, 120–1, 134
Cuckoo's Egg, 142–6, 183
cui bono, 102
Cutting Sword of Justice, The, 43,
95
cyber attack, definition of, 15–17
Cyber Command, US, 37
Cyber Squared, 129
CyberWar (Clarke and Knake),
14–15, 38, 137
Cyberdeterrence and Cyberwar
(Libicki), 153
Cybersecurity Information Sharing
Act (2015), 6
'Cyberspace Policy Report'
(2011), 6
'Cyberspace Policy Review'
(2009), 6
cypherpunk, 21–4, 37
Czech Republic, 197–8

Daily Beast, The, 179
Dardar, Firas, 180
DarkSeoul, 41, 72–5, 183
Data Security Council of India, 165
DataStream Cowboy (Richard
Pryce), 87–9, 91, 129, 159
Davis, Jake, 51
De Mont De Rique, Alexey, 116
Deeb, Hatem, 180
Defense Intelligence Agency, 115
Deibert, Ron, 168

Demchak, Chris, 175
Democratic National Committee,
79
denial-of-service attacks, 16, 38,
47–8, 50, 93–5, 106, 134, 140,
148, 168, 170, 172, 180
Department of Commerce, US,
194
Department of Defence, Australia,
157
Department of Defense, US, 6, 7,
43, 52, 102, 103, 106, 125, 143,
152
Department of Energy, US, 144
Department of Foreign Affairs and
Trade, Australia, 157
Department of Homeland Security,
US, 4, 44, 139, 195
Department of Justice, US, 33, 83,
100, 125–6, 129, 180
Department of State, US, 2, 67,
147, 166, 195
Deutsche Telekom, 196
Diabl0 (Farid Essebar), 61–2
DigiNotar, 169
Digital Agenda, 19
Digital and Electronic Forensic
Service, 149
Dipert, Randall, 147–8
Director of National Intelligence
(DNI), 41, 51, 60, 79, 115, 147
Donilon, Thomas, 127
Doody, John, 73
drugs, 37, 142
DuPont, 144
Duqu, 96, 120–2, 128, 130, 134,
172, 183
Durham University, 171

Easton, Nina, 119–20
Eberle, Christopher, 67
Economist, The, 115

294

INDEX

INDEX

INDEX

INDEX